Slices and Lumps

Slices and Lumps

Division and Aggregation
in Law and Life

LEE ANNE FENNELL

To Bob, with all best wishes

The University of Chicago Press
Chicago and London

The University of Chicago Press, Chicago 60637
The University of Chicago Press, Ltd., London
© 2019 by Lee Anne Fennell
Published 2019
Printed in the United States of America

28 27 26 25 24 23 22 21 20 19   1 2 3 4 5

ISBN-13: 978-0-226-65026-5 (cloth)
ISBN-13: 978-0-226-65043-2 (e-book)
DOI: https://doi.org/10.7208/chicago/9780226650432.001.0001

Library of Congress Cataloging-in-Publication Data

Names: Fennell, Lee Anne, author.
Title: Slices and lumps : division and aggregation in law and life /
Lee Anne Fennell.
Description: Chicago ; London : The University of Chicago Press, 2019. |
Includes bibliographical references and index.
Identifiers: LCCN 2019001789 | ISBN 9780226650265 (cloth : alk. paper) |
ISBN 9780226650432 (e-book)
Subjects: LCSH: Law—United States—Philosophy. | Law—Economic aspects—
United States. | Law—Psychological aspects—United States.
Classification: LCC KF380 .F455 2019 | DDC 340/.1150973—dc23
LC record available at https://lccn.loc.gov/2019001789

♾ This paper meets the requirements of ANSI/NISO Z39.48–1992
(Permanence of Paper).

For Chris

CONTENTS

Introduction

If you were a superhero, what would be your superpower?[1] Flying? Invisibility? Time travel? I would pass up these familiar options in favor of the profoundly important but woefully underrated power of *configuration*—the ability to divide things up that arrive in lumps and to put things together that arrive in pieces.[2] These feats might sound simple, but they are extraordinarily valuable and often maddeningly elusive.

To see why, think of all the things that might do you more good if they were sliced up differently. Perhaps you would prefer a job that involves a third less work and a third less pay, or a home that is half its size except when you are entertaining, or a car that materializes only when needed and is priced accordingly, or a dog that provides half the affection and requires half the walking. Next, think of the many things that arrive in fragments but that gain much or all of their value only when put together. The pieces necessary to build a complete rather than partial bridge. Votes to create a political result. The increments of studying necessary to pass a high-stakes exam. Patent licenses to produce a particular product. Or the bits of extra space between parallel-parked cars that you wish you could aggregate together to create a space large enough for your car. Getting part of the way there doesn't always get you a proportionate share of the total benefit (think of a partial bridge or a partial parking space).

Superpowers throw human limitations into plain view, and a central goal of this book is to explore why reconfiguration is both important and difficult. Once we look carefully, we see that difficulties in slicing and lumping shape much of the way we have organized our lives, and a great deal of law and policy as well. From hot button issues like eminent domain and habitat conservation to developments in the so-called sharing economy (better termed "the slicing economy," I argue) to personal struggles over work, risk, money, time, diet, and exercise, how things are divided up or aggregated together matters tremendously. Understanding the nature of configuration problems enables us to deal more effectively with them. By exerting control over how things are divvied up or pieced together, individuals, firms, and governments can shape outcomes in every domain of life, law, and policy.

Configuration, in short, is power. It is a power that has become increasingly pressing to understand and harness. New technologies and growing urbanization have made it easier than ever to bring people together in both real and virtual space to share ideas, make new things, and join forces on projects of all kinds. At the same time, emerging forms of unbundling, from jobs to cars to homes to entertainment, have refined the slices in which we produce and consume. It is no exaggeration to say that the future of the city, the workplace, the marketplace, and the environment all turn on questions of configuration, as do the prospects for more effective legal doctrines, for better management of finances and health, and much more. Yet the art and science of configuration is not a recognized field of inquiry. This book aims to make it one.

By the end of the book, I hope to have convinced you of the power of configuration, and to have illuminated how indivisibility and fragmentation generate—and sometimes help solve—a wide range of legal and social problems. My inquiry uncovers some unappreciated and often surprising ways that the increments into which choices or resources are divided or aggregated can influence human behavior. This book highlights how governmental actors, markets, and households slice and lump (often in unacknowledged ways) and how they might do these things better. I offer strategies for recognizing and harnessing the power of slicing and lumping in law, policy, and everyday life. I hope to make *configuration entrepreneurship* salient—both as a focus of private and public innovation and as a crucial form of life-hacking.

The evocative economic concept of "lumpy goods" offers a starting point for my analysis. In a classic paper, Michael Taylor and Hugh Ward observe that some goods, like bridges and rail lines, "cannot be usefully provided in *any* amounts but only in more or less massive 'lumps.'"[3] Lumpiness sometimes refers to a desired end state, like the complete bridge. In other cases lumpiness represents an *impediment* to reaching a preferred end state—one wants only part of a job, say, or a share of a car, but (for whatever reason) the good is produced or provided in an all-or-nothing fashion. The inability to divide things up also limits the ability to make things *incrementally* bigger. For example, production or computing capacity can often be added only in large chunks.

Some constraints are physical or technical in nature and may be surmounted, if at all, at great expense. For example, the *Silver Spirit* cruise ship, a 642-foot-long vessel in Silversea's fleet, was recently cut in half to insert a new forty-nine-foot midsection that will add about 12 percent to its passenger capacity.[4] This ship-splicing represents a rare engineering feat—one that will consume roughly 450,000 worker-hours—and its difficulty and cost attest to the inherent lumpiness involved.[5] Evolving technology is making rapid inroads on other kinds of indivisibility, however, as we see with new platforms for dividing access to houses, cars, clothing, and more. Many other forms of lumpiness are intentionally constructed by government or private actors—minimum lot sizes or product bundles, for example—and thus represent potentially malleable features of social, legal, and transactional settings.

Despite the evident centrality of lumpiness and divisibility to law and policy, these concepts have received only scattered attention from legal scholars. This might seem surprising, especially given the prominence that the economic analysis of law enjoys. But economics itself also tends to neglect these matters.[6] This is partly for reasons of mathematical simplicity—models are more tractable if a linear relationship between inputs and outputs is assumed.[7] And in the large-number settings that much economic analysis focuses on, indivisibility is not especially consequential: for a factory making hundreds of widgets per day, it hardly matters that producing each widget is an all-or-nothing proposition.[8] Moreover, economists have long recognized that although individual decisions may be lumpy—a stable owner cannot reduce his team by a fraction of a horse when oat prices rise slightly—markets as a whole exhibit what Andreu Mas-Colell calls "the regularizing effects of aggregation."[9] At a large enough scale, lumps come out in the wash.

Yet for individuals—workers, consumers, household members, risk bearers, taxpayers, and citizens—lumps matter profoundly. As Hagan Bobzin observes, making one more car "is of little significance for an automobile company, whereas a household faces considerable consequences depending on whether it has got a car or not."[10] People cannot successfully navigate the interactions that are most important to their lives without at least an intuitive understanding of the significance of slicing and lumping. For related reasons, law and policy cannot afford to ignore matters of configuration. Not only is legal analysis frequently concerned with the structure of individual decisions, but social policy regularly addresses unique, indivisible goods and large-scale goals that are not amenable to the marketplace's alchemy of averaging.

Take conservation, a context in which recognizing lumps of value can upend established ways of pursuing goals. Mary Ellen Hannibal recently observed: "For more than one hundred years, conservation has functioned by drawing a boundary around a special area and limiting human impacts there . . . . But science today tells us this approach is failing. Nature doesn't work without connection."[11] In other words, the world is lumpy, and some of the most significant lumps of value may not correspond to the ways in which resources like land have traditionally been sliced up. This reality is now being recognized through efforts to create migratory pathways and wildlife corridors. Here, as in other contexts, it is impossible to devise meaningful solutions without appreciating the lumpiness lurking in natural and social phenomena.

Lumpiness can also produce or explain behavior that seems to defy basic economic principles. For example, the law of diminishing marginal returns suggests that the next unit of a good will add less value than the previous unit. Lumpiness inverts that relationship: at times, one needs more of something to get any return at all. The lumpy or fragmented features of a given situation may also elicit behavior that is mistakenly attributed to behavioral biases. For instance, a person who plays the lottery or elects a lump sum over a larger payment stream may not be irrational or myopic, but rather simply expressing a strong preference for a lumpy consumption experience that is difficult or impossible to attain in any other way. Paying attention to configuration forces us to rethink our assumptions.

This is an especially exciting and crucial time to be studying questions of slicing and lumping. As increasing urbanization and environmental threats raise the stakes for land configuration choices, a technology-fueled entrepreneurial explosion is underway that is dividing goods, services, and jobs in novel ways, from Airbnb to Zipcar. This book highlights the connections between these and other social and economic developments, and examines the opportunities and concerns they present. It also sheds new light on chronic intrapersonal struggles, from overeating to the management of time and money, as well as persistent legal and policy puzzles, from the best way to deliver benefits to the best way to address risky behavior.

A few words about the book's methods and goals will help to frame what follows. My approach here is primarily analytic. I seek to understand and explain configuration problems, to get inside them and see how they work, rather than advocate for particular solutions to them. Yet in so doing, I mean to shed light on the ways that configuration matters to human well-being, and on the potential for better configurations to improve our lives. This book emphasizes the significance of the lumps and slices we encounter, and the need for our analyses and habits of thought to account for them. But this does not mean we must accept configurations as we find them. Even when indivisibilities arise from ecological or other natural phenomena, human reactions to them are malleable, making configuration an active enterprise, not a static fact. The words in my title are verbs as well as nouns.

For concreteness, my exposition is intensely example driven. There are large and deep literatures attached to many of the specific contexts I touch upon, which I cannot do justice to here. My aim is not to offer a comprehensive analysis of each of these situated examples, but rather to highlight the common structure they share—a forest that has been largely ignored in favor of individual trees. The book thus engages in a type of meta-lumping by highlighting connections and commonalities among diverse configuration challenges that have previously been treated in isolation. At the same time, this book distinguishes problems involving lumpy or indivisible goals or goods from the other types of collective action problems that tend to dominate the popular and academic imagination—a form of meta-slicing.

The first four chapters of the book lay the conceptual groundwork, starting with an overview in chapter 1 of the types of indivisibilities that appear in markets, communities, personal life, and law. Chapter 2 shows how lumpiness arises in high-profile contexts like eminent domain, which involves the forcible assembly of land, as well as in settings where resources that are currently co-owned must be split up among claimants. I show that these two types of problems—assembly and division—are not distinct, as is usually assumed, nor is one inherently harder to solve than the other. Instead, they share a common structure: each type of reconfiguration requires *both* assembly (of consent by the affected stakeholders, or an overriding of their lack of consent) and division (of the surplus that is thereby created). In both cases, what is really being pieced together—whether voluntarily or through coercion—is cooperation in pursuit of a lumpy goal, the resource's reconfiguration.

Chapter 3 extends this theme of assembling cooperation to collective action problems more broadly, whether saving a fishery from collapse or collecting funds to cure a disease. I show how lumpy social goals—ones that are all-or-nothing—present different, and generally more favorable, prospects for success than the standard tragedy-of-the-commons scenario.

Also significant are the ways in which the resources to be harvested or the tasks to be contributed are divided up. Chapter 4 then considers how choice menus—whether sizes of sodas or technologies for fighting pollution—affect behavior by defining the increments in which people can take actions. When alternatives are chunky rather than continuous, people often must produce or consume either less or more than they would prefer—with overlooked and sometimes surprisingly positive implications for behaviors that have spillovers on others.

Chapter 5 turns to the ways in which aggregation and division impact intrapersonal dilemmas. Many of the same considerations that we observe in collective action problems among different people also apply when the players are different versions of oneself. Likewise, the chunkiness of the choices one encounters can edge decisions closer to one's overall long-term interests or push them further away. Finding ways to strategically engineer and personalize choice menus offers new avenues for addressing self-control problems. Chapter 6 extends these ideas into the realms of personal financial management and public finance. Recognizing the significance of aggregation and division in saving and spending can improve how households manage their budgets and how governments formulate taxes, incentives, and benefits.

The next four chapters show how aggregation and division crop up in several important domains: the workplace, the marketplace, the home, and the city. Transformations are underway in all of these settings. Chapter 7 explores how new business models that slice time, effort, attention, and risk in unprecedented ways are changing how people work and play. The gig economy represents one manifestation of this shift, and the ambivalence surrounding it can be understood in terms of lumpiness: delumping the working experience has also meant decoupling work from many of its standard accompaniments, including health insurance. Chapter 8 examines the developing slicing economy in the marketplace for products and services. Here I explore the prospects and limits of swapping full-strength ownership for on-demand access. I also show how indivisibilities crop up in product bundling, sizing, pricing, and standardization, with implications for consumer choice.

Chapter 9 turns to housing, where innovative new forms of slicing abound, from platforms like Airbnb to social housing designs that deliver partial homes. At the same time, legal and policy choices often contribute to a discontinuous, chunky menu of housing alternatives that omits or limits options that people might prefer—such as very small units suitable for one-person households. Analyzing this constructed form of lumpiness in housing raises questions about the scope of the home, ones that require examining complementarities between individual dwellings and the surrounding community. Chapter 10 widens the viewfinder to take in the city, where the questions of land assembly that appear early in the book are reconsidered in connection with agglomeration benefits (urban vitality) and costs (congestion). Perhaps the most pressing economic question of our day is how to make the most of our cities, which are themselves a paradigmatic instance of the power—and challenges—of aggregation.

The final pair of chapters extends the analysis of aggregation and lumpiness into legal decisions and doctrines. Chapter 11 begins with the observation that law often constructs cliffs or generates all-or-nothing outcomes. For example, judicial decisions are very often binary in nature (one party wins entirely and the other loses entirely). Messy facts drawn from a continuum of possibilities are rendered into all-or-nothing outcomes. Much turns, then, on the "thresholding" processes that the law uses to generate these on-off results. Questions of aggregation play a decisive role: a momentary lapse of judgment, for example, might fall on one side of a legal line if viewed in isolation and on the other if considered as part of a larger pattern of careful or careless behavior. Chapter 12 shows that many legal and policy debates boil down to disagreements about bundling—whether of precautions, property interests, behavior, regulations, or legislation. Because the power to bundle or unbundle can dramatically change results, battles over bundles are some of the most interesting and consequential disputes in law and policy.

The book concludes with takeaways for policy makers, lawyers, academics, and anyone else who is interested in understanding and leveraging the lessons of lumpiness. Issues of lumpiness and divisibility touch nearly every corner of human experience, and they offer countless opportunities for innovation and entrepreneurship. Although the contexts I cover are necessarily illustrative rather than exhaustive, I hope that this book will spur others to identify additional arenas where the ideas explored here can be applied and extended. There are, of course, many other ways that the terrain I cover could have been broken up and heaped together. But I hope that the current configuration will let through enough light to intrigue you, and to inspire your own efforts at lump building.

ONE

Surveying Lumpiness

Picture a bridge spanning a chasm. Removing one chunk of the span renders it worthless—indeed, it is no longer even a bridge. Because bridges are useless unless they are complete, they offer intuitive examples of lumpy, indivisible, or "step" goods. Lumpiness is found not only in large-scale infrastructure like bridges, highways, and railroad lines, but also in ordinary products and services. Some goods, like car tires or developable land, are more valuable if consumed in particular quantities or combinations. Others, like cars, jobs, houses, and pets, are often available only in difficult-to-divide chunks. Conditions like species survival or election wins depend on maintaining or reaching critical thresholds, not merely coming close. Legal rules and litigation outcomes may also exhibit lumpiness, operating in an all-or-nothing fashion, or producing results only when some threshold of compliance or deterrence is reached. And the lumpy fixed costs that attach to many endeavors—from introducing a new product to passing a new law to learning a new skill—make choices fewer and chunkier for firms, consumers, citizens, and workers than they otherwise would be.[1]

These and many other examples will be explored in the chapters that follow. Here, I take up two foundational questions: What counts as "lumpy"? And why do we care? The answers to these questions will preview the range of aggregation and division problems taken up in this book. Many of these problems involve desired, attempted, thwarted, or contested reconfigurations—attempts to slice up things that are difficult to divide or to aggregate things that start out in pieces. Others concern the appropriate legal or practical treatment of naturally occurring or constructed lumps, whether in regulatory policy, legal analysis, informal order, bargaining settings, or the realm of self-control.

What's Lumpy?

The idea of lumpiness seems intuitive, but the term is used in more than one way and encompasses a variety of phenomena. Some distinctions and definitions will help to set the stage.

Supply, Demand, and Lumpiness

We might refer to a good as a *lumpy* or *indivisible* either because this is how the good delivers its value (in a lump, like a bridge) or because the good arrives in a lump and is accompanied by constraints (natural or constructed) that make it difficult or costly to divide (think of the full-time position that does not allow for part-time work). These are, in a sense, opposite meanings. In the first, lumpiness describes a desired end state (the completed bridge). In the second, lumpiness describes a suboptimal starting point (the full-time job). In both cases, there is a mismatch between the starting point and the desired end state, but what is necessary to span that gap differs. To build the full bridge, many smaller pieces must be assembled. The lumpy job comes preassembled, and that is exactly the problem—a slice of the job would be preferable for the employee.

One way to express this distinction is between goods that are *lumpy in demand* (people want full bridges) and goods that are *lumpy in supply* (cars and pets come in whole number units). Some goods might be described either way. For instance, we could say that an employer supplies jobs in full-time increments or demands labor in full-time increments. Regardless, lumpiness becomes interesting where what is desired (by someone) takes a different form than what is provided (by someone else). A good that is lumpy in demand, like a bridge, often must be assembled from inputs— bridge segments, labor, financial contributions, and so on—that are fragmented in supply. A good that is lumpy in supply, like a car, may need to be split into smaller use-slices to effectively meet consumer demand.

Often lumpiness is of no consequence because it can be addressed through ordinary markets or informal transactions. For example, if the smallest unit of candy that can be economically produced and sold separately is a 1.5 ounce candy bar, and if most people have no desire to purchase candy in smaller increments than this, whatever theoretical lumpiness may exist presents no difficulties. Lumpiness becomes problematic when the supplied units are much larger or smaller than desired (think of a mammoth candy bar or a single chocolate chip) *and* there are significant impediments to dividing up the larger unit or aggregating the smaller ones. The obstacles may stem from physical constraints or the costs of engaging in market transactions.[2] They may even be social or psychological in nature. Philip Henry Wicksteed, writing in 1910, observes that the commercial standard of supplying ink in one-penny measures effectively precludes people from acquiring smaller quantities, given the "awkwardness and humiliation" involved in negotiating with a stationer for a smaller amount.[3]

Lumpiness can also cause difficulties when everyone agrees that the initial (lumpy) configuration is the most valuable one, but there is more than one plausible claimant. A vivid example is the dispute over the baby that featured in King Solomon's famous decision.[4] Babies, it turns out, are extremely lumpy. Luckily, there are alternatives to physical division, and the Solomonic outcome illustrated one of them—an award to the claimant who clearly valued the child more. As the literature on this topic has noted, indivisibilities may be addressed through a variety of techniques, including slicing the good temporally (e.g., through rotation systems); converting the good into something divisible like money, as by auctioning it off; giving claimants chances at the good that are proportionate to the strength of their claims; or giving the good to one claimant while compensating the others.[5]

Temporal slicing of goods is an especially intriguing solution because it can bridge the gap between the physical configuration that maximizes value and the amount of the good that a particular individual wants, needs, or is entitled to receive. It works well for goods that are far more valuable when physically intact, where people do not want, and are unwilling to pay for, the whole thing. No formal slicing is necessary if people can agree to share the resource. In some cases we manage to do exactly that.[6] People form clubs or enter communities to consume certain kinds of indivisible goods—swimming pools, tennis courts, clubhouses, and so on. Other varieties of time slicing are longstanding and familiar: library books, hotel rooms, rental cars, and so on. Entrepreneurs are now finding a multitude of ways to create small-scale market transactions that further fine-tune slicing, as evidenced by Airbnb, Uber, and many other business models. An extreme example is Recharge, an app that allows people to buy "microstays" at hotels and apartments, priced by the minute.[7]

Consider another innovation in temporal slicing, pet sharing.[8] Companion animals, like babies or bridges, are lumpy and can't be physically divided. But the unit in which pets arrive is not necessarily the optimal unit in which their companionship is consumed. Suppose that for one individual, Angus, dog ownership is great fun for a few days a week, but the burden continues to grow as the week wears on, and the benefits diminish apace. If the unfun days of Angus's dog-owning week could be transferred to other people who similarly experience declining returns from dog ownership (Beth and Cam, say), the dog could deliver a larger total quantum of enjoyment to its (now plural) owners.

There may be problems, of course. Time-share dog owners may shirk on bathing the dog or taking him to the vet. The dog may never get properly trained, or the constant parade of owners may produce anxiety or confusion for the dog. Some of these issues might be overcome by, for example, having a platform manager who coordinates tasks, establishes minimum time blocks, and sets care standards, but these solutions add to the costs of time slicing. BorrowMyDoggy.com, which currently operates in the UK and Ireland, enables a pet owner who retains primary responsibility for her pup to offer short-term "borrowing" in exchange for dog walking, care, or socialization, while the platform provider collects a fee that covers veterinarian access and insurance.[9] This model offers an approximation of informal interactions over pets among friends and family, adapted to urban settings where people often lack preexisting social networks.[10] Here, as in many other contexts, from ride sharing to home sharing, we see new models for managing lumpiness emerge as earlier (and mostly unremarked) ways of informally aligning supply and demand break down.

Some Terminology

The notion of lumpiness connects tightly to the concepts of *indivisibility* and *complementarity*. To say that a good is indivisible or that it exhibits indivisibilities does not usually mean that the good literally cannot be divided, but rather that it is considerably less valuable when divided, or that it is expensive (perhaps prohibitively so) to divide successfully.[11] The idea of complementarity refers to the fact that certain goods and services produce more value when consumed in particular combinations. Right and left shoes are a standard example. Because most people have two feet of similar size and follow the social custom of shodding them identically, a pair of shoes typically delivers far more than twice as much value as a single shoe. Likewise, the segments that make up a full bridge span are strongly complementary; subtract just one, and the bridge becomes useless. A partially fenced yard does no better than an unfenced yard at containing animals, a car with three tires drives no better than a car with no tires, and small and scattered patches of land are useless for large-scale development.

In these familiar examples, indivisibilities are a function of comple-

mentarities. A set of tires or a pair of shoes exhibits indivisibilities not because tires or shoes are physically hard to separate from each other, but
rather because splitting them up would be self-defeating—they are much
more valuable when consumed together. Not all indivisibilities track complementarities in this way. Other things that we might characterize as indivisible (cars, jobs, pets, houses, and so on) might be more valuable in
pieces (whether time slices or physical slices) but dividing them up is for
some reason technologically or administratively difficult.[12] I will use the
term *indivisibility* in this book as a synonym for lumpiness. The notion of
complementarity represents a general purpose explanation for why goods
or services might be more valuable when aggregated in certain ways.

Two other terms associated with lumpiness are *discontinuities* and *nonlinearities*. Returns from activities like studying or voting are often *discontinuous*: making it over some threshold makes the difference between passing and failing, or between winning and losing an election. *Nonlinearities*
occur when outcomes do not increase smoothly and proportionately in
response to inputs. There may be increasing returns (economies of scale),
diminishing returns (diseconomies of scale), sharp steps or notches at particular thresholds, or some mix of these effects. The economic tool of the
production function, which maps inputs to outputs, provides traction on
these ideas.

Lumpy Production Functions

Lumpiness can be understood as a certain kind of relationship between inputs (units of effort, money, or resources) and outputs (conditions, events,
products, or services). Consider, for example, the connection between dollars contributed to a charity and the benefits that the charity generates in
the world. If this relationship is plotted on a graph with well-being improvements on the vertical axis and dollars on the horizontal axis, what
shape will the curve take?

There are many possibilities.[13] Perhaps the relationship is linear, at least
within a particular range, so that each additional dollar generates the same
uptick in benefits. Think of assistance that buys increments of soup, medical care, or clean drinking water, which in turn produce a corresponding
improvement in well-being among the recipient population. In other cases,
a plateau may be reached after which additional dollars do less good than
the dollars that went before—after every household has mosquito nets, say,
the next best uses of the money may be less effective at producing marginal improvements. Conversely, there may be a snowball effect, so that

as more contributions are added, each does more and more good, at least up to a point—think of class sessions added to an educational program, or inoculations against communicable diseases within a community. Or the curve may be S-shaped, with a range of increasing effectiveness followed by a range of diminishing returns.[14]

Production functions for lumpy goods deliver outputs not in smooth, regular increments as individual units of input are added, but rather in large jumps after a series of inputs.[15] At the extreme is a pure step good that delivers all of its utility in one large chunk or "step." Think again of a bridge. Suppose you need to span a chasm that is a thousand yards long, and the bridge material arrives in one-hundred-yard segments.

As shown in figure 1.1, value to users remains flat as the first nine segments are added, one by one. But when the tenth unit is added to create a completed bridge, suddenly value steps up all at once. There is a sharp discontinuity, illustrated by the dashed line in figure 1.1. The step not only marks out a threshold under which no benefits are provided, but also represents a plateau from which no further incremental improvements are possible. Adding more lengths to the bridge once the span is complete does no good.

In fact, such pure step goods are rare. Even a bridge can be supplied at many different quality levels, as Russell Hardin has noted.[16] An election is also a common example of a step good—here, the inputs are the votes that either do or do not reach the critical point that enables one's preferred

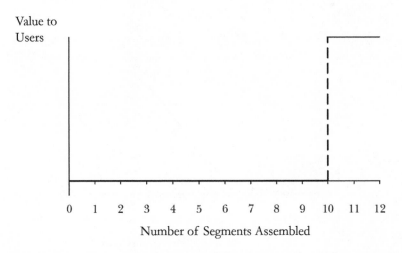

Figure 1.1. The Bridge. Source: Fennell, "Lumpy Property," 1958, fig. 1.

candidate to win.[17] Votes short of the amount necessary to win are use-less in generating the desired outcome, while extra votes beyond that level are superfluous. Of course, if one defines political objectives slightly more broadly than choosing a winner in a particular contest, the step function looks less sharp. Often we think that landslides produce at least somewhat better results for the winner than do narrow victories, while near-misses provide greater political impetus for another try than would a crushing defeat. Nonetheless, these examples provide an intuitive sense of what a lumpy or step good looks like.

Equally rare are perfectly linear goods—those with a smooth, continu-ous production function in which each infinitesimally fine unit of input is matched by a corresponding adjustment in output or utility. Few prod-ucts can be produced, purchased, or enjoyed in literally any quantity. Often some minimum threshold must be crossed to obtain (or enjoy) the thing at all, and many goods must be transacted over in integer units (bananas, for instance). Even readily divisible goods—Wicksteed uses the example of pudding servings for children—may be relatively valueless below a certain quantity threshold.[18]

Between the extremes of a perfectly linear good and a single-step good, we find different degrees of nonlinearity or indivisibility.[19] Consider fig-ure 1.2, which depicts an S-curve. This curve corresponds to a relatively lumpy good that does not take a pure step form.

Although this good does not deliver all its value in a single shot, its pro-

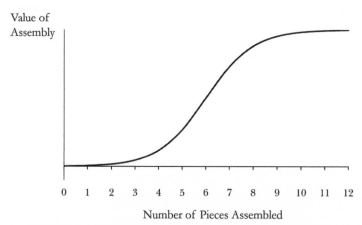

Figure 1.2. The S-Curve. Source: Fennell, "Lumpy Property," 1960, fig. 2.

duction function contains ranges over which the marginal effect of added pieces is sharply increasing or decreasing. The S-curve describes many collective goods that require a critical mass of participation to succeed, but that at some point plateau.[20] It might also fit with certain kinds of land assembly projects, where value increases sharply once a certain number of parcels are aggregated, but where having all the parcels is not essential.[21]

Lumpiness, as used in this book, refers to severe discontinuities or nonlinearities in the production function, whether or not those functions take a pure step form or intersperse segments of sharply increasing or decreasing returns with ranges exhibiting linearity.[22] These differences in shape are important, however, because they can influence the prospects for cooperation and the risks of strategic behavior, as we will see in chapters 2 and 3.[23]

What's in the Lump?

So far, I have spoken of "segments" or "pieces" that produce value when aggregated together. Lumpiness or indivisibility often refers to quantities of relatively fungible inputs—segments of a bridge, lengths of railroad track, tires for a car, units of work, and so on. Yet it may also refer to systems made up of heterogeneous elements, such as a machine that cannot operate without each and every one of its parts.[24] I will use the notion of lumpiness broadly and functionally here to refer to both heterogeneous and homogeneous aggregations, given that both forms of lumpiness can generate similarly structured problems.

In the context of land assembly, for example, the unique spatial location of each parcel makes the component parts of the desired assembly unique and nonfungible. But this sort of nonfungibility is neither necessary nor sufficient to produce an assembly problem. Even if a group is building a bridge out of identical, interchangeable segments, there may still be an assembly problem if there are no outside sources of bridge material and each individual in the group holds a segment essential to the whole. Conversely, a car may require many different mechanical parts to run (none of which could substitute for each other), but there will be no difficulty assembling the necessary pieces as long as each part is readily available on the open market. The car is still lumpy in that its parts are interdependent and all of them are needed, but this lumpiness may pass unnoticed as long as the underlying markets for its inputs remain competitive. What matters most to the shape of an assembly problem, then, is not whether the necessary components are interchangeable *with each other*, but rather whether close substitutes exist for each of the components required for a given assembly.

As this example suggests, the lumpiness of a good or service is distinct from the market conditions that influence whether, or how easily, the full lump will be obtained. Familiar examples of lumpiness, like large-scale developments that require assembling many pieces of contiguous land, often confront the holdout power held by the various owners of the component parts. But the lumpiness of the project would remain (though it would likely go unremarked) even if the property were all initially held by the developer. Thus, lumpiness tends to announce itself as such when some impediment stands in the way of achieving it or breaking it down—whether monopoly power, technological limits, or other factors.

The components making up a given lump may also be segments of time. Some goods, such as private residences, can become disproportionately valuable when consumed over lengthy, unbroken periods. Often, the most valuable temporal chunks are defined by reference to external events, such as the length of a life, a job, or an educational program, or the time that it takes for a particular risky investment to yield returns—all of which can be uncertain. Property rights that let owners hold onto things long enough to realize distant or uncertain payoffs respond to this temporal lumpiness.

Finally, sometimes lumps represent not the way in which goods generate value, but rather technological or natural constraints on how goods are produced or supplied. As we have seen, it is possible to have goods that are lumpy in supply that become more valuable when divided (temporally or physically) among different people. This kind of lumpiness indicates a discontinuity or nonlinearity in the production process, perhaps due to high fixed costs or other economies of scale. Once the good is supplied, the challenge is to come up with a plan for dividing the consumption experience. Indeed, without a plan for dividing the consumption experience, the good may not be profitable to supply in the first place.

Subdividing Lumpiness

To get a better sense of the scope and variety of lumpiness-related issues that crop up in the real world, and to more clearly see what is at stake, it is helpful to consider some other ways of subdividing the category.

Goods and Bads

So far I have spoken of lumpy *goods*. But sometimes an undesired end state takes a lumpy shape. Russell Hardin gives the example of a power blackout to illustrate a step bad: the blackout will occur all at once if aggregate electricity usage exceeds a critical threshold.[25] Or consider a population crash that will cause the demise of a fishery.[26] Below some threshold of harvesting, nothing much changes, but once the threshold is crossed, disaster ensues—a lumpy bad. When the goal is to avoid a catastrophic end state (rather than to achieve a desired end state), the challenge becomes one of limiting the piecemeal acts of harvesting or destruction that can combine to push beyond the threshold of sustainability. This challenge can be recast as one of assembling forbearance from those who are otherwise entitled to draw from the common supply. Assembling enough forbearance to keep the lights on or pull the fishery back from the brink can be reconceptualized as achieving the lumpy *good* of "avoiding a blackout" or "avoiding a population crash."

In other cases, what is a lumpy good for some people is a lumpy bad for others. Göran Bostedt analyzes the case of the Swedish wolf, whose preservation constitutes a public good for many Swedish nature lovers, but a public bad for reindeer herders whose herds suffer depredation from the wolf.[27] Although it is possible to have more or fewer wolves, if the population threshold that is robust enough to satisfy the wildlife lovers also creates a serious threat to the herders, this is a lumpy state that will be sought by some and opposed by others.[28]

Differences of opinion may also emerge as to whether a given resource is more valuable when split up or when maintained as a unit. For example, what appears to be a problem of lumpiness in supply (a pet or job that cannot be divided in half) may in fact be the most efficient arrangement. Maybe nobody wants to sign up for half of your dog or the last three hours of your job each week, at least not at a price you would find agreeable. Splitting the resource might, in fact, destroy rather than create value. In these cases, the key question is whether there is any gain to be had by reconfiguring—and the answer may turn on private information about valuations, as the next chapter discusses.

Natural versus Constructed

There is little mystery why bridge crossers demand a full rather than partial bridge—they are susceptible to gravity, and this fact about the physical world is reflected in the lumpiness of bridge structures. Likewise, a lumpy bad like the extinction of a species turns on an ecological reality, the threshold at which overhunting or habitat loss will render the population unsustainable. In these examples, lumpiness stems from naturally occurring discontinuities. In other cases, lumpiness is a function of technological constraints, such as a Coke machine that can take only nickels, or a manufacturing process that requires a minimum production run to cover high fixed costs. In yet other cases, the lumpiness is constructed by law. For example, a square footage minimum for apartments makes housing lumpy for reasons that stem not from physical or technological limitations on construction, but rather from (often contested) societal judgments.

Both private parties and policy makers may intentionally construct lumps that are hard to break apart in order to force people to make choices that are bundled, take-it-or-leave-it propositions. For example, the inability to negotiate over boilerplate terms in a lease or contract has the effect of making the leasing or contracting decision lumpy. Even seemingly mundane decisions about the size or quantities of products can influence choices quite profoundly. Think of sugary sodas or cigarettes—goods often viewed as bads when consumed to excess. The inability to choose one's preferred size or quantity of these items might result in reduced consumption for both psychological and economic reasons—or, alternatively, could make matters even worse (if, say, one buys multiples of a smaller size that amount to a larger total). Counterintuitively, even very large sizes might at times be part of a strategy to reduce consumption, if it puts people to an all-or-nothing choice in which "all" is unpalatably large.

An especially interesting form of constructed lumpiness involves property rights. To what degree do these rights correspond to cohesive "things" (from which the owner can categorically exclude others) rather than bundles of entitlements that are either endlessly flexible or at least socially and culturally contingent? Henry Smith puts it this way: "Property organizes this world into lumpy packages of legal relations—legal things—by setting boundaries around useful attributes that tend to be strong complements."[29] Property ownership characteristically structures access to these presumptively complementary resources through a block of delegated control that excludes the uninvited and extends unbroken through time, bundling access today with access tomorrow and tomorrow and tomorrow.[30] This setup allows people to reap what they have sown (both figuratively and literally) and to hold onto the land or other asset as long as necessary to see returns on their investments.

But property is not just lumpy; it is also sticky. Attributes that were at one time complementary may tend to remain together as chunks of ownership (an entire car, say) long past the time when they continue to generate more value aggregated than disaggregated. New business models that offer thinly sliced rights in resources—from rides to tools to toys to lawns to clothing—highlight the inherent lumpiness in traditional property ownership, as well as the possibility of alternatives.[31] In other words, if the strong complementarity that originally made us draw property lines *here* and not *there* is contingent on social, cultural, and technological factors, rebundling becomes necessary as conditions change. And we are currently seeing a groundswell of changes along just these lines as new ways of slicing up access to goods and services become central to everyday life.

Property, then, provides an especially compelling setting in which to consider foundational questions about natural and constructed lumps of value. Do particular sets of rights (or particular physical or conceptual objects) possess some inherent unity that resists splintering, or are lumps instead largely of our own making? Gregory Alexander has recently explored similar questions in considering parallels between the "thing-ness" of works of art and of property—both of which can prove much less stable than is often assumed.[32] Those same concepts can assist in examining other legally or socially constructed lumps to see whether they correspond to valuable complementarities that should be maintained or whether they are merely artifacts of past complementarities that exist no longer.

More broadly, the issue of composition—when (and whether) components may be said to form a coherent thing—is a subtle and philosophically interesting one. Peter van Inwagen presents a thought experiment in which people believe they are seeing black tigers or "bligers" in the distance, when in fact they are seeing sets of six separate animals—four monkeys, a sloth, and an owl—moving in concert so that they appear to compose single creatures.[33] As the bliger tale suggests, the fact that components are in contact with one another does not necessarily make them part of the same organism.[34] Conversely, what might look like many separate entities may instead be a single thing. Consider Pando, an aspen forest in Utah made up of an estimated forty-seven thousand genetically identical trees joined by a shared root structure, which is reputed to be the planet's largest living organism.[35]

Even when entities are intentionally constructed, questions remain about what is inside and what is outside. Ronald Coase famously explored the boundaries of a firm by considering the relative costs of conducting transactions inside and outside the envelope of the business entity—the make-or-buy decision.[36] In urban contexts, the question of what counts as part of the same city can have more than one answer depending on whether one is referring to jurisdictional boundaries or functional interactions. Yet even the former is open to redefinition, as can be seen in a plan to split Sydney, Australia, into three separate cities.[37]

Law too must often make judgments about what counts as part of the same entity or event. What counts as a single crime, for example, and when does it begin and end?[38] Should a person's past pattern of conduct be relevant in a tort action, just the moment that caused the accident, or something in between?[39] Is a person's whole life or some smaller slice the relevant unit when assessing inequality, pursuing societal well-being, or setting tax policy?[40] Similar aggregation questions run through all of law.

Rival versus Nonrival

Another dimension for classifying indivisibilities involves the distinction between rival and nonrival goods. Certain goods like ideas, songs, landscapes, and lighthouses do not get used up as people consume them— this makes them "nonrival" in consumption. Nonrival goods are inherently lumpy in supply: supplying such goods for many people costs no more than supplying them for one person.[41] Nonrival goods are frequently lumpy in a more familiar sense as well: they cannot be enjoyed at all until a certain threshold is reached and gain nothing from inputs beyond that level.[42] As Fred Thompson explains, "half a lighthouse is, perhaps, worse than useless, more than one is redundant."[43] These lumpy or "discrete" nonrival goods are effectively one-offs; only a single unit of the underlying good is ever produced.[44] They are all-or-nothing propositions, where the question is not *how much* to produce, but whether to produce the thing at all.[45]

Two opposing observations highlight the complex role of indivisibility in this analysis. First, lumpy nonrival goods can be easier to supply through voluntary cooperation since anyone (or any set of anyones) who cares enough about consuming the discrete good should be willing to underwrite its production, even though others will benefit. The fact that others will benefit may produce strategic behavior—everyone would prefer to have others fund the good while enjoying it for free—but people may still find contributing to be in their rational self-interest.[46]

Second, and cutting in the other direction, nonrivalry disables the most intuitive basis for divvying up access and payment among users: consumption. Because my eating a pint of berries precludes you eating the same pint of berries, it seems only natural to charge me for the berries that I wish to eat and to assign me exclusive rights in those berries. I am getting what I paid for. Yet it is probable that the berries would be produced at exactly the same scale even if I did not buy my marginal pint. It is unlikely my purchase caused the berry patch and workers' hours to be incrementally expanded exactly one pint's worth. Instead, investments in berry production are large scale and lumpy, but the units of berries are priced to cover the production costs. Seen in this light, the nonrival good does not seem much different—there is still a lump of production to fund—but because the most intuitive basis for assessing payment obligations is absent, another funding approach is required. Chapter 3 will consider this question further.

Types of Lumps

We can round out our survey of lumpiness with a nonexhaustive list of categories in which indivisibilities in supply or demand can be found, including goods, services, events, conditions, goals, and laws.

Goods

As we have seen, consumer goods may be offered in indivisible units, such as an entire car or an all-the-time pet, when some consumers would prefer smaller increments of ownership, such as a car for weekday mornings only or a pet that is one's own only on alternate weekends. Similarly, purchasing a minivan or a three-bedroom home means owning the full structure all of the time, even if a vehicle half as large would suffice for the majority of car trips and the third bedroom is only used a dozen days each year. Firms and other large organizations like universities face related constraints: expansions in capacity may be available only in relatively large increments (a new plant, a large chunk of network capacity, or a new building), producing a forced choice between inadequate capacity and capacity that will appear excessive, at least in the short run.[47]

Another aspect of lumpiness in supply, recently explored by Joel Waldfogel, relates to the fixed costs of production, which can limit the variety of goods produced.[48] Here, the problem is not that individual customers are forced to purchase more of a good than they desire, but rather that consumers must collectively purchase a threshold amount of a given good in order for its manufacture to be cost justified. Changes in the technologies of production and distribution have enabled a larger set of consumer preferences to be served in many markets,[49] but those with nonmainstream tastes may still find themselves out in the cold, especially for goods and services that must be consumed locally and thus cannot draw on a larger market. For example, commercial airline routes serving particular cities depend on a critical mass of passengers for their viability—a fact that has led to federal subsidies for service to smaller communities.[50]

We have seen that goods often must be consumed in particular quantities or combinations in order to deliver value—whether matched sets of shoes or tires, or complementary goods like printers and ink cartridges—a fact that presents few difficulties if the relevant markets are competitive. But when monopoly power exists over some or all of the components, aggregation can become difficult. Land assembly is a special case of this general problem. Similar issues exist for products or creative works that depend on inputs to which others hold intellectual property rights.

Services

Like the manufacturer who has a minimum efficient size for a production run or product, entities or persons providing services may not be willing or able to supply those services in minutely divided segments. For example, because a plumber cannot make half a service call, the amount paid for the call must cover the cost of time and vehicle use necessary to actually complete the call. To be sure, the plumber can do greater or lesser amounts of work while out on the call, can use more or less expensive materials, and greater or lesser amounts of skill. But the client must at least cover the cost of getting out to the site and spending some minimum amount of time there or the service input will not be made at all.

The flip side of lumpy service inputs is lumpy service requirements. Here, think of the many young lawyers who complain that they would prefer to work somewhat shorter hours for lower pay, but find this alternative unavailable to them at major law firms. Here, the operative lumpiness may have little to do with the indivisibility of their own inputs—many could, in fact, easily work 10 or 20 percent fewer hours.[51] Rather, the problem is that their employer requires a certain minimum amount of service in order to offer them jobs at all. If they fail to put in the requisite hours, the result is not a proportionately downscaled salary, but rather withdrawal of the employment opportunity altogether. The indivisibility in service requirements may be driven by the economics of hiring, training, and offering benefit packages to larger versus smaller numbers of workers. In some cases, however, such indivisibility may be artificially constructed by firms in an effort to screen out workers who are less willing to work hard or who have significant outside demands on their time that might tend to reduce their productivity or availability.[52]

Often indivisibilities exist in both supply and demand for services, but are at least roughly congruent with each other. Dentists presumably prefer to provide complete dental procedures rather than partial ones, and patients strongly concur—no one wants to buy just the "drilling out" portion of a cavity-filling procedure. In this context, lumpiness presents few problems, although the full lump may be financially unattainable for some patients. It is interesting, however, that the lumpiness is much more acute for the patient. A holdup problem might occur if dentists could perform the drilling-out portion and then renegotiate the price for the filling's completion. Luckily, professional norms, law, and repeat play protect consumers against this strategy, but we can see a similar problem in some other contexts.

For example, a leading actor who performs for an entire season of a television show or an entire run of a play may generate many times more value than if he appears for only part of the series. Even if the performer *also* gains a greater lump of value (in terms of fame or reputation) from completing the entire series than quitting midway through, he may have much less to lose from dropping out than the show's producers do. What is to stop such an actor from threatening to walk off the project partway through unless the contract is renegotiated on more favorable terms? This is exactly what James Gandolfini, star of *The Sopranos*, did at one point (and it worked—he got more money).[53]

More broadly, indivisibilities present the potential for contracting parties to apply leverage to each other. Renovations, auto repairs, medical procedures, and many similar services exhibit indivisibilities that make it difficult for consumers to readily switch to a competitor midway through. Information asymmetries may also make it difficult to know whether an announced change in price as the work progresses represents a strategic ploy to exploit the leverage provided by the lumpy situation or simply a response to new information that has been uncovered in the earlier phases of the work. In some contexts, dual sourcing or similar approaches can alleviate switching costs and potentially police strategic efforts to extract more surplus.[54]

Events and Conditions

Many important outcomes have a lumpy or binary quality—a population of animals crashes or remains sustainable, a candidate is elected or defeated, an accident occurs or it does not. When investments made by different parties combine to produce outcomes, the problem has features that resemble those involving contributions to a step good such as a bridge. The key is to induce each party to contribute amounts that, when combined, will be just sufficient, but not excessive, to produce the result. In the examples just given, the events and conditions feature the same lumpy demand patterns as we have observed with goods and services.

Inputs to these desirable or undesirable conditions may themselves be lumpy as well—a form of lumpiness in supply. Consider the goal of avoiding an accident. Some variables, like driving speed, are continuous, but others are all-or-nothing: a car either has antilock brakes or it doesn't. Getting to the no-accident condition requires combining *enough* contributions to safety, but figuring out how to get there when some contributions are binary and others are incremental can be challenging. Similar issues arise in keeping pollution below particular thresholds, where some inputs (like adding a scrubber to a factory) are indivisible and others (like reducing operating hours) are incremental. In addition to finding the "cheapest cost avoider,"[55] it may be important to identify who is the cheapest precaution slicer—the party best able to scale precautionary inputs to avoid a lumpy event like an accident.

Personal Goals

Often people set goals for themselves (or have goals set for them by others) that have a lumpy or all-or-nothing quality. People may create rules that bundle together all instances of a given type of behavior (such as not drinking or not eating meat), or they may come up with plans that help them realize lumpy personal goods (like a fitness target or writing a book) or avoid lumpy bads (such as alcoholism or other forms of addiction). The ability of people to achieve their goals may be heavily influenced by the way their choice sets are configured, which depends in turn on how markets and law interact. Lumpiness plays a large role in human cognition more generally. Indeed, many common aphorisms testify to the ubiquity of these considerations in everyday life, such as "in for a penny, in for a pound," "it's only a drop in the bucket," "well begun is half done," "it's now or never," or "it's the least I could do."

Law

Law interacts with many forms of lumpiness that have already been introduced. Perhaps most obviously, law can make it easier or harder to slice up unified things or assemble fragmented things. For example, eminent domain allows certain kinds of land aggregations to occur more easily, while other legal rules address the slicing up of unified property interests. There are many laws and regulations that encourage or discourage, even when they do not mandate or forbid, particular ways of dividing up everything from risk to contractual obligations to families to jobs to units of housing. The law may also specify minimum or maximum lumps of production or consumption (such as minimum lot sizes or maximum soft drink sizes).

Moreover, law is often used to bring about or avoid circumstances, conditions, or occurrences that have a lumpy or step quality. The tax system, for example, mandates contributions that ensure that enough money will be aggregated to purchase lumpy public goods like bridges. Regulations operate to keep a fishery sustainable or to keep pollution below a critical threshold. Likewise, there may be a threshold level of enforcement of criminal laws that must be met within a given jurisdiction before inhabitants enjoy a sense of "law and order," and a minimum level of property rights protection that is necessary to induce widespread investment and reliance. Uniform accessibility requirements like curb cuts or wheelchair ramps can enable mobility throughout an entire community, producing an aggregate value analogous to that of a completed highway.[56] And even the mundane legal restriction of banning smoking in bars lets barhoppers dodge the lumpy bad of smelly clothing that even one smoke-filled bar would inflict.[57]

Finally, law *itself* may exhibit lumpiness. Many legal outcomes are all-or-nothing—a defendant is guilty or not guilty, liable or not liable, required to hand over a disputed piece of property entirely or allowed to keep it forever.[58] In making these binary choices, law must also decide how the process of choosing a winner will proceed, including how the inputs to particular legal outcomes—such as pieces of evidence—will be aggregated together or considered separately. When a driver suffers a lapse of attention, for example, should we look just at the fateful moment or at her larger pattern of driving behavior in assessing liability?

There may also be lumpiness in the supply of legal rules, if there are high fixed costs or other considerations that make producing additional laws or legal classifications costly.[59] Consider *numerus clausus*—the notion that only a fixed, limited number of property forms are permissible and that further customization is disfavored. In Thomas Merrill and Henry Smith's account, the limited number of forms economizes on information costs.[60] People interacting with the property system may prefer that property interests be delivered in a small number of familiar forms, not only to make transacting easier, but also so that they can understand their own holdings and avoid encroaching on those of others.[61] Likewise, regulations may be easier to produce and understand when they cluster around a few standard property forms than if different laws must be created and heeded for an infinite variety of alternatives.[62]

Why Should We Care?

This survey of lumpiness might seem to prove too much. If so many everyday phenomena can be recast as lumpy or indivisible, we might wonder how significant the concept can really be. Why should it merit our attention? This book will answer that question in some detail. To preview, there are three main reasons we should care about lumpiness—and, by extension, about problems of segmentation and division.

First and most obviously, the concept of lumpiness bears on a wide range of efforts to optimally configure resources, from land assembly to car sharing. I show how problems of dividing and aggregating are not distinct problems, but rather share a common structure, one that is informed by attention to lumpy production functions.

Second, an understanding of lumpiness allows us to recast many collective action problems, legal puzzles, and social conflicts in terms of indivisibilities and complementarities, which makes it easier to resolve them. Many of the most difficult problems known to law and policy involve choosing between two (or more) sets of complementary goods, and lumpiness offers a framework for doing so.

Third, lumpiness can be intentionally leveraged to advance personal or social goals by altering or constructing the choice sets that actors confront. Interactions with others and even with oneself look different if moves can only be made in certain-sized chunks than if they can be selected in fine degrees from a continuous menu.

Through these channels, lumpiness influences private and informal governance regimes, formal law, and even the efforts of individuals to manage different temporal versions of themselves. Its significance extends from the most personal realms (an individual's efforts to complete a project or stick to a diet) to the largest and most public concerns (such as eminent domain, housing policy, or environmental protection). The balance of the book will show how lumpiness cashes out in a range of contexts.

TWO

Assembly and Division

In 2005, the US Supreme Court upheld the City of New London's right to condemn Susette Kelo's little pink house (along with the homes of her neighbors) to make room for the redevelopment of an economically languishing area.[1] Outrage and backlash followed.[2] The Court's decision was not a surprise to legal scholars, even those who disagreed with the ruling. *Kelo* did no more than reiterate a principle that had been clearly established in other cases decades earlier: the US Constitution allows the government to use its eminent domain power to advance public purposes, even when it does so by transferring property from one set of private hands to another. But the decision applied that principle in a context that struck so close to home (literally) that it opened up a new dialogue about eminent domain's rationale and scope.

The power of eminent domain lets the government coercively reconfigure property entitlements. It is controversial because it pits two deeply held values against each other. The first is the right of property owners to hang onto their holdings unless and until they choose to sell, at a price they find agreeable. The second is society's interest in achieving lumpy, large-scale goals that could otherwise be stymied by a single holdout. The notion of complementarity introduced earlier stands on both sides of the question. The fee simple absolute, the form in which most real property is held, bundles together possessory rights that extend over time, in perpetuity. This continuity supports long-term attachments to the land and encourages people to make investments in their properties, including gambles that may take a long time to pay off.[3] In other words, property rights allow owners to enjoy complementarities between their right to possession today and their right to possession tomorrow—and all the tomorrows thereafter. But this *temporal* complementarity can conflict with *spatial* complementarities, such as those between different segments of a proposed highway path or different portions of a large-scale redevelopment or conservation area.

Significantly, it is not always clear whether a particular resource like land is more valuable if kept in separate parcels or assembled together. The values that parties subjectively place on their current holdings will typically be unknown, while the value to be produced by the new configuration will often be uncertain. Market transactions are the usual method for assessing who is the higher valuer of a particular resource, yet holdout problems can gum up the works and keep worthwhile transfers from occurring. Eminent domain can coercively cut through bargaining impasse.[4] But it cannot resolve the underlying uncertainty about whether the new configuration will actually be more beneficial on net. And it may dampen investment incentives for property owners.[5]

In this chapter, I examine the challenges that accompany attempts to reconfigure property entitlements, whether by assembling pieces of land or other resources held by separate owners, or by dividing up a larger whole into separately held pieces. Although dividing and aggregating might initially seem to be distinct problems, they turn out to be two sides of the same coin. Putting together land for a highway means landowners must relinquish their claims over the component parcels in exchange for some form of compensation. Dividing a common field into separate parcels similarly requires every commoner to relinquish her free access to the entire commons in exchange for an exclusive right to a subset of the land. In both cases, we see aggregation (of existing claims over the resource) *and* division (of the surplus produced by the new configuration). Given the entwined nature of slicing and lumping, it is a conceptual error to view the problems as distinct, or to regard one kind of problem as inherently more difficult to solve than the other.

In practice, division problems often seem easier to solve than the aggregation problems that we most commonly encounter, but this is not *because* they are division problems rather than aggregation problems. Rather, it is a function of the number of parties who must agree to a given reconfiguration, and the monopoly power that each of those parties holds. If one person owns a big piece of land and wants to divide it up and sell the pieces to other people, this reconfiguration can be readily accomplished as long as our landowner can find enough buyers. Notably, these buyers don't have to be any particular individuals—there is a large pool of potential purchasers, any combination of whom will do—so none of them can single-handedly block the owner's plans. Contrast this situation with the prototypical aggregation case, where different specific people hold the parcels that are going to be assembled together. If all the pieces are needed, the reconfiguration requires the consent of all the parcel holders, and it must be *those exact people* who unanimously agree—each is a monopolist with respect to her own essential contribution.

These prototype scenarios do not begin to exhaust the possibilities, however. If we introduce a set of permitting agencies who must each sign off on the division of property, or a set of co-owners who must all agree to the division, then dividing land suddenly becomes harder.[6] Conversely, assembly becomes far easier if it is not necessary for *all* the pieces held by a set of identifiable owners to be assembled, or if the assembled property does not have to be in a particular location, or in a particular shape—or indeed, even contiguous at all.[7] Take radio spectrum, for example. The traditional goal of establishing a nationwide radio presence depended only on acquiring (any of many) thin bands of spectrum in a sufficient number of local markets.[8] This was a much easier form of aggregation to accomplish through market processes than the more recent efforts to reassemble large contiguous blocks of spectrum.[9] In all of these cases, we must consider who has to agree to the reconfiguration and the extent to which each contribution is unique and essential. The ultimate difficulty of dividing or aggregating also depends on whether and how the owners' lack of consent can be overridden, such as through eminent domain, spectrum repacking, judicial partition, or other mechanisms.

Assembly Problems

Consider land assembly. Why is it often both valuable and difficult to put together separately held pieces of land? Suppose land is currently broken up into half-acre lots for residential use, but consolidating the lots would generate more value by enabling a larger-scale use.[10] The stakes grow higher if the preferred new use takes a lumpy or step-like form. Stephen Shmanske and Daniel Packey give the example of a golf course that requires a minimum of ninety-one acres to be viable.[11] If the golf course would be the best use of the land, but only ninety acres can be assembled, the land will be relegated to a lower-valued use, such as a park.[12] Similar analysis would apply if a species requires a minimum amount of habitat, or a particular (complete) migratory corridor, to remain sustainable.[13] Likewise, bringing a new invention or drug to market may require assembling licenses from all of the relevant patent holders—including ones who come out of the woodwork after the manufacturer has already committed to a particular product development path.

These examples involve lumpiness in demand (such as an entire golf course or the right to market a whole product) that is not matched by lumpiness in supply (land may currently be in half-acre segments, and patents on components may be scattered among many holders). Moreover, the ingredients to the assembly are defined by past allocations of rights. Land does not arrive from nature with lot lines marked on it; rather, the units in which land is supplied depend largely on past patterns of land ownership and use.[14] Each current property owner has a spatial monopoly on her own parcel of land—a fact that does not matter as long as there are plenty of alternative parcels to choose from.[15] But that monopoly power becomes significant if each parcel is needed in order to undertake a new use of the land at a different scale.[16]

Who, Exactly, Must Agree?

The difficulty of an assembly problem is less a function of how many owners must agree than of the *specificity* of the participation requirement. Must all or a large proportion of *particular* owners agree to sell in order for a given shopping center, golf course, highway, or wildlife corridor to come about? Or will just about any set of landowners do? The degree of specificity depends on several features of the situation. Consider first the tightness or looseness of geographic constraints on the assembly, which we can capture with the term *tethering*. Are there mountains that require the highway to run through a narrow valley? Are there only certain physical locations where habitat can be viably maintained? Must a particular spot (such as a historic landmark) be included within the envelope of the assembly? How many and how robust are the points of adhesion that tie this assembly to precise geospatial locales? In short, how spatially tethered must this assembly be?

It is possible to imagine assemblies that are almost entirely untethered. Suppose any twenty acres within a medium-sized city will serve equally well as a centralized storage facility for certain equipment or records. There is still some tethering even in this example, insofar as the facility has to be within municipal boundaries, but it is of a very loose sort. At the other end of the spectrum, if there is only one site that will serve as the right place for a certain assembly (perhaps due to its unique geographic features), the assembly is precisely tethered to that spot. Specificity is at its height in this context, because every owner who holds property within the relevant geographic footprint must agree to the assembly. Even if there is only one owner, a problem of bilateral monopoly may emerge as the parties vie over surplus. But if there are many owners, the risk increases that the individual prices that the parties choose will combine to preclude a mutually advantageous assembly.[17]

If tethering is not complete (and usually it is not), then other factors help determine the specificity of participation, including the intuitive criteria of *contiguity* and *shape*. Perhaps the assembled acreage can be anywhere, but the assembly must be fully contiguous and in a regular, rectangular shape. Or perhaps the assembled land can be any shape, including an unusual "barbell" or "tentacles" formation as long as there is sufficient contiguity to enable unimpeded travel between the portions of the holdings. The combination of tethering, contiguity, and shape determines the flexibility of the assembly and how unique the components are that make it up (in other words, how many good substitutes exist for each). These factors together determine the ratio between the number of property owners who *can* contribute and the number who *must* contribute. If the relationship is one to one, the agreement of every specified party is required, a form of unanimity. Coercion or changes in property rights protection are often employed to sidestep such a harsh participation requirement, as the following sections discuss.

Coercion

Eminent domain is often (at least implicitly) justified by property assemblies that take a lumpy or step form.[18] At the extreme, a highway or pipeline requires a full contiguous stretch of land in order to realize large gains; missing pieces defeat the purpose. In other cases, like an urban redevelopment project or the preservation of habitat, having all the pieces of a contiguous holding would significantly increase the value of the entire holding, even though it would be possible to glean some substantial positive returns from a partial or incomplete aggregation. When it comes to assembling land or other property entitlements, we can again think in terms of production functions. There may be minimum assembly thresholds necessary for any return at all, maximums beyond which no further returns are enjoyed, regions of increasing or decreasing gains, sharp steps, or any combination of these effects.

We might wonder why the necessary pieces of property cannot be assembled through ordinary market transactions. In some cases, this is indeed feasible, especially if the parties from whom the property is being purchased remain unaware of the assembly efforts.[19] But often, such awareness is inevitable, whether due to government disclosure or transparency requirements, or the public process involved in clearing the necessary land use permits. Knowing that their entitlements will serve as essential inputs to a much more valuable configuration, owners of the separate parcels may each attempt to hold out for a larger share of the assembly surplus.[20] Private efforts to reconfigure property may, therefore, run aground due to strategic bargaining problems.

The potential for this result is baked into the structure of property entitlements. Interests in property are usually protected by what Guido Calabresi and Douglas Melamed call "property rules," which grant the owner the right to veto any transfer outright, unless and until she is offered a price that she finds agreeable.[21] This arrangement protects each owner's subjective valuation of her property, but it also lets holdouts thwart valuable land assemblies.[22] In Calabresi and Melamed's terms, eminent domain swaps in a "liability rule" for a property rule.[23] The owner loses the right to veto the transaction, and the government can force the transfer to go through by paying compensation (typically fair market value) to the owner.[24] Such coercive overrides solve the holdout problem but introduce new difficulties, as the controversy over the *Kelo* case suggests.

Aside from vivid concerns about the loss of autonomy that comes from a forced sale, the compensation provided by the government is often thought inadequate to make up for the owner's loss, given subjective attachments to the property and other uncompensated elements of value.[25] The problem is not just that undercompensation can seem unfair, but also that it may make it unclear whether the assembly of land generates more value than leaving the property pieces unassembled, in the hands of their original owners. Even if we think that the government fully internalizes the pain of paying compensation for the properties that it acquires, its condemnation choices will be distorted if it is not required to pay as much as the properties are worth to their owners.[26]

Relying on private transactions to assemble land tends to filter out assemblies that would reduce rather than add value, since each owner will have voluntarily chosen to part with the property at the offered price. But bargaining impasse can block value-enhancing (efficient) assemblies that would produce large social benefits. Eminent domain and other coercive transfers can solve the impasse problem, but at the potential cost of allowing some value-reducing (inefficient) assemblies to go forward. In other words, the tool that society uses to overcome the bad stickiness of strategic behavior can also cut indiscriminately through the good stickiness that keeps losing reconfigurations from occurring too easily. Choosing between approaches means deciding whether to tolerate more false positives (inefficient assemblies produced through coercion) in order to reduce the number of false negatives (efficient assemblies that fail to occur), or to do the opposite, tolerate more false negatives in order to reduce the number of false positives.[27] Scott Duke Kominers and Glen Weyl explain: "Any successful mechanism for reducing holdout must strike a delicate balance. While full protection of property rights can preclude any possibility of efficient assembly, excessively weakening sellers' property rights may encourage frivolous and exploitative assemblies."[28]

Holdout Risk and Property Protections

Explicitly recognizing lumpiness—and the holdout risk that it can generate—provides one basis for striking this balance. Consider a prototypical assembly project: buying land to build a railroad. The assembler needs enough contiguous segments to form a complete route and also wants to minimize twists and turns that will add to the cost and risk of the route. A textbook on railroad construction advises starting with a straight line between each set of points and trying to "find a general route which will have the least possible variation from that straight line, without sacrificing the limits of ruling grade, curvature, and general type or cost of construction."[29] If there is only one viable route that meets these criteria, the railroad project is like a bridge—we need all the pieces or we have nothing of value. It is a step good. In cases like this where strict complementarities are present and all the parcels are essential to a valuable assembly, coercion may be the only way to overcome strategic holdout problems.

If there are multiple viable routes, the problem may be easier—at least at first. Given routing constraints, the problem is not quite like that of the spectrum assembler who just needs *some* bits and pieces in multiple locations—everything needs to connect up in a sensible way. The ability to route around recalcitrant landowners is not unlimited, given the financial and accident-related disadvantages of adding deviations to the track.[30] But when the land assembler is initially scouting out possibilities, even a limited set of alternatives can create sufficient competition to ease holdout concerns.[31] Once the railroad has committed to a particular route, however, its options dwindle, and the monopoly power of the landowners grows accordingly.

This same basic pattern can be seen in the patent context. Here, a product designer faces what Carl Shapiro dubbed a "patent thicket," which he describes as "a dense web of overlapping intellectual property rights that a company must hack its way through in order to actually commercialize new technology."[32] A product designer might initially be able to take any number of engineering approaches—map any number of pathways through the "patent thicket" to assemble rights over the necessary components. But once a manufacturer has committed to a particular pathway, the firm needs *all* of the necessary rights that lie on that pathway.[33] This is why so-called patent trolls generate such angst.[34] The term is usually applied to a party who strategically acquires a patent with the express purpose of later licensing it (and with no plans to practice it), and who then lies in wait as other business entities develop products or services for which the patented material is an integral part.[35] Once reliance on the patented element has reached a very high level, the troll emerges and threatens devastating legal action unless a licensing agreement is negotiated.[36] The threatened shutdown of BlackBerry email service in 2006 is a commonly cited example—one that led to a $612.5 million settlement shortly before a judge was expected to issue an injunction.[37]

The patent holder's ability to exact leverage (and payments) depends on what the law will do about an infringement. In the 2006 case of *eBay v. MercExchange*, the Supreme Court held that patent holders are not entitled to an automatic injunction that would enable them to shut down the infringer.[38] Instead, a set of four factors determines whether a patent holder will be granted an injunction or merely damages. Justice Kennedy's concurring opinion, joined by Justices Stevens, Souter, and Breyer, expressed concerns about patent trolls, although he did not use that term:

> An industry has developed in which firms use patents not as a basis for producing and selling goods but, instead, primarily for obtaining licensing fees. . . . For these firms, an injunction, and the potentially serious sanctions arising from its violation, can be employed as a bargaining tool to charge exorbitant fees to companies that seek to buy licenses to practice the patent. . . . When the patented invention is but a small component of the product the companies seek to produce and the threat of an injunction is employed simply for undue leverage in negotiations, legal damages may well be sufficient to compensate for the infringement and an injunction may not serve the public interest.[39]

Here we see how a seemingly esoteric question of legal remedies becomes quite momentous—it determines whether an owner of intellectual property has "property rule" protection that gives her the right to stop the use of her component outright or merely "liability rule" protection that limits recovery to damages, allowing the assembler to continue to use the component if he pays. Recall that in the landowner context, eminent domain is a way of downgrading protection to mere liability rule status to enable forced sales—a very controversial move. Courts can effectively do the same thing by deciding what remedies a property owner can get against an encroacher.

Liability rule solutions have cropped up not only in intellectual property contexts but also in settings involving real property, including situations where a landowner accidentally builds over a neighbor's property line.[40] For instance, in a New Jersey Supreme Court case, *Mannillo v. Gorski*, a homeowner built exterior steps and a walkway without realizing that they extended fifteen inches over a neighbor's property line. The court observed that in certain cases of mistaken improvements, "the true owner may be forced to convey the land so occupied upon payment of the fair value thereof."[41] In remanding the case for a determination of whether such an outcome was appropriate, the court emphasized considerations that should by now sound familiar, such as whether the forced conveyance would leave the "balance of the [original owner's] parcel unusable or no longer capable of being built upon by reason of zoning or other restrictions."[42] In other words, the lumpiness of the stairs and walkway might compel a conveyance, but only if this would not destroy another lumpy interest in keeping the encroached-upon parcel whole.

In the patent and railroad examples, complementarities were strict (or became so after development had reached a certain stage); all the pieces were needed. This setup generates significant monopoly power for the component holders if the law gives them property rule protection. But when complementarities are not strict (that is, not all the components are essential to achieving the goal), the bargaining dynamic changes. Consider an urban redevelopment zone or a shopping center that requires some critical mass of contiguous space but can be shaped in a variety of different ways. Now, would-be holdouts risk being left out of the assembly altogether—which may not only deprive them of a deal they would have viewed as worthwhile, but leave them adjacent to uses that may not be compatible with their own. For example, most homeowners would not want to be the lone holdout whose dwelling is surrounded by an industrial complex after all her neighbors have departed. In such cases, ordinary market forces may be sufficient to assemble the necessary land.

Indeed, we might worry that market dynamics will at times create too much pressure toward assemblies—again, for reasons relating to lumpiness. Gideon Parchomovsky and Peter Siegelman offer a case study in which a power company was able to acquire an entire town, in part due to the close-knit nature of the community.[43] Once a certain fraction of households in the community sold their homes, the rest of the residents found that they no longer placed much value on staying put.[44] Here, the town's cohesiveness can be viewed as a lumpy good that required a critical mass of established neighbors. Once enough people left, the community was fractured in a way that destroyed much of the area's appeal for those who remained.[45] As Susan Kuo and Benjamin Means explain, a similar dynamic can arise when the government offers buyouts to owners affected by flooding, as New Jersey did in the wake of Superstorm Sandy.[46] Homeowners deciding whether to return to a flood-affected area may find the prospect less appealing once a critical mass of their neighbors have accepted buyouts. For this reason, even voluntary buyouts can contain an element of compulsion.[47]

As these examples suggest, when valuations are interdependent, a "divide and conquer" strategy can make large-scale transformations easier to achieve, whether assembling pieces of property in the hands of a developer or keeping a flood-prone area from being resettled.[48] This is especially true if there is a certain threshold of departures beyond which value drops sharply for most or all who were considering remaining in place.[49] The fact that these goals become easier to accomplish does not tell us whether they *should* be accomplished, however. To answer that question, we need to know how much value the neighbors would have cumulatively derived from the property had they all resisted selling, and compare that with the value to be gained by moving the property into new hands. But people's valuations of their property are chronically difficult to discern, as the next section discusses, making it uncertain whether a given reconfiguration represents an improvement. This uncertainty, which can attend even voluntary assemblies of property, sharpens concerns about using government coercion to bring about assemblies.

Information Problems and Solutions

Suppose a landowner, Lani, holds a piece of land that is essential to a development project. The would-be assembler, Acme, offers Lani more than twice the fair market value of her property, but she refuses to sell. How should we interpret her price resistance? Perhaps she is a holdout who hopes to extract more of the assembly surplus from Acme. If she is simply bluffing, her strategizing may prevent assembly of the interests in the hands of a higher-valuing Acme. But she might instead be what Gideon Parchomovsky and Peter Siegelman have termed a "holdin"—someone whose refusal to sell is based on her honest subjective valuation.[50] In that case, the land may be more valuable in pieces (with Lani retaining her parcel) than it would be once assembled. A liability rule solution like eminent domain would allow the deal to go through over Lani's objection, which is the efficient result if Lani is just a holdout, but not if she's a holdin. Knowing how to proceed would be much easier if we could know Lani's true valuation. Yet simply asking her is unlikely to produce a reliable estimate.

Instead, we might consider self-assessed valuation mechanisms, which have long been discussed by scholars, and have even been implemented at times.[51] The basic idea is simple: the person whose entitlement is at stake decides what it is worth, but offsetting consequences attach to that valuation in order to create pressures toward honest valuation. For example, homeowners might be required to state the value of their homes for purposes of both property taxation and eminent domain compensation.[52] Assess your property too high, and you have to pay too much tax. Assess it too low, and you risk losing the property at a price that is inadequate. Such mechanisms offer a twist on coercion: they override an owner's ability to *block* the transfer but allow her to control the *price* of the transfer. Fine-tuning the mechanism to induce honest valuations presents challenges, however, as those writing on the topic have well noted.[53] Another complication involves complementarity: the value an owner places on her own property will vary depending on what she expects to happen to other nearby properties. Nonetheless, self-assessment represents an intriguing approach to one of the largest problems with assembly efforts—the lack of accurate information on valuations.

Adding Division

Although I have focused so far on assembly problems, the same structural problems can plague efforts to *divide up* resources. Suppose two siblings part ways and need to split up a plot of land that they jointly own. At the outset, each sibling owns an undivided share of the whole parcel. Splitting up this holding requires physically dividing the land, or selling it and divvying up the proceeds, or some combination of the two.[54] If the pair cannot agree on how to break up the property, they can resort to the courts for a coercive solution—judicial partition.[55] Like eminent domain, judicial partition accomplishes a reconfiguration of property by coercively overriding the veto power of at least one party.

Lumpiness can play a role in the court's choice of a solution. If economies of scale make the land significantly more valuable when it is kept together than when it is physically split into pieces, this weighs in favor of keeping the land intact and selling it as a single unit.[56] And often courts do exactly that.[57] However, these partition-by-sale solutions can conflict with the strong interests that some parties may have in continued physical possession—a form of temporal lumpiness. This interest in unbroken possession can sometimes cause courts to order partition in kind and physically split up the land, even when market assessments suggest it is more valuable unified.[58]

Of course, the question of whether property is more valuable in pieces or together may be hard for a judge to assess. People often possess private information about their own valuations that is difficult to verify. Suppose one of the siblings in our story, Carly, is especially attached to a portion of the property that she has lived or worked on for a long time. Carly's subjective valuation of that segment may be so great as to make splitting up the property the highest-value alternative. Still, we might think she could simply outbid her sibling in a partition sale, keep her favorite part, and sell the rest.[59] But she may lack the liquidity to do so. Should the law privilege the (apparent) lump of value associated with keeping the land in one piece over the (asserted) lump of value associated with keeping it in Carly's hands?

As in the case of land assembly, we might consider mechanisms for eliciting truthful information about valuations. A familiar example is the procedure for dividing a cake between two kids.[60] Player 1 cuts the cake into two pieces, and Player 2 decides which piece to take. By making the pieces equal in her own eyes, the cutter insures that she will receive what she views as half the value of the cake. The solution is not perfect—maybe part of the cake contains features like cherries that one player knows the other player loves (or detests), allowing for strategic division gambits.[61] Nonetheless, there are significant pressures toward honest efforts to divide the cake equitably.

The "Shotgun" or "Texas Shootout" technique for dissolving a business enterprise operates on similar principles.[62] It works like this: Partner 1 states how much a share of the enterprise is worth to her. Partner 2 then has two choices. First, he can buy out Partner 1's interest at that price. Or, alternatively, Partner 2 can demand that Partner 1 pay that much to buy out Partner 2's own share. Just as the cake cutter does not know which piece she will end up with, the Shotgun mechanism gains its power from the valuer's ignorance of whether she will wind up as a buyer or a seller.[63] The intuitions behind these approaches can be adapted to tackle other division problems. For example, Yun-chien Chang and I developed an approach to judicial partition of co-owned land that relies on self-assessed valuations;

like the other approaches, it hinges on parties not knowing whether their stated values will end up being the basis for making payments or receiving payments.[64]

The rules that govern division do not just determine how things get split up; they may also determine whether things get split up at all, and how the parties are likely to behave prior to the split.[65] Yet this is not unique to the division context. The rules that determine when and how coercion can be used to produce an assembly and the way in which compensation will be calculated can also influence the prospects for assembly and the kinds of investments that owners make in the shadow of a potential assembly.[66] This is just one way in which the problems of division and assembly share a common structure, as the next section explains.

Assembly and Division Together

Slicing and lumping problems both begin the same way: with a resource that is, at least allegedly, suboptimally configured. Two basic things are involved in any reconfiguration of that resource. First, the consent of those with stakes in the resource must either be obtained or the lack of consent overridden. Second, surplus from the reconfiguration must be divided up somehow. The two elements may occur simultaneously or as two separate steps. For example, when a developer buys up parcels of land to assemble a large, unified tract, the same purchase prices that buy consent to the reconfiguration also parcel out the share of surplus that each parcel holder receives. Likewise, co-owners of property who are seeking partition must assemble everyone's consent to a voluntary agreement carrying out the terms of the split (which will determine the division of surplus), or have the lack of consent overridden through judicial partition, with surplus parceled out in the process.

The exercise of eminent domain overrides consent, while the rules governing compensation payments determine what portion of the assembly surplus, if any, will go to the original landowners. If the compensation payments are lower than the landowners' valuations (as will typically be the case if only fair market value is provided), then the landowners do not receive any of the assembly surplus and will instead bear losses. As an alternative, a group of neighboring landowners might agree in advance to a particular way of splitting up the proceeds from a sale of their collective holdings (e.g., based on parcel size or square footage), should the group as a whole decide to sell to a developer. They might then adopt and employ a voting mechanism through which their lack of unanimous consent to the sale could be overridden.[67] Similarly, a court order to dissolve a condominium ("strata property") in British Columbia can be obtained based on an 80 percent dissolution vote; the entire property is then sold and the sales proceeds are split among the former owners.[68] The possibilities are many, but one way or another, both steps—aggregating agreement and dividing surplus—must occur.

The Trouble with Fragmentation

Seeing that slicing and lumping are structurally identical problems exposes the flaw in assuming that putting together fragmented entitlements is an inherently harder problem than splitting up resources that are consolidated in some way. This point sheds light on the "anticommons"—a theoretical construct that highlights problems with assembling entitlements. Frank Michelman, who originally introduced the concept, cast the anticommons as the opposite of a commons—a situation in which resources may be wasted not because too many people have access to them, but rather because too many people hold vetoes over their use.[69] If entering a park requires going through a gate locked with ten separate padlocks, and ten people each hold one of the necessary keys, any one of them can keep a would-be park-goer from entering. Using the park as a resource requires assembling keys, which in turn requires assembling consent.

Later work by Michael Heller extended the idea of the anticommons and applied it to a range of legal problems, from land use to patents.[70] The same problem of assembling consent that we saw in the gated park example arises when a developer wishes to put together many tracts of land or a manufacturer needs to assemble a large set of patent rights. Heller argued that dividing property entitlements among a large number of owners could have tragic consequences, because reconsolidating the pieces would often be prohibitively costly.[71] To be sure, tragedy is not inevitable, as anticommons theorists have well recognized. But concerns about reconsolidation have nonetheless been cited as a reason to avoid unduly fragmenting property interests.[72]

Sometimes fragmented property rights do present assembly difficulties, as we have seen. If each of a set of independently held entitlements must be acquired to make use of a given consolidated resource (whether a bridge, enough land for a highway, or a product that relies on licenses for multiple patents), then each entitlement holder has an effective veto over the entire useful resource. But the resulting holdout potential arises not because the resource *itself* is fragmented, but rather because our system of property grants certain strong rights—and associated remedies—to the holders of these fragments. In other situations, such as land concurrently owned by more than one person, each individual has a stake in the whole property, which the law will again protect. Here too, there may be difficulties reaching unanimous agreement; if this occurs, the law provides mechanisms for the parties' lack of consent to be overridden.

As Michelman emphasized, the problem lies not with the way a given resource is held (in separate private ownership or in common), but rather with the potential for self-interest to get in the way of the resource being usefully exploited.[73] It is the need to assemble *cooperation*, not the property itself, that creates the dilemma. This is true whether the reconfiguration in question involves slicing up things held in common or lumping together things currently held separately. Indeed, one of the most famous eminent domain cases decided by the Supreme Court, *Hawaii Housing Authority v. Midkiff*, involved the use of condemnation not to assemble land but rather to break up a land oligopoly.[74] Fragmentary property interests may create reconfiguration problems serious enough to require coercive overrides, but so too may consolidated holdings.

Property rights might also be intentionally fragmented to make it more difficult to bring about changes in existing arrangements.[75] For example, if a number of neighbors have effective veto power over shifting a nearby park into some more intensive use, the park cannot undergo a radical change without broad consensus among these stakeholders.[76] This stickiness may or may not be efficient in a given case. But the fact that fragmentation of rights can entrench existing configurations may at times be beneficial rather than harmful. Recall that it will often be unclear which configuration will actually generate more value. The fact that a reconfiguration is difficult to accomplish does not necessarily bespeak inefficiency; perhaps the reconfiguration should not occur.

Sometimes pieces of property work best for some purposes when kept in separate ownership, but best for other purposes when consolidated. Suppose several parcels of farmland overlay a large oil reserve. The farmland may be most efficiently managed by separate owners, but the oil reserve would be most efficiently managed as a unit. In other words, the scale that optimizes exploitation of one resource (soil) is different from the scale that optimizes exploitation of another resource (oil).[77] Consolidating the farmers' holdings would make the oil operations more valuable but would make the farming operations less valuable. Here, creative solutions may enable both resources to be managed efficiently.[78] Oil unitization, in which the landowners collectively manage the oil reserve (while preserving their separate interests in the farmland) offers one solution, but it presents fresh challenges in assembling landowner consent to the unitization arrangement itself.[79] Compulsory unitization laws, enacted in many oil-producing states (but not Texas), allow a supermajority of landowners to force the others into a collective oil management arrangement.[80] This, of course, is a coercive solution, resolving some concerns and raising others. As with land assembly, unitization involves both aggregation of consent (or a coercive override) and the division of surplus.

Keeping Options Open

Decisions made today, such as whether to fragment property holdings into smaller pieces, will have lasting repercussions tomorrow. Some legal doctrines—from minimum lot sizes to the rule against perpetuities—have been justified as attempts to improve or conserve opportunities for the future reaggregation of property entitlements.[81] Indeed, Heller and other scholars posit a "one-way ratchet" or Humpty Dumpty effect in which entitlements are easy to break apart but very difficult to piece back together again.[82] Yet the analysis above shows that reunifying fragmented entitlements is not inevitably more difficult than pulling apart consolidated ones—Humpty Dumpty notwithstanding. What really matters is how the law assigns and protects claims on property, whether those claims are to fragments or to shares of a unified whole.

Significantly, it is currently unknown what configuration will later be most valuable.[83] Keeping property in a large tract today preserves the option of using the land at that scale later on without having to reassemble dispersed parcels. That's a valuable option, but it is not infinitely valuable. It must be traded off against the opportunity costs of keeping the land unified today—as well as the possibly higher future costs of dividing the land, should *that* configuration turn out to be the optimal one. Even if we had a rough sense of whether future needs would call for more consolidation or more division, we still would not know whether to encourage larger or smaller holdings today.

Imagine, for example, that a developer needs eighty-five contiguous acres within an area containing one hundred acres in total. Will her chances of assembling the necessary land be better if she faces five owners who each own twenty-acre lots, or one hundred owners who each own one-acre lots? It is impossible to be sure without more information. For example, we would need to know about any constraints on the shape or configuration of the assembled parcel, to determine the degree of complementarity and substitutability among pieces.[84] But we can say this much: each owner's cooperation will be critical in the case of twenty-acre holdings, whereas fifteen owners' cooperation will be unnecessary where the pieces are smaller.

Counterintuitively, the larger parcels make the assembly a pure step good, whereas the smaller ones make it merely lumpy (since not all pieces are needed, the complementarity is not as strict). Given the ability of a single holdout to thwart the assembly in the first case (and the incentives that each landowner will have to hold out), smaller holdings might be *more* conducive to this sort of later assembly. Thus, even if we could predict that larger-scale uses would be more valuable in the future, it might still be counterproductive to prevent people from subdividing their twenty-acre parcels in the hopes of easing later reconfigurations.

Conversely, suppose that a currently unified nine-acre parcel will later be most valuable as nine separate one-acre building lots. At the moment, a judicial partition action is pending before the court, and a decision must be made about whether to split the land physically among four siblings (so that each would get 2.25 acres) or keep the land intact through a partition sale. Again, the ability to predict that a smaller-scale use will be more valuable in the future would not be especially helpful in deciding what to do now. As figure 2.1 shows, splitting the property four ways (along the solid lines) creates a situation in which all four siblings must cooperate in

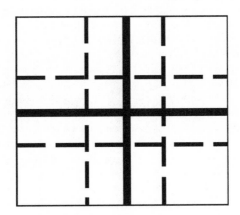

Figure 2.1. Division Problems. Source: Chang and
Fennell, "Partition and Revelation," app. D, 12,
fig. D1, https://perma.cc/P752-7CVL.

order to generate nine parcels (indicated by the dashed lines). By contrast, a single owner of the full parcel could simply subdivide the property into nine lots at some future date.

Of course, we can imagine counterexamples that go the other way. The point is simply that attempting to hedge our bets against the need for future reconfiguration by doing more or less division or aggregation today is not likely to be a winning strategy. Instead, if we truly wish to keep our options open as to land configuration, we could make use of actual options—instruments that would provide the right, but not the obligation, to reconsolidate or reconfigure land in the future. Such an approach would allow land to be used in whatever way is currently best, but bake in the possibility of changing its use in the future. Flexible alternative modes of holding property may become increasingly important as urbanization makes the need for reconfiguration a more frequent and pressing concern.[85]

Reconfiguration problems differ along a number of dimensions, as we have seen. The most obvious distinction—whether the reconfiguration involves dividing up a resource that is presently aggregated or aggregating resources that are currently split up—turns out to be less significant than is commonly assumed. Grasping the essential similarity between different kinds of reconfiguration problems enables us to see that what really must be assembled is cooperation, which might be aggregated either to put things together or break things apart. This same assembly of participation recurs in collective action problems that take a step or lumpy form, as we will see in the next chapter.

THREE

Lumpy Goals, Segmented Resources

In 1949, the Oklahoma City Zoo acquired a young elephant named Judy. The pachyderm arrived with much fanfare, including a parade down Main Street, and remained a favorite at the zoo until her death in 1997 at the age of fifty-two.[1] Judy's purchase was funded by donations of pennies, nickels, and dimes from fifty thousand Oklahoma schoolchildren (my mother among them) through a campaign sponsored by a local newspaper, the *Oklahoman*. In this case, small inputs that were initially divided among many different people were successfully assembled to achieve a lumpy objective. Judy's story connects to a central question for social policy: When and how can people cooperate to achieve collective goals without legal coercion?

Physique aside, it's obvious why an elephant qualifies as a lumpy or indivisible good—one must buy the whole animal. Judy was also a lumpy *public good*.[2] The two signal characteristics of a public good are nonrivalrousness and nonexcludability.[3] Judy, although just one elephant, was nonrival in that she could be viewed and enjoyed by large numbers of zoo-goers without diminishing the enjoyment of other zoo-goers. While it is true that Judy was, strictly speaking, excludable—the zoo was gated and a nominal admission fee was charged to enter—it was neither feasible nor desirable to limit access to Judy to those who had contributed to her purchase. Not only did many people visit the zoo over the decades Judy resided there, many more had the option of doing so, and still more enjoyed virtual access to Judy through photos and news stories.[4]

Economic analysis tells us that public goods like Judy tend to be underprovided due to free-rider problems. The benefits from these goods go to everyone within range, while the costs fall only on those who contribute. Similarly, common-pool resources like fisheries, which feature depletable (rival) resources, are usually viewed as highly susceptible to tragedies of the commons.[5] Not only may some fishers fail to cooperate in restricting their catches, but the efforts of the most cooperative fishers may be undone by noncooperators who respond by stepping up their own extractive efforts. Yet we know that at least sometimes, people can solve collective action problems informally, without resorting to legal coercion. People find ways to provide public goods privately,[6] and communities are often able to successfully manage common-pool resources.[7]

I will focus here on two factors that affect the likelihood that collective action problems can be noncoercively resolved: (1) the lumpiness of the collective good or bad in question; and (2) the way in which the resources being harvested (or contributed) are broken up or segmented. These two factors interact. Lumpy collective action problems may be overcome by making a cooperative strategy focal—and segmentation provides a way of doing exactly that.[8]

Lumpiness in Collective Goods and Bads

Resource problems and their solutions often take a lumpy or step form.[9] For example, fishing from a common pool may do little or no harm up to a certain threshold, but then produce a population crash that destroys the resource altogether.[10] Keeping the crash from occurring may require the cooperative forbearance of *all* the local fishing operations—even one holdout who intensively overfishes could doom the effort.[11] Similarly, curing a disease or addressing an environmental hazard might require a high fixed expenditure on a new technology; in such a case, falling short by a thousand dollars could be as bad as falling short by millions of dollars. Other collective efforts, like exiting from a burning building in an orderly manner or carrying out a successful boycott, similarly depend on attaining certain thresholds of cooperation.[12]

Large literatures have examined how collective action problems play out under different assumptions, and scholars have identified and analyzed a number of evocatively named game structures, including the Prisoners' Dilemma, the Stag Hunt, and Chicken.[13] Rather than revisit that literature in detail here, I want to start with a single, crucial distinction that separates collective action problems involving lumpy goods from collective action problems that involve a steady, linear relationship between inputs and outcomes: people confronting lumpy collective action problems will not invariably find it rational to "defect" (choose the noncooperative option). This is true even if we assume the most narrowly self-interested vision of human rationality, and even if no mitigating factors like social norms or repeat play are involved. Instead, what is rational for one player to do depends on what she expects others to do.

This does not mean people will always cooperate—far from it. In game theory lingo, such lumpy problems feature *multiple equilibria*, which means that no single outcome can be predicted from the payoff structure.[14] We can see how the possibilities play out by examining three basic elements that define any collective action problem: production functions, participation requirements, and payoffs.

Production Functions

As we saw in chapter 1, a production function for a particular good or bad is simply the relationship between inputs and outcomes. What happens as each segment is added to a path between two parks, each additional dollar is contributed to a charity, each successive unit of pollution is expelled from a factory, or each boatload of fish is extracted from a fishery? Do the benefits or harms come all at once in a single large step, in several big jumps, in a smoothly proportionate manner, or something in between?

A social goal with a lumpy or step production function has an all-or-nothing quality—the result is indivisible. This indivisibility matters in two ways. First, it raises the stakes for getting (or avoiding) the required level of inputs. Depending on whose cooperation is required to secure those inputs (participation requirements), strategic behaviors like free riding and holding out can be a significant barrier to success. At the same time, the all-at-once payoff structure creates powerful incentives toward cooperation, since nothing can be enjoyed by anyone until the threshold is reached. As we will see, this structure departs radically from the Prisoners' Dilemma template that legal scholars overwhelmingly conjure up when analyzing collective action problems.[15]

Participation Requirements

Consider a lumpy good like a wildlife corridor. By connecting otherwise isolated patches of habitat, a corridor allows for greater movement and dispersal of species.[16] The completeness of a corridor, like that of a bridge, is central to its function. Although a fragmented corridor would still add area to the habitat patch (or patches) to which it is adjacent, generating some benefits, the value uniquely delivered by connectivity between the patches would be lost.[17] Who must contribute dollops of cooperation to make (or keep) the corridor complete? The answer, setting aside possibilities like eminent domain, is each of the landowners who control pieces of the would-be corridor. Put in terms introduced in chapter 2, the situation features high specificity—each and every one of these *particular* landowners must agree, unless there are other viable routes. Each of them holds a monopoly on an element that is essential to the overall assembly.

Contrast this situation with another lumpy good, funding a major acquisition for a charity (a piece of expensive technology for saving lives, say, or Judy the elephant). Here, contributions may be sought from a wide range of individuals, but there is no particular set of people who must cooperate in order to fund the outcome. Money is fungible and can be supplied by any subset of the potential contributors, including just one large donor. No one has a monopoly on money, although people obviously have different quantities at their disposal. Unlike the habitat corridor, the funding problem features low specificity (no particular set of people must cooperate—any subset capable of raising the requisite funds will do).

Another standard example of a step good, an election win, lies in between these two extremes in terms of the specificity of participation requirements. Here, participation by enough voters is necessary to supply the good. Each person has a monopoly on her own vote. But not every person must vote for a given candidate in order for that candidate to win. A sufficient block of votes are necessary (strictly complementary to each other) in producing the outcome, but any set of votes within the relevant voting unit can form that block. This distinguishes the election case from the wildlife corridor or standard land assembly cases, where all (or most) of a *particular* set of participants must be on board.

Participation requirements can generate two distinct obstacles: holding out and free riding.[18] The holdout problem is strongly associated with the highly specific participation requirement of unanimous cooperation. Each person always holds a monopoly on her own cooperation, whether that cooperation involves contributing a property interest or other input, casting a vote, or simply choosing one's own behavior. If someone else's cooperation can readily substitute, then that nominal monopoly power generates no holdout problems. Yet the very fact that someone else's cooperation *can* substitute lies at the heart of free-rider problems. Whether these free-rider problems can be overcome may depend more on expectations (and on methods for coordinating them) than on the number of players.[19] Samuel Popkin describes how entrepreneurial leaders can surmount free-rider problems by segmenting "a larger goal into many steps with critical thresholds," thereby creating a situation in which "each person has a monopoly on a necessary factor for the final goal, [and] all contributions are essential."[20] Manipulating the participation requirement in this way can be effective where norms or other aspects of the payoff structure make people unwilling to withhold a critical input—that is, in situations where holdout problems are unlikely.

Another complication involves the way in which participation requirements are distributed over time. Once inputs have been made toward achieving a lumpy good (or avoiding a lumpy bad), will those inputs stay put, or are they vulnerable to raiding? For example, if contributions to fund a lighthouse are made over a period of time and take a fungible form (money, or building materials that can be readily repurposed), the store of inputs might be dissipated before they accumulate to the lighthouse-provision level. Contributions toward the lighthouse are, however, largely locked in place once the lighthouse is constructed; it is a nonrival good that does not get depleted as more ships use its beacon. By contrast, keeping a habitat sustainable is an ongoing project. Here, the inputs involve resources that are not only rival (trees, say) but that remain rival forever, requiring constant cooperation (e.g., not chopping) by those with access to the area.

Payoffs

Whether participation requirements will be met—whether enough parties will choose cooperative actions—depends on the payoff structure. Economic analysis posits that actors who do not bear all the costs or enjoy all the benefits of their actions will do harmful activities too much and beneficial ones too little. The standard tragedy of the commons story equates to a multiplayer Prisoners' Dilemma in which each party always does better by defecting, no matter what anyone else does.[21] But people do not always defect in real life. Indeed, as the work of Elinor Ostrom demonstrates, common-pool resources are often managed in the real world without tragedy.[22] There are many reasons this might be so, including social norms and repeat play, but one crucial factor is the payoff structure, which may look nothing like a Prisoners' Dilemma.

Let's start by looking at an actual multiplayer Prisoners' Dilemma—a simple public goods game in which defection is the dominant strategy. Each of a group of ten players can choose to contribute up to $5 to a common fund in which all contributed dollars will be tripled and divided equally among the players.[23] One of the players, Zoe, quickly realizes that no matter what anyone else does, she will always do better if she hangs onto her entire $5 rather than contributing any of it. If no one else contributes anything, she'll still have her $5, versus the $1.50 she would wind up with if she turned over her money to the magic pot, where her $5 would be tripled to make $15, but then divided among all ten players. If everyone else dutifully puts in their $5 and Zoe contributes nothing, she will collect $13.50 from the group and still have her $5, for a total of $18.50—better than the $15 she will get back if she contributes her money along with everyone else. The same logic holds for all intermediate points. Assuming pure rational self-interest and the lack of any repeat play, norms, or other confounding factors, there is a single all-purpose strategy that dominates no matter what anyone else does: defect.

Notice that this multiplying-pot game features a linear relationship between contributions and payoffs.[24] Each additional contributed dollar produces exactly the same increase in per capita payoffs—thirty cents, in the example just given, where the multiplication factor is three and the group includes ten members. There is no threshold beyond which payoffs jump up or fall off sharply. This explains why Zoe rationally chooses to contribute nothing at all—thirty cents on the dollar is never a good deal—and it also explains why we might expect all of the other players to follow suit. On the other hand, if the magic pot multiplied contributions by a factor larger than the number of participants (say, by twelve rather than by three), each player would always do best by *cooperating*, no matter what anyone else did. Either way, there is a single dominant strategy that does not depend on the actions of others.[25]

Suppose instead that we have a lumpy payoff structure in which no one can receive any payoffs until a particular threshold is reached. For instance, imagine our group of ten players can supply a completed bridge, worth $60 in total benefits ($6 each), if they cumulatively contribute $20. No one will receive any benefit from a smaller contribution, nor will anyone enjoy any increase in benefits from a larger contribution. Now Zoe's reasoning operates differently. It would be worth it to her to contribute the full $5 if the bridge will be supplied (net payoff of $1)—as long as it will really be supplied. Each player's best strategy now depends on what she expects others to do. In short, changing the shape of the problem changes the prediction of universal rational defection.

This hardly means the group's difficulties are over, however. If there is a hard cap of $5 on contributions, the participation of at least four players is necessary to secure the bridge. Because there are ten players in the game, there is no single individual who is in a position to hold out. There are, however, two other problems. First, there is the risk that not enough other people will contribute, which could leave a contributor like Zoe with nothing to show for her trouble except a view of a useless partial bridge. This fear can be allayed by specifying that contributors do not have to pay if the funding threshold is not reached—a model that the crowdfunding platform Kickstarter uses.[26] Such contingent payment schemes have long been of interest as a potential mechanism for increasing contributions.[27] But a refund system cannot address a second worry: that one will pay more than one's fair share for the bridge, while others free ride. In fact, a money-back guarantee may make the free-rider problem worse, if participants now predict that others are more likely to contribute.[28]

Zoe does not relish the thought of contributing to a bridge that others can enjoy for free. Indeed, she would get the highest available payoff ($6) if she could manage to free ride herself and let others make the necessary contributions. However, if the other nine players cumulatively contribute anything between $15 and $19.99 and can credibly commit to paying no more, Zoe will be better off making up the difference herself. Not wanting to be suckered, she may feign disinterest in the bridge construction project and attempt to convince others that she will not pay anything for it. Others will act likewise. The result of all this strategizing will be either the provision of the full bridge in all its spanning glory or no bridge at all.

Sometimes one or more participants would find it worthwhile to pay for an entire lumpy public good. Consider a shipping firm (call it Nightship) that will get so much benefit from a lighthouse that it would be better off paying for the whole thing rather than having to do without it. Yet even if Nightship's payoffs would be high enough to justify paying the lighthouse's full cost, Nightship will still try to convince another firm to pay for part or all of it (since this would make Nightship's payoffs still higher). Features of the situation that single out a particular person or entity as the best provider of the good can break this logjam. Perhaps a larger operator, Amazhip, would use the lighthouse much more intensively than any other shipper, and everyone knows it, making it a matter of good public relations for Amazhip to kick in the lion's share of the funding. Property rights or proximity can also single out a party as the best provider of a local public good, whether putting out a nearby fire or clearing ice from a sidewalk.[29] Thus, if Edgeowner owns a large swath of coastline property, it might be best situated to provide the lighthouse, given its ongoing interest in not having ships run aground in the vicinity.

The lumpiness of the good matters in these cases because it affects the payoff schedule that the firm or individual confronts. The potential provider of a lumpy public good may be forced to an all-or-nothing choice:

contribute what is necessary to provide a complete lighthouse, or do without it altogether. If the "all" choice is justified based on the chooser's own payoffs, the fact that others also benefit will not matter—except to the extent she can convince them, singly or collectively, to contribute to the good's provision. Our contributor might well undersupply the good if it were available in any-sized increments, but because she must decide on an all-or-nothing basis, undersupply is not an option. In other words, we need not worry that the wrong amount of the good will be provided, only whether it will be provided at all.[30]

This analysis assumes that those who make contributions toward a good like a lighthouse will actually be able to enjoy it. This will be the case if the good in question is nonrival, since no one else's consumption will interfere with the consumption of the contributors themselves. Under these circumstances, a contributor can determine her net payoff from supplying the good by simply subtracting the cost of her contributions from the value the good produces for her. Common-pool resources that can be depleted, like a fishery prone to collapse, present a different situation.[31] Keeping the fishery sustainable is a lumpy social goal that involves rival resources. Contributing enough of one's own conservation efforts to save the fishery today may not ensure that the fishery is there to enjoy tomorrow, since other fishers may undo those gains with increased harvesting of their own.

The fact that resources like habitats and fisheries require ongoing participation or forbearance by users to maintain their existence makes their provision sound like a harder nut to crack. But this might not be the case, especially if only a limited number of people have access to the common pool.[32] More sustained participation is required to achieve the lumpy goal than in the nonrival case, but it may be easier to secure if the rival resource units (the extracted fish, say) also provide an observable basis for the equitable allocation of burdens, such as through agreed-upon catch limits.

Importantly, payoffs can include nonpecuniary elements like esteem or shame associated with upholding or breaking social norms. The power of norms to influence behavior in close-knit groups is one reason why commons theorists distinguish between an open-access commons that anyone can use and a limited-access commons open only to a defined and bounded group.[33] An undefined, open-ended user group already makes a common-pool resource problem harder to solve because it directly increases the participation requirements (more people must forbear to preserve the resource). But payoffs also operate differently in such an environment: an open-access commons is more likely to include users who are insensitive to local norms and who, by defecting, may cause cooperative norms to unravel more generally.

Segmented Draws and Contributions

So far we have focused on the lumpiness of collective goals. But we must also consider the granularity of *the inputs* toward those collective goals—a factor that can matter whether the social goods or bads in question are lumpy or linear. How easily groups can achieve cooperative solutions may depend on whether inputs into or draws from the collective good are broken into segments that make the cooperative strategy focal and easy to monitor. This is true even in very simple harvesting situations: a milkshake is harder to share equitably than a pie that has been cut into single-serving slices. Similarly, the success of a common project that requires contributions of effort or money may depend on how the solicited contributions are broken up. For example, Yochai Benkler has emphasized the significance of divisible, granular segments of effort in sustaining peer production models that rely on widespread volunteerism.[34]

People may do their best to equitably share resources that lack visible segmentation, such as a natural gas reserve lying under land held separately by a number of neighbors, but it can be difficult to gauge whether one is taking more or less than one's share. Perceptions may be clouded by a self-serving bias that leads to more generous assessments of one's own appropriations and more critical evaluations of the amounts others are taking.[35] Likewise, in the absence of clear markers that help people see what they are contributing to a collective enterprise, each may assume she is doing more than her fair share.

Segmenting Resources

Resource segmentation can help solve collective action problems by providing a measuring rod for assessing draws on, or contributions to, common pools. Proper segmentation can support cooperation in two interlocking ways. First, appropriately divided resources allow participants to monitor each other's behavior and enforce compliance with social norms.[36] Second, and often as important, participants can use segmentation to monitor their own behavior. For example, studies on the importance of feedback regarding energy use have demonstrated how simply making people aware of their usage, and of how it compares to that of others, can influence their behavior.[37]

This combination of reciprocal monitoring and self-monitoring can buttress internalized norms of fairness by allowing participants to compare their behavior to that of others in the group, and to see whether their contributions and acts of restraint are being reciprocated. Robert Ellickson's study of Shasta County ranchers found that close-knit communities rely on a "rough mental account" to sustain cooperation.[38] Segmentation can act as a handy heuristic to aid similar accounting efforts in a broad range of circumstances. David Lewis gives an example in which ten friends routinely share a plate of twenty shrimp, with each person willing to limit herself to two shrimp as long as the others do the same.[39] While Lewis does not focus on the discrete nature of the food units and their ready divisibility by the number of sharers—nor on the fact that retained shrimp tails may help the eaters keep track of their consumption—these factors would appear to make the sharing equilibrium easier to maintain. Popkin similarly observes that segmentation can deter shirking in an ongoing collective project like keeping a village canal weeded. If each worker is assigned a particular section of the canal to keep clear, monitoring becomes easier (and free riding harder) than if the workers were simply asked to devote a certain amount of time each month to weeding.[40]

Some forms of segmentation occur naturally (individual trees, animals, and so on), but often segmentation is artificially constructed. Land is a good example: aside from irregular boundaries like rivers and mountain ranges, it is a continuous, unsegmented resource. Yet land can be surveyed and broken into parcels suitable for claiming. Likewise, the lines demarcating parking spaces serve as highly visible focal points that generally induce motorists to occupy asphalt in specified chunks, even in free lots where the risk of enforcement is minimal.[41] Segmentation can also be built into harvesting methods. Standardized or shared harvesting equipment (serving spoons, fishing nets, and so on) can divide up resources that do not fall into appropriately sized natural units.

Think of cattle grazing on a shared pasture. The actual resource units in question (blades of grass) are too small, numerous, and difficult to observe to serve the monitoring or benchmarking purposes associated with resource segmentation. The cattle themselves, by contrast, represent a highly visible form of "harvesting equipment" with a (roughly) known capacity.[42] The common-pool resource can thus be segmented de facto based on the number of cattle grazed on the pasture. Fishing nets and boats can operate similarly if they have relatively standardized capacities. Elinor Ostrom explains: "The cost of monitoring an apportioning scheme based on an easily observable factor—what technology a boat is using—is much lower than the cost for one based on the quantity of fish harvested."[43] Even when a designated harvesting method does not physically dole out chunks of a resource in the manner of a net or a spoon, it may nonetheless place a practical limit on the amount of a resource that can be appropriated over a particular timespan. Such a method might then be paired with temporal segmentation (such as a daily or weekly rotation system).[44] The divvying work performed by harvesting technologies explains why new technologies capable of generating higher yields can disrupt existing commons arrangements.[45]

Similar points can be made about limited-access commons in which resources are harvested only for immediate, personal use. Think of a pond from which a set of neighbors may catch fish for household consumption, but not for commercial resale.[46] In this case, the consumption capacities of the commoners place an effective cap on extraction—and if those capacities are low enough and the resource plenteous enough, the arrangement may be sustainable without the need for further restrictions. Such an equilibrium can be disrupted if an active market develops for selling resource units to outsiders. For instance, a Vermont man sparked opposition from his neighbors when he sought to bottle 250,000 gallons of water per day from a Montpelier spring.[47] Here we see how certain forms of capacity-based segmentation implicitly depend on limits on alienability, whether legal or de facto.[48] An all-you-can-eat buffet doesn't work if people can carry out food to eat later or to sell to others.

Although segmentation often helps commoners avoid overdrawing a resource, appropriate segmentation can also prevent *underuse* by making clear what one can legitimately claim without encroaching on the interests of others. For example, people may sit closer together on public benches that are divided by armrests than on undivided benches.[49] Of course, bench armrests may instead be motivated by concerns about perceived overappropriation since they also keep people from lying down—and pointed concerns have been raised about street furniture being intentionally designed to drive away homeless people.[50] Softer forms of demarcation, like the intermittent bench backs and slightly tilted seats shown in figure 3.1, might encourage more use without precluding people from lying down.

Similar in spirit, and likewise potentially addressing both underappropriation and overappropriation, is a product called Soarigami (aka "Portable Armrest Extender/Divider").[51] This device, shaped something like a paper airplane, is designed to clamp onto armrests on airplanes and divide the available armrest area into two equal segments, each of which is also made a bit wider by the "wings" of the product. It's a clever way of divvy-

Figure 3.1. Street Furniture in Santiago, Chile. Photo by author.

ing up often-contested space, although some might prefer a rotation system to subdividing an already small ledge of space. By contrast, the Knee Defender—a set of plastic clips that attach to one's tray table and prevent the person sitting in front from reclining—represents an absolute claim on an ambiguous space, and one that has sparked high-altitude fights.[52] A segmentation solution (timed reclining or partial reclining) seems elusive without some focal point around which expectations can form. An airline attuned to the significance of segmentation (and equipped with sufficient technology) might make a cooperative strategy focal by giving a small reward (a drink coupon, say, or some free airline miles) to any traveler who reclines her seat for less than half of the flight time.

Even small pressures can interact with resource segmentation to control draws against the commons. The pricing structure of some city bike-sharing programs offers a simple illustration. Chicago's Divvy system, for example, allows a patron who has purchased either an annual membership or a twenty-four-hour pass to borrow a bike for free—but usage surcharges will accrue if she keeps the bike out for more than thirty minutes without returning to a Divvy station to check it out again.[53] There is no limit to how many thirty-minute use segments one can rack up seriatim.[54] But returning to a station repeatedly is a minor hassle, and it reinforces the idea that the bikes are meant to be kept in circulation, not hogged by one person for an extended period. Like a tiny serving spoon, the setup communicates something about how much each patron is meant to take.

Segmenting Contributions

Contributions to a resource system, goal, or project (time, money, effort, forbearance, and so on) can also be segmented in a variety of ways, some of which will work better than others in fostering and sustaining cooperation.[55] Innumerable collective projects, from quilting bees to barn raisings, depend on the ability to parcel out appropriately segmented tasks to be completed before and during the interactive event. Making effective use of volunteers requires a similar slicing of time commitments into discrete and manageable segments. For example, the One Brick volunteer program that exists in several cities touts "commitment-free volunteering" in which participants attend discrete volunteering events on an à la carte basis.[56]

Charitable organizations, which must solve large-scale collective action problems, commonly include suggested or recommended contribution amounts rather than issuing open-ended pleas for funds. Often the requested donation is conceptually concretized and quantified by reference to a discrete and tangible unit of assistance, such as a goat or a mosquito net.[57] In the case of large, indivisible goals, a particular challenge is overcoming the sense of "causal impotence"—the idea that one's own contribution will be too small to matter.[58] Yet, interestingly, successful strategies may include wide appeals for very small suggested donations, as in the case of Judy the elephant. The 1938 March of Dimes campaign employed a similar strategy in tackling the indivisible goal of eradicating polio. The campaign's name, coined by entertainer Eddie Cantor (playing off the popular newsreel *The March of Time*), focused attention on a broadly attainable contribution level—a dime.[59] Following Cantor's radio appeal in January 1938, $268,000 in dimes were mailed to President Franklin D. Roosevelt.[60]

Communicating to a potential donor that even a small amount is useful and acceptable can help spur contributions. In a 1976 paper, Robert Cialdini and David Schroeder found a positive effect on contributions when door-to-door fund-raisers added the statement that "even a penny will help"—an effect known as "legitimizing paltry favors" that has been replicated in later studies.[61] It is not clear that the "paltry favors" effect holds for fund-raising that is not conducted face to face.[62] But recent experimental work by Indranil Goswami and Oleg Urminsky found a related phenomenon in written solicitations: setting a low default contribution amount appears to spur a higher rate of contribution.[63] Although Goswami and Urminsky did not find that including a message like "every penny helps" altered the effect of the default,[64] the low default itself plausibly communicated a similar message. By inviting participation at an affordable level, the authors hypothesize, the default may allow people to experience the "warm glow" of giving "at a discount."[65] Although lumpy goods were not part of Goswami and Urminsky's research design, the default might also effectively counter "drop in the bucket" or futility concerns by signaling to potential donors that the charity has calculated the level of contributions necessary to achieve the critical threshold. At a more basic level, the low ask may simply remove the usual excuses to say no.[66]

Goswami and Urminsky's research revealed another side of the story, however, one that makes setting defaults tricky: even though contribution *rates* go up when defaults are low, people may scale back the *amount* of their contribution to match the default.[67] These two effects—the "lower-bar effect" and the "scale-back effect"—may cancel each other out, masking the effects of each.[68] Nonetheless, it may be possible to find a default level for a given audience for which one effect would dominate the other.[69] Research also suggests the efficacy of establishing contribution tiers or categories in encouraging people to "round up" their contributions to achieve the next level.[70]

Empirical work on these issues continues, and findings have been mixed.[71] Yet the potential remains for a well-crafted contribution menu to influence behavior in significant ways. For example, menu options might be designed to reassure lower-level donors that they have given enough while also communicating to higher-level donors that they are not contributing too much. Alternatively, defaults—or even entire menus—might be customized based on the donor's (inferred) willingness and ability to donate.[72]

Parallel points apply to in-kind contributions of effort to collective projects. A volunteer project that can be broken into smaller modules, just like a charity solicitation that calls for a trivial contribution, is likely to attract more participants. As Benkler explains, "the number of people who can, in principle, participate in a project is . . . inversely related to the size of the smallest-scale contribution necessary to produce a usable module."[73] Concerns about a "scale-back" effect among those who would otherwise contribute larger increments of effort might be addressed through a tiered structure capable of accommodating different degrees of involvement based on skill sets, interest, and time.[74]

When Segmentation Goes Wrong

As the foregoing discussion suggests, segmentation can render draws and contributions visible and salient, and hence easier to meter and monitor.[75] But segmentation can also go wrong. Increments that are not clearly demarcated or that are too large, too small, too heterogeneous, or too hard to observe will not serve these beneficial purposes. Demarcation problems can plague even private land holdings, where irregular shapes yield more boundary disputes.[76] Similarly, surface boundaries that sufficed for placer (surface mining) claims proved insufficient for subsurface quartz claims, because in the latter case it could be hard to tell whether the same or a different vein was being tapped.[77] At the extreme, ozone depletion is extraordinarily hard to manage because it involves "small (effectively invisible), highly mobile substances that are distributed throughout the earth's atmosphere."[78]

Mobility of resources can make attempts at segmentation ineffective, even when the individual resource units are visible. Elinor Ostrom observes that a self-organized approach to resource management "is less likely with mobile resource units, such as wildlife or water in an unregulated river, than with stationary units such as trees and plants or water in a lake" due to differences in the costs of observation and monitoring.[79] Mobile resource units not only make extractions difficult to see and police, but they can also mask the danger of overextraction. Consider the astonishing trajectory of the passenger pigeon from overwhelming abundance to extinction as a result of intensive hunting.[80] Without any meaningful way to segment the (initially) massive population, there was no way to track, much less arrest, movement toward the lumpy bad of complete species loss.

Segmentation problems can also arise when the claimable units, although clearly delineated and easy to observe, are sized inappropriately. Take the example of college classrooms that are kept open during nights and weekends to be used as study rooms. Research undertaken several decades ago yielded results that seem likely to remain true today: "The standard custom seems to award the whole room to the first student to take possession by squatter's rights."[81] Here, too-large units induce people to claim too much. But segmentation that leads people to take or accept less than is really useful presents a problem as well. For example, Terry Anderson and Peter Hill observe that the Homestead Acts, which variously granted allotments of 160 acres, 320 acres, or 640 acres to those who lived and worked on the land for five years, "specif[ied] a claim size that was generally inappropriate given the aridity of land on the frontier."[82] As they explain, much of the Great Plains could not be farmed but only grazed, and twenty to thirty acres might be required per head of cattle per year. Thus, even a parcel of 640 acres could only support a herd of twenty to thirty cattle—not nearly enough for a viable ranching operation.[83]

Similar issues exist on the contribution side as well—asking too much or too little can backfire.[84] Writing in 2005, Benkler gave the example of the collaborative online textbook site Wikibooks, which had not caught on with anything like the success of its parent, Wikipedia. Benkler blamed segmentation. In his view, the modules required of participants were too large-grained to elicit widespread interest, given the need to make the books cohere through their entire length and (in the case of texts for public school children) comply with various state requirements. Unlike Wikipedia, which could rely on very small contributions from a very large number of participants, textbook projects required so much from each contributor that it "led many of those who volunteered initially to not complete their contribution."[85] Although the nature of the work itself may have made recalibration of contributions difficult in the textbook context, there are other settings where it may be feasible to improve prospects for cooperation simply by adjusting the ask.

Putting It Together

We have now separately considered two factors that can influence the resolution of a collective action problem: the lumpy or step shape that the social goal takes, and the way in which the inputs toward that goal are segmented. This section will examine how these two elements interact.

Collective action problems involving lumpy goods vary along many dimensions, but they all share one signature feature: there is no single dominant strategy that is always rational for all participants to pursue. Instead, the choice whether to cooperate or defect in a situation involving an indivisible goal depends on what one expects others to do. Because expectations are critical, anything that helps to align (or disrupt) those expectations can influence the prospects for a cooperative, noncoercive solution. Focal points—salient features of the environment that can help parties land upon a cooperative solution—are especially significant in this regard.[86] And the segmentation of resources or contributions can serve as just such a focal point.

As the examples above have suggested, people tend to respond to visible markers that divide up resources, whether parking spaces or pie slices. The same appears to be true of nonhuman species. A study of a type of cichlid fish, the blockhead, showed that two pairs of fish could peacefully share an aquarium when a line of rocks placed at the bottom of the tank visually segmented the space into two sectors.[87] Without these landmarks, there was conflict between the pairs of fish that in nearly every trial resulted in one pair taking over the entire territory, while the other pair was compelled "to leave the floor of the aquarium and to hide on heaters or filters, or to remain swimming on the water's surface."[88] By allowing markers to segment their territory, the fish enjoyed the indivisible goal of aquarium peace. Boundary markers appear to work in roughly similar fashion in many real property interactions among humans.[89] Using segmentation to elicit cooperation is not logically limited to territorial contexts, however; the partitioning of resources can help coordinate behavior whenever any all-or-nothing goal is at stake.

Social norms provide another mechanism for coordinating expectations, and may even override the tendency to defect in linear collective action problems like the multiplying pot. Where lumpy goals are involved, norms carry even more power, because parties may already find it in their own interest to cooperate. If it is unclear whether cooperating is one's best strategy in a given instance, norms can provide the necessary push. The segmentation of resources and contributions provides a mechanism through which norms can be communicated and enforced, by enabling measuring and monitoring. Moreover, norms themselves seem lumpy: once they have become internalized, people tend to follow them consistently, rather than pick and choose when to adhere to a norm and when to flout it.[90] Where people are already inclined to be cooperative in a given context due to deep-seated norms, and are already interested in helping to produce a lumpy good, appropriately segmented resources or contributions can provide the guidance necessary to coordinate inputs.

One interesting context in which lumpy goals and segmentation interact is the production of creative works like novels or songs. These goods are discrete or lumpy, in that they are generally valuable only when provided in whole-book or whole-song units, not isolated batches of words or notes. They are also nonrival: My enjoyment of a given work does not (as a rule) diminish your enjoyment of the same work.[91] Once the work exists, it exists for everyone. But how to get it produced in the first place? Copyright, by granting a limited monopoly to creators, provides one way of funding the creation of new works. But it does so in a manner that requires exclusion from the nonrival good by those who do not pay—a challenge in a digital world, and a deadweight loss given that these additional would-be consumers would not raise production costs. Could there be a better way to fund these works?[92]

The analysis above suggests that the lumpiness of the goal (a whole book or song) could make voluntary cooperation more likely. But is it possible to sequence production and contribution so that the producer has an incentive to produce and the contributors also have an incentive to contribute? As Glynn Lunney has noted, Stephen King employed an iterated voluntary funding strategy for his novella *The Plant*. King committed to complete each new chapter if readers voluntarily paid enough per download on average to access the prior chapter (he asked for a dollar per download, but would write the next chapter if receipts averaged seventy-five cents per download).[93] Although nominally paying for the past (accessed) chapter, the readers were effectively paying King to produce new work—or, rather, signaling their willingness to "cooperate" in an iterated game in which additional increments of work would be followed by additional increments of payment. And indeed the experiment was successful until King indicated the series was ending, producing predictable endgame behavior.[94]

King could have instead set a "make me write" threshold that his fans needed to cumulatively meet in order to spur the next round of production—a more explicit way of soliciting the funding of new production, and one that would have divided surplus differently between King and his readers.[95] Yet the analysis of segmentation above suggests that the prospects for voluntary funding will be brighter if requested contributions can be divided among contributors in an intuitive fashion that appears fair. The goal is to enable parties to "coordinate their expectations," as Norman Frohlich and Joe Oppenheimer put it.[96] As Lunney observes, a per-copy contribution system "may have helped consumers reach a Nash equilibrium by establishing a standard against which each consumer could measure their contribution."[97] From a contribution segmentation standpoint, then, it may work better to ask readers to pay a set amount for each download of an existing work than to fund an amorphous share of a future writing project.

A per-download payment mimics familiar ways of acquiring rival goods and services. When nonrival goods were primarily consumed through rival media (physical books or records), selling the rival object served as a handy vehicle for dividing up access and collecting contributions. A ticket, code, pass, wristband, or key can serve the same purpose. Other complementary rival goods that must be consumed along with the nonrival one can offer choke points for requiring payment—think of parking fees near open-air festival grounds or port fees for ships that use lighthouses.[98] Similarly, access to nonrival creative works could be tied to the rival complements used to access them, such as computers, smartphones, or internet service subscriptions.[99] Like grazing fees keyed to the number of cattle rather than the amount of grass consumed, this approach would make the harvesting equipment, and not the harvested goods, serve as the basis for allocating both access and required contributions.

There are plenty of similar models, from coffee mugs that come with a right to infinite refills, to bundled subscription services of all sorts.[100] There are also plenty of complications—many more than I can go into here—about how the system would work and how creators would be paid. What is interesting about this approach as a thought experiment, however, is the way that it approaches a segmentation problem (the lack of any obvious basis for splitting up the funding of a lumpy nonrival good) by making access choices even lumpier. Under a bundled approach, consumers would no longer make marginal decisions about paying for specific content, but would instead decide in an all-or-nothing fashion whether, say, to own a smartphone. Although it's an empirical question, it seems likely most current users would opt for "all" unless the fees were quite high indeed, rather than inefficiently choose "nothing."[101] The next chapter will consider more broadly the implications of making choices lumpier.

FOUR

Increments and Incentives

Chicago is renowned for its summer festivals along the lakefront. No matter how good the music or the food, however, a festival is never festive unless there are a sufficient number of exuberant (but well-behaved) people in attendance. Indeed, Carol Rose describes a festival as an event that "is exponentially enhanced by greater participation."[1] To be sure, a festival could become unpleasantly overcrowded if the numbers grew too large. But within wide bounds, additional attendees create positive spillovers for others. There is no way for festival-goers to extract payments from those whom they collaterally benefit by their presence. Yet festivals may not suffer any loss of festivity as a result.

This claim might seem surprising—economic analysis teaches us to regard externalities, whether positive or negative, as portents of inefficiency. When the payoffs that actors internalize diverge from the payoffs that society as a whole enjoys or suffers, we might expect actors to underengage in acts with positive spillovers (like attending festivals or planting flowers) and overdo acts with negative spillovers (like polluting or littering). Yet this result is not inevitable; often actors who generate externalities would behave no differently if they fully took into account all external effects. In other words, sometimes externalities turn out to be irrelevant to efficiency.[2]

This chapter focuses on one reason that the presence of externalities may not produce inefficient results: the lumpiness of the choice set.[3] Often actors do not face a continuous spectrum of alternatives but rather a small number of discrete choice nodes—and sometimes just a binary on-off decision to take or not take a particular indivisible action. If the alternative that an actor selects for her own reasons also turns out to be the socially optimal choice, then no inefficiency results—even if the choice produces a lot of spillovers for others. The alternative that the actor will select for her own reasons depends on what the menu looks like, which depends in turn on whether the choice set is broken up into fine-grained alternatives or large, discrete chunks.

For example, if "attending the festival" is a discrete choice that you must undertake completely in order to gain any returns at all, you will do it whenever your private returns from the choice make it worthwhile. The fact that it also benefits others is of no consequence. Suppose instead that a festival-goer faces a continuous choice set regarding the festival, so that she can attend the festival to greater or lesser degrees (either in terms of time spent or the intensity of her participation). Here, she might stop short of optimal festival-going due to her inability to internalize the externalities she is bestowing on others. The way the choice set is structured, then, can affect the efficiency of the arrangement.

Sometimes choice sets are limited in particular ways by nature (it is impossible to add half a steer to a grazing pasture), but they are often malleable. The "attend the festival" choice, for example, can be made chunkier (less divisible) if feasible transit options are only available during certain hours before and after the festivities. Conversely, adding more buses to the schedule allows festival consumption to be sliced more thinly. A decision to televise the festival would offer a different way of slicing servings of festival consumption. A would-be reveler might then choose to consume the festival remotely rather than participate firsthand. Thus a choice *not* to televise the festival makes festival consumption lumpier.

As these examples suggest, social policy can greatly influence the choice sets that people encounter. Recognizing this point opens up the question of when it would be desirable to consciously structure choice sets to make them chunkier or less chunky. A real-world example of engineering along this dimension was the 2000 change in stock pricing from a fractional system that priced stocks by sixteenths to a decimal system that prices them by cents.[4] Finer calibration promised more precision in pricing and lower trading costs.[5] But there were concerns that the smaller "tick size" would reduce returns for providing liquidity (an activity with positive spillovers) and lower costs for trading practices associated with volatility (an activity with negative spillovers).[6] In 2016, the SEC launched a pilot project to examine the effects of raising the minimum tick size to five cents for the stocks of small companies, and scholars continue to study the trade-offs involved in choosing pricing increments.[7] Similar design choices exist in many other less-studied contexts, with important but often overlooked implications for policy.

In the sections that follow, I show how the increments in which actions can be taken influence people's choices and the spillovers these choices have on others. Standard economic models miss this point because they assume that choices are made from a continuum, rather than in discrete steps. Past work in behavioral economics has recognized a variety of "menu effects" relating to the way that the slate of options frames a given choice.[8] But the lumpiness of the choice increments themselves is a distinct issue, and one that transforms the analysis of incentive structures even in the absence of any psychological effects that menus might produce. Recognizing lumpiness in choice sets also queues up new questions about whether adding or removing intermediate options would induce better decisions.

Bundled Spillovers

Spillovers represent bundles of a sort: by doing an act like gardening or widget-making, one produces effects for oneself and also, simultaneously, for others. We know from common experience that people often undertake acts with positive spillovers, like gardening, and refrain from acts with negative spillovers, like polluting, even when they do not enjoy all the benefits or bear all the costs from these acts. Economists and legal scholars have recognized that spillovers do not always distort people's choices—in other words, that externalities can at times be *irrelevant* to efficiency.[9] But this idea and its implications remain underappreciated. Nonetheless, two related lines of analysis have appeared in the existing literature.

The first involves cases where an actor has more intense preferences than anyone else who is affected by her behavior, such as a gardener who makes her rose garden as beautiful for her own enjoyment as she would if she could collect viewing fees from her neighbors.[10] Suppose a gardener, Gina, is deciding how much work to put into her rose garden. Gina has high aesthetic standards for what counts as a proper rose garden, and finds it personally worthwhile to maintain her garden at the "breathtakingly gorgeous" level. Gina's garden is positioned where many of her neighbors are able to see it on a daily basis, much to their delight. However, truth be told, these neighbors have only the most rudimentary appreciation of roses and would hardly notice if the beauty level dropped to "near-gorgeous" or even just "fairly nice." Since Gina has no interest in constructing a wall to occlude sight lines to her garden, and cannot realistically collect viewing fees from her neighbors, her own consumption of gardening beauty is inextricably bundled with that of her neighbors—a package deal.

Will the fact that Gina's gardening efforts produce large positive externalities for everyone within viewshed cause her to cultivate an inferior garden? Of course not. Gina's intense preference for gardening beauty already surpasses that of everyone else within viewing range.[11] By providing the garden at her ideal level of floral beauty, the demand of everyone else for gardening gorgeousness is thoroughly satiated.[12] No one would be willing to pay Gina enough to make further improvements or upgrades, because she is already making the garden as lovely for her own enjoyment as anyone else would want it to be. Gina would garden in exactly the same way even if she could collect micropayments each time a neighbor caught a glimpse of her roses.

Externalities like the ones Gina's gardening produces are irrelevant to efficiency because there is no bargain that could be struck, even in theory, to improve matters overall.[13] These externalities may still have worrisome distributive effects—is it really fair for Gina's neighbors to enjoy those beautiful views for free?—but they do not distort decision making or produce inefficiencies.[14] Notice that in economic terms Gina's garden is a public good within viewing range, as it is both nonrival (the neighbors don't use up the beauty) and nonexcludable (Gina has no good way to charge for views).[15] This is a form of lumpiness: provision for one means provision for all. However, it does not matter whether Gina's enjoyment of her garden smoothly increases as she ramps up the beauty level or jumps up all at once when she hits the threshold of breathtaking gorgeousness; what matters is that the level of beauty that she pursues for her own reasons exceeds the level of beauty that anyone else would be willing to pay to achieve.

Another situation discussed in the literature involves the reciprocal production and receipt of positive spillovers. Suppose a company, Acme, engages in activities like research and development that cause large knowledge spillovers for others in the industry. Acme may engage in these research and development activities at an optimal level, notwithstanding the fact that doing so generates positive externalities for others, if those same activities also enable it to *absorb* the reciprocal spillovers of other industry players.[16] Here, the lumpiness takes a different form than in the gardening example. Acme is unable to disaggregate the acts that will render it receptive to the spillovers of others—that is, acts that develop its "absorptive capacity"—from the acts that bestow benefits on others.[17] A low-tech version of the same idea might be found in many social interactions: it may be impossible to get anything out of a party without contributing to others enjoying the party as well.

These examples show a robust connection between indivisibilities and irrelevant externalities. In the next sections, I will explore a slightly different form of lumpiness in choice sets that has not received much attention but similarly has the capacity to influence efficiency: that which comes about when actors cannot choose to move in any-sized increments, but rather only in certain discrete jumps.

Chunky Choices

Suppose a widget-maker uses a production process that pollutes the air in the surrounding neighborhood, and the law does not provide any relief to the neighbors. Imagine further, and realistically, that the neighbors would find it too costly and difficult to bargain with the widget factory over its external effects.[18] Will the widget-maker pollute more than is socially optimal, given that it is externalizing some of the costs of its production process? Standard analysis, which assumes people always choose from a continuous menu of options, would lead us to believe the answer is yes. But, in fact, people and firms often face *discontinuous* choices—and, at the extreme, all-or-nothing, binary decisions. Perhaps widgets can only profitably be manufactured in one-thousand-widget batches, or perhaps scrubbers come only in certain discrete sizes, or perhaps widgets cannot be made at all without releasing a fixed burst of widget-fumes that causes the harms in question.

When choices are chunky rather than continuous, externalities may not cause an actor's decision to diverge from the socially optimal one. Thus, the granularity of the choice set—the increments in which actors can make moves—can influence whether externalities will turn out to be relevant to an actor's decisions. Because discussions about externalities tend to omit the concept of irrelevant externalities altogether, little attention has been given to the important effects of choice set construction. To see how recognizing chunkiness in choices changes the analysis, it is first necessary to step back and look at how the problem of externalities is typically presented.

Standard Graphs and Stopping Points

Given the centrality of incentives to law and economics, it is puzzling that legal scholarship has largely ignored the role of lumpy or discontinuous choice sets in influencing those incentives.[19] One explanation can be found in standard models and graphs used to depict externalities, which generally assume that parties confront a continuous spectrum of choices about externality-producing behaviors like polluting or planting flowers.[20] These analytic tools suggest that any externality, positive or negative, will cause the actor to make inefficient decisions, whether by polluting too much or

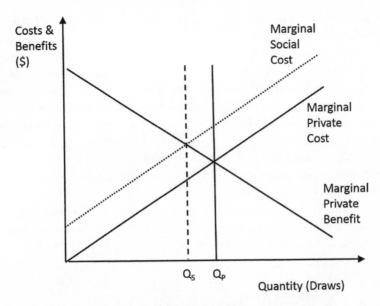

Figure 4.1. Externalities with Continuous Choice. Source: Fennell, "Slicing Spontaneity," 2379, fig. 1.

planting too little. Figure 4.1 illustrates this point in the context of negative externalities.[21]

The horizontal axis in figure 4.1 represents the quantity of a particular behavior that an actor (call her Aza) engages in—here, a behavior that will have negative externalities on the neighbors. I therefore refer to the behavior as making "draws" against a shared resource (as through pollution). The vertical axis reflects the impact in dollars. The solid sloping lines show the private cost-benefit calculus of the actor. Suppose Aza is making widgets and polluting in the process. Setting aside the impacts on others, at some point her marginal cost of making more widgets outweighs her marginal benefits. This is the place where the solid lines cross, at quantity Q_p—Aza's private stopping point. The dotted social cost line reflects the higher marginal social cost of the draws, counting the impacts of the pollution on others.[22] If these costs were taken into account, Aza would stop where the dotted marginal social cost line crosses the marginal private benefit line, at Q_s—the social stopping point. Here, the negative externalities make Aza stop too late in making draws. A similar graph could be shown in which positive externalities make her stop too soon in undertaking acts that benefit others.[23]

A graphical setup like figure 4.1 seems to suggest that an individual's private stopping point will *always* be different from the socially optimal one where externalities are present—assuming the parties have not been able to bargain their way to the optimal point. And this is how externalities are usually discussed in basic economics texts. As Gregory Mankiw summarizes, "Negative externalities lead markets to produce a larger quantity than is socially desirable. Positive externalities lead markets to produce a smaller quantity than is socially desirable."[24] Yet sometimes the opposite assumption is made, at least implicitly. Consider the argument that writers, musicians, and inventors will create their works even in the absence of intellectual property protections. Lumpiness can help to make sense of these claims. What happens when choices occur not along a continuum, but in discrete chunks? Let us start with an optimistic story in which the chunkiness of the menu helps to align private choices with the social optimum, and then consider the converse situation in which a limited menu makes decisions worse.

Fortuitous Lumps

Figure 4.1 assumed that Aza could select any stopping point in making draws against the common resource. That setup led her to stop too late in making draws, because she did not internalize the costs to others. But what if she were instead limited to just a few discrete nodes or "stops"? I will start with a stylized example to illustrate this idea and then show how recognizing lumpiness might change the analysis suggested by figure 4.1.

Suppose a train runs along a track emitting negative externalities (sparks) or positive externalities (locomotive charm) as it goes. The level or intensity of the train's activity can be concretized as three stations along the track; it can do the activity a little bit (stop at the first station), a moderate amount (stop at the second station), or a large amount (stop at the last station). The train, let's assume, cannot choose an intermediate stopping point; it can only stop at one of the three stations, if it operates at all. Will it choose the socially preferred stop?

Consider first the case where the train emits sparks (negative externalities). If the privately internalized costs and benefits of running the train were put onto a graph on the assumption that the train could stop at *any* point along the track, the crossover point would come, let us suppose, a little past the second station. If the social costs and benefits of running the train were similarly graphed on the assumption that the train could stop at any point along the track, the proper stopping point would come a little before the second station. But in fact, the train cannot stop just anywhere; it can only stop at a station. For the train's operator, the cost of proceeding to the third station is not justified by the benefits, so the train stops at station 2. The owners of neighboring fields are still made unhappy by the sparks, but they could not pay the train operator enough to scale back her operations all the way to the first station. If we take the limited menu as given, the second station is the efficient choice.

The same point operates in reverse if we imagine the train is instead emitting charm (positive externalities). The train's operator would prefer to stop a little before station 2, say, whereas society's preferred point would be a little past station 2. Yet again, both private and public payoffs are maximized at station 2; the neighbors who would like more train activity would not be willing to pay enough to justify the shift to station 3, nor is it worthwhile to the train operator to cut all the way back to station 1. In both cases (sparks and charm), the externalities are not Pareto-relevant: Given the constraint of the fixed stations, there are no value-maximizing trades that could improve matters. Put another way, the externalities do not cause the actor to make any decisions differently. Where actions are constrained to a limited menu of stopping points and externalities are relatively small, convergence may render the externalities in question irrelevant.

Figure 4.2 shows how a menu comprised of such discrete, lumpy choices changes the conclusions suggested by figure 4.1's analysis of externalities.[25] As before, the horizontal axis represents draws against a common resource, and the monetary impact is mapped on the vertical axis. These draws generate negative externalities, so the dotted marginal social cost (MSC) line again lies above the solid marginal private cost (MPC) line. And, as before, an actor like Aza would prefer to continue to point Q_P, where her MPC line intersects her marginal private benefit (MPB) line, even though society as a whole would do best if she stopped at Q_S (the social optimum, where MSC crosses MPB).

But there is an important difference: as in our train story above, it is now no longer possible for Aza to choose any point along the horizontal axis as a stopping point; instead, there are only three possible stopping points, as indicated by the vertical lines labeled 1, 2, and 3. Because she cannot stop at Q_P, her ideal private stopping point, Aza must choose between stopping a little sooner, at line 2, or stopping a lot later, at line 3. Given those options, she will choose the former. Doing so causes her to lose only a little relative to her ideal point (the rightmost small light-gray triangle) compared with the large loss (rightmost dark-gray triangle) that

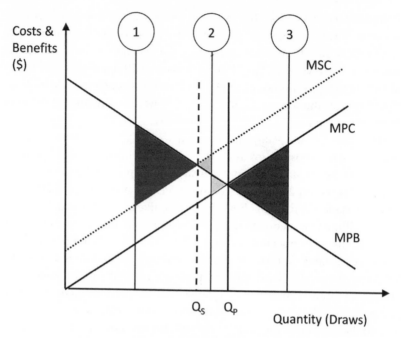

Figure 4.2. Externalities with Lumpy Choices. Source: Fennell, "Slicing Spontaneity," 2380, fig. 2.

she would incur if she were to move ahead to line 3. Her neighbors or fellow commoners might be happier if Aza scaled all the way back to line 1 or even 0, but they could not pay her enough to do so. Counting everyone's payoffs, including Aza's, more would be lost by moving back to line 1 (the leftmost large dark-gray triangle) than by settling for line 2 (the leftmost small light-gray triangle).

Thus, in this example, the lumpiness of the choice set fortuitously causes our actor to behave a bit better (stop a bit sooner) than she would if her choices were unconstrained—at least if we assume that the parties would not have been able to reach a bargain that would bring them closer to the socially optimal position.[26] This analysis also sheds light on choices that generate positive externalities, including the production of creative works. Whether they will be underproduced if an author, artist, or inventor cannot capture the full benefit may depend on the increments in which the works are typically produced.

Some creative efforts seem quite lumpy. A novelist must write in units of entire books. Even if finishing a novel generates some disutility that cuts into the returns the writer realizes, such that she would prefer to stop with 10 percent still unwritten, she cannot receive any returns at all until she finishes the full book. She might, of course, be tempted to do a sloppy job finishing up the book or write a poor or nonsensical ending. But if we assume some reputational stake (or editorial gatekeeping) that imposes a minimum quality standard, finishing the unit in an acceptable fashion may be close to an on-off toggle. If she will enjoy enough private returns to make finishing the book worthwhile, she will do it, even if it also produces positive spillovers that would ordinarily incline her to underproduce. Another interpretation, in line with the gardening satiation example above, would be that if the novelist's own standards for the book are so high that she continues improving it until she is personally satisfied, she may have exceeded the level of quality that any combination of readers would have paid her to achieve.

Other discontinuous efforts might be analyzed similarly. Mark Gergen gives the example of a real estate agent who must decide whether to incur costs to advertise a house on a multilist service.[27] This is a lumpy decision that cannot be made to just a certain degree; the house is listed (entirely) or not at all. As Gergen explains, a real estate agent will go ahead with the listing if the returns she internalizes from doing so are great enough to justify the effort, even though most of the rewards flow to her client. The fact that listing the property is a lumpy and indivisible act produces this result; if the agent could choose any effort level at all, she would likely do less than the optimal amount. But if she tries to cut corners in the listing by posting inaccurate or incomprehensible information, this would likely preclude her receiving any returns at all, yet it would cost nearly as much as posting an acceptable listing. Thus, the lumpiness of the decision can help to overcome a problem of misaligned incentives.[28]

There is a flip side to the point. If the payoff from the lumpy expenditure of effort involved in listing the home is inadequate to motivate the real estate agent, she might not undertake this action at all, at least not in the absence of some well-structured incentives that would lead her to take the first step.[29] Similarly, if the writer does not receive enough private returns from the whole book to make it privately worthwhile for her to finish it, she will not even start, even if she would prefer to write 90 percent of the book and receive 90 percent of the returns, were such a thing possible. Thus, lumpy choices have a pernicious side to them as well, as the next section explains.

Tragically Lumpy

We have seen that sometimes a chunkier choice set will push an actor in the direction of a more socially beneficial stopping point. But the opposite may also be true, as the case of the nonstarting novelist suggests. If a socially beneficial lump falls just short of being privately worthwhile, it may not be produced at all—even if the actor would have been willing to undertake most of the socially desirable action if it had been sliced up into smaller increments, with proportionate costs and benefits attached to each increment. The observation is a significant one for policy. Sometimes spillover-producing actions might be provided either in continuous increments or in large lumps—and policy makers can influence which decision unit applies.

Suppose there is an exciting technology store (call it Dapple) that generates a lot of positive agglomeration spillovers for the surrounding community—foot traffic for nearby retailers and restaurants, valuable interactions among people, buzz and activity on the street that make the area more vibrant. Dapple is quickly outgrowing its present downtown location and has a choice between expanding its existing store and opening a second store in an uptown location. If it decides to open the new uptown store, there is a minimum size threshold that the store must reach in order to be privately profitable to Dapple, and there would be little advantage to Dapple in going beyond that scale in that location. This makes the decision of whether to open the second store a binary one—open the store, or not.

By contrast, Dapple's decision regarding expanding the current store would be selected from a continuous menu. Although Dapple would presumably not find it worthwhile to expand the store in very small increments, such as a few additional square inches, it can profitably add a new wing that is significantly smaller than the minimum efficient scale of the new uptown store, and it can choose among many different possible sizes for that wing. Assume that in both locations the positive externalities that the store would generate for the surrounding community are proportionate to the square footage that Dapple adds. The question then becomes whether confronting the lumpy choice (opening an uptown store or not) or the more thinly sliced choice set (adding a new wing) will induce Dapple to add more square footage. Land use policy can determine which of these alternatives lies open to Dapple, and it can also influence the relative price of each.

Suppose the law makes it essentially impossible to expand a store but fully possible to open up the new one uptown. If Dapple's private returns from the uptown store are sufficient to justify the investment, Dapple will open the store; it does not matter that doing so will also create positive spillovers for commercial and residential properties nearby. And, significantly, Dapple may do this even though it would have chosen to add less square footage had it been able to choose the "new wing" strategy that enabled moving in smaller increments.

Yet lumps will not always induce the socially superior choice. Suppose instead that Dapple's private returns to the uptown store fall just a hair short of what is necessary to induce it to open up that store. Here, an entire socially efficient store is lost. If Dapple could instead design a new wing at nearly any scale it wished, it might have found doing so worthwhile. Even though it would likely choose a socially inefficient stopping point in adding square footage, since it will not take into account the spillovers for the community, it would still be generating *some* positive spillovers.

Lumpier choices render intermediate alternatives unavailable and thereby force parties to all-or-nothing (or lump-or-nothing) decisions. This raises the stakes for society, even as it tends to make small differences between private and social payoffs less consequential. The dynamics resemble those associated with grading increments. A small quality difference in an exam is less likely to matter to a student's grade at schools that use just two or three large grade buckets—but when it does turn out to make a difference, it makes a large difference. Conversely, a small quality difference is more likely to translate into a different grade if there are a dozen or more grading increments in use, but the effect of it mattering is much less for the student's overall grade point average.

Making (or keeping) choices chunkier can similarly increase the chances that the privately and socially optimal course of action will "land" on the same choice, but the fallout when this does not occur may be much greater. Conversely, as the Dapple example shows, society can make choice sets more continuous, as by permitting a store expansion of any size. The next section examines the effects of including more or fewer intermediate choices.

Adding and Subtracting Menu Options

As we have seen, chunky choices can sometimes make externalities irrelevant to efficiency. By limiting the choice set to discrete moves, the actor may be led to select the choice that also turns out to be the socially best alternative—on the limited menu, that is. But we need not take the menu as given; law, policy, and norms can influence the granularity of the choices that actors face. And the menu itself may be a source of inefficiency if adding—or subtracting—intermediate stopping points could make everyone better off.

Adding Intermediate Choices

Imagine that the choice under consideration is how high an actor, Builder, will build a fence—an act that will influence not only Builder's own payoffs, but also those of her (only) neighbor, Avian, a birdwatcher.[30] Assume that the law places no binding constraints on Builder's freedom to build as high as she wishes. If any height of fence is possible, as in figure 4.1, Builder will stop at the private stopping point, when the costs of more fencing material outweigh the privacy and containment benefits of going higher. If she were to fully take Avian's concerns into account, including the way that her fence will occlude his views of a nearby nature preserve, she would stop building sooner, at the social stopping point. The negative externalities are relevant ones.

However, if fences only come in three prefabricated heights: a short fence, a medium fence, and a tall fence, corresponding to lines 1, 2, and 3, respectively, in figure 4.2, Builder will choose the medium fence for the reasons recounted above. And, although Avian would prefer a shorter fence, the social losses of downgrading from medium to short are greater than the gains. There is no bargain that can make both parties better off, so although externalities persist (the fence is still taller than Avian wishes) they are irrelevant ones.

Our fence height constraint has turned what were previously relevant externalities into irrelevant ones. Should we celebrate this result? Should we rush to mandate uniform fence height menus in order to render more fence externalities irrelevant? Of course not. Fence height choices are not given by nature. By constraining the choice set, we remove opportunities for Pareto improvements—moves that could make Avian *and* Builder better off than the medium fence.[31] If fence heights were unconstrained, there is in theory some side payment Avian could make that would motivate Builder to move to society's ideal stopping point, represented by Q_s—a "medium minus" fence. The limited menu of fence heights takes that alternative off the table.

Notice that constraining available choices to our three prefabricated heights shields us from observing an unexploited opportunity for improvement. It looks as if Builder is doing the best possible thing, and she is—given the available choices. But this appearance of optimality is an illusion, made possible only because our limited set of fence heights artificially suppresses the opportunity for improvement itself. Fence innovation that allows for intermediate choices increases the likelihood that we will see efficiency-relevant externalities simply because it introduces the possibility of gains from trade. We can now understand relevant externalities as discomfiting signals that, similar to pain, are functional in showing us places where we could do better. The limited fence menu keeps us from feeling that pain. Adding more choices introduces the discomfort, but with it the chance of improvement.

Introducing intermediate choices is not an unmitigated good, however, if transaction costs are large. Suppose we take as a baseline our limited fence menu and the medium fence alternative that Builder would choose under it. Now we add intermediate alternatives. The possibility that a superior intermediate option like "medium minus" might simply go unused due to transaction costs does not militate against adding more options; we would be no worse off than before if Builder simply continued with the baseline medium fence. But she might not. The more finely sliced choice menu not only allows for bargains that come closer to the social optimum, but also allows actors who generate externalities to stray further from the social optimum—here, by choosing the privately preferred fence height, Q_P ("medium plus"), rather than the socially preferable medium fence.

How should society decide between a more continuous choice menu and a more limited set of discrete increments? This question will be taken up in specific contexts later in the book. For now, we can highlight two considerations that bear on the choice.

First, we want to consider the relationship between changes in inputs (draws and contributions) and changes in the social value or harm that is produced. Suppose, for example, that negative externalities exist at all levels of a given activity, but when those spillovers accumulate to a critical threshold there is a large jump in costs—a fishery collapses, say, rather than just becoming incrementally less robust.[32] This is a different form of lumpiness than we saw in figure 4.2, where we focused only on lumpiness in increments of action, while the marginal cost curve smoothly increased. The fishery collapse situation would involve a sharp upturn in the marginal cost curve at the critical threshold—a large chunk of indivisible harm that lands all at once. Here, society's primary concern is keeping aggregate fishing below that critical threshold.

Although there are many ways that law could approach this goal, one interestingly counterintuitive possibility would involve specifying *larger* increments in which harvesting choices must be made.[33] If fishers themselves typically face increasing marginal costs as they expand their harvesting efforts, fishers would be induced by the limited menu to select a lower choice point based solely on their own private returns from the available activity levels. A jump to a higher harvesting choice point would only be undertaken by those rare fishers who had developed methods that gave them extraordinary returns. We would need to know something about the number of fishers in these categories, the profile of their returns, and the likelihood of entry by new fishers to assess the effects of this alternative. But it is worth considering how increment adjustments might compare (both politically and ecologically) with the more familiar alternatives of catch limits or taxes designed to control overfishing.[34]

To take another example, suppose that instead of the proportionate spillovers posited above for Dapple's increases in square footage, the community does not benefit much at all unless Dapple either opens a new store or undertakes a major expansion that would cost the same as a new store. In other words, the marginal benefit curve for society steps sharply upward at the point where this minimum addition is met. Here, keeping the choice set chunky by disallowing smaller expansions does not come with much of an opportunity cost for the community. This is true even though it may keep Dapple from doing what would be privately most profitable—and could lead to a social loss if Dapple does not find the chunky investment worthwhile.

A second consideration that interacts with the first is whether there exist mechanisms to push an actor confronting a very lumpy choice toward the more socially valuable solution. We might fear that private returns will fall just short of being sufficient to catalyze a large, lumpy act with positive externalities, or that private costs would fall just short of deterring an actor from undertaking a large, lumpy act with negative externalities. In these cases, it may be possible to edge the actor toward the efficient lumpy choice by slightly changing the incentives. For example, Rose observes that public choices about roads and waterways encouraged commerce, an activity with increasing returns to scale.[35] Likewise, easy transit to the festival grounds might cause a would-be festival-goer to decide to attend rather than sit it out, providing the full lump of socially valuable activity, rather than none of it. Similarly, a tax on polluting activities—even one that fell far short of matching the external effects of the behavior—might be sufficient to induce a factory to make the socially preferred choice from a sufficiently chunky menu. A small push in the right direction may do the trick.

That small push might in some cases be supplied or assisted by social norms. As discussed in the previous chapter, resource segmentation also enables metering and monitoring that can influence behavior beyond the pecuniary payoffs that an actor internalizes. Consider, for example, a community in which many homeowners must make decisions about how high to build their fences. We might expect owners making this choice to trade off privacy for themselves against the impact the fence will have on their own pocketbooks and views, while ignoring the impacts of the fence choice on their neighbors. If fences come in only a few standardized sizes, however, a social norm may develop around a particular height—say five feet—even in the absence of any formal governance regime. Suppose a person, Paisley, would prefer a fence that is five feet seven inches if she could choose any height at all. In a world where only whole-integer fences are possible, she is very nearly in equipoise between the five-foot fence and the next available height of six feet, but would edge just slightly toward the latter based on her internal hedonic calculus. Yet if she is even slightly sensitive to social pressure, she may comply with the five-foot fencing norm. Notably, these social norms may be harder to develop, monitor, and enforce if fence heights can be chosen from a continuous menu. Moreover, it might well require stronger social pressure to move Paisley away from her *ideal* fence height (were it available) than it does to edge her toward choosing the five-foot rather than six-foot fence, when these two alternatives rank very close to each other by her own reckoning.

It is possible that an even better outcome for Paisley and her neighbors could be produced through bargaining if fences could be built at any height at all. But we might suspect that bargaining would be difficult to initiate over this issue, given the number of neighbors involved. Moreover, there would likely be no clear consensus about the socially preferred fence height in an any-fence-height world, making it harder to get enough neighbors on board to begin the process. In such situations, restricting the choice menu through relatively chunky alternatives may not mean forgoing any realistic opportunity to generate a finer-grained solution that would leave all actors better off. At the same time, the limited menu may help edge actors toward more socially desirable actions than they would select on their own if those pro-social choices are reinforced through social norms and reciprocity.

These examples suggest that in repeat-play contexts involving common-pool resources, where informal governance considerations loom large and reciprocity is important, the lack of open-ended freedom to choose degrees of action may be a feature rather than a bug. At the very least, the significance of resource segmentation and choice construction should be taken into account in thinking innovatively about how to address externalities.

Removing Intermediate Choices

The discussion above established that it will not always be advantageous for society to offer actors every decision point along a spectrum. Under some plausible conditions, constricting an actor's choice set to a few widely spaced nodes can produce better outcomes than leaving open all intermediate alternatives. This point should sound familiar to anyone who has ever studied (or practiced) bargaining, whether in markets or other contexts. Because the constrained menu puts the actor to a forced choice between nodes, it produces dynamics similar to those of a take-it-or-leave-it (TIOLI) offer. A bargainer who can credibly issue a TIOLI offer holds a powerful advantage over her counterparty: she can position the "take it" node so as to claim the lion's share of the gains from trade.[36] Likewise, a choice may be framed as "now or never" to force a party to the "now" node, even when a later point (short of never) would be preferred.

Suppose Cedric wants to buy a Neptune Blue 1959 Karmann Ghia from Devon. The overlap between the maximum price that Cedric will pay ($9,000) and the minimum price that Devon will accept ($8,000) represents a surplus from trade of $1,000, which will be divided between the parties in some fashion. Each party would like to be in the position of putting the other party to a TIOLI choice because of the bargaining leverage this confers. If Devon can set a TIOLI price of $8,999, Cedric would be expected to pay it. Conversely, if Cedric can make a TIOLI offer of $8,001, Devon would be expected to accept it.

One wrinkle in this story is suggested by empirical work on the "ultimatum game." In this widely replicated laboratory experiment, one party (the proposer) is given the power to offer the second party (the responder) a TIOLI offer as to how a sum of money will be divided up. The responder can either accept the offer, in which case both parties receive the proposed split, or reject it, in which case neither receives anything. Responders will often reject offers below 20 percent, suggesting a willingness to incur a loss to punish another party's perceived unfairness.[37] This effect is likely buffered in any real-world bargaining situation, however, given the uncertainties parties are likely to harbor about each other's reservation prices. When Cedric offers $8,001, he is not transparently telling Devon that he wants to divide the surplus 999:1 in his own favor; Devon may simply think this is all Cedric can afford. On the other hand, if parties actually have very poor information about each other's valuations, Cedric may fail to construct a TIOLI offer that lies within Devon's acceptable range (perhaps offering

$7,999 rather than $8,001). Thus, TIOLI offers can run aground due to insufficient information—or too much information.

As our earlier discussion suggests, analogues to the TIOLI offer can often be detected in law and social policy. For example, some laws designed to protect workers, consumers, or tenants operate by removing alternatives from the set of possible bargaining outcomes. Whether these protections turn out to be advantageous or counterproductive for their intended beneficiaries depends on how employers, sellers, and landlords respond to the pared-down menu—the nodes of which can be seen as TIOLI offers that society is making on behalf of the protected individuals. If an employer must choose between offering a minimum package of working conditions and wages and offering no job at all, what will she do? A similar question arises for a landlord who must offer a specified package of rental quality and pricing, if she is to offer a unit at all.

We might predict that employers will employ fewer employees, and landlords will provide fewer units, if such constraints reduce their profitability. Lumpiness may arise here as well. An employer may not be able to reduce the workforce below a certain level without compromising certain lumpy goals associated with her business model. Likewise, a landlord may own properties in lumpy quantities (like entire buildings) that make marginal adjustments infeasible. This lumpiness in individual decision making might be smoothed out across the market, just as small changes in the price of oats will generate a market response even when oat buyers must make decisions based on whole-horse consumption units.[38] But the magnitude of the response is empirically unclear.

Downward adjustments, to the extent they occur, might not visit net harm on workers or tenants. Individuals might rationally prefer arrangements that leave them with a somewhat lower chance of a better job or home, rather than with a higher chance of a suboptimal job or home.[39] Certain minimum packages of these goods may themselves be lumpy or bridge-like in enabling gains and avoiding "poverty traps" that can lock families into cycles of disadvantage.[40] If this is so, then social policy that spreads jobs or housing more thinly across more individuals may prove counterproductive. I will have more to say about these points later in the book. For now, it is worth observing that, just as in the fishery collapse example above, there may be discontinuities in the consequences associated with different points along the feasible spectrum. These discontinuities should be taken into account in choosing whether and how to prune down the choice set.

Lawmakers may also prune menus in an effort to influence individual consumption decisions. Consider recent attempts to limit the permissible volumes of sugary drinks.[41] While an individual could still consume as much as she likes of a given beverage by simply buying more units of the smaller size, there are reasons why this may not occur. One set of effects, considered in more depth in the next chapter, has to do with norms of consumption that might be communicated by product sizes.[42] But even if we posit an individual who is unmoved by such factors, size restrictions might still have a behavioral impact for reasons identical to those discussed in the examples above.

Suppose an individual would prefer to consume seventeen ounces of sugary soda, but the maximum permissible soda size is sixteen ounces. She now must choose between consuming sixteen ounces and consuming (or at least buying) thirty-two ounces. Her private calculation may push her back to the sixteen-ounce node, given the high cost of moving all the way to the next node. On the other hand, the restriction could backfire if most individuals would consume around twenty-five ounces if left to their own devices. Now, the constrained menu may push many people to routinely buy two drinks—and perhaps consume even more than they would have consumed if all alternatives lay open.

As a final example of how legal choice construction can produce TIOLI offers, consider the muddled doctrine of unconstitutional conditions.[43] At its core, the doctrine stands for the idea that the government cannot require people to give up their constitutional rights in exchange for government benefits, even though the government has no obligation to provide those benefits at all, and even though an individual might prefer to give up her rights in order to get the benefits. In the absence of the doctrine, the government would be able to issue a TIOLI offer to the citizen: take it (benefits coupled with the surrender of rights) or leave it (keep your rights and forgo the benefits). With the doctrine in place, the *government* is put to a TIOLI offer: take it (provide the benefits to the citizen without requiring any surrender of rights) or leave it (don't give the citizen any benefits). The intermediate option of offering the benefits on the condition of a surrender of rights is removed from the government's choice set, making the government's choice (and the potential outcomes for the citizen) lumpier.

Often, one supposes, such a restriction will have the effect of pushing the government to the "benefits without rights surrender" node.[44] Political pressures may induce the government to provide the benefits without strings, and there may be other constraints (such as equal protection) that keep the government from arbitrarily or discriminatorily trimming the number of eligible recipients. But the government might instead revert to the "no benefits" node, especially in highly discretionary realms like land use permitting where this can be done on a case-by-case basis.[45] Perhaps one of the reasons that the doctrine is so disordered is that removing intermediate choices plays out differently in different contexts.

What is most important to emphasize here is the common thread of strategic menu pruning, which cuts across a wider range of settings than has been generally recognized. Subsequent chapters will extend this line of inquiry into a variety of additional contexts, starting with intrapersonal dilemmas.

FIVE

Intrapersonal Dilemmas

People often have trouble achieving their goals. In some cases, these difficulties cannot be blamed on other parties, but rather only on other versions of themselves. Lumpiness is one reason why. Consider, for example, the lumpy goal of "writing a book." Like a bridge, a book may be close to a step good if the benefits for the author will largely go unrealized until it is completely finished. But the inputs that the author must make do not come in book-sized chunks, nor even in chapter-sized chunks. Rather, inputs must be made on a minute-by-minute, day-by-day, task-by-task basis—with full knowledge that failure to complete *all* the tasks will render the entire enterprise futile. How does an individual secure the cooperation of her different temporal selves when payoffs are distant? The problem bears a family resemblance to assembly problems we have examined already, translated to a more intimate scale.

In this chapter, I will focus on how lumpiness and segmentation feature in intrapersonal dilemmas. I start by framing the problem of assembling the cooperation of different selves over time. I then consider how resource segmentation and the chunkiness of choices can leverage or undermine self-control—and how people can strategically create their own choice intervals.

Getting Your Selves Together

Individuals often pursue goals that deliver benefits in relatively indivisible lumps but that require many small contributions of effort or time over a sustained period. Familiar examples include dieting to reach a weight goal, training for a marathon, writing a paper, studying for a test, or saving enough for a major purchase like a car or a down payment on a house. Even when the goal is not a single, sharply defined step, it may nonetheless be lumpy. For example, amassing enough savings for a comfortable retirement or studying enough to pass an exam may require reaching some minimum threshold, even if further improvements in living standards or academic achievement are possible beyond that point. Assembling the participation of one's temporally distributed "selves" is no simple matter, however, as a large literature on willpower and self-control has recognized. A central problem is what Drazen Prelec has termed "scale mismatch," where the relevant benefit (or cost) is experienced only at an aggregate scale, while the corresponding inputs must be made at a far smaller scale, decision by decision.[1]

Just as in the multiplayer problems considered in previous chapters, achieving a lumpy personal goal requires assembling cooperation (here, from the various selves) and dividing up surplus (again, among the selves). Production functions, participation requirements, and payoffs remain crucial in the intrapersonal context, although certain aspects of these elements operate somewhat differently.

Production Functions

I have already suggested that many of the goals that people try to achieve have a lumpy or step function: writing a paper, meeting a particular fitness goal, passing an exam, or saving up for a major purchase like a car, vacation, or home down payment. Notice, however, that the shape of the production function may depend on just how the individual frames the goal in question and how she derives value from its achievement. Some goals are very nearly binary by their nature and difficult to define in any other way—for example, passing a state bar exam to practice law. Failing by a tiny increment is just as bad as failing by a wide margin, and arguably worse given the presumably higher studying costs. Likewise, passing by a hairbreadth is just as good as getting a perfect score, and arguably better given the presumably lower studying costs.

Few goals have this all-or-nothing character, however. Unlike a bridge span or a bar exam, further gains are generally possible after a large initial "step" has been achieved. For most academic enterprises like exams and papers, there is a sharp step associated with doing enough to earn a passing score, but the production function continues upward beyond that threshold to the extent that better performance brings greater rewards. The number of grading or scoring increments determines the shape of this portion of the curve. An exam that is graded using just two or three grading buckets

will have correspondingly few steps, while those with many more grada-
tions (like the SAT) look more like a smooth upward slope. If a scholarship
or other benefit turns on getting a specific score, however, then an individual may experience a sharp step at that point and set her goals accordingly.

Similarly, one might set a very specific and ambitious goal like running
a five-minute mile and gear one's training to achieving that lumpy outcome, or one might simply aim to "run faster." Or a runner might have a
goal of completing a marathon (a binary result) but experience additional
improvements for faster times or better finishing positions. Reaching a
weight target is lumpy, but "losing weight" is linear. "Being a vegetarian"
is lumpy, but "eating less meat" is linear. The way in which goals are defined should reflect the way outcomes generate well-being for people. Goal
definition also influences which selves must participate and what kinds of
payoffs they will receive.

Participation Requirements

We can distinguish situations in which *every* temporal self must cooperate to achieve a lumpy good (veganism or sobriety, say) from situations
in which *some* (often very large) number of selves, distributed over time,
must cooperate (finishing a book manuscript, losing significant weight and
keeping it off, training for a marathon, becoming proficient in a language,
or mastering a musical instrument). Both of these patterns can also be distinguished from situations in which *one or a few* temporally concentrated
selves can achieve a given goal, but it will benefit many of the individual's
other selves as well (going to the dentist, getting an unpleasant medical
test, doing one's taxes, cleaning out the closet).

We can also distinguish situations in which in-kind contributions of effort are involved, as in the examples just given, and situations in which the
required contributions are monetary (to fund a lump of consumption like
a car, say). Goals reached through in-kind contributions may demand participation from many temporally dispersed selves. For example, "training
for a marathon" cannot be accomplished by my "today self" alone, as motivated as she may be. Sometimes physiological realities place limits on the
way that burdens can be concentrated, as in this example. In other cases,
a task is simply too large to be accomplished (by an individual anyway)
without spreading it across time. As much as my today self wishes to complete the book I am now writing, she cannot do it—the job is too big.

Monetary goals have looser participation requirements, just as in multiplayer situations. One wealthy donor can single-handedly fund an entire

lighthouse or a new wing of an art museum, even though many others will benefit. Likewise, one or a few selves with access to funds can make large contributions to meet a monetary goal. But the flexible fungibility of cash is a double-edged sword. Cash assembly is easier in one way—contributions need not be made at particular times or in particular patterns—but more difficult in that withdrawals are generally possible. In order to amass enough money to buy a car, for instance, intervening selves must not only faithfully set aside some portion of "their" paychecks, but also must refrain from raiding the store of funds already set aside by other selves. Of course, when money must be assembled rather than effort, other options often open up, such as financing a purchase rather than saving for it in advance. These options carry obvious advantages in expanding liquidity but have drawbacks as well, as we will consider in the next chapter.

Participation requirements in intrapersonal contexts are complicated by questions about how to define the players in question. Suppose a student, Adam, has to write a research paper that is due in ten weeks. Achieving this lumpy goal requires a succession of Adam's temporal selves to relinquish various short-run leisure opportunities. This presents a strategic dilemma among Adam's selves.[2] Because the paper can be written by some subset of the temporal "Adams," each Adam will be tempted to believe that he should be exempt from the contribution requirement, on the grounds that the other Adams are better positioned to make the contribution. Of course, the other Adams will reason the same way.[3]

We might define these different selves as "Adam at Week One," "Adam at Week Two," and so on.[4] But it is somewhat arbitrary to designate temporal selves based on weeks, as decisions about whether to contribute effort are actually undertaken at a much finer grain, moment by moment. Richard Thaler and Hersh Shefrin suggest another way to frame intrapersonal problems: as an ongoing conflict between a "planner" self and a succession of present "doer" selves.[5] The planner self serves as a kind of general contractor trying to coordinate projects in a way that will serve the person's long-term interests. As present doer selves parade past, at some point the planner begins ordering them to start working on the paper. But each one angles for an easier assignment (such as going to the gym, doing the laundry, or posting updates on social media), pointing out the massive number of future doer selves coming along behind who can easily handle the paper task. Even Adam's planner self knows in his heart of hearts that the entire job could be completed—hastily, badly, and with much misery and sleeplessness, but completed nonetheless—in the week before it is due.

Suppose Adam procrastinates for nine weeks and then begins work.

This seems irrational, yet the delay does engineer for Adam a collective action problem that is simpler to solve than that which the ten-week writing period originally posed. With a time horizon of many weeks, there was always something more pressing that each present self plausibly needed to be doing. This plausibility offered cover for free riding on later paper-writing selves and effectively muffled the protests of the planner self. But once the final week arrives, the planner self's voice takes on an air of authority and urgency: the problem has become one in which *every* self absolutely must participate at full engagement, with no more room for free riding.

This situation is far from ideal, however. For starters, it is possible that Adam has miscalculated and begun work too late, so that even by working full throttle the paper cannot be completed in time. In other words, there may not be enough remaining temporal selves to handle the job. Even if existing "personnel" can manage to cross the threshold of paper completion, they may not be able to go further to achieve a preferred grade. A more serious problem is that some of the remaining selves might decide not to cooperate. This is not because they hope to free ride (it is far too late for that) and not because they are trying to hold out for a better deal (there is no easy way for Adam's Tuesday midnight self, for example, to strategically demand a larger share of the gains from the paper). Rather, as Adam's exhaustion level increases, one or more self may come to value sleep more highly than the returns to be gleaned from the paper's timely completion. Borrowing from the terminology introduced in the land assembly context, such a self would be not a holdout, but rather a "holdin."[6]

When one landowner truly values her parcel so highly that she refuses to sell it at any price, the failure to achieve an assembly is not inefficient; the land is producing more value when unassembled. The same could be said in the intrapersonal case if we focus just on the selves situated in that crucial last week. But there were many other selves who were initially available to make contributions, and their opportunity costs would have been much lower than that of the sleep-deprived self who decides to throw in the towel as the deadline looms. Getting some of those earlier selves to participate could have produced the efficient outcome of paper completion without undue pain. But those selves were still in a position to free ride, because the deadline was far away.

Participation requirements can be adjusted by breaking the goal of paper completion into subgoals involving different phases of the paper, such as research, outlining, rough drafting, revision, and so on. If these phases have to be completed by various interim deadlines, then the work cannot all be bunched into the last week where a unanimous participation requirement produces both a spur to action and a potential stumbling block. Creating deadline-quality urgency around intermediate milestones can be a crucial strategy in solving intrapersonal dilemmas.

We must keep in mind another possibility: that it may not actually be beneficial for Adam to write the paper at all. Maybe there is *no* sufficient set of selves about whom it can be said that their opportunity costs of writing the paper are lower than the benefits achieved from completing it—too many would be holdins who more greatly value spending their time in other ways. We might think that the odds are fairly high that Adam should write the paper, given that he has apparently placed himself within some academic degree program that requires it. But the planner self who chose the program may not have had full information about what the day-to-day work would entail, or may not have foreseen what later selves would value. It can be difficult for anyone, including Adam himself, to tell whether he is experiencing a passing recalcitrance that can and should be overridden by the application of grit or whether the entire endeavor is a misconceived one that will subtract rather than add to his lifetime utility if it is pursued further.

This information problem is not unique to intrapersonal dilemmas. A developer surveying a neighborhood for redevelopment may be similarly uncertain about whether the people living there are so attached to their properties that they will refuse to sell at any price. Yet the developer may take a gamble and attempt an assembly effort. Similarly, I might buy a membership to a gym with the hope of getting in shape but lack insight into how much my future selves will dislike going to the gym under a wide range of highly plausible circumstances such as: it is raining, I have a cold, I have a deadline, and so on.[7] Failing to achieve goals does not necessarily represent a failure of willpower; it may instead be the triumph of rationality once more information is available.

This point relates to a larger issue lurking in discussions of self-control: which self's preferences should get priority? An earlier self who attempts to bind her later selves to a particular course of action may benefit from being at some temporal distance from the choice point, but may lack information about the circumstances she will face at that time or insight into what is in her own long-term best interest. Botand Köszegi and Matthew Rabin give the example of a woman who wishes to give birth without pain medication.[8] When she changes her mind while in labor, is she making a mistake or correcting an earlier mistake? One way to approach the problem is to ask what a person would do if all of her selves could costlessly bargain with each other.[9] This thought experiment brings us to the question of payoffs.

Payoffs

In multiplayer dilemmas, payoffs are critically important. They determine how the gains from cooperation (if there are any) will be distributed among the players. Payoffs are also important in the intrapersonal situation, but are a bit more slippery to delineate. In one sense, payoffs are always shared among selves—a person has a continuing identity that links past, present, and future—at least to some degree.[10] But conflict among selves often arises precisely because present selves prefer an immediate reward over a more distant one that is larger in magnitude (after being discounted to present value). Adjusting the payoffs of the various selves to induce their cooperation is no easy matter. Penalizing oneself for shortfalls is both difficult and counterproductive. And there is typically no simple way for a later self to offer the present self a meaningful side payment for cooperating.

In-kind rewards to oneself for making progress toward a goal may interfere with the achievement of that same goal. For example, watching a movie as a reward for work may use up time that cannot be spared, and rewarding oneself for a period of dietary restraint with a calorie-rich treat—or for a period of sobriety with a drink—may send an individual down a slippery slope.[11] A more congruent form of in-kind reward might be administered concurrently with, and made dependent upon, the self's cooperation. For example, someone who avoids going to the gym but enjoys listening to audiobooks could precommit to listening to audiobooks only at the gym—and a recent study showed that people would be willing to pay to make just such a precommitment.[12] Similarly, people are advised to choose workout routines that are intrinsically fun and that thereby deliver positive payoffs in real time, even if the ultimate fitness goal is distant and somewhat lumpy.

Third parties also might be enlisted to deliver payoffs. One particularly horrifying manifestation of this idea is presented in Stephen King's short story "Quitter's, Inc.," in which the protagonist is referred to a mysterious self-help clinic that boasts a high success rate for smoking cessation and weight loss.[13] Its methods turn out to be unconventional, to put it mildly— lapses are punished with escalating physical violence against the client's loved ones. A far more palatable form of third-party enforcement was introduced in 2008, when Ian Ayres, Jordan Goldberg, and Dean Karlan launched a company called StickK.[14] It works like this: You sign a contract committing to a particular goal, like losing weight or stopping smoking, and can choose to put up stakes that you will lose if you fail to keep your commitment. You can decide whether the forfeited money (if any) will go to a designated person ("Friend" or "Foe"), to a charity (one of several on a list, but you can't choose which one), or to a specified "Anti-Charity" that pursues goals you dislike.[15]

StickK's stake-forfeiting approach is a far cry from the ominous methods used in the Stephen King story, but it still relies on punishment to coerce participation—a stick rather than a carrot. It is possible to imagine a CarrotK version of this approach in which one's future self elicits the participation of present selves by sharing some of the surplus from the improvement scheme. Suppose I decide it is worth $500 to achieve a certain fitness target, one that I calculate I can reach in six months with diligent effort. I create a savings account that essentially works like a certificate of deposit, locking up the $500 until six months hence. However, I authorize a third-party enforcer to access the fund for one reason: to reward my current self, in preapproved amounts provided at prespecified intervals, for making progress toward my fitness benchmark. Ideally, this money would be earmarked for enjoyable current consumption for today's self. After all, she's the one doing the work! Such an approach is far from fail-safe, but it would at least ensure that either the goal of saving or the original goal of self-improvement would be delivered to the future self.

DIY Lumping and Slicing Solutions

As intriguing as third-party enforcement schemes like StickK are, most people rely on do-it-yourself solutions to self-control problems. Here, people might harness the principles of lumping and slicing that we have seen in other contexts to address their intrapersonal dilemmas.

Segmenting Consumption

In chapter 3, we saw how the way in which resources are broken down can influence the chances of successful coordination. The same is true when the harvesters are different temporal versions of the same person. Consider a person who is trying to control her diet. Portion sizes have been found to influence consumption, making attention to serving size a sensible strategy.[16] For similar reasons, people may avoid bulk purchases of tempting goods in an effort to ration their consumption, even if it means forgoing volume discounts.[17] People may also be influenced by a "unit bias" in which one unit of a food item is regarded as the appropriate amount to consume—at least within limits.[18] For example, many people may be inclined to take exactly one cookie in a social setting, whether the cookie has a diameter of three inches or five inches. This suggests that simply changing how food is configured and segmented can alter consumption choices.

The metering and monitoring benefits of resource segmentation discussed in chapter 3 apply in intrapersonal contexts as well. For example, the physical partitioning of chocolates (by individually wrapping them) has been found to slow consumption among those who are attempting to control their diets.[19] The partitioning may be effective because it draws attention to each increment of consumption.[20] For similar reasons, physical traces of consumption, such as pistachio shells, may aid in self-monitoring.[21] Yet even in the absence of such visual markers, simply dividing tempting foods into smaller pieces (e.g., dividing a cookie into halves) seems to reduce consumption—an effect that has been observed in children as well as adults.[22] As David Marchiori and his coauthors hypothesize: "reducing [food item size] alters the perception of the appropriate quantity of food to consume by providing more cutoff points at which a person can reassess his consumption."[23]

Research has shown inconsistent effects of plate and bowl sizes on overall caloric consumption.[24] Some researchers have suggested that extra space on a larger plate would more likely be used to expand servings of unsegmented or "continuous" side dishes such as vegetables, pasta, or rice, rather than individuated "unit" items like pieces of fish or steak.[25] In the case of vegetables, this effect seems beneficial (at least if the vegetables are actually consumed, rather than merely offering a visual offset that makes one feel freer to consume other items), but expanded servings of starchy foods may be more problematic.[26] Here, the effect of other methods of segmenting continuous foods, such as serving spoons, would be a useful avenue for further investigation. The USDA's "MyPlate" heuristic likewise encourages the habit of mentally segmenting one's plate so that it contains appropriate proportions of the various food groups.[27]

Segmentation can also help people avoid *underconsuming* or taking less of a resource than is actually in their long-term interest—again, if the segmentation enables metering and monitoring. In one computer simulation of a replenishing resource game, each participant was given exclusive control of a sector of the (virtual) harvesting terrain, which turned the experimental game into a self-control problem.[28] When this manipulation was accompanied by a feature that made the count of available resource units visible, participants got closer to the optimum harvesting strategy than in any other treatment. But when the resource units were not visible, participants were overly cautious and took too little of the resource.[29] We might see the same effect where sessions of work must be aggregated to complete a project: if it is opaque to the individual how much progress she is making, she may not take as many breaks as she should. Likewise, a dieter might make too many caloric cutbacks, miscalculating how much curtailment is necessary in order to achieve his personal goals. An excessively strict diet is likely to end in failure, but even if it "succeeds," it will reduce the dieter's well-being.

Tempting snacks that are packaged in single-serving pouches might be expected to produce both a constraining effect (by limiting portion size) and a liberating effect (by reassuring consumers that having a treat need not derail one's diet). Such single-serving packages are increasingly available and people appear willing to pay extra for them, but studies of these packaging efforts have yielded mixed results.[30] Holding the size of the food morsels themselves constant, dividing treats up among a larger number of smaller packages can at times actually lead to more consumption. For example, one recent study found that packaging six brownie pieces in one bag led to *less* brownie consumption than packaging the same six brownie pieces in three smaller bags containing two pieces each.[31]

A possible explanation for this result is that packaging recalibrates the choice menu.[32] Whereas the single sack containing six segments may have appeared to offer six discrete consumption intervals (one for each piece), the three-sack arrangement may have reduced the perceived menu to three nodes: two pieces, four pieces, and six pieces. While a participant could have chosen to eat just one piece of brownie from a given sack, the bundling format that places the two brownies together may have made it more likely that both would be consumed once the choice was made to open a new sack. Thus, packaging may help define choice intervals and shape how people experience the menu of options. More explicit menu manipulations are also possible, as the next section explains.

Strategic Menu Construction

Suppose a consumer, Constance, habitually buys a medium-sized salted caramel frappé at her local coffee shop every Tuesday afternoon. One such Tuesday she is disappointed to learn that the medium size has been eliminated—there's now just small and large. Will she splurge on the large or make do with the small? The answer is unclear, as is the long-term effect of the menu change on Constance's well-being. As we saw in chapter 4, when an activity generates externalities, the chunkiness of the choice might push the actor's behavior either closer to or further away from the social optimum. Analogous points apply when "internalities"—unaccounted-for impacts on other selves—are involved.[33] Thus, if Constance would find it in her long-term interest to consume fewer ounces of frappé, she might find that the elimination of the medium size brings her closer to her goal—or drives her further from it.

Although the effects of the menu change seem ambiguous overall, they may be knowable in an individual case. If we knew enough about Constance's preferences for iced coffee and her sensitivity to its price, we could predict whether she will respond to the menu change by consuming more frappé or by consuming less. Potentially, consumers could use data on their own past consumption patterns to determine which effect would dominate if menu items were removed. Armed with this information, people might consciously control the sizes and quantities that they encounter—effectively precommitting to a constrained menu.[34] While coffee purveyors may be unable to tailor the sizes of their beverages for each customer, it would be entirely feasible to offer online ordering apps that are customized to include or omit particular menu items, or to allow customers to prepurchase blocks of electronic coupons that can be redeemed only for particular sizes or varieties of a product.

One counterintuitive aspect of this analysis is that the options that people would most benefit from taking off their personal menus would not necessarily be the largest or most unhealthy. Indeed, sometimes having only a very large size could effectively constrain consumption. Imagine, for instance, that you have a sudden craving for a candy bar and stop by a drugstore to buy one. You discover to your dismay that the store doesn't sell individual candy bars, but the clerk helpfully directs you to a multipack containing six bars of the candy you had been planning to buy, at a price four times higher than what the single candy bar would have cost. Do you buy it? It's certainly possible, but you may well decide to pass. It's more candy—and more money—than you had in mind.

Consider how predictions about one's own future behavior would factor into such a choice. People well attuned to their self-control struggles might say, "I'm not getting that big pack of candy because then I'd just eat it all." Others with similar self-control problems but without awareness of those problems might say "I'm not buying that big pack of candy since I'd just eat one bar and throw out the rest—it's not a good value." In other words, both sophisticated and naive individuals with self-control problems might well resist buying the multipack, but for opposite reasons—one because she expects to eat all the candy, and the other because she doesn't.[35] Even though the naïf is wrong about how much of the chocolate she would actually eat if she bought the pack—from a value-for-money perspective, the purchase would probably work out just fine—her reluctance to make the purchase on value grounds turns out to protect her from a purchase that would have tempted her into overconsumption. Scholars have previously examined other mechanisms that similarly leverage economic self-interest into self-control, from a tax-and-subsidy scheme that rewards healthy food choices that the naive consumer expects to make anyway,[36] to a higher interest rate for placing funds in an illiquid savings instrument that the naive saver does not anticipate wanting to access.[37]

An extreme version of attempting to influence consumption choices through lumpiness was hypothesized by Ted O'Donoghue and Matthew Rabin.[38] Their idea was to require smokers to obtain a costly "smoking license" that granted them a volume discount on cigarettes: $5,000 up front for 2,500 tax-free packs. This would be a rotten deal for anyone who was planning to smoke for just a little while and then quit; it would only make sense for those who had already decided to become addicted smokers.[39] If many long-term smokers start out intending to be short-term smokers, decisions made on value grounds could sidestep a self-control trap.

Although this particular supersizing strategy may seem far-fetched, the underlying principle could prove relevant to current policy debates like those surrounding the sizing of sugary drinks—an area in which scholars are currently exploring the impact of menu choices and portion sizes.[40] Tools that enable people to customize their own menus as a form of precommitment could offer alternatives to untailored taxes or absolute size limits. And the insight that *lumpier* choices could benefit some people who struggle with self-control issues suggests new ways to meet those challenges.

Segmenting Effort

Just as the segmentation of consumption items can influence intrapersonal cooperation, so too can the segmentation of units of effort or time. There are two factors in play here—how easy or feasible it is for different temporal selves to make contributions, and whether the different selves will be motivated to make those contributions. The first factor is a function of the *granularity* of the inputs, while the second factor depends on the *payoff structure* that the selves confront—which often turns on how goals are defined and how different inputs stack together to achieve them.

Consider first granularity. In multiperson collective projects like barn raising or quilt making, as well as more newfangled collaborative computing projects, much turns on the segments in which tasks or other contributions can be parceled out to participants. The ideal, as Yochai Benkler explains, is to find the right level of granularity so that people can make contributions that are meaningful, yet manageable enough to fit within the envelope of excess capacity that a particular person has available.[41] So too when the collaborators are different versions of oneself.

Sendhil Mullainathan and Eldar Shafir use the metaphor of packing to illustrate granularity, contrasting the ease with which jelly beans can be packed into a bag with the difficulty of bagging up an assortment of whole fruit.[42] Because the former is highly granular, the different pieces automatically settle around each other and efficiently use the available space, whereas it takes careful positioning to fit bananas, pineapples, and oranges into a grocery bag.[43] The same point applies to fitting tasks into one's available time—the smaller the grains, the easier it is to fit everything in.[44] Bulky time commitments, especially irregular ones, require more strategizing to accommodate.

As Mullainathan and Shafir emphasize, granularity must be assessed relative to the available space.[45] Filling a boxcar with oranges looks nearly as simple as filling a bag with jelly beans. The tighter one's "space budget," the harder it is to fit in bulky or awkwardly shaped items relative to the same volume of objects cut into finer-grained units. The same is true of time budgets. For people with tight schedules, finding ways to resize and reconfigure tasks—and make use of the interstices around larger ones— represents a core challenge. Yet packing too full eliminates valuable slack capacity—whether one is talking about leaving space in a suitcase for last-minute items or space in a schedule for unplanned exigencies and opportunities.[46]

Making tasks more granular, just like dividing up the tasks among quilters or computers, can make it easier for people's various temporal selves to make contributions. A book can be broken up into chapters, and chapters into subsections, so that it is possible to fit work into the smaller time slots that are interspersed throughout the author's schedule. If tasks do not come in easy-to-divide segments, however, more time and effort must be devoted to slicing them up and reaggregating the results. And dividing up work among more selves, just like dividing up work among more workers, presents management challenges and raises concerns about shirking. This brings us to the second factor—the question of motivation.

When faced with a large project, people are often advised to break it down into manageable chunks, so that each is less daunting to accomplish.[47] One break-it-down approach is the Pomodoro Technique, developed by Francesco Cirillo and named after a tomato-shaped kitchen timer.[48] The technique requires users to devote a block of twenty-five uninterrupted minutes (a "Pomodoro") to a given task, with a short break after each Pomodoro and a longer break after a set of four Pomodoros. Each Pomodoro is itself indivisible, which makes it easy to track the time spent on tasks (measured in Pomodoros).[49] This approach incorporates some of the metering and monitoring advantages associated with segmentation that were discussed in chapter 3. However, if the time blocks do not align well with the tasks one is trying to accomplish or with one's method of working, the segmentation may be distracting or counterproductive. Apps building on this method (as well as kitchen timers themselves) allow for customized work intervals and breaks, although too much tinkering could erode the benefits of having standard-sized segments that can be allocated among one's selves.

Sometimes break-it-down advice is meant as a kind of trick to get a person started on a task that is, in fact, inherently lumpy or indivisible in character. As we saw in chapter 4, when tasks are lumpy, a small initial push may be enough to alter incentives.[50] For example, Joan Bolker's *Writing Your Dissertation in Fifteen Minutes a Day* recommends a facially inadequate unit of effort that may nonetheless get a writer working on a large project.[51] Like asking for small amounts in charity drives, the fifteen-minute approach helps to eliminate excuses and legitimize a trivial contribution. Once someone has committed even fifteen minutes to the project, the theory goes, they will have become so engrossed in the work that they will keep going. If they can continue to trick themselves into beginning their work day after day, eventually they will end up with a dissertation.

Breaking things down comes with a downside, however. The smaller the chunks, the easier each one is to schedule and complete, but the more each may seem like a drop in the bucket relative to the overall goal, and the less it might seem to matter whether any particular task gets accomplished on any particular day. Recognizing this fact can sap motivation, especially if the tasks are not intrinsically engrossing. If units of effort are highly granular but goals are lumpy, the problem of scale mismatch arises. Setting subgoals may allow success to be experienced at shorter intervals. Consider, for example, the mantra of "one day at a time" often associated with twelve-step programs. Even though a sustained pattern of conduct like abstinence from alcohol requires the cooperation of many selves over an extended period, this framing of the problem enables each day's self to feel a sense of accomplishment.

Personal rules offer a different way to address the problem of scale mismatch, one that relies not on breaking apart contributions but rather on artificially bundling them together. This lumping strategy can be effective at overcoming self-control difficulties, but it comes with some drawbacks, as the next section explains.

Rules, Exceptions, Acts, Patterns

One of the most common self-control strategies is to adopt bright-line rules to be followed in all circumstances.[52] Personal rules (like "no cake" in the dieting context) conceptually bundle together all instances of a given choice and proclaim a once-and-for-all answer that eliminates the need for case-by-case deliberation as each tempting situation arises.[53] Adopting a behavioral rule to govern tempting choices aligns well with a prescription Mullainathan and Shafir formulated for dealing with the common problem of needing to repeat good behaviors over and over: "whenever possible, convert vigilant behaviors into one-time actions."[54] Of course, adopting a rule is not the same thing as always following it! Nonetheless, rules change the payoff structure associated with the choices that they govern, both by reducing the costs of making the "better" choice by rendering it more automatic, and by artificially raising the costs associated with departing from it.

This stake-raising characteristic of personal rules has both positive and negative effects. On the plus side, it tends to enlarge the decision unit, so that people view the operative choice as one between aggregate patterns of conduct, rather than merely between individual acts.[55] This reframing can be extremely helpful in settings where one pattern, such as sobriety, plainly dominates another pattern, such as alcoholism, but at each decision point the chooser would prefer having a drink to not having a drink.[56] As Howard Rachlin explains, a similar structure occurs whenever complementarities are present that make one pattern more valuable than another, but the reverse preference exists for the pattern's subparts.[57] To borrow one of his examples, a person who would prefer to listen to a one-hour symphony in its entirety rather than hear twenty songs lasting three minutes each might nonetheless prefer each song to a three-minute segment of the symphony, if considered in isolation.[58] For the symphony, the whole is greater than the sum of its parts—it is lumpy, like a highway or bridge, and must be enjoyed in its entirety to be enjoyed much at all. Yet a person who always chooses based on what she most prefers to do with the next three minutes will never get to hear the symphony, and so will miss out on the more valuable overall pattern.

Similarly, many people who would enjoy and benefit from regular exercise might nonetheless find that they would rather spend any given free hour relaxing at home rather than running down a track. The advantages of exercise are cumulative, nonlinear, and indivisible, while the choice whether to get off the couch must be made at each moment. By making firm rules for gym-going (or play-attending or novel-reading or symphony-listening or dieting), people can try to break the grip of disaggregated decision making and choose a preferred pattern. Rules widen the viewfinder to encompass an entire complementary pattern and powerfully fortify self-control in the process: breaking the rule would set a precedent and would be tantamount to choosing the less-preferred pattern.[59]

But rules have their costs as well. By raising the stakes, they make each failure more monumental than its direct implications would suggest. Like take-it-or-leave-it offers in bargaining settings, rules strategically remove intermediate alternatives (e.g., "cake once in a while") to push actors toward the preferred chunky choice ("no cake")—but not without the risk that the actor will decide to switch to a different chunky choice ("cake anytime"). A lapse, instead of causing the lapser to redouble her efforts, may too often have the opposite effect of undermining her efforts and inducing further failures.[60] Thus we observe what has been termed the "what the hell" effect, where failure to live up to a goal such as a daily caloric restriction leads the individual to eat with abandon for the rest of the day.[61] This result is clearly counterproductive. The rule has constructed a cliff or discontinuity based on a daily calorie target, but there is in fact no natural discontinuity—if someone's target caloric intake for the day is 1,800 calories, going one thousand calories over the line is ten times as bad for purposes of reaching one's dietary goals as going one hundred calories over the line and half as bad as going two thousand calories over the line.[62]

Would extending the time period over which a dietary rule applies—to, say, a week or month—improve matters?[63] It would remove the daily cliff effect, but introduce a temptation to save the real dieting for later in the sequence. The diurnal cycle does come with a limited benefit: lapses are psychologically confined to the day on which they occur, allowing the dieter to start anew the next morning. We might even wonder whether the one-day observation period to which the rule is applied is actually too long rather than too short. Breaking the day up into separate goals for each meal would enable people who had overeaten at one point in the day to still experience some success during other periods the same day. But it would leave in place a cliff effect at the meal level, while perhaps making violations more likely as they become less consequential.

This example illustrates a general principle about what we might call behavioral firewalls. Considered ex ante, the belief that no firewall exists can powerfully assist a person in sticking to rules and pursuing a preferred pattern of conduct. If an ex-drinker believes that a single drink will doom her to a life of alcoholism, if an ex-smoker is convinced that one cigarette will make her addicted again, if a dieter believes a single slip will lead to lifelong obesity, and if a PhD student believes that wasting a few hours on social media means that she will never finish her dissertation, then compliance with rigid, hard-and-fast rules (no drinking, no smoking, no cake, no social media) will be more likely. But once a slip up occurs, the situation reverses: it is now no longer in the individual's interest to see her single act as an irrevocable choice of the entire disfavored aggregate pattern of conduct. Instead, she wants firewalls that will protect her future choices—and her hope of obtaining her goal or preferred consumption pattern—from contamination by the lapse. Allowing a lapse (or any other failure) to infect other sectors compounds the problem, but believing that it *will* infect other sectors makes the lapse less likely to occur.

In dieting, firewalls reliably form at daily intervals, which is frequent enough to enable numerous fresh starts—yet the knowledge (and, ultimately, repeated experience) of the availability of such fresh starts may make slip ups more likely.[64] Alternatively, people may attempt to firewall off a lapse by creating an exception that covers it.[65] This can be tricky, however, because the same exception that is constructed to wall off the lapse from the instances to which the rule applies will also invite further lapses that meet that exception, as well as further exceptions that extend the logic of the initial exception into new terrain.[66] So, eating cake on one's birthday becomes eating cake on other people's birthdays, becomes eating cake at any celebration, becomes eating cake whenever one is feeling celebratory, becomes eating cake when one *wishes to* feel more celebratory.[67] The problem of firewalling off lapses illustrates both the value of exceptions and their vulnerability to expansion. Closely related to this dynamic is the undue rigidity that bright-line rules can create for their adherents.[68] Finding a way to make *bounded* exceptions turns out to be very valuable, yet also very difficult.[69]

Another way to put the point, following Rachlin, is to observe that sometimes people do not really want an all-or-nothing result in a particular domain; they'd prefer something in between.[70] But how to achieve it? We have seen that rules can enable people to choose among larger patterns of behavior. Yet by their nature, rules are hard to square with *mixed* patterns that involve some amount of rule following interspersed with some amount of rule breakage. A complicated rule filled with exceptions can easily devolve into an all-things-considered deliberation at each decision point. Where an act-by-act method of choosing would generate a deeply suboptimal overall pattern, a strict rule may emerge as the lesser of two evils.

Very often, then, goals are defined in a lumpy or step manner not because this is how they actually deliver value to people, but because defining them in less absolute terms makes achieving the underlying benefits difficult or impossible. In other words, the operative lumpiness may be in people's own technologies for producing personal improvements. Strict rules can harm even those who manage to stick to them, as we see in behaviors like workaholism and miserliness that diminish people's enjoyment of life. In many other cases, the perceived all-or-nothing nature of a goal causes people to give up on their efforts altogether, or to shun lesser efforts that might nonetheless prove valuable. For example, the person who breaks her going-to-the-gym-every-day resolution might still benefit from going to the gym once a week, or even just by taking the stairs at work, but she may fail to implement these lesser measures.

Some years ago, Ian Ayres suggested an interesting implementation of the mixed-pattern idea: one-day-a-week vegetarianism.[71] This approach cleverly maintains the power of a bright-line rule, but it arguably places higher informational burdens on those with whom the sometimes-vegetarian shares meals. Thomas Merrill and Henry Smith famously used the idea of Monday-only wristwatch ownership as Exhibit A in their information-cost case against idiosyncratic property forms,[72] and Wednesday-only vegetarianism might seem to raise related concerns. But information costs are dropping rapidly in nearly every domain, allowing for many more ways of accessing resources and customizing consumption than would have been imagined a generation ago. Mixed patterns—whether in watch ownership or dietary restrictions or anything else—are likely to become increasingly attainable and worth pursuing.

As this discussion has shown, people can consciously construct and characterize their goals, including how lumpy or all-or-nothing they will be. This flexibility offers both strategic opportunities and potential pitfalls, as well as room for policy innovation. The next chapter extends the analysis of intrapersonal coordination into the realm of personal finance, and also considers some implications for public finance.

SIX

Saving and Spending

Pop quiz: To avoid financial distress, a family should (a) cut out all frills, such as dinners out; or (b) make sure to treat itself now and then. This is a no-brainer, right? Cutting out extras seems like an obvious step along the path to financial security. Yet in *The Two-Income Trap*, Elizabeth Warren and Amelia Warren Tyagi make a case for option (b)—coupled with advice to scale back fixed, long-term financial obligations.[1] Although Warren and Tyagi do not frame it this way, the reason comes down to lumpiness. Fixed expenses, like those for housing, tend to be lumpy and indivisible—very hard to adjust on the fly. By contrast, expenditures for extras tend to be granular and easy to scale up or down depending on a family's fortunes.

Consider two possible budgets for a family that, let's assume for simplicity, has just two major expenses: housing and food. Budget A involves a mortgage payment that is a stretch for the family, so that it only has enough money left over to cover inexpensive meals prepared at home. Budget B involves a much smaller mortgage or rent payment that leaves enough room in the food budget for buying various treats and eating out now and then. Now suppose the household suffers a financial setback—an illness or a layoff. A family that has chosen Budget A has nowhere to cut back—they are already subsisting on rice and beans, so to speak. Their mortgage payment is lumpy; even if they would be willing to shrink their home by 30 percent (or choose a 30 percent less fancy neighborhood) in exchange for a corresponding decrease in the mortgage, they have no way to do this. A family that has chosen Budget B, by contrast, has the flexibility to quickly trim down household expenses by buying cheaper groceries and skipping dinners out.

A couple of caveats are in order. My simple example ignores savings, which are the obvious first line of defense for meeting financial shocks, and should without question be part of any family's financial plan. The point of the example, however, is that the choices that households make about whatever portion of their income they plan to consume can also enhance or reduce their financial resilience. A second caveat is that housing has become a little less lumpy in recent years, thanks to platforms like Airbnb that enable renting out one's extra space—a point to be explored in more depth in chapter 9. But a family's home may not be physically (or psychologically) easy to divide, even if a willing tenant can be found, and private and public land use restrictions may further limit the household's renting-out options. Extra slack that is built into the food budget presents no such difficulties—it is not necessary to consult or contract with anyone before cutting out the artisanal cheeses, nor is there any regulatory regime likely to interfere with one's plans to eat a more austere diet. Counterintuitively, an up-front decision to enjoy the little extras helps to ensure some slack in the system.

Distinguishing the lumpy from the granular is not just a useful household budgeting trick. It is also central to understanding personal financial decision making more generally, as well as important public finance issues. The following sections explain.

Lumpy Preferences and Personal Finance

Many valuable consumer goods (cars, vacations, tuition, major appliances, down payments on homes) are indivisible in nature and may require relatively large expenditures all at once. Financing is not always available to break down these payments into manageable chunks and may even interfere with certain consumption experiences (such as vacations that are more enjoyable if prepaid).[2] So it is easy to see why people might want or need to *spend* money in lumps. Do people also prefer to *receive* money in lumps—and if so, why?

Research suggests that people are willing to forgo some increment of present value in order to receive a lump sum at a later date—such as a bonus at the end of the year, rather than a slightly larger paycheck every two weeks.[3] A similar pattern, to be discussed in more detail below, is found in the prevalence of income tax refunds—lump sums that are built out of earlier tax overpayments. From an economic perspective, these preferences seem puzzling. Money does not have to be received in a lump to be spent in a lump—it could instead be received in dribs and drabs and saved up. Indeed, standard economic analysis assumes that individuals can spread their lifetime earnings over their entire life cycle and consume in any temporal pattern they desire.[4] Given the time value of money, we would expect people to always want money earlier rather than later, without regard to whether it arrives in lumps or fragments.

An important clue to this puzzle involves collective action problems among temporal selves, a topic explored in chapter 5. Although self-control problems can arise with respect to all sorts of goals, assembling an adequate lump of cash may prove problematic for two basic reasons. First, it may be difficult to get enough of one's temporal selves to *contribute* to the fund, given that money (unlike effort or time) might be supplied in greater or lesser amounts by any number of different selves. Second, it may be difficult to keep one's temporal selves from *raiding* the fund before the necessary amount is amassed, given money's liquidity and fungibility. Partial solutions to both of these problems exist in various forms but are far from foolproof.

Savings accounts from which withdrawals are not permitted until a specified date, such as the once-popular "Christmas clubs," can attempt to address the raiding problem.[5] Successive selves still must place money into such an account rather than spend it immediately, or the desired lump of cash will not materialize. A system of automatic paycheck deductions, which would require each self to consciously "opt out" of the plan to avoid contributing, can help in this regard.[6] Once the money is in place, the external control on liquidity keeps it from being raided on an impulse. Nonetheless, such raid-guarding is unlikely to be fail-safe; it is hard to create financial assets that cannot be borrowed against or accessed by paying a penalty.[7]

An interesting raid-proofing alternative that is commonly pursued in many countries is to put savings into a tangible, illiquid form—a partially built house that will be constructed over time as cash flow allows—although the disadvantages of this approach are manifest.[8] More broadly, people might wish to buy certain goods in advance of when they will be needed, to tie up money while they still have it rather than risk letting it dissipate. Abhijit Banerjee and Esther Duflo give the example of Kenyan farmers who had enough money to buy fertilizer just after harvest, when local shops might not yet have it in stock, but no longer had the money in hand when the fertilizer was needed (and available).[9] An initiative that allowed the farmers to buy a voucher for fertilizer right after harvest provided a simple solution.[10] As this example suggests, it is not necessary to put money directly into tangible goods if another form of earmarking can be used instead. In a related vein, Mullainathan and Shafir see potential in "impulse savings" cards picturing particular goals (such as a car or a home), offered in place of standard checkout-aisle impulse items like candy bars.[11]

Rotating savings and credit associations (ROSCAs) offer another way of overcoming the twin problems of collecting contributions from one's selves and preventing self-raiding. Under this informal financing model, a group of people can join forces to enable each of them to acquire a lumpy good that otherwise would require a fairly lengthy period of saving. Timothy Besley and Alec Levenson give the example of ten people who each would like to buy a good that costs $100, but each only has ten dollars per week to put toward that goal.[12] With a ROSCA, everyone in the group pools their ten dollars each week, which allows one group member per week to acquire the good.[13] A major advantage of the ROSCA is that, on average, it lets people acquire goods much more quickly than they could acting alone.[14] Only the last person to receive the good must wait as long as if she had saved up for it on her own.[15] Yet even this last person gets something valuable out of entering into the arrangement: a raid-proof savings instrument with mandatory regular contributions.

Some raid-resistant savings programs use subsidies to encourage contributions. For example, the federal government's Retirement Savings Contributions Credit ("Saver's Credit") offers earners under certain income limits a nonrefundable tax credit of up to half of their retirement contributions up to $2,000 ($4,000 if married filing jointly).[16] Individual Development Accounts operate similarly: sponsoring organizations (governmental entities and nonprofits) provide matching funds to people with low income and wealth who lock up savings for approved purposes like buying a home, starting a business, or pursuing higher education.[17]

One barrier to participation in such programs is the temporal lumpiness of the savings behavior involved. As Adi Libson has observed, taking advantage of the Saver's Credit requires forgoing liquidity—the option value of money—for what may be a very lengthy period.[18] Libson proposes an intriguing alternative, the "Saver's Continuous Credit," that delumps the incentive structure. Under his plan, savings could be rewarded bit by bit while leaving open the option of withdrawal.[19] Instead of receiving a lump sum subsidy at the initial point of committing the money to the retirement fund, individuals could choose to receive the subsidy in installments as they complete each period of savings.[20] People unwilling to lock up money for a long time ex ante might nonetheless turn into long-term savers over time—and even those who do not may find themselves better able to weather periods of financial stress.

There are downsides to this approach. Just as breaking up a difficult task into smaller chunks makes each chunk easier to complete but harder to motivate, the existence of continual exit ramps from the savings plan could draw more people into the program but cause a larger percentage of them to defect from the desired behavior. Although the aggregate empirical effects are unclear, it seems likely that a finer-grained saving option would be beneficial on net for some subset of potential savers. Here, as in other contexts, finding ways to personalize financial tools to meet the needs of particular individuals and families represents an important avenue for future work.

Traditional borrowing can also serve as a means of precommitment. A person who finances the purchase of a car, for example, is able to access a powerful mechanism for coordinating her selves. Once the purchaser takes the car home, the prospect of losing possession will induce her to make payments on it faithfully, if she can possibly do so. And payments made on a car, unlike savings building up in an account, are somewhat harder to raid. Nonetheless, raiding remains possible even after the car is paid off, through, for example, title loans. And financing a purchase can be an expensive method of cash assembly.

Home mortgages present a related set of issues, but with much higher stakes. As David Laibson has observed, people can use illiquid goods like homes as a form of forced savings, although the ability to readily access their equity through mechanisms like home equity loans can undermine the potency of this strategy.[21] Another concern, underscored by the recent financial crisis, is that some mortgage products may leave people unable to repay, however willing they may be. Adjustable rate mortgages that caused payments to reset to much higher levels after two or three years were very popular because of their initially low "teaser" rates, but they were marketed to many households that could not actually pay the higher rates. For such households, these mortgage products would only be viable under conditions of sustained home price growth that would enable refinancing before the payments reset. When home prices went down rather than up, many households ended up in positions that no amount of willpower could resolve.

More broadly, financing a purchase has two opposing effects. One is that the acquisition powerfully harnesses loss aversion to coordinate the selves on a course of action—repayment—that will facilitate continued possession. The other, however, is that it raises the overall cost and risk associated with the lumpy purchase, presenting the possibility of default and associated dispossession. In short, financing makes the selves more willing, but less able, to cooperate.

Unlumping and Segmenting

As the discussion above suggests, the lumpiness of the home is a mixed bag—it can serve as a vehicle for forced savings, but it can also greatly limit flexibility. These points relate closely to the budget puzzle at the start of the chapter. Leaving slack in the budget for extras does make it more likely that the slack will be dissipated on unnecessary expenses unless it is greatly needed to address some budgetary shock. But tying up all of one's money can constitute an excess of precommitment when such shocks arrive. In short, liquidity may be tempting, but illiquidity is dangerous. This brings us to the question of delumping illiquid goods like the home.

Imagine a family has made payments on a house for years and has built up a cushion of home equity. Perhaps the household suffers a financial setback such as job loss and needs to access funds that are tied up in the home, or perhaps the household simply wishes to engage in some additional spending. Home equity loans offer a way to open up the piggybank of the home and extract funds—but not without cost, and not without risk.[22] Home equity loans spiked in popularity during the run-up to the housing crisis, but often included terms that made them difficult or impossible to repay when home prices failed to continue rising.[23] Regulatory responses have since made credit significantly harder to access. This benefits homeowners who might be overly tempted to access credit for frivolous reasons, but it also limits the ability of families to address legitimate financial crunches.

What the home equity conundrum reveals is that often people want neither an ironclad and unopenable lockbox for their money nor an open-ended ATM machine that can be accessed at a whim, but rather something in between. Could a form of partitioning similar to that which appears to slow food consumption help in achieving this balance? Work by Dilip Soman and Amar Cheema in the savings context offers some support for this idea.[24] They conducted a study in rural India with participants who were married laborers with children, all of whom were engaged in the same occupation and earning the same amount.[25] The experimental design involved setting aside part of each worker's weekly pay in sealed envelopes, earmarked as savings. Some of the workers had all of each week's earmarked savings placed in one envelope, while others had it partitioned into two envelopes; the experimental design also varied the savings target across these conditions so that some workers had about 6 percent of their wages sealed into either one or two envelopes, while others had a target twice that high, 12 percent, sealed into either one or two envelopes.[26]

Finally, half of the participants received their earmarked savings in plain white envelopes while the other half received the savings in envelopes printed with photographs of the worker's children.[27]

The study found that partitioning had a significant effect in increasing savings. Even though the two-envelope households with high savings targets were very likely to open *one* envelope during a given week, the partitioning helped to guard some savings from being raided. This partitioning effect was accentuated when children's pictures appeared on the envelopes.[28] Those with the high savings target and an unpartitioned single envelope saved the least.[29] The researchers concluded that "a high saving target helps when partitions are present but hurts when partitions are absent. Because the high saving target is difficult to maintain, the presence of partitions prevents households from sliding down a slippery slope of goal failure."[30] This kind of partitioning calls to mind not only the physical partitioning of food portions discussed in chapter 5, but also the psychological firewalling of days of dieting from each other, so that failure on one day does not necessarily portend failure on the next day.

The idea of using partitions to segment and earmark money is not new; many people grew up in families that used envelope or coffee-can budgeting systems. An interesting question is whether the effects associated with physical partitioning can be replicated in virtual space, within ordinary bank accounts. People can already partition their money into different bank accounts, and they may mentally partition accounts based on the source of income (feeling more free, for instance, to spend a bonus than an ordinary paycheck).[31] Soman and Cheema discuss the possibility of software that could visually represent different "envelopes" or earmarked categories within a single bank account.[32] The virtual representations of these envelopes could be digitally adorned with pictures designating goals, could have sound effects or animations accompany "opening an envelope," or even require more steps (or time delays) to open certain envelopes.

A similar partitioning approach could be extended to borrowing contexts. For example, policy innovations could enable homeowners to segment their home equity and selectively restrict their own access to it by adding delays or procedural steps. Unlike a hard legal cap on the amount of equity people can take out of their homes, such an approach would not preclude people from ultimately accessing more of their equity. But doing so would require the equivalent of opening another envelope.

Lumpiness and segmentation also carry interesting implications in the context of debt repayment. The psychological boost associated with clearing an entire line of debt underlies Dave Ramsey's popular financial advice to pay off debts in reverse order of size, gaining momentum as one goes.[33] Yet this segmentation-sensitive advice clashes with the basic economic principle that debt carrying a higher interest rate should be repaid before debt carrying a lower interest rate. Could the two ideas be reconciled? Imagine an app that would order a consumer's nonmortgage debts based on interest rates but artificially recut the loans into ascending size segments for repayment. These debt segments could be concretized by naming or color-coding them, so that instead of paying back loans for "Acme Department Store Card" or "Used Car Loan," one instead pays off "Red Debt" and then tackles "Orange Debt." The underlying loans would remain unchanged; the app would simply calculate the amounts necessary to retire each constructed segment, and prompt the consumer to make the appropriate payments to the appropriate creditors in the appropriate order. Suitably gamified, such an app might deliver the same satisfaction and momentum as paying off discrete debts that correspond to specific creditors, while allowing consumers to retire their most expensive debts first.

Lumpy Preferences or Irrationality?

The preceding discussion shows that techniques for reconfiguring one's finances exist, but may be difficult to access or implement. If do-it-yourself cash assembly efforts often go wrong, we should not be surprised that people show preferences for receiving money in lump sums—and will even forgo some expected value to obtain money in that form. More broadly, lumpy preferences can explain seemingly anomalous or irrational conduct that might otherwise be attributed to inconsistencies in time preferences or in risk preferences. The sections below illustrate these possibilities using two familiar examples. First, I discuss the common practice of income tax overwithholding, which generates lump sum refunds. Second, I discuss lottery play—losing bets that people frequently make despite binding economic constraints.

Income Tax Refunds

Close to three-quarters of US taxpayers receive tax refunds annually.[34] Refunds are primarily generated because people have more income tax than necessary withheld from their paychecks or because they are receiving the Earned Income Tax Credit (EITC). Overwithholding seems like an odd choice, as it runs directly counter to the rational preference to receive money earlier rather than later. The EITC is currently only available in a lump sum, so the refunds it generates do not reflect any choice on the part of recipients. However, up until the 2010 tax year, the EITC *could* be received in advance installments—but very few families elected that option. These behaviors seem especially puzzling given that many tax filers prove willing to pay to accelerate receipt of the refund through refund anticipation products or to incur interest costs on debts while waiting for the refund to arrive. Many possible explanations have been explored in the literature, and there are no doubt a number of reasons for the overall pattern.[35] But one explanation deserves attention in the present discussion: that people find it valuable to receive a preassembled lump of cash, given difficulties in saving—or, for some people, difficulties in *spending*.

Consider overwithholding. Self-control problems may make it difficult for an individual to translate small amounts of money saved from paychecks throughout the year into a lump sum. In addition, people may not feel as free to make large expenditures from their regular income.[36] The withholding system provides an easy way to generate a lump sum in the form of a tax refund at the end of the year. Income tax withholding incorporates two features that can help coordinate temporal selves. First, the automatic payroll deduction harnesses the human tendency toward inertia by making contributing in each period the default choice.[37] Second, bureaucratic delay is likely to tamp down any momentary temptation to change the default selection: the requested change in withholding may not be reflected in one's paycheck for weeks.[38]

The EITC is also paid out as lump sum after recipients file their tax returns. This design choice seems anomalous on its face—after all, the EITC is a means-tested program for low-income people, who we might expect to be on very tight budgets and in need of funds earlier rather than later. Yet decades of experience with the Advance EITC (AEITC) alternative, which allowed families to receive the EITC in advance installments, suggested little recipient interest in delumping the payment. Only about 3 percent of EITC recipients chose AEITC in tax years 2002 through 2004.[39] When efforts at increasing awareness of this alternative failed to substantially increase take-up, the Government Accountability Office offered this explanation: "IRS officials, other experts, and our prior work suggest that individuals often do not elect the AEITC because they prefer receiving the entire EITC as a lump sum when filing their tax return."[40] The option to receive advance EITC payments was eliminated after the 2010 tax year.[41]

Self-control issues may combine with the need for lumpy outlays to explain these preferences for lump sum tax refunds.[42] With average refunds in the neighborhood of $2,900, a significant lump of spending can be financed all at once.[43] Many recipients prioritize using the money to get current on bills, something far more satisfying to accomplish all at once.[44] Others focus on funding large purchases—vehicles and vehicle repairs, tuition, a new wardrobe for a child, household furniture, major appliances and electronics, or down payments on housing.[45] The large payment also seasonally grants many recipients something else that may be lumpy in nature: a sense of financial plentitude, the wherewithal to indulge in special treats like dinners out or preferred grocery items without having to carefully attend to each dollar spent.[46] Finally, many refund recipients plan to save a portion of their refund[47]—an intention that might depend on starting out with a lump that seems significant enough to save.

One controversial wrinkle in the tax refund story involves refund anticipation products offered by tax preparation services, which can accelerate taxpayers' receipt of expected funds. These products have been widely used by EITC recipients and to a lesser extent by other tax filers.[48] Although some details have changed over the years (refund anticipation loans were effectively eliminated by a 2010 regulatory change, so refund anticipation checks are now the operative product), the puzzle remains: why are people both willing to delay receiving money by several months *and* willing to pay to speed it up by about a week?[49]

Lumpiness supplies an explanation. Conditional on being able to receive money in a unified lump sum, people do wish to receive money as soon as possible. Nonetheless, the desire for the lump sum overwhelms their desire for earlier piecemeal payments. A person who desires lumpy consumption as soon as possible, but cannot manage to assemble a lump sum for herself, might quite consistently make choices that first look *hyperopic*—the opposite of myopic—to assemble the necessary lump, and then switch to choices that look myopic (to obtain the lump sum as quickly as possible).[50] Refund anticipation products have another compelling practical advantage: a filer can have her tax preparation fee taken out of the refund after it arrives, rather than have to pay up front before the return can be filed.[51]

That we can explain the existing pattern does not mean that it is optimal, and there are a number of reforms (including tax simplification) that might improve matters. One promising avenue, much in keeping with the theme of this book, involves splitting up the refund.[52] Some individuals may plan to use part of the refund for a big-ticket purchase, but would not mind waiting a little longer to make that expenditure if they could immediately receive a portion of the refund to address especially pressing financial needs—including the need to pay for tax preparation services in order to get the refund in the first place.[53] For families that have fallen behind on their rent and utilities, even slightly quicker access to funds can make the difference in avoiding eviction or keeping the power on.[54] But the funds necessary to get current on essential bills and to pay for tax preparation need not be accessed at the same time as the rest of the refund that enables more discretionary spending—or saving.

A step in this direction is the IRS's "split-refund option," which allows taxpayers to designate up to three separate accounts to divide their refunds among.[55] This approach allows for refund recipients to put a portion of their refund directly into one or more savings accounts while placing the balance into an account for immediate spending—an approach that may harness the partitioning benefits discussed above.[56] Similarly, Brett Theodos and his coauthors describe a low-cost program in which recipients were able to access 80 percent of their anticipated refund right away. The rest of the refund, which was provided after the IRS had processed the return and issued the refund, reportedly "tends to stay in the customers' accounts."[57] Other ideas for deferring or advancing a subset of the EITC payment have gained traction in recent years, including a recent pilot project in Chicago that allowed recipients to receive half of the credit in four advance payments.[58] These approaches reflect the possibility that even those with lumpy financial needs can benefit from artful slicing.

Lotteries: Buying a (Lumpy) Dream

State-run lotteries present another policy conundrum. On one hand, they are capable of raising significant revenue through what amounts to voluntary contributions.[59] On the other, they do so by encouraging constituents, including many with severe resource constraints, to take losing gambles.[60] The expenditures are significant: Melissa Schettini Kearney and her coauthors observe, citing 2008 data, that US households spend more on lottery tickets, on average, than on dairy products or alcohol.[61] What should we make of this behavioral choice—is it a mistake, or simply a vindication of consumer sovereignty? The expected value of the ticket is too low to induce the purchase on its own, so something else must make the purchase worthwhile in the eyes of lottery players.[62] This added component might simply be "lottery fun" or an overoptimism bias that makes people believe their personal chances of winning are larger than the odds would suggest.[63] But lumpiness points to another explanation: the payoff may be inflated in the player's eyes because it represents the large, indivisible good of substantial wealth.[64]

A lottery player's goal might be to achieve a particular absolute level of wealth, perhaps understood in functional terms, such as enough money to never have to work again, or enough money to move solidly into a different socioeconomic class.[65] If so, lottery play may not reflect a player's engrained "love of the gamble" but rather her desire for something that, given her budget constraints, can *only* be achieved through a gamble.[66] It is far from clear that we should regard this sort of risk-leveraging behavior as a mistake.

Nor should we be particularly surprised if we see a lottery player also buying an insurance policy. As Milton Friedman and L. J. Savage explain, this combination can occur if people experience sharp drop-offs in well-being at low wealth levels and large jumps in well-being at high wealth levels, but have a much gentler utility slope in the middle income ranges.[67] In other words, living a relatively comfortable life may be close to a step good, and achieving fabulous wealth may be a higher step good. People might insure to avoid the step down in utility associated with the worst outcomes, but be willing to gamble on a chance to step up to a much better payoff.

Another way of reconciling lottery play and insurance is suggested by Markus Fels, who argues that "both insurance and gambling are desirable . . . for the same reason: their ability to concentrate wealth into a subset of states in order to overcome affordability constraints."[68] Fels's observation builds on Ng Yew Kwang's insight that indivisibilities sometimes explain gambles.[69] Suppose we think of the lottery prize as a large, indivisible sack filled with lovely goods and experiences. The sack is far out of our price range, and there is no way to buy just the slice of it that we can afford. Even if we could somehow afford to rent the sack for an hour, say, that would not be long enough to enjoy its contents in any meaningful way. So we do something different. Instead of dividing up the sack itself, we divide up our possible futures into millions of different pathways and, for the price of a lottery ticket, populate one of those pathways with the sack. By constraining the sack to one possible (and very unlikely) state of the world—the one in which our number is drawn—it becomes affordable.[70]

Insurance works similarly. Again, we can start by recognizing that there are many possible futures that we may experience. But here, we notice that some of those potential futures are already populated by bad things— poor health, accidents, fires, and so on. If we leave our funds spread evenly among all the possible states of the world and wind up in a future containing one of these severe negative events, we will be deep in a hole with insufficient resources to dig our way out. Insurance allows us to heap resources into just those states of the world that are already populated by the negative events.[71] We do this by removing money from the many other states of the world where the negative events do not occur—that is, by paying insurance premiums. These premiums buy us a kind of lottery ticket that hedges against bad events and pays off only when we draw a losing ticket in the game of life.

This slicing-by-state-of-the-world is not so different from many of the other kinds of slicing that we have seen already and will see later in this book. Recall the EITC recipients who are able, through a lump sum refund, to enjoy a season of relatively free spending at tax time. Such a spending pattern is too expensive for the family to enjoy year-round, but the refund allows freer spending to be concentrated into just one segment of the year, where it conveys a sense of plentitude. Similarly, services for sharing or slicing cars, tools, and other durable goods concentrate resources into just those states of the world where they are needed, rather than requiring that they be available on a constant basis.

Public Finance Implications

The allure of the lottery, and of lump sums more generally, suggests some interesting directions for policy innovation. Prize-linked savings accounts represent an emerging example.[72] These bank accounts incentivize savings not through interest payments, which would be fairly paltry on small balances, but rather through automatic entries into lotteries that offer the chance at a significant, perhaps life-changing, lump of cash. Importantly, even those who lose in the lottery are induced to save, and to thereby assemble their own lumps of cash. Research suggests that prize-linked accounts can indeed increase net savings, in part by reducing expenditures on traditional lotteries.[73] Recent federal legislation, the 2014 American Savings Promotion Act, has removed a major regulatory barrier to the adoption of prize-linked savings products, clearing a path for more experimentation with these models going forward.[74] One incarnation of this approach ties back to our earlier discussion: Save Your Refund (sponsored by the nonprofit Commonwealth in partnership with America Saves) offers chances at cash prizes to those who sign up for the IRS's split-refund option and direct at least fifty dollars into savings.[75] Here we see lottery lumps being used to encourage delumping moves.

More broadly, it may be possible to incentivize socially desirable behavior at a lower cost simply by changing how payoffs are lumped and sliced. In one study, survey data suggested that people might be more willing to delay retirement for an incentive formulated as a lump sum rather than as a stream of payments—even if the lump sum had a lower expected value.[76] Lotteries have also proven effective as incentives in at least some contexts. One experiment investigating tax compliance found that offering a lottery entry for a clean audit induced more compliance than a fixed reward.[77] Similarly, a recent study in Rimini, Italy, found that compliance with the requirement to purchase a public transit ticket (rather than attempt to free ride) increased significantly when each ticket purchase entered the rider in a lottery.[78] These findings suggest that the format a payout takes, and not just its expected value, can be an important policy lever.

Lotteries do not always outperform fixed payments, however.[79] One study found that survey respondents who were asked to recruit other respondents (a methodology known as "snowball sampling") were much more likely to pass along a survey to others when it was accompanied by a fixed monetary incentive, as compared with a chance of winning a prize— even though people given a choice about their own reward preferred the lottery.[80] The fixed payment opportunity may have seemed more appropriate to share since it was guaranteed to pay off and would not risk the sharer's credibility in the way that telling someone about a losing lottery might. A recent attempt by United Airlines to replace employee rewards with entries in a prize lottery also misfired; workers saw it as an unfair and arbitrary way of allocating compensation among colleagues.[81] Much work remains to pin down the mechanisms driving the observed pattern of results, but it appears that social norms play a role in determining when lotteries will be viewed as an appropriate and attractive substitute for a flat payment.

Lotteries and lump sums also feature in the delivery of social benefits and might be made more effective in those roles. Currently lotteries are used to allocate lumpy public benefits like housing for which demand far exceeds supply. Rather than supplement these tools with long waiting lists, as currently occurs, people might be allowed to choose whether to buy more or fewer chances at the indivisible good by accepting larger or smaller amounts of a divisible benefit like cash assistance.[82] States and localities might also offer other sorts of actuarially fair lotteries that would give people a chance at a lump of money sufficient to, say, start a business.[83] These ideas come with drawbacks and may be unsuitable without a sufficient floor of assistance to make choices across goods meaningful. But the basic insight that people often prefer a chance at a lumpier good over the certainty of a divisible benefit deserves careful policy attention.

Lump sums also feature in state welfare "diversion" programs that permit families with acute, short-term needs to access a one-time payment in lieu of applying for regular welfare benefits.[84] Under a number of state programs, lump sum recipients must agree to forgo the right to receive regular monthly benefit payments under the Temporary Assistance for Needy Families (TANF) program for some period of time.[85] Such programs usefully recognize that a lump sum payment can have the power to rapidly lift families out of dire financial straits. But if people weight lump sums more heavily than other payments, the risk exists that some families will fail to seek longer-term assistance when it would be more suitable. One question that this analysis raises is when the heavier weighting of lump sums is a rational reaction to the lumpy realities that people must surmount to exit poverty, and when it instead represents a hardwired bias that may prove self-defeating.

Related issues surround the segments into which in-kind assistance is divided. The Supplemental Nutrition Assistance Program (SNAP), formerly known as food stamps, delivers food assistance to households via electronic benefit cards on a once-monthly basis.[86] Food purchase and consumption tends to be skewed toward the date of the benefit reload, with less food purchased and consumed later in the monthly cycle.[87] This pattern might make the benefit increments appear unduly lumpy for households' budgeting needs. On the other hand, the monthly cycle of plenitude and scarcity could be more attractive to some households than more evenly spread consumption, for reasons that resonate with the EITC refund discussion above. Offering recipients the choice to receive their SNAP payments semi-monthly is one alternative that has received attention.[88] Another option would be to segment the benefits so that each week or two-week allotment is partitioned off in a manner that requires the electronic equivalent of deliberately opening an envelope. This alternative would offer more flexibility to families with fluctuating purchase needs, while still providing a useful budgeting nudge. More generally, the electronic benefit format should make it relatively inexpensive to let recipients slice up their benefits in ways that best fit their preferences.

Just as questions arise about how to split up assistance provided to the same family over time, so do questions about how to divide up assistance among different recipients. How can the desire to provide assistance in truly meaningful increments be reconciled with the goal of serving as many qualifying low-income families as possible? The answer depends, in part, on how lumpy or indivisible particular chunks of public assistance really are.

One facet of benefit lumpiness can be distilled from Banerjee and

Duflo's analysis of poverty traps—situations in which people lack the resources to increase their future earnings and thus slide into deeper poverty.[89] A push that enables an individual to get past a critical threshold can place her on a different part of the earnings curve where she is able to leverage current returns into larger future returns.[90] A small business owner may need to make a crucial capital investment to make the leap from a floundering or subsistence-level business to a really profitable enterprise.[91] Falling even a little bit short leaves her with the equivalent of an incomplete bridge. Similarly, Charles Karelis argues that for those in deep poverty, additional increments of assistance can bring *increasing* marginal returns, rather than the usually posited diminishing marginal returns.[92] For instance, he observes that someone who lives six miles from work will find it disproportionately valuable to get a ride the entire way to work—five miles is not five-sixths as good.[93]

Thus, there may be discontinuities—gaps and jumps—in the good that assistance does for people. What do these observations mean for public policy? First, these examples suggest the importance of providing functionally adequate assistance—what David Super calls "functional entitlements."[94] In other words, enough assistance to "do the trick" (which requires, in turn, defining what the trick is in a given context, whether escaping a poverty trap or getting to work in the morning). As a corollary, the fact that results are not observed at a particular funding level does not prove that assistance is futile; shifting to a slightly higher funding level could make all the difference.[95] The second takeaway is that the same amount of assistance can do different amounts of good depending on how it is divided up among people. Just as distributing bricks to many families is less helpful than building an entire home for one of them, assistance can be more effective if it is aggregated in certain ways. By the same token, there are points beyond which additional increments of assistance to the same individuals or families will do less good than shifting those increments to others.

Public policy, informed by an understanding of lumpiness, might consciously focus on aggregating assistance into units that are functionally adequate to extricate families from poverty. But this extricating increment is not the same for every household. What is functionally adequate for people who are very close to escaping a poverty trap, or people who live just two miles from their workplace, will not be functionally adequate for people who need a much bigger boost out of a poverty trap, or who live eighteen miles from their workplaces. To deliver functionally adequate assistance to as many families as possible, however, would mean concentrating assistance on those who were very close to self-sufficiency already. To do the opposite—offer functionally adequate assistance to those in the deepest need—would mean helping fewer families escape poverty. Yet those closer to self-sufficiency might have other alternatives available for self-help that those in greater need lack. Moreover, the consequences and meaning of poverty might be far worse for those in greater need, making their extrication more valuable both to themselves and to society.

These decisions are difficult and controversial ones.[96] My point here is not to resolve them but rather to show that these kinds of trade-offs lurk just below the surface of debates about welfare benefits. The way in which aid is doled out inevitably makes these choices, even if not explicitly. Thinking about poverty relief from the perspective of functional adequacy—the lumpy amount needed to get from a bad situation to a sustainable one—can alter the discourse around welfare policy. At the same time, the amount that society chooses to put toward poverty relief is not fixed in advance but is instead sensitive to how that assistance is framed.[97] Recognizing the role of discontinuities and thresholds in poverty extrication can reframe poverty relief as an investment in human capital. The next chapter will take up some related questions about how lumpiness intersects with choices involving employment, leisure, and risk-bearing.

SEVEN

Work, Play, Risk

As the sun sets and the streets outside buzz with rush hour traffic, the young lawyer gets another cup of coffee and settles in for a long night of work. She went to a top law school, and the law firm job she has secured pays extremely well. It is even interesting most of the time. But the hours are crushing. She cannot recall the last time she got home before eight in the evening, and even then there are always more emails to answer and loose ends to tie up. Weekends are a blur of chores crammed in between the projects she must finish; any bits of downtime thrum with low-level panic about the deadlines ahead. She would gladly trade half her salary if she could reduce her working hours by a third, down from the sixty-plus hours a week she averages to something closer to a forty-hour week—without losing her chance to make partner. But this option does not exist. Her job, in short, is very lumpy.

At the other end of the spectrum, the emergent "gig economy" features highly granular work that can be sliced up finely and aggregated into patterns suited to each worker. Platforms like TaskRabbit and Uber are enabling significant segments of the population to replace—or supplement—traditional employment relationships with alternatives that involve supplying small chunks of effort to many different purchasers. Bureau of Labor Statistics data from 2017 indicate that about 10 percent of the US workforce is employed in alternative arrangements as their "sole or main job,"[1] and a 2017 Federal Reserve study of US households found that "three in 10 adults work in the 'gig economy,' though generally as a supplemental source of income."[2]

These new ways of working add tremendous flexibility. For example, Keith Chen and his coauthors recently found that, despite some disadvantages to the working arrangement, Uber drivers derive substantial benefits from the ability to choose their own work hours.[3] But there are significant pitfalls as well. For one, unbundling the job into granular work units may also unbundle the job from the legal protections and benefits that typically accompany employment. Indeed, firms may strategically pursue such unbundling in an effort to dodge regulatory mandates, whether by reducing work hours or the number of employees below a particular threshold or reclassifying workers as independent contractors.[4] Thus, delumping work may also mean altering a worker's legal status and rearranging the risk that she bears.

In this chapter, I will consider how lumpiness in time and risk interact in the realms of work and play to shape and structure people's lives. Understanding the core challenges of aggregation and division in these arenas will enable policy makers and entrepreneurs to improve the fit between supply and demand.

Jobs and Gigs

Consider again the problem of the too-lumpy job—a common complaint, and one that is by no means limited to the legal profession. Job lumpiness has at least two facets. First, most jobs are *economically indivisible* in that employees cannot freely split them up into smaller commitments comprised of less hours and less pay. This indivisibility would constrain workers even if they were entirely free to choose which hours and days to work (consider our overworked young attorney, who would find cold comfort in being able to select *which* sixty-five hours to work each week). Second, many jobs feature *temporal indivisibility* coupled with *temporal immobility* or *fixity* in that they occupy fixed and contiguous lumps of time within the worker's schedule, such as a specific block of eight hours per day that must be worked during a week of five (specified) consecutive days. Temporal indivisibility and fixity are logically separable—a task could require eight consecutive hours of work that could be completed at any time—but typically they appear together.

Mullainathan and Shafir's packing metaphor, introduced in chapter 5, is apt here: fitting tasks into the available envelope of time presents a challenge much like fitting physical objects into an allotted space.[5] A person who has a job that is economically and temporally indivisible, as well as temporally immobile, is like a driver preparing for a journey who must fit her belongings around a large object that is bolted in place in the car's trunk. The larger this immovable lump is relative to the available space—that is, the larger the proportion of one's waking hours it takes up—the harder the challenge. But merely shrinking the lump's overall volume may be less helpful than freeing it from its fixed position, depending on the size, shape, and immobility of the other time commitments that need to be wedged in. The ability to shift the chunk of working time about or divide it up and move the pieces around into a different configuration can address certain kinds of time crunches, even if it cannot address the more foundational problem of overwork.

What Causes Indivisibilities and Rigidities?

Why do jobs embody these forms of lumpiness? At first blush, employment indivisibilities and rigidities seem to be unilaterally imposed by employers who require that work be supplied by employees in certain-sized chunks and in specified configurations—or not at all. But this just pushes the inquiry back a step: why would employers want these things? Perhaps the fixed costs of hiring and training make it infeasible to recut the work into smaller servings and distribute it to more workers. For example, if each new hire requires the employer to lose money upfront for months or even years before positive returns can be realized, then the employer will want to incur that cost as few times as possible. Indeed, the fixed upfront cost of learning a new skill offers an explanation for labor specialization more broadly—an idea that goes back to Adam Smith.[6] There may be other indivisibilities as well: difficult-to-share amenities like an office or a laptop (although this is changing, as we will see), or fixed administrative or benefit costs that are not scaled to working hours or to salary. These factors too might push employers to shape jobs into particular minimum configurations.

Alternatively, a lumpy job may screen out those employees who lack stamina or who will be shirkers, offering a way of simplifying promotion decisions.[7] Other possibilities relate to the way that the worker's inputs generate returns for the employer. Perhaps there are increasing returns in a given workweek, so that the first two dozen hours generate much lower returns than the next two dozen hours. This might be the case, for example, if the employer is constantly taking on new clients or new projects, for which steep learning curves exist. Or particular projects may demand attention from the same person from beginning to end, and completing them within the necessary time envelope requires sustained work over a given period. Similarly, an eight-hour workday or a five-day workweek might be useful in accommodating projects that require cumulative inputs that build on each other or lengthy periods of preparation or cleanup. In such cases temporal indivisibility helps minimize the time spent ramping up and ramping down. Temporal indivisibility and fixity may also arise from the need to coordinate the work of multiple people at once or the need to coordinate supervision. Thus, features of the work's production function, as well as features of the regulatory environment, may push employers to demand certain lumps of work.

Yet recent research suggests that the problem may run deeper than employer demands. A study of employees in Dutch organizations found that even when firms accommodated worker requests for shorter working hours—as the Working Hours Adjustment Act of 2000 requires employers to do if the company's interests will not be put at serious risk—many workers still reported working more hours than they wished to work.[8] Specifically, the authors found that "a third of the part-time employees still work overtime even though they would rather not do so," and despite the fact that "for the majority (75%) of these employees, overtime is unpaid."[9] Thus, even workers who successfully negotiate a part-time position end up working closer to full-time hours than they had planned, contributing to what has been termed "the part-time illusion"[10] or "schedule creep."[11] The reason, the authors of the Dutch study posit, is "a *new form of lumpiness*: The employer does not forbid adjustment of the working time, but . . . work itself comes in 'lumps' of tasks" that require sustained attention and timely completion.[12] Under these conditions, workers' own choices can sustain a gap between preferred hours and actual hours.[13]

One way of understanding this phenomenon is to see that the wages paid by the employer are only part of the payoff that workers get from their jobs. Employees also receive intrinsic, reputational, and career-building returns from producing certain results for clients in a timely fashion and maintaining certain standards of quality as they do so. If the contract with the employer serves to get workers started on a task, then the returns that employees internalize from finishing the entire project may carry them beyond the agreed-upon hourly terms—even though most of the surplus goes to the employer.[14] We have seen this phenomenon in other guises already. Like the dissertation writer who forces herself to work for fifteen minutes per day, but then becomes sufficiently engrossed to make real progress, the worker who contracts to work for thirty hours a week may find herself putting in fifty anyway.

More broadly, as we saw in chapter 4, many all-or-nothing decisions like attending a festival or listing a home for sale may be undertaken even when most of the returns go to others—as long as enough returns are realized by the actor to make the action worthwhile. In some of our earlier examples, such binary choices were benign or beneficial, but here we might be concerned that employers will get the better end of the bargain if they can pay only for the early units of work and get the balance for free. The data on the Dutch experience suggest that simply requiring employers to accommodate employee requests for shorter hours may not accomplish a durable slicing of the job at the contractually specified point. In many cases the tasks themselves may provide the binding constraint. Yet these features of work are not given by nature; they may be due to (malleable) client expectations or other upstream decisions. A strong enforcement mechanism, such as required overtime pay when a purportedly part-time employee goes over the weekly limit, might encourage employers to recut assignments in ways more amenable to part-time schedules.

To be sure, some tasks are just more difficult to divide than others, or exhibit engrained rigidities that affect scheduling. Certain tasks, like teaching a class, performing in a play, or driving a bus, have to be performed in specified blocks at definite times and cannot be subdivided, aggregated, or rearranged at will. Other tasks that appear thinly sliced and flexible—Uber driving is a current example—still have indivisible chunks embedded within them, such as trips that must be completed once begun.[15] In other cases, lumps of work are not inherent to the task but rather arise from past procrastination that creates a bottleneck around a deadline. Similarly, sometimes several lumpy tasks that could each be absorbed with little difficulty will happen to randomly converge in ways that increase the overall lump of work beyond capacity.[16]

A related issue is that work lumps may not be ever-present but may emerge at certain critical junctures. Having sufficient capacity to handle these lumps requires one of two things: either a means by which to expand and contract the supply of labor (or "attention") or periods in which excess capacity will exist in the form of idleness or "slack."[17] If it is easy to hire seasonal or temporary workers to handle peak loads, it may be possible to get by with a smaller standing workforce. Conversely, a larger standing workforce will come with a lower opportunity cost if lower-priority tasks can be taken up during downtime (which may depend on the granularity of those tasks) or if there are ways to reallocate workers across firm sectors that have different cycles of high and low demand. In theory, a firm could contract out its workers to another firm during slow periods, although administrative hurdles may make this avenue impractical.

The same idea of granularity that we examined before in the context of fitting tasks into one person's schedule also applies to fitting work into a firm's business model. The larger the firm, the easier it will be to absorb unusually large chunks of work without running into capacity problems, as long as the timing of work lumps is not highly correlated and workers can move among tasks freely. This is another example where lumpiness at close range looks smooth when we scale up and zoom out. For a solo lawyer with only a few clients, a major filing deadline can create a large lump of work that requires unusually heavy work hours, the hiring of extra help, or some of both—it is like a tall hill in an otherwise flat landscape. For a firm with many clients, the filing deadlines form so many peaks of activity that the workload ends up looking smooth—the hills are so numerous that they effectively merge into a continuous mesa, with a few small crevices here and there into which stray tasks or extra leisure time can fit.

Changes over Time

Some tasks that seem by their nature hard to divide may change with technology and shifting business models. Writing in 1969, Charles Frank observed that it was typically impossible to hire half a manager, explaining that "even if two firms were willing to share the services of one manager so that each could hire him part time, the physical location of the manager may be so important that it might be impractical or impossible for him to manage two operations at once."[18] This may still be true to some extent, but undivided physical presence may have become less crucial in providing many kinds of services—perhaps even surgery. Although controversial, it is apparently now common for some surgeons to "run two rooms" where surgery is being performed simultaneously, intermittently supervising and assisting trainees who are carrying out the bulk of the procedures.[19] Many types of collaboration no longer require people to be physically present in the same place or to work on a project at the same time. Indeed, offset schedules can speed up certain kinds of joint work, as I learned a few years ago as a Chicagoan working with a coauthor in Taipei: Each of us could knock off work in our respective evenings, hand off the draft by email, and wake up to a new and improved version—no downtime!

Other workplace rigidities seem destined to fall away as the nature of offices and equipment change. Computers need not be permanently assigned to a particular user, but can instead be used by multiple workers who log in under their own profiles and access data that resides elsewhere. The rise of "hot desking" or "office hoteling" likewise makes individual desks or offices less dedicated workspaces than access nodes that workers can move among.[20] Many employers have already implemented unassigned seating arrangements in the workplace, and the trend seems likely to continue.[21] Assigned offices can seem like anachronistic space hogs when the things traditionally kept in them (even personal touches like family photographs) increasingly take a digital form and the employees themselves frequently collaborate in various other locations or work off-site.

But the news is not all good: floating workspaces can be alienating and inconvenient for employees, and employers may find that their workers resist or resent the change.[22] Some scholars have suggested that open seating may run counter to engrained notions of territoriality.[23] One case study found that a hierarchical structure developed in response to hot desking, with some workers "settling" in particular areas that they occupied consistently over time, while others were left in a "vagrant" status to float among the now-depleted set of communal workspaces.[24] Yet a similar slicing-by-rotation is common and accepted in many other arenas: think of bus and airline seats, amusement park rides, and classroom chairs and lecterns. What makes people resist time slicing in some contexts and not in others?

The answer may have less to do with innate territoriality than with social norms or expectations that have developed around particular arrangements. More concretely, a worker may fear negative externalities from her temporal neighbors, such as crumbs left in the keyboard by the previous occupant of the workstation. There may also be losses in continuity (in routines, in interactions with workmates) associated with moving too frequently. Some "turnover costs" can be managed through rules and procedures, such as cleaning between uses. The architecture firm Perkins + Will, for example, helps maintain its unassigned seating plan by having sanitary wipes readily available, which workers must use to clean any desk they will be leaving for more than two hours.[25] But other costs, like the loss of continuity in interactions, remain—although they may be counteracted by the benefits of a wider network of interactions. An important question that ongoing research may address is which kinds of work are strongly complementary to having fixed work locations and which are served as well or better by floating access.

Significantly, hot desking is often introduced as a cost-saving or space-saving measure. Indeed, the term itself nods to the practice of "hot bunking" in which multiple people use the same bed in shifts—a practice common on submarines and other vessels featuring tight quarters. Like hot bunking, hot desking allows less space and fewer amenities to serve more people by squeezing out excess capacity and slicing access thinner. A similar principle explains why more cars can be served by street parking that is open to all on a rotating basis than by a set of assigned parking spaces. Perhaps some resistance to hot desking involves resentment of a change that benefits the employer's bottom line at the expense of the individual's preferences.

Where thinner slicing has been readily accepted, it has often been in peer-to-peer contexts like Airbnb where individuals glean benefits from capturing and exploiting excess capacity, not where excess capacity was simply stripped away in a top-down move. The same physical arrangement can carry quite different valences depending on who controls its terms. Arthur Ripstein provides the vivid thought experiment of an intruder who sneaks in and takes a nap in one's bed while one is out of the house.[26] Although the visitor does no damage and is careful not to leave any traces, even supplying his own sheets and pillowcase, the conduct still feels deeply objectionable.[27] But make this man a paying Airbnb guest and the creepy offense disappears, replaced with the host's sense of entrepreneurial agency.

This line of reasoning suggests a testable hypothesis: would workers be more amenable to hot-desking arrangements if the workers themselves could control the terms on which "their" workspace would be shared with others, and reap the associated benefits? Granting control over the interaction to the original possessor would harness rather than conflict with territoriality. A similar leveraging of territorial impulses has been proposed in the street parking context: allowing homeowners who might otherwise possessively hoard the spaces in front of their homes to profit from fees collected from nonresident parkers.[28] Similarly, points-based and swapping systems that untether vacation time-share owners from a fixed week in a fixed location have made time-shares more valuable.[29] Adapting these ideas to the workplace might involve crediting workers who are willing to give up their customary workstations with points that could be used to bid on other preferred spaces, or to gain time off, schedule flexibility, or other perks.

More broadly, changing conditions should prompt careful thinking about which apparently indivisible features of the work environment are fixed and which are malleable. As the returns to more thinly sliced employment rise, the frontier of work possibilities expands, but not without bringing new management, coordination, and policy challenges. Indeed, one potentially important facet of the rise of the gig economy is the amount of work that will be devoted to the task of dividing up work into useful and sustainable new configurations.

Work, Play, and Home Production

The temporally lumpy and immobile workday also has significant implications for how people spend their time when they are not at work. Working time shapes leisure activities and what economists call "home production" (unpaid activities like meal preparation, laundry, housework, home
repairs and improvements, and caring for the kids). A standard nine-to-
five, Monday-through-Friday schedule rules out certain activities, but it
also leaves regular, predictable, unbroken blocks free. If indivisibilities and
rigidities in the workday begin to break down, ripple effects—whether positive, negative, or some of each—will spread through other dimensions of
workers' lives.

Consider some of the implications of an increase in the granularity of
paid work. If workers already have other immobile and temporally lumpy
obligations in their schedules (such as school or child care responsibili-
ties), greater granularity allows more hours of work to fit into the schedule.
Think again of the metaphor of packing items into a car's trunk—if there
are some large items in one's "trunk of time" already, granular work obligations can flow into the interstices and around the edges in a way that
lumpy work obligations cannot. Likewise, greater work granularity enables
workers to take on a wider range of lumpy and immobile temporal obligations; they need not limit themselves to just those pursuits that can fit in
the spaces left open by a fixed workweek. Of course, more granular work
might also simply accommodate *more work*. There may be a heightened
risk of overwork that does not present itself in the traditional model where
work hours are fixed and therefore limited.[30]

The granularity of leisure is changing as well, in ways that interact with
the granularity of work. The advent of VCRs, followed by DVRs and stream-
ing services, virtually eliminated temporal fixity, allowing television and
movies to be consumed at any time. There may still be substantial chunkiness, however, at least if we assume that dividing up a movie or an episode
of a show diminishes it. Indeed, many people seem to enjoy aggregating
larger units of content in the form of binge watching. At the other end of
the spectrum, social media that can be consumed in very short segments
(thirty-second YouTube videos, instant messages, or tweets) can accommodate lumpy work arrangements that leave only stray scraps of time here
and there throughout the day. Conversely, smartphones enable people to
slice off tiny pieces of labor (or more highly preferred leisure) and insert
them into, say, a lag in a dinner conversation. The opportunity cost of the
lull has become manifest, something to be repurposed rather than merely

endured. (On the other hand, people may be more willing to have dinner with those likely to bore them, since spending time with another person is no longer an all-or-nothing proposition, attention-wise).

Changes in leisure activities may also influence work patterns. For example, a recent paper draws a connection between the rise in online video gaming and the drop in employment among young men.[31] An interesting question is the extent to which certain aspects of the games, such as quests that build upon each other and generate esteem for players as their participation grows, exhibit temporal or functional indivisibilities. Such lumpiness could make serious immersion in game play an especially poor complement to paid employment, while at the same time making it a very good substitute for paid employment in the degree to which it structures time and engages the player's attention.

Lumpiness in working arrangements also impacts the coordination of nonwork time.[32] It is possible for workers to have fixed, indivisible working hours that are nonetheless unsynchronized with those of others. For example, the Soviet Union adopted the *nepreryvka* "uninterrupted" five-day week in 1929, assigning workers to staggered days off to keep factories continuously in production—a plan that was abandoned in 1931 in favor of a six-day week with a common day off.[33] But lumpy work schedules are often synchronized to a standard Monday-to-Friday, nine-to-five pattern, and workers place a premium on working "normal" hours. A recent study of seven thousand applicants who responded to a national call center recruitment drive found that employees would be willing, on average, to forgo 20 percent of their wages to avoid the risk that their employer would assign them evening or weekend hours.[34] Being off work at the same time as others facilitates spending time with one's family and friends, as well as attendance at all sorts of gatherings, from dinner parties to bowling leagues to book clubs to PTA meetings. Synchronized leisure may be especially valuable for activities that feature increasing returns as more people participate, such as festivals, concerts, and sporting events. Yet despite workers' aversion to working nonstandard hours, working at night and on weekends is more common in the US than in continental Europe.[35]

There are some downsides to synchronized work, including crowding of certain venues during times when everyone is off work. Child care requires outsourcing when every adult in the household is away at work simultaneously. Doctor and dentist appointments, as well as interactions with many institutions and service providers, require taking time off from work. Some relief may come in the form of technological changes that enable certain kinds of virtual interactions. For example, J. J. Prescott has recently studied the capacity of online portals to courthouses to improve access to justice.[36] One platform technology adopted by some Michigan state courts, Matterhorn, allows litigants in small-stakes cases like traffic ticket disputes to interact online and asynchronously with decision makers, eliminating the need for individuals to come to the courthouse and wait around for hours to have the matter decided. As flexibility is added in more domains, remaining rigidities may become less constraining. The overall picture is a dynamic one in which not only work but many other facets of life are simultaneously undergoing changes in granularity and fixity in both time and space. The advantages are evident. But as it becomes increasingly possible to interweave work, play, and errands throughout all of one's waking hours, people will have to make greater efforts to assemble contiguous blocks of time, especially if they mean to share them with others.

The finer slicing of labor may also eliminate some previously unappreciated forms of slack capacity. Just as periods of idleness or slack in an organization may be necessary to enable it to meet periods of heightened demand, slack working capacity within a household can be useful in responding to exigencies. A household member's nonparticipation in the formal workforce creates a reserve of human capital that can be deployed as needed either episodically (help with errands, repairs, or child care) or on a longer-term basis when the family's configuration or the employment prospects of its current breadwinners change.[37] While maintaining such a large reserve may be neither tenable nor desirable for many households, keeping some gaps in a worker's schedule (rather than filling them with extra work) provides valuable flexibility.

It is also worth observing how various forms of excess capacity interact, and how the slicing economy may alter that interaction. Extra rooms in a home can absorb unemployed adult children, for example, who might in turn help out with errands, repairs, and child care—matching excess capacity in housing with excess capacity in labor. In the new slicing economy, the spare room may be rented out through Airbnb, and the previously unemployed adult child who would have occupied it gratis may work for an outfit like TaskRabbit to do odd jobs in other people's houses in order to fund her own Airbnb lodgings. Meanwhile her parents may use the money they derive from the room rental to buy needed services through TaskRabbit or equivalents. There are efficiency gains from employing all resources more fully, increasing specialization, and achieving a tighter fit between what is required and what is provided. There may also be psychological benefits and greater independence for all concerned; we should not idealize informal arrangements that may embed indignities or advantage taking.[38] But the gains do come at the price of eliminating some of the play in the joints that can help to buffer unexpected shocks or simply ease the difficulty of day-to-day life.

Work and Risk

New employment arrangements can alter not only the configuration of work, but also the division of risk. In a traditional employer-employee relationship, the employer bears the bulk of the investment risk while the employee sells a stream of labor inputs at an agreed-upon price. Full-time paid employment is often bundled with certain risk-buffering products, such as health insurance. By contrast, a worker who is self-employed and operating as an independent contractor or entrepreneur bears all of the upside and downside investment risk and must buy her own risk management products. Yet there is room in the labor spectrum for alternatives that slice up risk in new ways.

For example, people embarking on entrepreneurial projects might wish to alienate at least part of the associated earnings potential. The 2012 JOBS Act enables one mechanism for doing so: by loosening restrictions on crowdfunding, start-ups can divide risk and reward with their backers in previously unavailable ways.[39] A major impetus for such arrangements is a need for up-front liquidity in order to make the necessary initial investments. Lumpiness plays an important role here: reaching a particular funding threshold may be essential to an income-producing project. Banerjee and Duflo give the example of Xu Aihua, a Chinese woman who was able to build a garment company only by making a large outlay on modern automatic sewing machines that enabled her to move into the export market.[40] For people who are liquidity constrained and unable to access sufficient funding through conventional lending markets, the sale of equity in a new enterprise may be an attractive way to assemble the necessary lump of cash—whether it buys equipment and materials to launch a new business, or simply a block of time to write a novel.[41]

Sometimes people wish to rearrange the risk associated with their own human capital, quite apart from immediate liquidity concerns. Professional athletes with front-loaded earning profiles, for example, may be interested in hedging career-ending injuries. Similarly, an academic who is widely viewed as standing a significant chance of winning the Nobel Prize might alienate the right to the proceeds from that prize in exchange for a sum certain if she preferred the sure thing to the gamble. And anyone who anticipates an uncertain future earning stream—even one that is expected to trend upward—might prefer to off-load some of the associated upside and downside risk to third parties and invest the proceeds in a more diversified portfolio.

Selling equity shares in one's earnings potential, although it has long been of academic interest, might seem unusual.[42] Yet recording and publishing contracts offer a close parallel for particular slices of work and income. Future payoffs from creative works can be highly uncertain, and artists and authors often sell much of the upside potential in exchange for a sure gain. That gain can include an advance on royalties, which effectively insures the author against receiving an outcome below that benchmark, as well as the in-kind provision of production, distribution, and publicity services.[43] To the extent new production, distribution, and publicity channels opened up by the internet make the in-kind component easier for artists to supply or contract for on their own, more artists may be interested in selling equity shares in their future earnings à la carte.[44]

Many other ways of rearranging risk can be imagined. For example, Robert Shiller suggests that people might hedge against changes in their chosen profession by buying financial instruments tied to indexes capturing trends within particular fields.[45] If demand for canine ophthalmology decreases, for example, the veterinarian who has specialized in that subfield would receive a compensating payout. Conversely, consider academic jobs that come with tenure, which protects employees from being terminated without cause. Presumably, some currently tenured professors would be willing to accept a sum of money in exchange for being exposed to the same risk of termination as an at-will employee. Steven Levitt, for example, has stated that he would gladly give up tenure for a $15,000 salary increase.[46] Or people might wish to "double down" on future income gains to intensify their own incentives using "anti-insurance," as Robert Cooter and Ariel Porat have suggested.[47] For example, a worker could pay the expected value of a possible future bonus to a "reverse insurer" who agrees to match the actual value of the bonus if the worker receives it.[48]

These and other potential ways of recutting risk interact with the widespread re-slicing of work that is currently underway. Risk reconfigurations are important to consider in this context because they can make emerging alternatives more attractive or viable than they otherwise would be. One of the largest questions involves the treatment of risk-buffering benefits (such as health insurance) that have been traditionally bundled with a particular model of work. Changing ways of working may require new assemblages of risk pools that stand outside of the traditional employment model—in other words, new forms of lumping as well as of slicing.[49] The project of making affordable health insurance available through nonemployment channels is not just a public health issue, then, but also a labor market issue.[50] Policies that help workers manage risk outside of traditional employment are a way to support entrepreneurism and innovation—both on the part of the workers themselves and on the part of those devising new and better ways to slice and dice work.

In considering different policy approaches to work and risk, it is also important not to misinterpret the risk-related choices that we observe among workers. In studying global poverty, Banerjee and Duflo have suggested that the prevalence of small businesses may reflect less a widespread entrepreneurial spirit than a dearth of the kinds of jobs that can lead families out of poverty.[51] This observation connects to questions about what kinds of working arrangements the law should encourage or permit. It is possible that certain minimum packages of benefits, hours, pay, and working conditions make up a much more valuable lump—what Banerjee and Duflo call a "good job"—that greatly enhances the ability of individuals to gain wealth and achieve upward social mobility.[52] As Banerjee and Duflo explain, "if good jobs mean that children grow up in an environment where they are able to make the most of their talents, it may well be worth the sacrifice of creating somewhat fewer of those jobs."[53] In other words, lumpiness makes it thinkable to trade off the quantity of jobs for the quality of jobs, a calculus that mirrors ones we see in other poverty relief contexts.

Lumpiness and Risk Attitudes

There is another connection between risk and lumpiness: sometimes risks are incurred or avoided because of a strong desire to obtain lumpy goods or achieve lumpy goals. We have seen this already in the context of lottery play, but it extends to nonmonetary risks as well.

Consider George Stigler's famous assertion that if you've never missed a flight, you're spending too much time at the airport.[54] Before we can agree or disagree with Stigler on this point, it is important to recognize that making a flight is a step good—*almost* making it doesn't get you any closer to your destination. Moreover, the person who misses the flight loses all of the time spent getting to and from the airport, without getting any return from that investment at all. The size of the step determines how bad the mistake of getting to the airport too late will be, while one's opportunity cost of sitting at the airport determines how bad of a mistake it is to arrive too early. Notice that this second kind of mistake generally follows a linear path, so that each extra increment of waiting has a proportionate cost—unless getting to the airport at a particular time precludes some other lumpy goal, such as completing a deal or attending an event with an inflexible ending time. Balancing the mistakes cannot be done categorically for all people under all circumstances, but the shape of these two mistakes matters.

If it's really important to arrive at the destination on time (for business or professional purposes, say, or to connect to other legs of travel), the cost of missing the flight can be enormous, whereas the incremental cost of showing up a bit early is often slight. Significantly, since the time Stigler spoke on this issue, changes in technology have made waiting time at the airport more productive and enjoyable for many people, shrinking the cost of the "too early" error. The cliff associated with a missed flight may also have diminished in some contexts due to technological advances—if one misses getting to the meeting in person, Skyping in might be an option, for example—but it often remains very significant. These sorts of "cliff versus continuum" trade-offs may prompt rational actors to act in ways that would look excessively risk averse if continua lay on both sides of the balance.

We can observe similar patterns in many other contexts. It will often be unclear exactly how many inputs of money or effort are necessary to achieve a lumpy goal. Consider studying for a high-stakes exam with a binary pass-fail outcome, such as a state bar exam. As noted in chapter 5, passing the bar is a pure step good—failing by a little is no better than failing by a lot, and there is little point in getting a score higher than the minimum necessary to pass. Here, we might expect people to overstudy relative to their best estimate of how much studying is necessary to pass. As in the airplane example, a miscalculation in one direction is much more costly than a miscalculation in the other direction. Study too little, and you fail the bar and must wait months to retake it, often suffering adverse employment consequences in the meantime. Study too much, and you only lose the extra increment of time that was spent overstudying. What might look like extreme risk aversion may simply be a reaction to the lumpiness of the goal and the asymmetry between miscalculations in two directions.

There are some settings in which people commonly choose to *raise* the stakes associated with a lumpy binary outcome, effectively making the cliff effect larger. Think of sports events, which typically have a step good quality for fans—almost winning is not nearly as good as actually winning, and winning by a single play just before the buzzer may bring as much satisfaction (if not more) than crushing the opponent in a shutout. Yet most people making friendly bets choose to bet for, rather than against, their favorite team—a choice that will make the high of winning higher and the low of losing lower. One way to understand this pattern is to see the monetary winnings (and perhaps their ability to fund a really good celebration) and the psychic payoff of a win as complementary goods that together form an even more valuable lump than either would in isolation.[55] People might similarly bet on good vacation weather, favorable medical outcomes, or any other event or condition that would make an infusion of money unusually valuable.

Sequences and Lumps

People typically prefer sequences of experiences that introduce variety, build on each other, or improve over time. The full sequence is a special kind of intertemporal assembly—a valuable lump. Rearranging or removing elements will reduce the sequence's value to the person experiencing it, perhaps dramatically. Preferences for sequences thus provide an additional point of contact between work, play, and lumpiness.

Consider people's preferences for wage profiles that grow as one progresses in one's career.[56] Notably, such preferences cut against the usual economic assumption that people engage in positive time discounting—that is, that they prefer to enjoy good things as soon as possible.[57] What explains this preference for improving sequences? Adaptation is one answer. Because people quickly incorporate changes into a new baseline, downward shifts from a previously attained consumption level will be coded as a loss— something people are likely to experience as more painful than the deferral of an economically equivalent gain.[58] Improving sequences shield individuals from painful downward shifts and instead provide them with a continuing stream of favorable contrasts.[59] This does not entirely explain, however, why people might want to receive *money* in improving sequences, since one could simply save up one's money and carry it forward (with interest) into the future to fund an upward-tending sequence of consumption.[60]

Of course, people might want their wages to increase over time in recognition of their growing proficiency in their chosen professions.[61] A limited rebuttal of this proficiency-recognition hypothesis is found in a study by George Loewenstein and Nachum Sicherman comparing reactions to sequences of wages with reactions to sequences of payments unrelated to personal merit or skill (rental income from an inherited building). They found that while a larger majority rejected present-value maximization in favor of upward-sloping sequences where wages were involved, a majority also preferred such sequences for the non-merit-based payments.[62] Something else appears to be in play as well, such as a desire to address self-control problems that make it hard to assemble the necessary cash to fund an improving sequence of consumption unless the money arrives in that pattern.[63] It is also possible that people simply enjoy the experience of receiving increasingly larger checks over time, for reasons related to adaptation to the income figures. Whatever the reasons, the fact that people prefer increasing wage sequences makes the *shape* of one's lifetime income, and not just the total amount, relevant to human well-being and hence to social policy.[64]

There are many other contexts in which sequences of consumption matter. This might be because certain components build on one another, such as shows in a series or acts of a play.[65] Alternatively, the spacing of certain experiences or their contrast with other experiences can enhance them. For example, more total enjoyment may be derived from a pattern of restaurant meals that intersperses some dinners that are *not* at one's favorite restaurant.[66] We already observed in the self-control context that considering a pattern of conduct as a whole can yield a different choice than considering each separate act on its own.[67] More broadly, we often cannot say what we prefer without knowing what else we have consumed or will soon be consuming. To borrow examples from Mark Machina, one's preference for red or white wine at dinner likely depends on what main course will be available, and one's preference for viewing *Star Wars: Episode I* rather than *Star Wars: Episode II* probably depends on whether one has just finished viewing *Star Wars: Episode I*.[68]

These forms of lumpiness—the complementarity between different parts of an integrated whole—reveal human choices to be more complex than they seem when considered piecemeal. These indivisibilities influence not only small-scale decisions about what to eat or watch, but also large-scale interactions between jobs, leisure activities, and home production, as well as between each of these components and other facets of human life, from managing risk to maintaining relationships.

As this chapter has emphasized, indivisibilities and complementarities are not confined to physical, spatial, and financial phenomena but extend to the way that people use their time and manage their exposure to risk. New ways of dividing up work and play offer potential gains, but also carry drawbacks if the changes eliminate useful (but previously underappreciated) slack, sever labor from risk-buffering arrangements in unintended ways, or interfere with valuable sequence-building efforts. The next chapter will extend the analysis of the new slicing economy into consumer markets generally.

EIGHT

Buy, Own, Split

Cows are lumpy. This presents a problem for people who wish to obtain grass-fed beef directly from small ranches that maintain high standards of animal care and meat quality but have large minimum purchase requirements. Buying a quarter of a cow equates to about 110 pounds of meat—more than most households have the appetites or the freezer space to handle.[1] Enter Crowd Cow, an intermediary that enables people to buy much smaller shares of a particular farm's bovines (and to select desired cuts of meat as well) through an online platform. This crowdfunding arrangement allows buyers to enjoy "craft beef" in modest quantities; typical purchases are between five and ten pounds.[2] The solution seems obvious, but it remained elusive until a mechanism existed for pooling the small-scale demand of many purchasers into a suitably large lump.

It has always been the case that some assets are too large or too expensive to be owned by one person. People can often collectively extract more value from lumpy or indivisible resources by employing property structures that extend use rights to nonowners or that involve some form of sharing or joint ownership. Informal sharing among family members and friends is a time-honored way to make use of excess capacity in cars, houses, and other large and hard-to-divide goods. Other models are found in common interest communities or private clubs where amenities like swimming pools, tennis courts, clubhouses, and golf courses are shared by members. What is new about some of the emerging ways of slicing access is that they do not require any preexisting connection among the parties who are obtaining slices.

Just as people can put together contributions to fund lumpy public goods, as we saw in chapter 3, so too can they coordinate to make joint purchases of lumpy private goods.[3] As in the public goods context, people need both a way of aggregating their inputs to obtain the good in the first place, and a way of dividing up access to it. Both steps are essential: without a workable plan for splitting up or sharing the good, it will be impossible to attract sufficient buy-in to acquire it in the first place. Sometimes a good's lumpiness can be addressed through physical division, as in the case of the cow; in other instances, delumping requires arrangements like shared use, renting, or turn-taking.

The problem is not a new one. Over a century ago, Philip Henry Wicksteed observed that a person who would like to own a piano on a part-time basis is forced to buy the whole thing or nothing at all, unless she can work out "some such method as combining with a friend for the joint use of the piano."[4] Yet he also recognized that "the system of hire" could overcome the dilemma:

> Hire may meet the difficulty of large units, relieving a man from the necessity of choosing between going without a thing altogether or supplying himself with a commercial or natural unit of it, when what he would prefer would be to purchase half or a quarter or a hundredth of the opportunities it puts at his command for half or a quarter or a hundredth of the price.[5]

What we are seeing today in the new slicing economy (misnamed "the sharing economy") is a dramatic expansion in the concept of hire.[6] All manner of assets—cars, bikes, backyards, clothes, pets, tools, toys, and more—are being subdivided in new ways.[7]

This chapter considers some of the implications of these unfolding changes in the way access to goods is structured. I will also work through several other facets of lumpiness in the marketplace, from limited product selections that stem from indivisible setup costs, to product bundling of various sorts, to prices that become sticky due to the lumpiness of money itself. A common theme connects these topics: confronting a potential mismatch between the lumps in which things are produced or provided and the increments in which they are demanded.

The Slicing Economy: Access, Ownership, and Use

The literature surrounding new resource arrangements typically juxtaposes "access" with "ownership."[8] But a better distinction is between traditional property ownership, on the one hand, and use rights (what property lawyers call a usufruct), on the other. Both represent modalities of access to resources; they simply structure that access differently. The newfound

emphasis on access gets two things right, however: first, that access to resources is what really matters; and second, that there are ways to grant
meaningful access to resources without granting a particular party full and
permanent ownership of the entire thing itself.

The Appeal of On-Demand

It is easy to understand why a new mode of resource access might gain
ground. When an owned thing takes a physical form, it takes up space
and may impose other demands as well—it has to be stored, maintained,
or lugged around if one is traveling.[9] Having a thing always on hand offers option value—an owned car or fondue maker is ready whenever it is
needed, even if it is needed only rarely. But ownership often imposes both
lumpy acquisition costs and a stream of ongoing maintenance and storage
costs associated with the thing's presence, while the associated benefits appear only sporadically, when the thing is needed. For a good that will only
be needed under certain rare conditions, these costs may make owning it
(or holding onto it, or taking it along on a trip) a losing proposition.[10]
This has always been true. But urbanization has put space at a premium,
while technology has made slicing off "right-sized" chunks of use cheaper
and quicker.[11] Increasingly, the use opportunities associated with constant
physical possession for long, unbroken spans of time can be approximated
at lower cost through on-demand access.

In some contexts we take on-demand arrangements for granted. Consider banks. One might keep a stash of cash (or precious metals) in one's
private vault where it would be continually available for any needs that
might arise. But banks simplify the storage problem without materially
impacting one's ability to derive value from the asset. (Note, however,
that this preservation of value depends on institutional arrangements, including FDIC insurance to forestall demand spikes.) Or consider electricity. Individuals, firms, and institutions with special needs for continuity
in power may acquire generators, but most users rely on the on-demand
system rather than commit to ownership of a power source. Again, careful
resource management is necessary to address surges in correlated demand,
but the system works satisfactorily most of the time, and at much lower
cost than if each customer had to generate her own power supply.

Even the ordinary workings of the market can be understood in similar terms. As Friedrich Hayek famously emphasized, the price system aggregates innumerable bits of dispersed information to match supply with
demand.[12] It is not necessary to own one's own cow to have a predictable

milk supply; the local grocery stores offer disaggregated access to the resource of interest in appropriate quantities. There may be occasional disruptions in markets, but such rare interruptions only serve to underscore how reliably and well the system works as a rule. Personally owning and managing all of the means of production necessary to run a self-sufficient household would be prohibitively costly (for most people anyway); the gains from specialization and trade are enormous.[13] And just as a cow represents a milk-production technology that most dairy consumers have no interest in owning outright, a car can be viewed as a little factory for producing transportation that is, increasingly, unnecessary to own outright.

For many assets, the biggest issue is not the acquisition price, nor even the fact that the asset might sit idle most of the time (we might say the same of a fire extinguisher).[14] Rather, it is the ongoing cost of ownership. A car that is needed infrequently may be far too costly to park during the balance of the time, even if its purchase price compares favorably with the service it renders during the times it is needed. These ongoing costs are not limited to cash outlays; there is also a significant hassle factor as well. The elaborate routines that some city dwellers endure in order to move their cars for street cleaning on particular days of the week, for example, have real opportunity costs.[15]

The capacity to conjure up resources just when they turn out to be needed and send them away when they begin to impose burdens—to make resources *selectively* available—is a valuable and elusive goal, and a key driver of new slicing platforms. People can attempt to self-administer this approach by purchasing a good when it is needed and selling it (or abandoning it) as soon as it is no longer of value or becomes too costly to transport. Lior Strahilevitz gives the example of a travel-crib that is cheaper to buy outright at one's destination than to rent, and cheaper to abandon there than to bring home, given baggage fees.[16] Umbrellas often receive similar treatment: inexpensive and only sporadically needed, they may be bought at odd times and carelessly lost after the rain stops. Costlier items are sometimes bought and sold to meet short-term demands as well—a used car bought for a sabbatical away and sold at the end of the term—if the costs of transacting are low enough.

The slicing economy promises to make such time-limited transactions increasingly possible and affordable. Sometimes this means bringing storage services and rental services together under the same (virtual) roof. For example, FlightCar (which has since shut down, selling its platform technology to Mercedes-Benz) offered a form of airport "parking" in which the traveler's car would be rented out to third parties during her time away.[17]

Another firm, Omni, has recently applied the same idea to household goods like camping equipment that are used infrequently enough to be good candidates for off-site storage, but which would also be useful to others for short-term rentals.[18]

Recognizing that the slicing economy may be as much about delivering relief from the burdens of constant possession as it is about making access more affordable helps explain why owners as well as nonowners have shown interest in platform exchanges. Over time, however, we might expect fewer parties to become full owners in the first place. The availability of slicing platforms works a curious alchemy by turning what had previously been a fairly passive enterprise—owning an asset for personal use—into a proto-entrepreneurial activity. But not everyone wants to be an entrepreneur. Traditional property rights amount to a kind of vertical integration of ownership and access. The development of slicing platforms makes ownership's perpetual stream of access more monetizable but less necessary to the daily lives of most people—a combination that is likely to lead to a specialization in owning by those with the greatest access needs, the greatest talent at managing access arrangements, or both. Seeing things from this perspective reveals that we are likely occupying a transitional stage in what will turn out to be a much larger shift in how resource access is structured.

The End of Excess Capacity?

Proponents of new modalities of resource access have celebrated the ability of platforms to tap into excess capacity—the bits and pieces of idleness or waste that had long lurked unnoticed in everyday products (the spare couch, the underutilized power drill, and so on).[19] This is indeed an exciting achievement, but it is not without its drawbacks, nor should we expect the current model to last long. To see why, consider where excess capacity comes from in the first place. It is not given by nature. It arises because of some preexisting lumpiness in products or services, some crudeness in the earlier slicing that gave people more than they really wanted or needed. Sometimes this lumpiness was a function of production realities or high costs of turning over goods among users. In other cases it related to fluctuating consumer needs that products could not readily expand and contract to fill. If you have a family of four, you need a car that can fit four people, even if there will be many trips of one, two, or three people; the car cannot expand and contract trip by trip. (A similar point can be made about housing, as we will see in the next chapter).

The excess capacity that accompanies product lumpiness is not entirely wasted even if there is no organized mechanism for exploiting it. The extra space or unused time slices offer option value—the flexibility to give a ride to a friend at a moment's notice, for example, or to let relatives stay overnight unexpectedly. But a good deal of this surplus has historically gone untapped because tapping it was simply too costly. In the early phases of harnessing excess capacity through improved technology, voluntary social production models emerged in which consumers simply gave away unneeded capacity for free (a model that truly fits the name of "sharing"). Now we increasingly see market-based models that more finely divide access to resources ("slicing"), both through peer-to-peer platforms (Airbnb or Uber) and new takes on traditional business models (such as ZipCar, which features ultrashort car rentals).

Yochai Benkler gives the example of SETI@home to illustrate peer production fueled by voluntary contributions of excess capacity.[20] SETI@home is a University of California innovation that cleverly aggregates the computing capacity contributed by millions of personal computer owners to search for patterns that might be associated with extraterrestrial life (the acronym SETI stands for Search for Extraterrestrial Intelligence). A widely distributed program puts each user's computer to work solving computational problems during times that the machine is sitting idle—a neat capture of excess capacity.

Yet the very neatness of that capture may be the model's downfall—or so posits Lior Strahilevitz in his review of Benkler's work. If philanthropic entrepreneurs can harness excess capacity, he observes, so too could a for-profit entrepreneur that "pays PC owners for their excess computing resources and then aggregates these resources for sale to proprietary pharmaceutical firms or defense contractors."[21] The transaction costs of doing so need not be prohibitive, especially if the transaction over excess capacity is bundled with another that the user will be engaged in anyway, such as procuring wireless internet service. Strahilevitz sums up the situation as follows: "Where we observe excess capacity, and social production is the only thing exploiting that capacity, a market opportunity exists."[22] And such market opportunities can crowd out charitable efforts.[23]

This account may be a bit too pessimistic. Consider initiatives to harvest unused bits of hotel soap—aggregating, cleaning, and recycling it for distribution in countries where the availability of soap could make a large difference in health outcomes.[24] The market for used soap may be thin to nonexistent among those who could pay enough to cover the relevant turnover costs. If this is so, then there may exist no money-making opportunity that hotels would value more than the positive publicity of the charitable arrangement. Nonetheless, the purely altruistic sharing of resources may become a rarer phenomenon as slicing technologies improve.[25] For one thing, the opportunity costs of simply giving away excess capacity will become visible—where before one saw only an unused thing that might as well be shared, now one sees dollars and cents.[26] People might not be as eager to have houseguests if it means losing the chance to rent the room to a paying guest, less eager to give someone a ride if it means giving up a seat that will otherwise be occupied by someone paying for it, less eager to run an errand for a friend or a family member if it means giving up money from one of the errand platforms.

In the short run, this ability to capitalize on unused capacity might actually make some people more willing to buy cars, large houses, and so on, recognizing the ability to rent out whatever capacity they cannot use. The longer-run solution is likely to be even simpler: consumers buy access to exactly the amount of resources they require, so they never get their hands on any excess capacity in the first place. For example, a computer need not be kitted out with a standard-sized dollop of ever-present computational power if it can directly access a pool of computational power on demand.[27] Advances in "tailoring the transactional unit," as Orly Lobel aptly puts it, are "ushering [in] the end of idle capacity."[28] Widespread participation in slicing markets may be only an intermediate phase in the evolution of resource access.

Once people can buy just the access they need, we would expect ownership patterns to change.[29] Firms that are good at delivering thinly sliced access arrangements—whether on their own or through configuration intermediaries—will specialize in ownership, while ordinary consumers will choose to own less. This shift could crowd out many consumer goods of "'mid-grained' granularity," to use Yochai Benkler's classification scheme.[30] Eric Johnson uses the example of a two-pound bag of jelly beans to illustrate mid-grained granularity—too much for one person to eat at one time, too little to launch a jelly bean business with, but an amount that lends itself nicely to sharing among office mates.[31] If one can access exactly the jelly beans one wishes to eat whenever one wishes to eat them, however, there is no need to acquire a whole bag, and hence nothing left to share with others.[32] Even if jelly beans seem unlikely to move to a bean-by-bean acquisition model, the slicing economy will increasingly enable consumers to acquire "fine-grained" goods tailored to their precise specifications as the need arises.[33] The requisite divvying-up work may largely be relegated to firms that can exploit economies of scale in bringing fine-grained goods to market.[34] As slicing technologies become better, fewer people will buy the full loaf, so to speak.

An access-only version of life reduces the chance that consumers will replace selfless sharing with market microtransactions, but it also reduces the prospects for sharing itself. This can actually be an important benefit, and one that people may already consciously seek when they buy goods on an as-needed basis. A recent study in Tanzania found that people willingly gave up volume discounts by making frequent small purchases, perhaps in part because having larger surpluses on hand tended to elicit requests from friends and extended family, as well as increased drop-in visits around meal times.[35] Limiting quantities to that which was immediately needed could help avoid this "social tax."[36] Similarly, cashless payment systems that allow customers to transfer precise amounts at the point of sale eliminate the need to carry "leftovers" in the form of small bills and coins. Opportunities for certain forms of spontaneous generosity become less possible as a result, although cashless alternatives may soon take hold. For example, a recently developed app, GivnGo, can round up credit card purchases to the nearest dollar and direct the difference to charities.[37]

The Promise and Limits of Slicing

New access arrangements are exciting, but their limitations should not be overlooked. Perhaps, as Shelly Kreiczer-Levy has suggested, it is not really necessary for everyone on a given block to own a lawn mower.[38] But the optimal number of lawn mowers on the block might be quite a bit larger that it would seem at first blush. For one thing, mowing demand is likely to cluster around certain peak times: weekends with good weather. Sharing arrangements add coordination costs (having to sign up in advance to mow one's yard, rather than just doing it whenever one happens to have a favorable alignment of time and weather) and some degree of inconvenience (schlepping the lawn mower back and forth to the various properties). Moreover, lawn mowers break down and wear out—and presumably do so more frequently if kept constantly in use through a sharing or lending arrangement. Just as organizational slack—and associated periods of worker idleness—can fulfill an important and often unsung role in the world of work, the periodic idleness of seemingly redundant assets does not necessarily bespeak inefficiency.[39]

A sharing or slicing arrangement may still be worthwhile. But it is essential to pinpoint the ways in which new resource arrangements tap into value that would otherwise remain uncaptured, as opposed to simply rearranging or speeding up resource exploitation. Platforms for slicing or sharing the use of consumer items like toys, tools, clothes, and cars contemplate employing these goods more intensively than an average user would. This raises empirical questions about how particular assets depreciate— whether it depends on the total use, the conditions of use, the chronological age of the asset, the speed with which its technology becomes obsolete, or some of each. A "wasting resource" like perishable food depreciates in the dimension of time independent of use, while consumer durables may be little impacted by the passage of time but greatly affected by use patterns. It is also important to account for all the resources in the picture, including the time value of the money used to acquire a given asset and the storage space that an asset takes up.

Suppose a group of ten households decides to share a single lawn mower. Presumably, this lawn mower will be used about ten times more intensively than an average household would use it (although one effect of the arrangement might be to make mowing more inconvenient and hence less frequent). Will the heavier use cause it to wear out about ten times quicker, or to require about ten times as much in maintenance expenditures to keep it running? Or is the real threat to the lawn mower's continued functionality the accumulation of rust and clogged fuel lines from sitting idle? If *time* is what wears out lawn mowers, then each lawn mower can produce more total functionality (more acres of lawns cut) when shared by ten families. On the other hand, if *use* is what wears out lawn mowers, then the ten households may ultimately burn through the same total number of lawn mowers through the sharing arrangement, and derive the same number of lawn-acres cut, as they would if each household had obtained its own machine at the outset.

In this latter case, slicing or sharing cannot be justified on the grounds that it wrings more functionality out of a given lawn mower (by assumption, it doesn't). But those acquiring a communal lawn mower may buy one that is heavier duty, perhaps professional grade, that performs better and longer than the machines individual households might ordinarily acquire. The ability to pool funds on just one lawn mower now, and defer further purchases into the future, also has value. Households likely won't have to take on debt to make the initial acquisition, as they might if they were buying lawn mowers of their own, and in any case can earn interest on the money that they save in the short run. A sharing arrangement could also contribute to a sense of community or foster a sense of thrifty virtue that holds independent value.

There are other potential advantages to slicing arrangements that intensify use. Many products become less useful as time passes not due to physical deterioration, but because technology advances in ways that render them obsolete, or tastes change and make them outdated. Parceling out access in ways that condense the working life of a product through more constant use can allow users to benefit from these changes in taste or technology and avoid the lock-in that comes from having a durable good with a long life span. The more frequent replacement cycle experienced by households who share lawn mowers thus has the upside of enabling them to acquire new and improved versions with greater regularity.

Commentators have also emphasized a related advantage of slicing arrangements: their capacity to increase the *variety* of goods that individuals can experience.[40] An owned car, like an owned house, cannot expand or contract at will as conditions change. Yet a series of rented or borrowed cars or homes can, like frames in an animated movie, create the illusion of just such useful morphing—minivan one day, Mini Cooper the next. The stakes are also lowered for experimentation with different types of products. Instead of getting one draw every five or ten or fifteen years, the slicing economy lets people take fresh draws on a daily basis. The shorter the time commitment, the more draws one can get, suggesting that ultrathin time slices will dominate even community-based sharing (like our block-owned lawn mower) where diversification across products matters most. On the other hand, if there is a learning curve associated with using a particular thing, variety may be less important than familiarity, and longer time slices, standardized choices, or outright ownership may be preferred.

The ability to increase variety likely accounts for the bulk of the potential gains from clothing rental platforms such as Rent the Runway. Less convincing is the claim that collaborative consumption in clothing conserves resources.[41] Presumably an outfit that is being worn constantly by different people will wear out more quickly than one being worn infrequently (and may even lose its fashionability more quickly as more people wear it). Given that there are many outlets for secondhand clothing and recycled fabrics, it seems unlikely that outfit sharing generates an appreciable net decrease in cloth production over the long term. There may, however, be potential savings in the domain of storage. Likewise, even if sharing lawn mowers among neighbors does not increase lawn-mowing functionality, it might nevertheless increase storage functionality by allowing for a seriatim rather than concurrent storage arrangement.

A similar point is often raised in the context of ride-sharing services like Uber and Lyft, whose business models are built in part on people's desire to avoid the hassles of parking.[42] Whether or not slicing is a more efficient way of using cars (again, we would have to consider the relative impact of time and mileage on a car's overall productivity), we might think it is a more efficient way of storing cars. This is not so clear, however, given recent studies suggesting that new transportation services increase traffic congestion.[43] Many cars are now effectively stored *in traffic* between uses, as drivers wait for the next request.[44] Related concerns have been raised about the storage of "dockless" shared bicycles, which may be left anywhere at all, including in the middle of the sidewalk. Private storage burdens are eased, but at the expense of public space. The ability to sever resource access from responsibility for resource storage is one of the attractions of new platform-based property models, but it also represents a way that these models can impose externalities.

Although new slicing technologies make it easier to wring excess capacity from many resources, not all goods can be sliced into units that correspond with user demands. John Horton and Richard Zeckhauser call these rigidities in the system "bringing to market" costs.[45] Some goods are just more difficult to successfully slice, whether because the units people want to use are too small to profitably parcel out, because there are high turnover costs (such as cleaning or disinfecting the item before passing it to the next user), or because the demand for use is so highly correlated that there is no way for a business model to account for it.[46] For example, snow-shovel sharing might sound great in theory, but everyone wants a shovel at the same time, right after a snowstorm, not a day later when the snow has hardened into ice and not when the pavement is bare. Here, the correlated local demand makes it difficult to devise a business model for short-term rentals that works any better than outright ownership or the direct purchase of snow-shoveling services from a third party.

Sometimes the lack of a short-term rental market is overdetermined, as in the case of toothbrushes (one of Horton and Zeckhauser's examples).[47] The shortness of each use might matter, as they suggest, but turnover costs (cleaning and disinfecting) are also high. More foundationally, there is simply no benefit to a slicing arrangement: having more people wear out a shared toothbrush more quickly offers no gains for an item that is inexpensive and easy to store and transport. In some contexts, outright ownership remains the best lump.

Standardizing and Customizing

As I was writing this chapter, it happened again: a product that had been an essential part of my life for years was discontinued by its manufacturer. This time it was a particular variety of contact lens solution, but the same thing has happened before with certain hiking shoes, microwaveable breakfast pastries, and more. And I'll wager this sort of thing has happened to you as well. Even apart from discontinued product lines (where we know full well what we're missing), there are no doubt many products that would have been perfect for us that never got made at all. As Joel Waldfogel (and the Rolling Stones) have observed, you can't always get what you want.[48] Why is that?

The answer has to do with the benefits of standardization or, put differently, the fixed costs of generating, marketing, and supporting each additional variety. If each style of shirt or flavor of ice cream comes with a fixed cost (whether due to production setup costs, regulatory compliance, or other factors), then only those that are popular enough—and hence profitable enough to absorb that fixed cost—will be worth producing.[49] Reaching the necessary threshold of consumer demand to make the good's production worthwhile resembles some of the other collective action problems we have already considered. Like assembling segments of a bridge or contributions to cure a disease, sufficient consumer demand for the product must be assembled, just as in the Crowd Cow example that started this chapter. Thus, even when a good is readily divisible into appropriate slices, producing it may be a lumpy enterprise. And there is often a limit to how many distinct "lumps" the market can support.

Consider Henry Ford's decision to offer Model T purchasers "a car painted any colour that he wants so long as it is black."[50] Ford's philosophy of standardization went deeper than paint color; although the Model T was initially produced in several varieties, in 1909 Ford announced the company would thenceforth make just one model, on one chassis, in one color.[51] As Paul Seabright explains, "Ford had understood that by drastically reducing variety in the things he produced and in the processes by which they were made, he could make so much more with his workers and his machinery that ownership of a motorcar could be brought within the reach of the ordinary working family."[52]

We might imagine that things have changed a great deal since Ford's time. There has been a marked uptick in customization and diverse, specialized product lines. Chris Anderson's book *The Long Tail* offers a thoughtful account of why that trend exists.[53] Certainly, some of the costs of bringing goods to market (and matching them to those who want them) have dropped dramatically. As fixed production or stocking costs drop, or as access to larger geographic markets becomes cheaper (as through digital or automated delivery), more specialized and narrowly held consumer preferences can be served.[54] But there are still constraints that create pressure toward standardization.

As Waldfogel observes, many real-world markets are in fact "lumpy" such that high fixed costs impact product availability.[55] The problem is acute in localized markets where it is impossible to draw on a nationwide or worldwide customer base. Air service along particular routes is an extreme example: without enough customers flying to a particular metro area, it is not worth the cost to the airline to fly the planes and staff the airport.[56] Air travel must be consumed in person, and there is no way to broaden the customer base beyond those who wish to fly to a particular destination. Federal subsidies help ensure air service to smaller communities, and have addressed underprovision problems in a number of other markets as well, such as for pharmaceuticals needed by narrow segments of the population.[57] In other contexts, however, the result may be nonprovision.

One might wonder whether the missing markets—the products that are not supplied—are ones that would be inefficient to supply. Sometimes this is the case, but not always. The reason is that manufacturers typically have to provide a single price to all customers, and thus cannot charge a higher amount to those who value a particular good or service more. People are effectively voting with their dollars to decide what gets produced, but they are unable to fully express the intensity of that vote.[58] Waldfogel makes the parallel explicit: "the way markets work entails shortcomings akin to the shortcomings of voting."[59] The ability of firms to personalize prices for different consumers based on data about their likely willingness to pay, while controversial, offers the potential upside of making a wider set of goods available. This is similar to the way that intense preferences can help solve collective action problems, as we saw in chapters 3 and 4. In all these cases, the key is getting enough contributions to fund something that is lumpy in character, whether a public good or a relatively unpopular private good.

Where demand levels are unclear, niche products may be offered to consumers contingently, with production triggered only if enough preorders are placed. For example, noodle maker Nissin Foods recently developed a "noise cancelling fork" (designed to disguise slurping sounds) that it offered to sell for 14,800 yen ($130) if the company received five thousand preorders.[60] Such contingent production models have a long history, as Ian Ayres recently observed: an illustrated edition of John Milton's *Paradise Lost* was published only after receiving the requisite number of subscriptions, and Mozart attempted to use a similar model for manuscripts of piano concertos.[61] With online tools for coordinating consumers and the proliferation of data about their preferences, firms may make fewer mistakes in failing to produce goods that would in fact generate sufficient demand to cover fixed production costs. This does not, however, help the person whose preferences are true outliers.

What happens when a consumer cannot find her preferred version of a given product? Often, she will simply switch to one of the remaining options. Recall again the way that the chunkiness of a choice set works to push a chooser to the nearest available option, if her ideal choice is unavailable. Suppose that for each consumer, there is an ideal variety or size of product (given her particular preferences). The consumer will seek out the existing product that lies closest to that ideal point, but if all available alternatives are too far away, she may buy nothing.[62] The structure is a bit like the take-it-or-leave-it (TIOLI) offers discussed in chapter 4. Manufacturers may lose some customers by failing to supply additional varieties, but those who remain will be more profitable, even if some of them are less satisfied.

Bundling and Sizing

Like standardization, bundling can represent a way of removing options— if consumers are not able to purchase the components individually to build their own customized package. It is a form of constructed lumpiness in supply. Anyone who has bought a new car has likely confronted some unwanted bundling, as where a particular trim level forces the costly purchase of things people would never otherwise imagine needing, like a small dust guard above the rear window that adds several hundred dollars to the price. Bundling (without the possibility of unbundling) can be another way of exerting bargaining leverage through something like a TIOLI offer. But TIOLI offers can be issued in other ways (as with no-haggle pricing conventions)—so why bundle?

Manufacturers' efforts to capitalize on consumer confusion or irrationality offer one explanation.[63] Price discrimination provides another. Manufacturers usually must set a single price for all consumers rather than scale the price depending on factors that influence customers' willingness to pay. Yet bundling offers a way to do just that where heterogeneous consumers place different values on different components of the bundle.[64] Hal Varian gives the example of two math professors who have differing tastes in journals: the addition expert would pay $120 for an addition journal and the subtraction specialist would pay $120 for a subtraction journal, but each would pay only $100 for the opposite journal. Varian explains:

If the producer sells both journals at the separate prices, his profit maximizing strategy is to set a price of $100 for each. Each mathematician will buy each journal, yielding a revenue of $400. But suppose that the producer offers a bundle of the two journals: If the willingness to pay for the bundle is just the sum of the willingness to pay for the components, each professor would then be willing to pay $220 for the bundle. This yields the producer a revenue of $440![65]

In this example, bundling serves only to increase the publisher's profits; by hypothesis, the journal sales would have happened either way. But sometimes the ability of a firm to price discriminate through bundling enables mutually beneficial deals that otherwise would not be possible. To take an example provided by Chris Dixon, suppose a cable television company bundles two channels: one that focuses on history, and another which airs sporting events.[66] Some customers value the history channel at ten dollars per month but get only a little bit of value (three dollars per month) from the sports channel, while others are in the opposite position. If required to set a single price for each component separately, the cable company might set a price for the sports channel that would be too high for history buffs, and a price for the history channel that would be too high for sports buffs.[67] If the two channels are packaged together, the supplier can choose a combined price that yields more revenue and that enables both consumer types to access both types of programming. Bundling will not always add value in this way—but it can do so in some cases.[68]

The same general principle, scaled up, can explain how very large bundles of digital content—think Netflix or Kindle Unlimited on steroids—might actually better suit heterogeneous consumers. There is a counterintuitive point here. The idea of "one size fits all" is generally considered anathema; after all, who would endorse the conceptual equivalent of a shapeless garment when smart tailoring is readily available? But if prices cannot also be custom tailored to fit the value each individual places on each component, a bigger bundle, priced uniformly, can allow each consumer to effectively pay more for what she values more and less for what she values less. Bundling is useful in these examples not because preferences are uniform, but rather because they are varied.[69]

Product sizing represents another form of bundling. Firms commonly make products in just a few standard sizes, which then represent indivisible units that buyers cannot split into smaller increments.[70] Although size standardization is often driven by economies of scale in packaging or by other production considerations, the choice about which sizes to offer may reflect a sophisticated pricing strategy. In a recent working paper, economists Ram Orzach and Miron Stano present a model in which a fast food establishment uses quantities and prices to differentiate (and price discriminate) between two types of customers: a high-demand type who wants to eat a large quantity of food, and low-demand type who wants a smaller quantity.[71]

Imagine these two characters, Hayley High-Demander and Louie Low-Demander, confront a menu that offers two choices: two mini-burgers (sliders) for $6, or five sliders for $7.50.[72] Louie has no interest in eating more than two sliders and so will not choose the larger order. Even though it features a better per-slider price, the last three sliders in the order are of no value to Louie (assume these sliders don't store or travel well) and are not worth the extra $1.50 in price. Hayley, by contrast, has no interest in the two-slider order. Even though the $7.50 order of five sliders is a good deal for her, she would only be willing to pay about half that amount to get just two sliders, not the $6 being charged. The resulting volume discount looks crazily large—three sliders for just $1.50 more! But the burger joint doesn't really sell three sliders for $1.50; it only sells a bundle of five for $7.50, which is still profitable.[73]

What if the customers were given a "right to split" the order in half, and pay half the price? Orzach and Stano propose exactly this remedy for strategic supersizing, as a way of addressing obesity and other health problems associated with consuming large quantities of fast food.[74] A "strong right to split" in their schema would let any customer order half the quantity for half the price, if the menu already includes a half portion or less sold separately (as it does in our slider example). This would undo the ability of the fast food purveyor to price discriminate between its low- and high-demand customers. A "weak right-to-split" would entitle the customer to have the full portion split in half and separately packaged for easier sharing or saving for later.[75] This second alternative could have important segmentation effects like those studied in chapters 5 and 6, since eating the second half of the meal would entail breaking open a new package. Of course, the supersized portion in all its unsliced glory may prove even more appealing to some consumers—even if future versions of those consumers might disagree.

Bundles are sometimes valuable for another reason: they make it easier for customers to rationalize a purchase that they might not get full value out of, and thus avoid the sunk-cost fallacy that would lock them into unwanted consumption. Suppose you have bought a nonrefundable ticket to attend a play on a particular night, but when the night arrives, you are exhausted from an unexpected crisis at work.[76] You would like nothing better than to lie on the couch and watch mindless television shows. Yet chances are good that you will still drag yourself to the theater, even though you can barely keep your eyes open during the show. This is economically irrational conduct. The ticket price is spent no matter what, so you might as well do what will make you happiest now (here, skipping the play). But people typically have difficulty doing that. Sometimes this tendency is helpful: the sunk cost precommits the chooser to a pattern of behavior that she really will find valuable, notwithstanding momentary temptations to the contrary.[77] In other cases, though, attending to sunk costs just makes people unhappy.

Suppose that instead of having purchased a ticket to an individual play, you purchased a pass that you could redeem for any four plays, on dates of your choosing. You have already seen three plays this season, all of which you greatly enjoyed. It is now the very last night of the season, when you had planned to see the fourth play. The same work emergency keeps you up the night before. Are you more or less likely to skip the play under these circumstances than if you'd purchased a free-standing ticket? A study by Dilip Soman and John Gourville addressed just this question, in the context of bundled or unbundled ski passes. Participants reported being more likely to skip skiing on the final day when conditions were poor and icy if they had bought a four-day pass and already enjoyed three days of great skiing than if they had purchased individual tickets for each ski day.[78]

Bundles apparently make it easier to ignore sunk costs, perhaps by allowing people to see that they have gotten some good out of "the product" (mentally framed as the whole bundle) rather than having an entire discrete expenditure be a waste.[79] It is well recognized that bundling can encourage people to consume more by removing any marginal cost for additional increments. This can be freeing, as where an all-inclusive vacation makes consumption more enjoyable precisely because it is unmetered. What is perhaps less well recognized is that bundling can also make people's lives better by giving them an excuse to consume *less* if they so choose. Here, it is helpful to recall that outright property ownership is a type of bundling. If one has the asset all the time, one perhaps feels freer to let it sit idle than if one has specifically purchased use rights for a given time span. Property ownership extends not only the flexibility of use at zero marginal cost, but also the option of regret-free failure to use, since the asset was valuable on other occasions already and perhaps will be again.

Prices, Sticky and Lumpy

Another facet of lumpiness in consumer markets relates to pricing itself. Consider this intriguing bit of consumer product history detailed by economists Daniel Levy and Andrew Young: Coca-Cola's price for a 6.5 ounce bottle of Coke remained unchanged—at one nickel—for over seven decades, from 1886 to 1959.[80] Why? Several factors seem to have played a role, but one is especially relevant here: the indivisibility of money itself, especially when coupled with the mechanical limits of Coke machines and the perceived need for the convenience of a "single-coin" transaction.[81] According to commentators writing on the issue, Robert Woodruff, who served as Coca-Cola's president from 1923 to 1954, believed that customers must be able to pay for a Coke with just one coin.[82] And it was very difficult for that single coin to be anything other than a nickel.

Consider first the chunkiness of the monetary units. Moving from one nickel to one dime is a dramatic price increase of 100 percent.[83] But no lesser increase would preserve the ability of consumers to buy their Cokes using a single coin. Not that Coca-Cola didn't try: Woodruff asked his friend, President Dwight D. Eisenhower, to push for the minting of 7½ cent coin (Treasury officials apparently nixed the idea).[84] A South Carolina Coca-Cola bottler took a different tack, which also proved unsuccessful: selling Cokes for a dime, but taping two pennies to the bottom of each bottle.[85] Another approach extended a kind of lottery to customers in an effort to raise the average price of a Coke: Coke machines would still be keyed to take nickels and dispense one Coke bottle per nickel, but one out of every nine times the customer would receive an empty bottle or "official blank."[86] A customer who drew the blank would have to deposit another nickel to get a Coke. Perhaps unsurprisingly, this plan was also abandoned after some experimental trials.[87]

Another problem, aside from the desire for single-coin convenience, was that Coke machines were set up to take only nickels. Retrofitting them to take pennies as well was expensive, both in setup costs and increased incidence of mechanical malfunction.[88] Oddly, Coca-Cola did not consider adjusting the *quantity* of Coke. As Frederick Allen relates, "the logical move, to a bigger bottle, was an innovation Woodruff obstinately refused to contemplate."[89] It is possible that this commitment to a standardized size was influenced by other forms of lumpiness, such as the fixed costs of changing the size of the bottles or of making vending machines compatible with a different size.

Size adjustments do appear to have been frequently used to effectively raise the price of candy bars.[90] Suppose candy makers' costs increase by 10 percent, but the only feasible price increase (whether due to vending machine limits or a desire to choose a "round" price that will maximize customer convenience) is 50 percent or 100 percent. Firms can span the artificial gap that the coin constraint imposes by reducing the size of the candy bar by 10 percent. Or they can offer a notably larger candy bar for the next highest price increment (pushing some consumers to join forces and share the candy). Or the candy maker might swap in lower-quality ingredients to keep the price the same. The point is a very general one: if there is lumpiness along one margin that rules out certain choices, we would expect it to be met by adjustments along another margin.

The lumpiness of money itself may seem a bit anachronistic these days, as many people eschew carrying or using coins altogether. Nonetheless, the increments in which monetary choices are made still matter, as chapter 4's discussion of tick sizes in the stock market illustrates. And psychological barriers to moves beyond certain customary price points can still create repricing lags,[91] which may be accompanied by cost-cutting along other dimensions. Whether these psychological barriers will lessen as people no longer make purchases using chunky denominations of cash or coin is an open question. But it seems a safe bet that lumpiness will continue to influence monetary decisions, as chapters 6 and 7 explained. In the next chapter, we will see how some of the other forms of lumpiness endemic to consumer markets resurface in the context of housing.

NINE

At Home

How lumpy is a home? Chilean architect Alejandro Aravena, winner of the 2016 Pritzker Prize, confronted this question head-on when he took up the challenge of rehousing one hundred families that had been illegally squatting in the city of Iquique.[1] The government's per-household subsidy was too low to build each of these families a complete home in the central location where they had been living, and where they strongly preferred to stay. So, Aravena explained, "we thought: why not build everyone half a good house—and let them finish the rest themselves."[2] His firm, Elemental, designed starter sets of housing, with framed spaces that could be filled in over time as the households' resources allowed—an "incremental housing" approach that has since been extended to other social housing projects.[3]

Incremental design debunks one form of lumpiness in housing by showing that an incomplete house can be a feasible option. Yet Aravena's innovation was powerfully driven by another type of lumpiness: locational indivisibilities. There would have been enough money to build each of the rehoused Iquique families a physically complete structure in the hinterlands, but this would have disconnected the households from employment opportunities and family networks.[4] Given two conflicting indivisibilities— the community network and the home's physical structure—the former seemed more important to preserve. Thinking about the ways in which housing is or is not lumpy, then, requires recognizing that dwelling units exist within communities. Homes are also embedded within built environments that profoundly shape the residential experience—ones that law plays a pivotal role in shaping.

This chapter considers the nature of housing and the indivisibilities that are implicated in its provision. This inquiry will require us to pin down what a home is meant to do, and what residential services fall within its scope. I will then turn to legal restrictions on housing that limit the slate of alternatives open to households: constraints on the size and quality of dwellings, limits on construction, and restrictions on the terms on which housing can be offered. The result is a housing menu that features gaps—unavailable choices. Why do these gaps exist, and how do households respond to them? Can we improve housing policy by expanding the menu options? Answering these questions requires examining how well legally constructed discontinuities—menu gaps—track the ways that housing delivers value to households or generates externalities for communities.

Lumpiness in Housing

At first glance, a home looks like a step good: a dwelling's four walls, roof, and foundation, like the segments of a bridge, together deliver the valuable good of meaningful shelter. Leaving out any one of these elements changes a fully contained private shelter into a windbreak, a cubicle, or a lean-to. Viewed in this way, there is a sharp discontinuity between the value of a nearly completed house and a fully completed house—just as there is a sharp discontinuity between an almost-bridge and a completed bridge. Although it is possible to build "half a good house," as Aravena's work shows, doing so is much different than just stopping halfway through the construction of an ordinary house. The initial modules or shells of incremental housing units must be sufficient to operate as functional dwellings and must also be designed to support later improvements and expansions, such as additional rooms or stories.[5] Even if the home is not finished, it must nonetheless be complete in some important, if provisional, sense.

Still, the step good analysis oversimplifies. Bridges do not come in just one style and price point,[6] and neither do houses. Accordingly, there is no single threshold that corresponds to "a completed house." Even if we specify minimum levels of durability, weatherproofness, and structural soundness, houses occupy a wide range of sizes, from newly popular "tiny houses"[7] to sprawling mansions. Another way to gain traction on what makes a house complete is to ask what a home is meant to do. Here too, it is hard to generalize. Although homes typically combine elements of shelter and privacy, and generally come with legal protections that allow occupants to exclude others, to secure and display belongings, and to leave and return at will, this hardly captures the full range of value that people derive from their homes.

Perhaps most important, the home is a portal for consuming local public goods and services and for experiencing all of the benefits and detriments that come with the dwelling's location.[8] A household's residential experience depends on the interplay between these local amenities and services and the individual housing unit. Whether an apartment seems large enough, for example, may depend on whether there are nearby coffeehouses, libraries, and parks that effectively extend the living space. Put differently, the home's scope is not fixed or immutable, but instead depends on what residential services will be contained within the home, and which ones will be provided outside of the home.

Including and Outsourcing

Choices about whether to include particular functions within the home or procure them outside the home resemble the make-or-buy decisions that firms confront. And just as a firm's scope is determined by the relative cost of coordinating inside and transacting outside, so too the scope of a home depends on the relative cost of managing functions within the home or outsourcing them.[9] Law plays a large role in determining not only the quantity and location of housing stock, but also in determining the proximity and availability of "outsourced" complements, from public parks to laundromats. These complementary services represent important facets of housing policy, with repercussions for the legal regulation of dwellings. Significant too are limits on a household's capacity to subdivide the dwelling (either temporarily or permanently) or to use platforms like Airbnb to transact over excess capacity in the home. As a result, the suitability of a particular dwelling for a particular household depends not just on its structural features and location, but also on the surrounding regulatory and market forces.

How large a dwelling needs to be, for example, depends on what functions we expect the housing unit itself to perform for the household. Many functions commonly associated with a home can be located outside of one's dwelling unit—whether procured privately or shared with a larger community. In cohousing communities, some activities commonly performed in private homes—cooking, eating, and relaxing with friends and family—are instead carried out in communal kitchens and other shared areas.[10] This outward shift of residential functions allows each household's private dwelling to be smaller than it otherwise would be.[11] Indeed, small private housing units might be desired precisely *because* they encourage (and effectively precommit) occupants to pursue more activities outside of the unit. Thus, dormitory rooms may be made intentionally small to push students out into common areas for study and conversation, and private backyards might be eschewed in favor of shared lawns or public parks—whether for purposes of conviviality or economy. Microapartment dwellers may similarly rely on surrounding neighborhood amenities to effectively augment the living space.[12]

There are indeed few examples of core residential functions for which shared or privatized alternatives do not exist. Shared bathrooms located outside the residential unit can be found in many places, from Beijing hutongs to the Lawn residences at the University of Virginia.[13] Private storage spaces (rented storage units, off-site garages, safe-deposit boxes, and so on) can safeguard and archive one's goods outside the home. Private gyms offer alternative places to exercise and bathe, entertainment venues can substitute for in-home entertainment centers, and laundromats and tailors allow clothing maintenance to be shifted off-site. Food and beverage services, pet care, child care, education, and many other functions—including sleeping—can be handled in or out of the home, or (often) some of each.

These observations cast doubt on any notion that housing demands a fixed amount of space or must include an immutable set of features. How large and amenity-filled a dwelling must be to constitute a suitable home depends on the cultural context, the functions the household wishes to carry out within the envelope of the home, and the surrounding structure of societal arrangements. The private home sphere can shrink as more and more of its functions are supplied outside—whether in common areas shared among a limited group of insiders, in public areas open to the community at large, or through privately contracted arrangements. Conversely, larger homes may encompass amenities like swimming pools, libraries, and observatories that are more often supplied jointly outside the household.

Transacting over Excess Capacity

An important limitation on the scope of the home is the fact that housing is cumbersome to resize. Because it is not easy to add or subtract rooms, homes may often include excess capacity to accommodate peak loads, such as times when all children are at home, or when guests visit. Similarly, homes may be sized in a manner that fits a family well at one stage in its life cycle but not another. This rigidity is to some degree a function of existing social and legal arrangements, which limit the ability to subdivide or reaggregate living spaces within the same building or on the same lot. Accessory dwelling units or "granny flats" offer one potential source of flexibility. For example, retirees might move into a garage apartment and rent out their main residence.[14] Matching platforms like Airbnb can help to manage excess capacity, and new models continue to emerge. For example, the Nesterly platform, which recently launched in partnership with the City of Boston, seeks to pair older homeowners who have extra space with younger people seeking affordable housing—with the potential for the "guests" to help their "hosts" with tasks around the house in exchange for a lower rent.[15]

There are some pockets of excess capacity in the home that are impractical to address, even with the most sophisticated platforms. For example, people often leave their homes for many consecutive hours each workday, during which the home's capacity to provide shelter and privacy goes unused. But transacting over those thin time slices of shelter would typically conflict with other important residential services that the home provides to the household. We use homes not just as places to personally occupy, but also as staging areas for a range of activities that can be suspended when we leave, and seamlessly resumed upon our return. The home is a place to store and display our personal property in the manner we prefer, and a habitat for pets and plants in our absence. It is also a refuge to which we can return at will if our plans change for the day, without having to negotiate with anyone about it. Here as in other contexts, what might appear to be slack capacity is actually a useful reserve. Similarly, certain appliances or amenities within the home, such as a washing machine or bathtub, may be used for only a few hours a week—but we value the option to choose when those hours will be, without having to consult a schedule or coordinate with other people.

A home's excess capacity can sometimes also serve as a form of precommitment for certain desired interactions and uses. People who hope to throw more parties may acquire a home that is well-suited for entertaining, those who want to spend more time gardening or playing outside with their dogs may choose a home with a large yard, and those who want out-of-town friends to visit more often may buy a home with a guest bedroom. It would be fully possible to outsource these functions: there are party venues, community gardens, dog parks, and local hotels. But a couple whose home cannot accommodate a large party may decide not to hold the party at all, the family without a spare bedroom may find that their out-of-town friends stop visiting, and inertia may keep the person without a yard indoors more than she had hoped. The ability to prepurchase large blocks of services outside of the home (gym memberships, for instance) can serve a similar precommitment function—or can at least attempt to do so.[16] The idea could be extended to prepaid membership in a "home extension club" that grants access to reservable guesthouse rooms, large dining and entertaining areas, lawn and patio spaces, and so on. Private residential communities already operate on a similar principle by providing shared amenities like clubhouses, tennis courts, and swimming pools.

Lumps of Time and Rights

A related dimension of lumpiness concerns the time scale for occupying housing. The option to remain in place as long as one wishes and to move only at a time of one's own choosing is of paramount importance for many households. This suggests that a home's value to its occupants often grows over time—and that an extended lump of ownership is far more valuable than the sum of shorter time slivers. A resident's subjective attachment may relate to the physical structure itself, especially if it has housed many significant moments in the family's past or has been adapted over time to the household's particular needs. But the increased value of a home over time may also reflect attachments formed in the surrounding neighborhood, such as a close-knit social structure among neighbors. This too represents a type of complementarity or lumpiness in housing to which law might respond—whether in setting eminent domain policy or by changing zoning regulations to make it easier for people to remain in the same community over time as their family configurations or income levels change.

Other rights associated with the residence may also be lumpy in nature. One aspect of rights-based bundling that has received empirical attention is the packaging of formal title with possessory rights. Secure title appears to increase investments in property.[17] For example, a study of the effects of titling in Buenos Aires, which took advantage of a natural experiment in which some squatters received title earlier than others for exogenous reasons, found that formalization was associated with markedly increased investments in the home, including higher probabilities of "good quality" roofs and walls.[18] Empirical work by Erica Field comparing titled and untitled squatter communities in Peru also shows that a lack of property rights often translates into a large proportion of time spent at home in order to guard the property.[19] With property rights in hand, by contrast, employment outside the home rises, and time spent at home decreases.[20] In other words, one kind of bundling (title and possession) makes possible another kind of unbundling (one's home and one's place of employment). Examples like this suggest that a simple, formal addition to the bundle can produce discontinuous gains.

Attention to lumpiness can help to identify low-hanging fruit—places where public policy can assist in the functional equivalent of bridge completion, as opposed to futile or superfluous efforts at adding bridge segments. At the same time, attention to how housing produces value may cause us to rethink some of the legal restrictions that withdraw alternatives from the menu of residential options, as the next section explains.

Limited Housing Menus

Housing is one area of life (among many) in which the law does not leave all possible options open to private parties, even if they would like to bargain for them. Law often regulates factors like unit size, lease terms, and housing quality, and may also constrain the ability of households to take on or shed risk—whether the risk of negative financial consequences or of physical displacement. For example, regulatory restrictions can thwart efforts to introduce new or redesigned varieties of housing: "microunits" with less square footage than traditional efficiency apartments; accessory dwelling units such as garage or basement apartments located on single-family lots; or modern single-room occupancy units with shared kitchens and baths.[21] Density limits or minimum parking requirements can also render certain kinds of housing units financially infeasible.[22]

To observe that a legal restriction or regulation removes options from the housing menu does not itself imply any particular normative judgment—but it should push us to ask why the restriction exists. Asking such questions becomes crucial when missing options contribute to housing affordability shortfalls or create a mismatch between housing stock and household composition. The dramatic rise in single-person households in the US over the last few decades, for example, has not been matched by an expansion in rental stock suitable for single-person households.[23] Where size minima or other restrictions on smaller units reflect entrenched practices rather than reasoned empirical judgments, they should be revisited.

There has been recent movement in this direction, as alternatives like microunits, accessory dwelling units, and reimagined single-room occupancy units have gained attention from scholars and policy makers.[24] San Francisco introduced a pilot program in 2012 that allowed apartments as small as 220 square feet, down from its preexisting minimum of 290 square feet.[25] In 2016, New York City jettisoned its 400-square-foot minimum for dwelling units, bringing it into line with a number of other major cities with lower square footage requirements.[26] Restrictions on the size of rooms within dwellings have also been eased. In 2015, the International Building

Code adopted by many US jurisdictions loosened its minimum habitable room area requirements. Previously, dwelling units were required to have at least one habitable room of at least 120 square feet; now all habitable rooms (with the exception of the kitchen) need only have a minimum size of 70 square feet.[27] In explaining this change, the International Code Council observed that "the minimum area of 120 square feet was not based on scientific analysis or on identified safety hazards but was generally accepted by code users and in the marketplace."[28]

Yet gaps in the housing menu remain. Even where law does not forbid particular forms of housing, the spectrum of available housing alternatives may be limited as a result of legal or policy choices that burden or subsidize particular configurations or by the way that market decisions interact with the regulatory environment. In all of these ways, law and policy determine what kinds of housing stock will be available and in what quantities. The result is a spectrum of legal housing alternatives that omits certain choices, as the next section explains.

The Spectrum of (Legal) Housing

Imagine (to greatly simplify) that interests in housing can be arrayed along a single spectrum from thinnest (point A, temporary sleeping rights) to thickest (point G, outright ownership in a high-quality dwelling with no mortgage), as shown in figure 9.1. Only certain housing packages are widely available, as indicated by the heavy line segments in figure 9.1. That leaves gaps on the spectrum—unavailable bundles.

For example, the lack of intermediate points between homelessness and legally permissible leaseholds creates a large gulf in areas with high housing costs, and one that many families will have difficulty traversing. Similarly, as Andrew Caplin and his coauthors put it, the unavailability of intermediate points between renting and owning "forces households to make the stark choice between rental accommodations' disadvantages and complete ownership's harsh financial realities."[29] As a result, a household trying to improve its housing situation may find that incremental moves

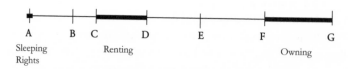

Figure 9.1. Residential Property Spectrum. By author.

are not available; it must stay where it is or make a large leap to the next available node.

Suppose a household is currently residing at point A, which represents homelessness on figure 9.1's spectrum. The family has only temporary sleeping rights in a public place, such as a sidewalk or shelter. Point C represents a rental unit that is up to code, of a certain size, and accompanied by certain basic legal protections. Setting point C as the minimum package for a legal leasehold outlaws formal transactions for housing falling in between points A and C. For example, a household cannot transact with a landlord for an undersized or below code unit that is located at point B.

At one level this seems counterproductive. Families who are now stuck at point A, but who could attain point B, are kept from improving their housing situation until they can make the leap to point C. Similarly, households who are at point C and suffer a small setback may be forced all the way back to point A: homelessness. Families whose resource levels do not allow them to rent a unit at point C must typically join a lengthy queue to have a chance at a publicly subsidized version of C. Alternatively, such families might double up with other families, perhaps skirting maximum occupancy limits set by landlords, to attain what amounts to a fractional share of C. What they cannot legally do, though, is transact with a landlord for the substandard housing represented by point B. Why?

Perhaps there is a concern that many of the families who are now at point C would slide down to point B if that option existed. Removing choice B creates strong incentives to obtain and retain C-quality housing. In other words, the gap in the housing spectrum might be expected to keep households from *choosing* substandard housing. But what about those families who lack the resources to choose anything better? Another possibility is that moving to point B somehow makes it harder to get to point C than making the leap directly from point A. This might be the case if conditions at point B trap residents in a demoralizing cycle of overpaying for unhealthy and unsafe housing. Or perhaps the prevalence of housing at point B would sap the political will to provide more housing at level C. If so, then removing this choice from the option set could, at least in theory, make low-income families as a whole better off.

Removing alternatives could improve outcomes if it alters the bargaining environment by putting landlords to a take-it-or-leave-it (TIOLI) choice between supplying a habitable package and nothing at all. Similar suppositions have at times caused even those who stand to lose out on possible transactions to endorse limits on bargains, such as minimum employment standards.[30] Even if not everyone will end up with a job or a home as a result, this outcome might be preferable to one in which everyone's working and living conditions are driven down by bargaining imbalances to a level that becomes nearly unbearable. Thus, under certain conditions, homeseeking families might welcome restrictions on their own housing choices.

Another possibility is that there is something special about achieving point C. Perhaps point C puts together such an important set of complementary rights that it is like adding the last segment to a bridge. In other words, maybe housing is so inherently lumpy that partial advances between A and C offer only trivial increases in utility, but reaching point C delivers a housing package that is fundamentally different in its capacity to improve a household's prospects. We have considered analogous questions in earlier chapters, whether examining how welfare assistance maps onto improvements in well-being[31] or considering the minimum funding push that would enable someone to escape a "poverty trap."[32] The question remains whether housing really operates in this fashion, and if so, what attributes are essential to providing the large step-up in well-being associated with point C.

Consider next the dearth of hybrid regimes lying in between renting and owning. Point E in figure 9.1, for example, might represent a thinner form of homeownership in which investors and occupants divide up housing market risks and returns in unconventional ways. For instance, a home buyer might go in with an investor who helps finance the home and who agrees to cover some of the risk of a housing market downturn in exchange for a share of the home's future appreciation.[33] Entrepreneurs and academics have long been interested in such possibilities, but they remain rare outside of specialized contexts.[34] Currently, households that cannot afford to own, or who don't want the associated housing market risk, must rent. Households that can't stand the strictures of renting—which often includes limits on pets, decorating choices, and much more—must own, full stop. The bundles of risk and control that these alternatives offer have been made indivisible; the choice is a chunky one.

Many reasons have been posited for this state of affairs, but an interesting one to consider in the present context is the degree to which the jump from the renting node to full ownership represents a package of upgrades that are far more valuable as a set. On this account, hybrid arrangements would deliver a half-bridge sort of residential package that few households would desire. This could explain the absence of these hybrids forms in the marketplace. Yet this explanation seems incomplete. Homeowners already off-load certain risks through insurance policies and no-recourse mortgages, a pattern that suggests bearing full risk is not integral to being a homeowner. It is unclear why rearranging some of the upside and downside risk associated with local housing market fluctuations would necessarily compromise the homeownership experience.

The presence of a hybrid housing form could also impact the overall composition of residential tenure forms in society. An intermediate tenure option might be expected to attract some families that are presently renting and some families that presently own their own homes—but in what respective proportions? The answer matters if there are certain tenure forms like homeownership that society strongly wishes to encourage. The question of effects is an empirical one, but it leads back to normative questions, including whether full-strength homeownership is worth encouraging.

Gap Filling

To evaluate gaps in the housing spectrum, we need to know how people respond to them. The discussion above focused on the subset of homeseeker responses that we might call node choice—how gaps pressure households to either attain the next legal node or drop back to the one below. But sometimes households respond by undertaking other kinds of efforts, ones that effectively fill in spaces between the nodes (albeit with different results than if the missing intermediate options were available in their own right). People might respond to legally constructed housing constraints by adjusting their behavior along margins that remain legally open to them, or along margins that are unpoliced or underpoliced. In this section, I will focus on the way that households might fill in the gap between homelessness and a legal rental—the portion of the housing spectrum where problems of housing affordability bite most sharply. But the law may create conceptually similar pressures at other points in the housing spectrum, such as by requiring home buyers to purchase residential lots of a certain minimum size.

One possible gap-filling tactic involves a change in household size. If it is impossible to select a smaller housing *unit*, then individuals might instead select a smaller *share* of a legal housing unit by expanding the household. For example, an individual who can spend $800 per month on housing may find that this amount would buy her only a two-hundred-square-foot apartment in the relevant market, where the minimum unit size (let us suppose) is three hundred square feet.[35] But if she joins forces with another individual with a similar housing budget, the two can together lease a four-hundred-square-foot apartment for $1,600 and split the cost. The result is gap filling in that it opens up new size-cost ratios that were unavailable when the household size was held constant.

Yet it also means expanding the household, which will have implications for all the tangible and intangible goods produced within the home.[36] Selecting the right household size often requires difficult trade-offs between prioritizing those residential services for which economies of scale are important, like space, heat, shelter, and meals, and those like privacy, autonomy, and intimacy, for which there tend to be diseconomies of scale.[37] Minimum size constraints (or other regulations that make smaller units unavailable) can skew this choice.[38]

As an alternative to permanent household expansion, people forced to buy or lease more residential property than they can use might find ways to contract over the resulting excess capacity. Business models like Airbnb support such an approach by allowing people to slice off portions of their holdings and transact over them separately and temporarily.[39] But Airbnb-style contracts over excess space may run afoul of regulatory constraints, or may violate private restrictions included in leases or covenants. The stronger these constraints, the more significant the bite of size minima is likely to be, and hence the lumpier the choice set. (The platform-based slicing of housing also presents concerns about discriminatory conduct that may be harder to address than in traditional housing models).

People may also simply choose to ignore legal restrictions if the missing alternatives become attractive enough relative to the expected sanctions.[40] The prevalence of such violations will depend on how binding existing legal constraints are, how good legal enforcement is, and how much people stand to gain, as well as on other factors such as social norms. If the physical size of rental units is an easy margin to measure, monitor, and enforce, then parties may pursue illegal options along other dimensions—allowing quality to deteriorate, say, or disregarding occupancy limits. If the subdivision of a dwelling into multiple smaller units cannot be effectively policed, illegal units are likely to proliferate where they offer size-cost combinations that are otherwise unavailable.

Where both parties to a transaction desire an illegal alternative and monitoring is difficult, enforcement will predictably falter. Nor is there much risk that a tenant, having struck such a deal, will then call for legal enforcement. Many tenants find themselves dependent on the landlord's forbearance to avoid eviction (an event that brings a formidable cascade of consequences, as Matthew Desmond has recently detailed),[41] and will be unwilling to make waves. Similarly, occupants of illegally subdivided units know that they will find themselves out of a home if they provide truthful information to building inspectors.[42] In New York City, an estimated one hundred thousand illegal units exist, ranging from accessory dwelling units in basements or garages to subdivided apartments or homes.[43] While some of these units are fully habitable and merely lack formal approval, others are overcrowded or unsafe.[44] The results can be tragic: illegal live-work spaces divided with wood and fabric partitions were implicated in a 2016 warehouse fire in the Fruitvale neighborhood of Oakland, California, that claimed thirty-six lives.[45]

The backdrop against which these choices play out in some American cities is a crisis of housing affordability. Indeed, it is the costliness of the alternatives at point C on figure 9.1's spectrum that makes the omission of alternatives in the range of point B so momentous for households, and creates pressure to find gap-filling alternatives. Housing prices are driven up and kept up when demand increases and supply cannot expand in response. Although the physical configuration of some cities makes expansions in housing stock more difficult, the most binding constraints appear to come from law.[46] As chapter 2 emphasized, strong property rights and attendant holdout powers can block land assemblies, including those necessary to redevelop areas at higher densities. Zoning and other restrictions on development also keep housing quantities from adjusting upward as demand rises, causing many families to be priced out of the market.[47]

Families who cannot afford a minimum suitable home in a hot housing market may be pushed to outlying areas or to other metro areas with less expensive housing. Here we observe yet another way that households can fill in the gaps in the housing spectrum: by finding lower-cost versions of legally permissible units farther away or in other housing markets. This response has caused a number of commentators to express concern that people are being pushed out of, or kept away from, places where their human capital would be put to its most productive use, so that they wind up trapped in places where their human capital is less productive.[48] We will revisit this issue in the next chapter. For now, we can observe that supply constraints that raise housing costs in a given market widen the chasm that must be traversed to secure a minimum legal housing unit at point C in figure 9.1. Zoning or other land use restrictions can limit or prohibit the addition of certain kinds of housing stock in a given area, inflating prices as supply fails to keep pace with demand.[49] Location is a margin along which families can make incremental adjustments that help to fill gaps in the otherwise chunky residential menu.

Rethinking Housing Policy

The previous section considered lumpiness in housing that the law creates by withdrawing intermediate options from the slate of available alternatives. One way to evaluate that constructed lumpiness is to ask how well it tracks indivisibilities or complementarities in housing itself. Is the minimum legal lump of housing (which might include certain size and quality standards, as well as a certain bundle of legal rights and protections) the minimum package that can reliably deliver essential residential services to the household? If so, then the law might seem sensible—though we might wonder why it is necessary. Why would people voluntarily strike bargains for what amounts to half a bridge? If people lack good insight into what bundles of attributes will deliver the largest lumps of value, or if they are likely to be pressured into bad bargains, then removing obviously inferior options might make them better off. But legal restrictions that remove intermediate housing options that well-informed people would find attractive require justification.

An alternative to opening up more space in the housing spectrum is to empower people to span the relevant gaps—through vouchers or direct provision of subsidized housing. But these alternatives also raise deep questions about the best way to deliver assistance. Currently, fewer than one in four eligible families in the US receives federal housing assistance.[50] For those who do, subsidies average $8,000 to $9,000 per year.[51] In a recent paper, Ingrid Gould Ellen asks: "Is it better to give smaller subsidies to all low-income households or to give larger subsidies to one in four of them?"[52] Housing assistance plausibly constitutes a "functional entitlement"—one that is provided (if at all) at a level necessary to meet a particular need.[53] But how should that need be defined? Providing a complete house to one household does a better job of meeting housing needs than doling out walls to one family, a roof to another, windows to a third, and a floor to a fourth. Yet smaller or less expensive homes might be provided to more families—especially if some housing assistance dollars go to helping people meet some of their needs outside the home, whether through parks, community gardens, jogging paths, or other complementary amenities and services.

There may also be creative ways to provide partial housing assistance to more families. For example, Ellen floats the idea of using an Airbnb-like platform to make portions of homes available to low-income people.[54] The incremental housing example that started this chapter provides another model for thinking about splitting up housing assistance. An interesting side note on that approach is that some of the housing that was initially designed to be incremental, such as Elemental's 2007 Renca project, managed to attract sufficient additional funding to be fully completed before the families moved in.[55] One possible interpretation is that funding is sensitive to apparent indivisibilities: committing to build half may draw more funding from the woodwork. Incompleteness in the physical structure contains the promise of a completed home and provides a spur to further investment—whether by private parties, the government, or the households themselves. By contrast, locating affordable housing in the hinterlands would have broken indivisibilities of community in a manner not only less visible, but also less remediable.

The idea that a partial home can serve as a kind of precommitment is even more vividly illustrated by the way that families in many developing countries use unfinished homes as vehicles for savings. In their book *Poor Economics*, Banerjee and Duflo note the remarkable prevalence of such partially completed homes, and the typical explanation for it: "If you ask owners why they keep an unfinished house, they generally have a simple answer: This is how they save."[56] To be sure, it seems inefficient for households to use a home-in-progress as a savings account. But there are important lessons embedded in this behavior—about the indivisibility that homes exhibit, and the desire for a precommitment mechanism that will allow a household to realize a large, lumpy good. Sinking costs into the home makes it impossible for this goal to be derailed by a succession of short-run demands for cash.

Some of these examples may seem far removed from questions of US housing policy. Yet they raise tightly related questions about how best how to package and deliver residential assistance, how to leverage inputs by households and those assisting them, and how to build in flexibility as people move through different stages of life. For example, incremental housing may seem unrealistic in the US context, but bungalows—with their flexible upper level that could be developed into bedroom space—historically provided just such an option for many families across the country. Allowing housing stock to respond more flexibly to changes in household configuration and enabling incremental inputs from the household itself could offer new traction on housing affordability challenges. Reducing regulatory barriers to housing reconfiguration, where this can be done without sacrificing safety, could facilitate more plentiful—and more useful—housing options.

Perhaps the largest policy question surrounding affordable housing in the US today is where it will be located.[57] Even if demand-side alternatives like housing vouchers are used, the way in which rental assistance is calculated will determine where the vouchers can—and cannot—be used.[58] This locational question sharpens the trade-offs between serving more families and providing a larger increment of assistance. Enabling low-income households to live in lower-poverty areas that offer better educational and employment prospects requires larger outlays than subsidizing homes in deeply impoverished neighborhoods.[59] The question again comes down to identifying the relevant indivisibilities and complementarities—should we be more concerned with the quality and size of the housing unit, or more concerned with where it is located?

The answers depend on yet more questions, including some crucial empirical ones. How much more valuable does a housing unit become to a low-income family if the unit is located in a lower-poverty neighborhood? Recent findings from the long-running Moving to Opportunity studies show a positive impact on outcomes like college attendance and earnings, but only for children who were younger than age thirteen at the time of the move to a lower-poverty neighborhood. Researchers attribute this pattern to longer periods of neighborhood exposure for the younger children, coupled with possible "disruption effects" for those who moved as adolescents.[60] This suggests an important temporal lumpiness in this kind of assistance, one that is undermined by a system that often requires families to wait years to receive a voucher.[61]

Another question is how much more expensive such assistance is to deliver, compared with housing assistance concentrated in higher-poverty neighborhoods. HUD recently rolled out a new approach to calculating allowable rental rates for vouchers that is keyed to market rents within specific zip codes rather than across entire metro areas; this makes it possible for families to use vouchers in more expensive areas where opportunities are greater.[62] Empirical work studying the effects of this approach is ongoing, but findings in the Dallas area suggest that such a change could generate savings (lower rental payments) in higher-poverty areas that counterbalance the higher rental payments in lower-poverty areas.[63] This does not eliminate the trade-offs involved, but it does suggest the potential for thoughtful design choices that could help target assistance to those families who stand to gain the most from them.

Finally, a point raised in chapter 6's discussion of poverty relief bears repeating here: the total amount of assistance available to dispense to recipients is not fixed, but rather is a function of political will.[64] Changing the way affordable housing assistance is delivered can change its magnitude as well. This should lead us to ask not only what kinds of housing assistance make the best use of available resources, but what kinds of housing assistance would be most likely to catalyze private and political responses that increase the pie of affordable housing. Even if building half a house is not a realistic option, other alternatives might work similarly, such as pilot projects in high-opportunity areas. As families thrive in these locations, could the political will emerge to keep them in place?[65]

Housing exhibits indivisibilities—both structurally and as a result of law and policy. Thinking broadly about the different sorts of lumpiness that housing embodies can inform a range of policy choices, from land use regulation to housing codes to landlord-tenant law to decisions about the types of tenure forms that law should encourage. Making it harder to transact over excess capacity—whether through reconfiguration of housing units over time or through the kind of short-term alienation of use rights popularized by Airbnb—makes housing lumpier, while deregulating these choices helps to open up the housing spectrum. Some of the most important housing-related indivisibilities relate to the home's connection to the surrounding community—a topic to be continued in the next chapter's discussion of the city.

TEN

In the City

Why do people live clumped together in cities, rather than spread evenly across the surface of the earth?[1] The question is foundational to urban economics.[2] The answer, unsurprisingly, has to do with complementarities and indivisibilities—in a word, lumpiness. The growing percentage of the world's population living in urban areas attests to the fact that putting together people, firms, ideas, and commerce can bring gains.[3] But urbanization brings conflict as well, and the rising costs of forgone opportunities. The lessons of aggregation and division developed in this book offer a conceptual tool kit for taking on this central challenge of the twenty-first century.

This chapter examines the dilemmas that arise in aggregating and distributing land uses—and land users—within and among cities. Communities can be vibrant or stagnant depending on how households, firms, amenities, and infrastructure are assembled or dispersed in space. Yet attempting to put together valuable new combinations can come at the cost of breaking apart existing units, such as established neighborhoods, that deliver value in chunks. Cities often present wrenching instances in which different lumps of value are pitted against each other. Urban areas are also the sites of many new forms of slicing—of jobs, products, homes, and experiences. As Nestor Davidson and John Infranca have recently emphasized, this shift to new modalities of access is an intrinsically *urban* phenomenon that builds on proximity and density.[4]

Agglomeration and Indivisibilities

It is impossible to understand cities without considering how patterns, combinations, and clusters—of people, industries, activities, and so on—

add and subtract value. Concentrating more people and more economic activity in close proximity generates both positive effects, or "agglomeration benefits," and negative effects such as traffic, pollution, crowding, and crime—often referred to collectively as "congestion."[5] Cities embody trade-offs between these two types of impacts.[6] The balance is tricky because the urban participants who contribute to valuable collaborations and interactions also burn up scarce resources, including space.[7] Making excellent cities requires fostering not just *any* clusters of activity, then, but the most valuable clusters.[8] As a corollary to this point, a given use of urban land does not have to be noxious to destroy value; it can diminish value simply by occupying critical "interaction space" that could be better used by someone or something else.[9]

Because cities are premised on lumpiness, it is essential that urban analyses account for it—a linear approach will not do.[10] Indivisibilities and complementarities come into play in a number of different ways. As the standard bridge example illustrates, urban infrastructure is often lumpy. Lewis Hopkins explains: "Indivisibility means that we cannot take arbitrarily small increments of action. A road is useful only if we build all of it to connect two locations. We must build a width of at least one lane."[11] These indivisibilities are highly consequential: infrastructure is intricately woven through private property holdings and facilitates their creation of value.[12]

As important as urban infrastructure is, it is only part of the story—a means for realizing the agglomeration benefits (and costs) that flow from the underlying clustering of complementary activities in cities.[13] The study of agglomeration benefits often uses the work of Alfred Marshall as a starting point,[14] emphasizing factors like knowledge spillovers among firms, deeper labor markets that can more easily match up workers with firms, and interactions between suppliers and customers.[15] Perhaps the most intuitive agglomeration benefit is the reduction in transportation costs produced by proximity. Indeed, Edward Glaeser boils down the benefits of agglomeration to the single idea of reducing transportation costs—for "goods, people and ideas."[16] New innovations and technologies have not eliminated these benefits, but have only changed how they cash out. Proximity has become less important for certain kinds of production, but cities remain important centers of innovation, as well as places to jointly consume experiences—entertainment, restaurant meals, cultural events, and social interactions.[17]

An influential recent taxonomy of agglomeration benefits uses the broad functional categories of "sharing, matching, and learning mechanisms."[18]

Parties who are physically near each other can share indivisible resources such as infrastructure, and can mutually benefit from shared access to the vitality and variety that urban areas offer.[19] More populous cities can support a wider array of localized products and services because businesses can tap into a larger customer base to cover the necessary fixed costs.[20] Clustering of people into urban areas facilitates matching, not only in traditional labor markets but also in dating, retail, and entertainment markets,[21] and through peer-to-peer platforms like Airbnb and Uber.[22] Proximity also enables people and firms to learn from each other in the course of regular, incidental interactions.[23] Marshall's classic statement of the learning associated with clusters of industry still rings true:

> The mysteries of the trade become no mysteries; but are as it were in the air, and children learn many of them unconsciously. Good work is rightly appreciated, inventions and improvements in machinery, in processes and the general organization of the business have their merits promptly discussed: if one man starts a new idea, it is taken up by others and combined with suggestions of their own; and thus it becomes the source of further new ideas.[24]

The magnitude and nature of these gains, as well as of congestion costs, will be sensitive to the spatial placement of households, firms, and land uses within the urban envelope. This brings us to the central question of location choices.

Choosing Cities

Every household has to decide where it will live, and every firm has to decide where it will locate. These choices, which are bounded by private and regulatory forces, cumulatively shape our cities. Some of these locational decisions take place at a small geographic scale, between different properties, blocks, neighborhoods, or districts. Homeseekers and businesses also make medium-scale judgments about whether to locate in a central city or in a suburban or exurban area. But we will start our analysis by looking at the large-scale choices people make among metropolitan areas—whether to live, for example, in greater Atlanta or greater Boston.

Housing costs play a primary role in the location decisions that individuals and families make, as the previous chapter emphasized. As housing costs have risen in certain highly productive cities, economists and legal scholars have expressed concern that housing supply distortions are relegating people to places where their human capital will not be put to its best use. Economists Chang-Tai Hsieh and Enrico Moretti have found that workers are spatially misallocated across US cities due to housing supply restrictions in the most productive locations.[25] Thus, some cities remain smaller than they should be, as work by David Albouy and his coauthors suggests.[26] In the absence of any regulation, popular cities might grow too large because each new entrant would not pay for the marginal increment of congestion that she adds.[27] But too much regulation artificially inflates housing prices and makes it less possible for people to migrate from less productive to more productive urban areas.[28] A recent paper by Edward Glaeser and Joseph Gyourko similarly finds that land use regulations in certain markets, like the San Francisco Bay Area, constrict housing supply and raise home prices above production costs, creating "a potentially profound distortion: people are unable to move into more desirable metropolitan areas."[29]

As these analyses suggest, location choices are not zero-sum. In a zero-sum game, every gain is offset by an equivalent loss, and every loss is compensated by an equivalent gain. In a zero-sum world, it would not matter to the overall welfare of society whether a particular firm or a particular worker located in Atlanta or Boston. If a worker chooses Atlanta because the housing is cheaper, the gains she produces there would perfectly offset whatever loss Boston would suffer by her absence, and vice versa. But there is no reason to believe things work this way in cities. Where interactions among firms and households generate agglomeration effects, location choices become a positive-sum game: some sets of choices are better overall than others. We cannot count on a firm or household to pick the location where its contributions will do the most good if it will not internalize all of the costs and benefits of its choice or if the inputs to its decision are mispriced. As a result, we may wind up with cities that produce less value on the whole.

The synergies that complementary uses produce within cities represent one important form of lumpiness in the urban context. Lumpiness also comes into play when considering the nature of the location choice set that people face. If there are a large number of cities that individuals and families tend to see as good substitutes for each other, the jump to a different metro area will be easier to trigger. Even minor distortions introduced through land use controls or housing policy could cause households to choose locations that are suboptimal matches for their human capital. But if the menu of cities looks very lumpy (e.g., if many people feel that only one major city in the US is a good fit for them), then a few distortions in the picture will be less likely to change people's decisions about which metro area to locate within. Not everyone will see the choice set the same way, of course. Some will find themselves tightly bound to a particular place because of family or social networks (another type of indivisibility), while others will be more open to alternatives.[30] The point is simply that the perceived chunkiness of the choice set helps determine how sensitive decisions will be to distorting factors like externalities or supply constraints.

The logic here is the same as in other contexts featuring lumpy or binary choices: if the payoffs are sufficient to induce a person to make a socially valuable choice for her own purposes, it does not matter whether there are external effects in the picture. Likewise, some degree of mispricing in housing in the most popular urban centers may not be enough to push a family to an entirely different metro area. Yet as we have also seen, a chunky menu produces cliff effects, so the stakes are higher if someone *is* pushed by distortions to make a suboptimal choice. A more thickly populated spectrum of city types might increase the chances that a firm or household won't locate in their first best location, but it also means that the costs of its suboptimal choice will be lower. These observations relate to the question of whether we have too many or too few urban centers in the US and whether they exhibit the optimal range of sizes.[31]

Surprisingly, lower housing costs in a person's "second choice" city do not necessarily increase the chance that she will end up there. The reason relates to some of the principles we considered in the context of gambles and is captured well in a scenario modeled by economist Rod Garratt.[32] To put his example into the US context, suppose an individual, Ingrid, really wants to live in New York City but will settle for her second choice, Houston, if necessary.[33] We might understand "living in New York" to be something like winning the lottery for Ingrid—an indivisible lump of urban bliss. Her current resources allow her to do little more than buy a lottery ticket, so to speak: she aims to spend a few weeks or months in the Big Apple and try to secure a job that will let her stay forever.

Ingrid knows her chances of striking it lucky aren't especially good, so she sets aside enough money to make a start in Houston if her dream job in New York fails to materialize.[34] Given the importance of making professional connections and the like, Ingrid's odds of finding a way to stay in New York increase the longer she can extend her exploratory gambit.[35] If housing prices are cheap in Houston, then she can afford more "lottery tickets" (months of rent, say) in New York and still have enough set aside to cover her fallback plan in Houston. But if housing prices rise in Houston, she will need to set aside a larger safety fund, and can afford fewer tickets for the New York lottery. Under these assumptions, higher housing costs in Houston actually *increase* the chance that she will end up moving there.[36]

This possibility adds a counterintuitive wrinkle to the current urban location discussion. There may be other factors in play, of course, that would change the result. Perhaps the rising Houston home prices simply induce Ingrid to choose a less expensive place for her fallback life, such as Oklahoma City. Here too, it matters how chunky the menu of cities is perceived to be, and whether different metro areas are viewed as close substitutes for each other.

Spillovers and the City

Next, let's zoom in and consider agglomeration effects within cities, whether in the form of a vibrant downtown district or an area struggling with crime or traffic congestion. Because these effects are not fully enjoyed or suffered by each person who decides where to live or work or how to act, they represent externalities in the economic sense. But they differ from traditional spillovers that emanate from land uses, such as factory smoke or the smells of neighboring livestock. This is not just because agglomeration effects are often positive rather than negative—agglomeration can also produce negative effects like crowding and crime, while traditional spillovers can include positive effects like a lovely view of the neighbor's rose garden. Instead, it is because of the cumulative and nonlinear way that agglomeration effects interact to produce indivisible effects, which differs from the straightforward "boundary crossing" impacts that are the stuff of nuisance and zoning.

As Paul Seabright explains:

> [Certain types of externalities] are neglected because they are extremely hard for us even to foresee, depending as they do on the idiosyncrasies and serendipities of the way in which individuals interact and the mutual spark they provoke. The history of urban planning is full of examples of cities that have worked hard to remove some of the most obvious causes of physical blight but have proved incapable of alleviating boredom, delinquency, and violence.[37]

One urban theorist who appreciated the complex and organic interplay of different elements within a city was Jane Jacobs, who saw that the separation of land uses through zoning could eliminate certain benefits from mixing together diverse uses.[38] Although research continues into both the negative and positive effects of mixing uses,[39] one thing is clear: the whole that emerges from a set of neighborhood interactions is different from the sum of its parts.

Urban areas face two basic risks, corresponding to the two ingredients necessary to produce positive agglomeration effects. The first is a lack of valuable participation. The second is a lack of appropriately sited interaction space. City dwellers impose costs on each other, but they also confer mutual benefits through their interactions in the city. Which story will be dominant depends on what is plentiful and what is in short supply. If interaction space is plentiful, the need for interacting parties (and their associated energy or vibrancy) becomes the focus. If interacting parties are plentiful but space for interacting is scarce, then congestion emerges as a problem. Because both inputs—people and space—are necessary to the alchemy that takes place within a city, the undersupply of one and the overcrowding of the other are both problematic. But it is not merely a question of having too few or too many people present in the city—it is also a question of where people are located relative to each other, and what they are doing. And the decisions that firms and households make on these dimensions—where to locate and what to do while there—may be distorted by externalities.

An important question is whether these externalities really matter. As we saw in chapter 4, externalities are often irrelevant to the choices that people make—an actor would behave no differently if she were to internalize all of the negative and positive effects of her acts.[40] This is true in the urban context as well. For example, an individual might still crowd into a popular part of the city even if she had to bear the congestion costs her presence imposes on others, or she might contribute just as much vitality to the urban scene as she would if she could reap all the benefits. On the other hand, externalities are not *always* irrelevant, and the distortions they introduce into human behavior account for a great deal of law. Can we pinpoint circumstances under which urban externalities are relevant or irrelevant to people's decisions about where to locate and what to do?

First, as we saw in chapter 4, externalities may be irrelevant when the choices involved are binary or very lumpy. If private returns are enough to trigger an entire lumpy action, the fact that positive spillovers benefit others will be irrelevant.[41] By contrast, we might expect a party who is choosing *how much* to contribute to a social good to contribute too little if she cannot capture all the gains. Second, acts that produce positive spillovers *for* others may simultaneously enable one to collect positive spillovers *from* others. For both reasons, positive externalities of the sort historically generated through participation in markets, festivals, and other interactive arenas may not have caused many people to undercontribute. These were often relatively binary actions (attend, or don't). In addition, each actor reciprocally gleaned roughly as much from others as she contributed to others through her participation. And, importantly, participants typically contributed and gleaned value through the same discrete actions in the commons, so that gleaning could not be unbundled from contributing.

When considered in light of these factors, how do modern urban externalities measure up? Consider first the lumpiness of the choice menu. An interesting and to my knowledge unexplored issue is whether increased urbanization may have changed the nature of the spillover-generating decisions that actors make. Perhaps, for example, positive externalities were historically easier for urban planners to ignore than negative externalities because the associated acts took lumpier forms that made them less relevant to efficiency. Activities that generate negative externalities like pollution or noise typically involve choices selected from a continuous menu (such as production levels) and may be highly relevant to efficiency: people tend to do too much of them when private and social payoffs diverge. Choices that generate positive externalities may have traditionally been more discrete or lumpy in nature—like the binary decision whether to attend a festival, open up a store, or plant a rose garden.[42] Here, the private and social payoffs might well converge on the same choice.

But that may be changing. Modern agglomeration benefits likely turn less on discrete on-off choices like garden planting and more on continuous choices about levels of economic investment in an area. One of the most significant choices that any urban participant makes is deciding where to locate. And, although this decision looks like a binary on-off choice as to whether one will locate in any given place, the decision process as a whole involves choosing from what amounts to a continuous menu of possible locations—right in the city center, a half block out, a full block out, and so on. The location that looks best from the individual chooser's perspective may well diverge from what is socially optimal, since she is not accounting for the spillovers she will bring with her. Her choice may be distorted as a result, even apart from other distortions associated with land use controls or other public or private restrictions on locational choice.

An important caveat is suggested by the possibility of reciprocal spillovers. Location decisions will not be distorted if an actor's own positive impacts within a given urban sector closely track the value she derives from the positive impacts of others in that same location—in other words, if only an excellent contributor to a local scene would value living or locating near that scene. In some cases this seems likely. For example, Brett Frischmann and Mark Lemley have suggested that a high-tech firm's "absorptive capacity"—its ability to benefit from the research and development (R&D) efforts of other firms—may depend on its own spillover-producing R&D efforts.[43] Similarly, perhaps households who enjoy crowds and excitement and therefore seek out urban residential areas are the very same people who are best positioned to contribute ideas and creativity to those areas. But the opposite might also be true. For example, a wealthy middle-aged couple might wish to soak up the hip ambience of a trendy neighborhood but do little or nothing to help maintain the neighborhood's hipness against the influx of moneyed, unhip people such as themselves. In sum, the characteristics that cause particular economic actors to derive value from a given location may not be the same characteristics that would lead them to contribute value to that location.

A second caveat connects back to the distinction between lumpy and continuous choice sets. I suggested above that the location choice is effectively a continuous one in an urban area: there are innumerable possible sites that vary slightly as to how they will generate value for the locating party and for her new neighbors. But this characterization of the choice set depends on spillovers being sensitive to small differences in locations. Suppose instead that there were just two meaningful buckets of sites in a metropolitan area—call them "core" and "hinterlands"—and the spillovers that a firm or household generates did not depend on where within the core or where within the hinterlands it located, only which of the two options it selected. Then we would be back to a chunky, binary, on-off choice, and it is quite likely that what is socially best and what is best for the individual would converge. Which characterization is more accurate? Figuring out the answer requires knowing more about how agglomeration benefits actually work.

Finally, I have focused here on efficiency, but distributive effects—who wins and who loses—also matters. It is possible that some apparent "mistakes" in locational choices actually contribute to a more just or inclusive metropolitan area. For example, an innovative business might add the most value in the city's core, but if pushed to the hinterlands as a result of distortions would wind up spreading benefits to people living there who (for whatever reason) would not be in a position to move to the city's core themselves. Although it is an empirical question, some degree of mismatch between the most productive uses and the most productive places could soften what might otherwise be an unduly sharp cliff between life in those places and everywhere else. Similarly, ensuring that people of all income levels can access a city's most vibrant interaction spaces holds independent value, regardless of how the economics works out.

Assembling Participants

One way to think about urban agglomeration is to focus on aggregating people—households and firms.[44] What is the best way to assemble them in close enough proximity to enjoy maximum agglomeration benefits, without at the same time producing problematic congestion? Significantly, not all land uses are equally capable of contributing to agglomeration benefits in a particular location. The challenge is to find ways for people to contribute to rather than block the most valuable patterns and combinations of uses. This is not easy to achieve. Land use patterns are sticky, and control over them is dispersed among individual owners who each hold a monopoly on the particular space that their real estate occupies.[45] When it is necessary to combine parcels or coordinate large-scale patterns of uses in order to capture agglomeration value, each landowner holds a crucial part of a lumpy whole.

This participant assembly problem echoes in some ways the problems of land assembly we have considered already. But it is not necessary for large swaths of urban land to be physically consolidated in the same owner's hands in order for agglomeration benefits to be realized. On the contrary, concentrating ownership may get in the way of more dynamic and organic interactions. Yet uncoordinated action has pitfalls as well: households and firms acting independently do not internalize all of the costs and benefits that their location choices inflict and bestow on the community.[46] Path dependence also plays a role: the order in which sites become occupied can foreclose patterns from emerging that otherwise would have been preferred.

Consider the following analogy: A campus dining room serves as a site both for quiet consumption of coffee or food by individuals who are reading or studying, and for larger lunchtime academic discussions. The best discussions are conducted around a round table that seats twelve, when all seats are filled (any fewer detracts from the energy of the conversation, any more is too crowded). Sadly, the dining room only has one table like this. Academic departments sometimes reserve the whole table ahead of time and occupy it en masse. But the conversations might be even better if the discussants arrived from a variety of different departments on a spontaneous drop-in basis. Yet this kind of spontaneity has its price. Unless reserved ahead of time, the table typically becomes partially occupied early in the day by several individuals or pairs of people who are reading or studying, and never fully opens up again until closing time. Individuals do not linger endlessly, but as they depart in ones or twos, their emptied seats are soon refilled with other independent studiers.

Here, the good of a "discussion table" is lumpy and can only be realized if all the seats are vacated simultaneously—something that is unlikely to happen in the ordinary course of events. If a would-be discussion group is especially enterprising, they might attempt to buy out the table occupiers. But because the seat emptying must be complete in order to be effective, we might expect holdout problems. Alternatively, the management might be called over and asked to displace the customers from the table to free it up for discussion—the equivalent of eminent domain in the land use context. But this is likely to produce outrage. The crux of the problem is that the customers in this story have an everlasting entitlement to stay where they are, as long as they continue to buy a minimum amount of coffee to sip (the land use analogue is a property tax). They do not internalize the opportunity cost of their protracted occupancy and staggered departures, which preclude the valuable assembly of discussants.

This analogy reveals some dimensions of the challenges cities face in putting core interaction space to its most valuable use. It is not only regulatory restrictions that keep people from making optimal use of urban space, but also the stickiness that comes with unrestricted property claims and the monopoly power they confer. Nor is it simply a question of kicking out obviously noxious or toxic uses—the quiet customers in the story were perfectly well behaved, but because they occupied crucial interaction space, they kept greater synergies from forming. This is because the public good of agglomeration benefits can only be realized through the consumption of the associated rival resource of physical space, as people come together to interact.[47] And when space is limited, every inclusion implies an exclusion.

Pursuing Patterns

Neither property markets nor traditional land use controls work well to address the core challenge of urban life: participant assembly. Markets are plagued by holdout problems and distorted by the fact that actors do not internalize all the effects of their location choices. Traditional land use controls work extremely well at controlling noxious cross-boundary spillovers like smoke and noise, and can even achieve certain kinds of homogeneity through zoning. But they cannot tackle the subtle problem of optimally assembling complementary uses—and leaving open the flexibility to create new assemblages as conditions change. The sections below briefly consider alternatives that recognize the interdependence and indivisibilities of urban life.

Refining Pricing

In theory, local governments could address agglomeration costs and benefits by applying differential pricing (say, in the form of property taxes) to different land uses based on their suitability to particular locations and the impacts that they generate for their neighbors.[48] Differential pricing is a common mechanism where participant assembly is important. For example, universities employ it to bring together a desired mix of students—some students are charged full freight while others receive various amounts in scholarships, stipends, and other assistance that allows them to attend at reduced or even negative prices.[49] Land use authorities engage in a form of differential pricing when they strike individualized bargains with landowners about land uses.[50] Their ability to so, however, is subject to doctrinal limits on bargaining laid out in a series of Supreme Court decisions, the full implications of which remain uncertain.[51] Regardless, the growing economic significance of agglomeration may create pressures toward liberalizing this practice.

Revising Zoning

Traditional Euclidian zoning, the type in use in nearly all sizeable communities, operates by specifying uses that are permitted in particular zones and banning all others.[52] This approach is ill-suited to the project of agglomeration, which centers on putting together the most valuable combinations of uses. But other forms of zoning might carry more promise in this regard. Performance zoning focuses not on uses but rather on their impacts, such as certain decibel readings or pollutant concentrations detected outside the owned parcel.[53] While usually considered in the context of negative externalities like noise or emissions, performance zoning would be interesting to consider in the context of positive externalities—things like drawing more people into a shopping district. Suppose, for example, that cameras or other technologies could determine the number of trips on foot to a given store from outside of a fixed radius of, say, a couple blocks. In a "high foot traffic" zone, new uses might be permitted only if they can guarantee (say, by posting a bond) that they will draw a certain amount of foot traffic into the area on average, over a particular span of time. In areas where only a few stores are likely to serve as "magnets" that draw in foot traffic, designating entire zones might not be desirable; instead, permission for larger or denser developments might be granted to those willing and able to meet this output target.

As another example, suppose that knowledge spillovers comprise the primary desired agglomeration benefits. Here, zoning in commercial or retail districts might specify that firms locating in the area have a certain minimum average number of employees on site each workday. Such a performance standard might be an imperfect proxy for spillovers, but it would at least ensure that one of the essential ingredients for interaction—workers—are present (although it would have the downside of discouraging liberal work-from-home policies that could benefit both workers and firms). More intrusively, performance standards might target meals consumed by employees in the immediate area. Along similar lines, Mountain View, California, recently enacted a restriction specifying that workers' meals within Facebook's new complex cannot be subsidized at a level higher than 50 percent on an ongoing basis, although meals can be fully subsidized at outside restaurants that are open to the general public.[54] The idea is to get the workforce out of cloistered workplaces and into the city, generating foot traffic and spending money at local establishments—a goal that is consistent with, even if not motivated by, nurturing knowledge spillovers.

Rethinking Everlasting, Rooted Estates

Another set of ideas strikes at the heart of existing property forms.[55] The assumptions that property rights must be granted in physically rooted locations and must be perpetual in length need not be accepted at face value. Our current way of holding property makes sense in an agrarian context, where an owner's inputs and outcomes are relatively well contained within the four corners of the parcel. It makes considerably less sense in a dynamic urban context where everyone's uses are interdependent, and the value generated by property depends crucially on the patterns in which it is held. We could instead build impermanence and portability directly into land ownership.

As we have seen, governments already hold what amount to call options on real property, in that eminent domain can override the rights of private landowners.[56] What if owners could affirmatively choose a less permanent type of ownership, priced accordingly, that would be expressly "callable" by the government after a certain period of time? Suppose certain urban areas were designated as less permanent by design, and firms and households could sort into (or avoid) these areas based on their own preferences. The added flexibility in these callable zones could reduce the need to resort to eminent domain in other areas. Under this approach, the core ingredient of noncoercive reconfiguration—consent by the affected landowners—would be procured in advance, based on a clear plan for compensation that splits up the resulting surplus equitably.

We might also rethink the assumption that real property interests must be forever tied to a particular physical location. What if city dwellers could purchase "floating estates" on the understanding that their property interest might be shifted to another location nearby, of equal or greater value, with relocation costs covered. As unusual as this may sound, there are antecedents. Land readjustment, although not well known in the US, has been used in other countries to accomplish something very similar to this idea.[57] To illustrate, imagine a low-density residential neighborhood that would be more valuable if it were replaced with a higher-density mixed-use development. The area might be razed and redeveloped with higher-density residences, shops, and green space. Each former resident might then receive a smaller residential site in the new development, but it would be of equal or greater value than the property she was initially required to give up because of the effects of the redevelopment. Entrepreneurial variations on these ideas could ease reconfiguration by collecting consent in advance, along with an agreed-upon method for dividing the surplus.

Clusters and Competing Lumps

Before deciding what strategies to pursue, we need to know what kinds of urban combinations or clusters produce which kinds of agglomeration benefits, and at what geographic scales. A recent paper by William Kerr and Scott Duke Kominers delves into these questions.[58] They sought to understand how one strand of the agglomeration literature, which shows that spillovers drop rapidly as distance increases beyond a few city blocks (and sometimes even within the same building), could be squared with another strand finding agglomeration effects at a much larger regional scale.[59] Kerr and Kominers's answer: very small zones of "microinteraction" overlap with each other in urban areas to produce the observed regional clusters.[60] This type of analysis opens up new avenues for research, with important implications for law. For example, Kerr and his coauthor Gilles Duranton recently observed that "there is a surprising gap in our knowledge about how skyscrapers affect the structure of interactions"—an important question given the controls that some cities have placed on building heights.[61] More broadly, research exploring the "'inner workings' of clusters" is needed—both on how clusters generate benefits, and what inequities they may generate as they do so.[62] This research can inform law and policy aimed at ensuring that cities are not only generative but also inclusive.

If small circles of interaction, or "microagglomerations," as well as larger clusters are important to urban agglomerations, the question remains of how to foster these groupings.[63] A core problem is that some urban improvements must happen in large, indivisible steps, if they are to happen at all. This is the same feature that made the discussion table problem presented above so challenging to solve. Even though there was some turnover at the table, the staggered openings did not offer meaningful opportunities to transform the table's use. Interspersing two or three people bent on group discussion around a table otherwise filled with people reading independently would be the worst of both worlds: the discussants would find it annoying to talk around the readers, and the readers would find the (attempted) discussion distracting. Here, the mixed pattern is dominated by both of the homogeneous patterns (all readers or all discussants)—a setup that goes by the name of "nonconvexity" in the economic literature.[64] Nonconvexities present difficulties because the path to the best solution traverses a chasm of inferior ones—like crossing a valley to get from a lower peak to a higher one.[65] In other words, the solution is lumpy; one needs a full rather than a partial bridge to get there.

This basic problem, that a desired goal may be unreachable by small intermediate steps, has been recognized in the land use context, although it remains underappreciated. Vicki Been and Robert Ellickson give the example of an area filled with vineyards that would be more valuable if switched to residential use—but only if the shift is total.[66] Introducing a few homes here and there would be a disaster; the vineyard's vistas would be broken up, yet the residents would be too few to attract the local services that they need. Any developer who takes small steps toward the residential transition will wind up with an unpopular project that is vulnerable to being undone before the transition is complete.[67] Thus, as Been and Ellickson explain, "although a complete shift to the all-housing outcome would be efficient, market forces would tend to stymie any first steps in that direction."[68] In other instances, a mix of uses might be superior, but a suitable mix at a large scale can be just as hard to achieve and maintain through uncoordinated action.[69]

Buying out everyone all at once is one solution, and brute force (eminent domain) is another. But it is difficult to accomplish large-scale land use changes when the existing pattern features a large number of land-owners with strong and perpetual property rights. Another problem is that we may be uncertain about the benefits that the transformation will actually deliver. Markets usually do a good job of aggregating information to move resources into the hands of those who value them most highly, but urban land markets feature a confounding cocktail of local regulations, locational spillovers, holdouts, and nonconvexities. What approaches can overcome these problems and assemble together the most valuable urban configurations?

A first step is to understand the nature of the problem. Casting urban dilemmas in terms of co-location—the placement of land uses and users relative to each other—usefully emphasizes the importance of assembling complementary elements. At the same time, it highlights the real conundrum at the heart of the most interesting and difficult land use conflicts: that producing some chunks of value requires breaking apart others. Whether the conflicts take the form of community versus highway, shopping district versus wildlife habitat, or historic neighborhood versus affordable housing, recognizing the role of lumpiness on both sides of the dispute helps to clarify what is at stake. Although discussions of urban development are generally quite sensitive to the problem of displacement, less attention is given to two related problems, both of which relate to lumpiness.

Suppose, for example, there is a neighborhood that lies along an otherwise ideal route for a highway. The highway is a lumpy good—we need the whole thing—and there may be few viable routes. But the neighborhood may also be lumpy, especially if it is a longstanding and close-knit one. We focus, appropriately, on the displacement that would occur as a result of building the highway. Sometimes we also focus on the newly placed highway, which may have negative spillovers for the remaining neighbors. But there is another effect that often receives less attention: breaking up the old neighborhood.[70] What is costly about running the highway through the neighborhood is not just that doing so will displace households, but also that it will break apart a cohesive unit. Community is destroyed as it is divided up, and even those who remain geographically rooted are no longer in the neighborhood that they once occupied. These and other "barrier" effects that result from transportation infrastructure are sometimes aptly referred to in the literature as "community severance."[71]

Taking into account the effects on the community members left behind has important implications for law and policy. Counterintuitively, what might seem on the surface to be the least harmful way of carrying out eminent domain, displacing as few families as possible, may appear artificially cheap to the government because it does not account for communities that are split apart as a result.[72] Similarly, private assembly efforts that successfully target a portion of a community for buyouts may leave the rest of the community worse off.[73] What would it mean to take these disrupted unities into account? One possibility would be to grant the remaining community members the power to force the land assembler—whether government or private developer—to buy their land at a fair price as well.[74] This would put the assembler to an all-or-nothing choice about the whole set of properties. The would-be assembler might decide that the condemnation or assembly is not worth doing after all, but if the project goes forward, it would have to take lumpiness into account.

There is another potential problem implicated in the highway versus neighborhood scenario. Suppose that the interests of the neighborhood win out and the highway is not built at all. This too is costly to society. The unbuilt highway may attract attention if the discussion surrounding it was high profile, but many other *potential* packages of complementary co-locations simply never occur. To return to our dining hall example, we may simply never know how many roundtable discussions failed to occur due to the existing pattern of use. Likewise, we may be unable to readily observe the households that can't locate near their preferred schools because no affordable options exist, or the businesses that can't locate close enough to each other to generate a critical mass of foot traffic, or the species of animals that can't locate together in habitats large enough to sustain their populations.

The fact that indivisibilities and complementarities often stand on both sides of a controversial land use decision presents real challenges for urban policy and for property theory more generally. Indeed, the temporal lumpiness of property rights themselves—the fact that the fee simple is perpetual in duration—is often at odds with achieving a spatial assembly. Similarly, giving individuals full control over each parcel of land can mean giving up the opportunity to pursue certain collective projects that span across many owned parcels. To take a now-uncontroversial case, airplanes can freely cross the airspace high above people's houses without permission.[75] But this was at one time an open and contested question: granting airlines the lumpy good of an unbroken path of travel meant paring down the chunky exclusion rights—ownership to the heavens and to the depths—that property owners were previously believed to enjoy.[76] Likewise, the law's commitment to enforcing antidiscrimination norms against private landowners[77] has won widespread acceptance, even though this means making an exception to the owner's right to exclude.

As new trade-offs continue to emerge, framing them in terms of indivisibilities, and examining which chunks of value matter more to society, will help to center the debate in a more analytically useful place. It may seem reductionist to try to boil down deeply contentious urban disputes to questions of lumpy production functions.[78] But as this book has amply shown, behind those production functions lie human values, and only by understanding how different effects aggregate together can we see how best to pursue those values. Moreover, casting trade-offs in terms of competing lumps of value offers a way for those who disagree to understand one another's concerns. It may seem simple for an owner to give up part of what she has in the name of social obligation, but if having "nearly all" is dramatically less valuable than having "all," her resistance can be better understood. Likewise, if a given social obligation is viewed as part of an aggregation that may be difficult to achieve through uncoordinated action, the interest in achieving it collectively, through a reconceptualization of property, may resonate.

The city is in many ways the quintessential lumpy good—it would be inexplicable as a human phenomenon otherwise. But beyond the obvious ways in which lumps of value within cities deliver value (and impose costs), it is important to see that the decisions firms and households make within and between cities also encompass varying degrees of lumpiness. Understanding how these choice sets interact is a first step to building better urban agglomerations. Law has an important role to play in this process, both by building choice sets and by regulating how parties interact in urban space. The next two chapters will examine how the law itself embeds lumpiness—cliffs and bundles—in setting regulatory policy, making laws, and controlling behavior.

ELEVEN

Law's Cliffs

Barry Bonds set a new single-season home run record at PacBell Park in San Francisco on October 7, 2001. As his seventy-third home run ball soared into the stands, it ignited a mad scramble—and a legal dispute.[1] The ball first made contact with the glove of Alex Popov, but before Popov could complete the catch, he was knocked to the ground by the surrounding crowd. The ball went rolling through the stands and was retrieved by another fan, Patrick Hayashi. Both Popov and Hayashi claimed ownership of the ball.

The baseball itself was lumpy—an indivisible good. Although it might have been physically possible to cut it in half, its value would have been greatly diminished if not extinguished altogether by that operation. Preserving its value required keeping it in one piece. The court was thus faced with a choice between awarding the ball to Popov, awarding it Hayashi, or coming up with some other solution that would split the *value* of the ball—but not the ball itself—between the parties. The court chose the third alternative: it ordered the ball to be sold, and the proceeds split between the parties.[2]

This was an unusual outcome, although not wholly unprecedented.[3] Typically, courts make all-or-nothing judgments that declare one party the winner and the other the loser, full stop. This is true not just in property disputes but also in other areas of law.[4] An injurer is liable or not liable in tort. A defendant is guilty or not guilty. A contractual remedy is granted, or it is denied. A law is struck down, or it is upheld. These are lumpy, discontinuous results. Legislation and regulations operate similarly insofar as they rely on classifying situations and engaging in other forms of line drawing. Unless the lines happen to correspond to large discontinuities in the real world, they will separate similar situations for different treatment.

Some theorists have considered ways to "continuize" the law so that each small change in behavior produces proportionate changes in outcomes.[5] This approach would address cliff effects that are prevalent in law, where minor differences in behavior or other inputs map onto large divergences in outcomes. Others have recommended "split-the-difference" or fractional approaches in at least some contexts.[6] But these solutions present their own problems, including raising the cost of administering the law. When decisions are made on an all-or-nothing basis, courts need not parse the relative strength of claims that fall short of the level necessary to win. There is also less to be gained by bringing a weak case when a partial victory is not a possibility, which reduces caseloads and associated litigation costs. Even though most cases settle, producing split outcomes on the ground, settlement negotiations take place in the shadow of the law's all-or-nothing propensities.

Binary outcomes mesh well with the indivisible entitlements that are frequently at issue in legal disputes. For example, physically dividing disputed land will often make it less valuable than awarding it intact to one party or another. Of course, a "sell the asset and split the proceeds" approach can be used even when indivisibilities are present, as they were in the baseball case of *Popov v. Hayashi*. Courts often employ this method in judicial partition cases among co-owners, where more than one party has an indisputable claim to the land, but physically splitting it into pieces would reduce its value.[7] But such split solutions tend to be confined to circumstances where it is unusually difficult or impossible to declare a single winner.

For better or worse, then, law depends heavily on all-or-nothing judgments to carry out its work. In so doing, law makes two interlocking judgments that implicate lumpiness. First, in evaluating behavior or events, law must determine the proper unit of analysis—how widely or narrowly to set its viewfinder—in assessing whether a given line has been crossed or a given standard has been satisfied. This process of *evaluative aggregation* asks, for example, whether individual acts should be stacked together and considered as a whole, or considered one by one in isolation. Second, law must decide how sharp or graduated its responses should be—whether to use a cliff-like or a sharply notched structure in which small differences in behavioral inputs can yield large differences in liability, or a more modulated set of legal responses.[8] This *liability cliff* question goes to the lumpiness of legal consequences. Where legal consequences are binary, a lot rides on what goes into the on-off judgment.

Legal Thresholding

In converting messy facts into binary judgments, law's work resembles the "thresholding" process used to convert grayscale images to black and white.[9] Although pixels may come in many shades of gray, each is translated into either a black pixel or a white pixel based on whether its shading falls above or below some specified value. Thus, two pixels that are nearly identical shades of gray may be rendered as black and white, respectively, if they lie on opposite sides of the threshold.[10] Likewise, two acts that fall on either side of a legally constructed line can yield dramatically different outcomes: substantial liability in one case, and no liability in the other.[11] These cliff effects make the choices that underlie legal thresholding highly consequential.

A core challenge in legal thresholding is choosing the appropriate unit of analysis. Consider image manipulation again. When converting pixels from grayscale into black and white, the question is whether the shading *of the pixel* is sufficiently dark to render that pixel in black rather than white. Sophisticated methods of image thresholding examine clusters, shapes, or pixel "neighborhoods" to figure out what threshold should be applied to pixels within a particular portion of a given image.[12] But the applicable threshold, however derived, is nonetheless applied pixel by pixel. Legal problems, by contrast, don't arrive in sharply demarcated pixels. Before a court can decide who will win a case, or on which side of a legislative or regulatory line someone's conduct falls, it must decide what to include within its viewfinder when making that up-down evaluation. This preliminary decision will often be outcome determinative.

Suppose a court is deciding whether a driver, Dora, was negligent. It is uncontroverted that Dora briefly took her eyes off the road for half a second just before the accident, and that if she had not done so, the accident would not have happened. Should the determination about negligence be based on Dora's conduct during just that half second of inattention, or should it be based on some larger sample of Dora's driving behavior? It is impossible for anyone engaged in an attention-intensive task like driving to avoid the occasional lapse of attention.[13] Thus, if Dora was generally a conscientious driver, it might seem unfair to hinge her liability on the single moment when her attention drifted. Yet this is exactly what the law does.[14]

I will have more to say about this example below, and will end up agreeing with the law's treatment of Dora's lapse. My point at this stage is simply to illustrate that it can matter a great deal when making an on-off judgment whether one zeroes in on a single moment or considers a larger pattern of behavior. In the example just given, widening the viewfinder could provide offsetting evidence that, if taken into account, might relieve the defendant of liability. In other instances, however, taking a larger behavioral sample would have the opposite effect.

Consider the infamous case of *Rex v. Smith*, which involved a man accused of drowning his bride in the bathtub.[15] The defendant, George Joseph Smith, maintained that the death had been accidental. Unfortunately for him, evidence surfaced that he had been married to two other women, both of whom had also drowned in bathtubs early in their marriages under similar circumstances (including, in each case, recently executed wills naming Smith as beneficiary).[16] Although the defendant insisted he had merely experienced a run of bad luck, the jury disagreed: he was hanged for murder.[17] Here, focusing in on the single pixel of one bathtub drowning might well have resulted in an acquittal, given the high threshold required for conviction in a criminal case, the lack of witnesses, and the fact that it would not be unusual for newly married people to engage in estate planning.[18] But broadening the viewfinder to take in *three* instances provided overwhelming corroboration for the prosecutor's case.

As these examples suggest, questions about what should be included within the analytic viewfinder are crucial for two basic but opposite reasons. Sometimes widening the frame to encompass a larger slice of behavior allows evidence to pile up in support of a conclusion that could not be reached, or could not be reached to a sufficient level of confidence, based on a thinner window of observation—as in the bathtub drownings. In other cases, widening the frame enables other observations to dilute or offset the ones of initial interest—the driver with the rare lapse. And sometimes expanding or contracting the field of vision will have both effects in various proportions, and it may be impossible to predict in advance which will dominate.

In cases like the ones above, we might understand the initial observation (the single tub drowning or the accident-causing lapse) as a draw from an urn.[19] We might worry both that this draw is an outlier (which might raise concerns about basing consequences upon it) and that this draw is characteristic (which might raise concerns about *not* basing consequences upon it). A central concern is whether "taking character evidence" in this manner is appropriate.[20] To even speak of behavior as a draw from an urn implies that human beings constitute the same urn over time, and that observations that form a pattern are not independent of each other. But in the law's eyes, this is questionable. To the extent that liability is meant to attach to a given act, and not to one's overall urn-pattern, peering into the urn may appear illegitimate, and plucking additional draws both beside the (legal) point and potentially prejudicial.

Yet in many contexts, people try to do exactly that, and it is generally regarded as not only sensible but essentially required. For example, it might seem rash to fail to obtain references about a potential hire. Likewise, an employer who suspects an employee of dishonesty might watch that employee closely to see if corroborating or exonerating patterns appear.[21] These are widespread informal mechanisms of aggregating information to resolve uncertainty, but more formal methods are possible. For example, Frederick Schauer and Richard Zeckhauser observe that the "recorder" system used by card players in contract bridge competitions facilitates aggregation of information about suspected misconduct.[22] Under this system, players submit complaints to a designated recorder, who then chooses whether to recommend that the matter be taken forward to a disciplinary committee. In making this judgment, the recorder can take into account whether a previous complaint has been lodged about the person in question. Schauer and Zeckhauser suggested adapting a version of this protocol to other settings where charges might be made under conditions that do not permit complete certainty, such as workplace sexual harassment.[23]

More recently, Ian Ayres and Cait Unkovic have proposed an escrowing system for reports of sexual assault and other kinds of wrongdoing,[24] and a real-world version of this approach now exists in the Callisto system adopted by a number of colleges and universities.[25] The idea is simple: a person who has experienced an assault submits information about it, but has the option of leaving the incident unreported to authorities unless and until one or more other people report being assaulted by the same perpetrator. Fear or uncertainty that might deter an individual from reporting an assault would be dissipated by the existence of a second complaint, submitted independently.[26] To investigate the effects of this alternative, Ayres conducted a sexual assault survey on Mechanical Turk (a platform offered by Amazon) that put respondents in the hypothetical position of a college student who believes he or she may have been sexually assaulted by a friend following a night of drinking.[27] Under these conditions, Ayres's findings suggest that a "matching" escrow like Callisto would primarily attract those complainants who otherwise would have done nothing, without eroding the rate at which people choose to go forward with a formal complaint.[28]

In the criminal context, aggregative efforts confront both evidentiary limits and deeper normative objections about compounding probabilities of guilt based on different incidents. What should be done about evidence that effectively reveals additional urn draws, like the additional bathtub drownings in *Smith*? As Sean Sullivan observes in his analysis of the case, the reason why the pattern of drowned wives seems interesting and relevant necessarily arises from a belief that the probabilities of the drowning deaths are not independent across cases, but rather are dependent on each other in some manner.[29] Yet character evidence is disallowed, so the inferred connection cannot be simply that the defendant is a "guilty urn" given to murder.[30] Nonetheless, evidence that shows other mechanisms through which correlation might flow (knowledge of how to commit the crime, or the existence of a plan or mode of operation) may be admissible—even if this effectively brings propensity in through a back door.[31]

An alternative proposed by Alon Harel and Ariel Porat would embrace the uncertainty that frequently accompanies efforts to determine guilt or innocence and allow aggregation of probabilities of guilt across different alleged offenses.[32] Under their approach, a defendant could be convicted if there is no reasonable doubt that she committed at least one of several offenses, even if it is impossible for the finder of fact to specify which one.[33] While this sounds like a radical departure from existing understandings of how criminal law is supposed to operate, the discussion above suggests it shares some common ground with existing approaches that aggregate information about behavior over time. The next section examines questions of behavioral aggregation that arise in the context of tort liability for momentary lapses.

Lumping Lapses

Consider again the case of the lapsing driver, Dora. Driving offers a familiar example of the general maxim that human beings cannot avoid occasionally falling short in their efforts to take due care.[34] Anyone who drives very often will experience the occasional lapse of attention. While usually harmless and quickly forgotten, these lapses sometimes produce an alarming near-miss, and in a tragic few cases, a terrible accident.[35] Should a momentary loss of focus generate liability if a driver was otherwise a very careful person? Is it appropriate to home in on a single pixel of conduct without considering the larger pattern it is located within? Should the negligence determination be based instead on a larger sample of behavior?

The answers are tricky for several reasons. First, it is generally impossible to observe entire patterns of behavior, so inferences must be drawn from available observations. Second, even if it were possible to observe entire patterns (as may increasingly become the case given smartphone-enabled monitoring of driving), it is not clear that we should make the consequences of a driver's lapse turn on her behavior on other occasions. Consider too that *some* of a careless person's lapses would have been made by even the most careful person—just not all of them. Yet we have no way of telling an "excess" lapse from one that comes from a human being's unavoidable allotment.[36] If we tolerate liability for unavoidable lapses when they are mixed in with avoidable ones by the same person, why not otherwise?

One rationale for charging *all* actors for their lapses (avoidable or not) relates to a well-known shortcoming of using a negligence standard to impose liability: that injurers will engage in risky activities to an excessive extent because they will never bear liability as long as they are sufficiently careful, even though their elevated activity level raises accident costs for victims.[37] For example, a driver might jump in the car on a whim to pick up a single grocery item without thinking about the risk she is creating, since she can avoid liability simply by meeting the negligence standard.[38] Because courts will not delve into whether a particular outing was really worth its cost in increased risk, but will instead consider only the care taken while driving, motorists might be expected to drive too much. This line of reasoning assumes that people can always comply with the negligence standard. But if unavoidable lapses occur in proportion to activity levels, then it is impossible for an injurer to increase her activity level without at the same time increasing her chance of being held liable for a lapse.[39] Thus, liability for lapses could help to check the tendency of injurers to overengage in risky activities by effectively taxing the activity in proportion to its volume.[40]

Distorted Decisions

Robert Cooter and Ariel Porat have suggested a reason that the law's harsh treatment of human lapses could produce behavioral distortions: the law may be relatively more lenient toward imperfections in other kinds of precautionary technologies that rely less on moment-to-moment human attentiveness.[41] This concern can be reframed as a divergence between the degree of aggregation used to evaluate due care in human actions compared with that used to evaluate due care in automated processes.

Suppose, to use an example from Ward Farnsworth and Mark Grady, that a surgeon will accidentally leave a sponge inside a patient in one out of every one million surgeries.[42] When that one-in-a-million case occurs, the doctor will appear negligent for failing to undertake a simple check that would have avoided a significant risk of loss. Now suppose a machine is available that keeps track of sponges used in surgery and counts them as they are removed. If the machine malfunctions one time per million surgeries, will its lapse be treated the same or differently from the lapse of the surgeon?[43]

Cooter and Porat's analysis suggests that the machine's error might be treated differently.[44] The surgeon's mistake will be evaluated in isolation by asking whether it would have been cost effective for her to spend an extra moment ensuring that she had all the sponges out before closing up the patient (a question that will always be answered in the affirmative). By contrast, the machine's error will likely be examined in terms of whether it would be cost effective to design and build a machine that had a lower error rate (to which the answer may well be negative). Cooter and Porat suggest that actors may choose mechanized precautions that will be assessed in the aggregate over individualized human actions that will be assessed one at a time, even if the cost-benefit ratio is better for the human precautions than for the mechanized precautions.[45]

Cooter and Porat provide examples of automated technologies—cruise control, traffic lights, and so on—that generate predictable patterns of results over time.[46] Because the full pattern can be observed, errors that would look like lapses in the individual human actor case are not picked out and evaluated in isolation but are instead aggregated with the far more prevalent instances of correct operation for purposes of evaluating whether the technology meets due care. In the case of a human lapse, by contrast, fact finders are observing a single draw from an opaque urn of behavior. Jurors will be uncertain whether the behavior they are seeing is indeed a rare lapse, analogous to the error of a generally sound machine, or whether they are instead glimpsing one instance of an overall pattern of unreasonably risky behavior. For this reason, it is perhaps unsurprising that jurors would latch onto even legally irrelevant cues that might help them form a judgment of the defendant's character and attitude toward risk.[47]

The activity level issue raised above only heightens the problem that Cooter and Porat identify. A party who cannot avoid using a technology—human judgment—that will generate actionable lapses as she increases the volume of a given activity may indeed curtail her activity level. But a party who can substitute a mechanized precautionary technology that meets the due care standard will have no such incentive. Rather, she can be certain that no matter how high her activity level, the technology will always protect her from liability because its overall low failure rate will be deemed to meet the due care standard. Thus a driver who relies on cruise control (or in the foreseeable future, automated cars) may be able to increase the number of miles driven without fear of expanded liability, while a driver whose own decisions about speed or other factors will be evaluated one by one could not do so.[48]

A Lapse Defense?

To avoid these kinds of distortions between different modes of precaution, Cooter and Porat recommend a "lapse defense" that would effectively permit defendants to demonstrate that they were suffering from an atypical lapse rather than a typical shortfall.[49] Liability would no longer turn solely on observation of a one-off event, but rather would require looking at a larger sample of behavior. One possibility would be to focus on some facet of the defendant's behavior that operates at a higher level of aggregation than the individual lapsing moment—what Cooter and Porat term "second-order precautions."[50] Examples might include routines, plans, or checklists that the defendant follows as standard operating procedure, even if there was a shortfall on a particular occasion. Grady has suggested that fact finders already tend to treat "precaution plans" differently from individual precautions: a surgeon's conduct will be assessed more leniently if she has adopted a plan of counting sponges but lapses on a single occasion than if she lapses in the absence of such a plan.[51] An explicit lapse defense could build on this approach, although it might induce wasteful expenditures on formalizing plans that are not consistently followed or that would perhaps even be inefficient to follow.

The immense amount of data that smartphones can collect (and indeed already collect) offers another likely avenue for accessing a larger behavioral sample. For example, some insurance companies offer discounts to drivers who submit to smartphone-enabled monitoring of their driving habits.[52] The data collected on risky behaviors like hard acceleration and braking, speeding, and erratic movements currently allow premiums to better reflect risk profiles. But these data could easily be repurposed in service of a lapse defense. Another possibility for accessing a larger behavioral sample might be a variation on the "How's My Driving?" reporting system that Lior Strahilevitz has recommended for driving and other behaviors.[53] Like the information escrowing approaches discussed above, the system would collect reports from observers. A record that is clean of complaints over an extended period could be used to show that a given lapse was an aberration. But some of these approaches could create perverse incentives to rack up large numbers of miles to increase the denominator against which a lapse would be evaluated, exacerbating concerns about excessive activity levels in a negligence regime.

A Disaggregating Alternative

There is another way to alleviate the imbalance between the law's treatment of human lapses and other kinds of failure rates: by imposing strict liability for accidents caused by mechanized or routinized systems. Thus, if an automated car or other machine malfunctioned and caused an accident, liability would follow without fail, regardless of how low the failure rate or how well designed the machine might be overall. This is in fact how products liability already works in the context of manufacturing defects. The individual defective product forms the unit of analysis for establishing liability, and it is no defense that due care was taken in mass production techniques. Just as careful human drivers will occasionally suffer lapses, manufacturing defects will slip through well-designed quality control systems now and then—but in neither case does inevitability protect against liability.[54]

Imposing strict liability on mechanical processes would be the inverse of Cooter and Porat's proposal. Instead of compiling a larger sample of human behavior, the "behavior" of the machine or procedure would be disaggregated: a failure would serve as a basis for liability, regardless of how many successes might have already occurred. This disaggregation would remove the distortion as effectively as would the creation of a lapse defense, because there would no longer be an incentive to substitute an automated or routine process solely for the purpose of taking advantage of evaluative aggregation. If the mechanical procedure were really superior to a particular set of human decisions, however, it would still be employed. Negligence would remain the standard for the human-mediated actions, and human lapses would still give rise to liability in the manner that currently occurs—with the accompanying favorable effects on activity levels.

Even though this approach would hold machines and humans to nominally different standards, the effect would be to level the playing field between them by counteracting differences in how human and machine conduct is typically aggregated for evaluation. Commentators worry that a strict liability standard will chill innovation and thwart moves to safer technologies.[55] But that argument assumes the human error to machine error comparison is apples to apples—when it is really apples to orchards.[56] Given a background tendency toward evaluative disaggregation in the

200 / Chapter Eleven

human case, and toward evaluative aggregation in the mechanized case, holding humans liable for their (inevitable) lapses is fully consistent with holding machines liable for theirs. And it conserves on information costs compared with an approach that would even things up by inquiring into the human's overall "error rate."

Luck and Insurance

Removing distortions between automated systems and human error does nothing to address what might seem most troublesome about liability for lapses: it strikes only the unlucky lapser who causes an accident, not the equally culpable lapser who is lucky enough to proceed without incident.[57] This speaks to a lumpiness at the heart of tort law: it responds not to the innumerable fine-grained acts of risk creation that each of us performs every day but rather to large, discrete, harmful events—"accidents." For those who are engaged in a large number of interactions, the lumps come out in the wash, just as they do in many other contexts. Indeed, this is one rationale for strict liability in high-volume, repeat-play contexts like products liability.[58] But for individuals, accidents are lumpy, discrete events—no one has exactly 0.13 car crashes, even if this is what one's risk profile might predict.

Insurance can replicate the large-number smoothing experienced by larger players. To the extent premiums are based on risk creation, they help to close the gap between the lucky and unlucky lapsers. Of course, neither insurance premiums nor repetition will produce appropriate price signals unless the underlying liability patterns reflect appropriate thresholding choices. Thus, insurance can answer the problem of bad luck, but it cannot paper over problems in the law's methods for determining liability—methods that in turn require attention to problems of aggregation.

Counting Problems

Puzzles of evaluative aggregation also crop up where discontinuous legal consequences depend on the answer to a "how many" question. For example, criminal laws attach consequences to each separate offense, while double jeopardy forbids prosecution for the *same* offense after an acquittal. Likewise, insurance contracts limit how much is paid out per covered event. In these and many other instances, we have to know what counts as "one" in order to assess consequences. And answering this question requires knowing something about the rationale underlying the counting exercise.

Consider the familiar grocery store checkout lane limit of "twelve items or fewer." Borderline cases are easy to imagine. Is a six-pack of beer one item or six? How about a bunch of bananas or a bag of apples? Two identical items united by a "buy one get one free" coupon? If the reason for the rule is to limit transaction time, then perhaps we can decide based on the number of bar codes that must be scanned (but then do coupons also count as "items"?). On the other hand, if the limit on items is meant as a rough proxy for the physical bulkiness of the order (perhaps because the item-limited lanes cannot accommodate large carts or have constrained bagging areas), then a different logic applies, one that might cast doubt on the customer with a dozen eight-packs of jumbo-roll paper towels.

Other counting contexts involve far more momentous consequences. For example, double jeopardy protections can turn on the answer to questions like this one raised in the Supreme Court case of *Brown v. Ohio*: How many offenses has an automobile thief committed when he takes a nine-day joyride in a stolen vehicle?[59] The Court held that because the applicable criminal statutes in Ohio "make the theft and operation of a single car a single offense," the extended joyride must be treated as a single offense for double jeopardy purposes.[60] Writing for the majority, Justice Powell opined that "the Double Jeopardy Clause is not such a fragile guarantee that prosecutors can avoid its limitations by the simple expedient of dividing a single crime into a series of temporal or spatial units."[61] Having chosen to define the crime in a unified way for some purposes, then, the state was not free to slice it up differently when it suited prosecutorial objectives.

To take another criminal law example that legal philosophers have examined, consider the person who shoots into a building five times, but hits no one.[62] Should that volley of shots count as one offense or five? If we say one, then it seems as if we are improperly giving the defendant a "volume discount" on his bad behavior.[63] But if we say five, it might seem to unfairly equate this defendant's behavior with that of another shooter who fires into the building one time on each of five separate days. Larry Alexander and Kimberly Ferzan suggest that considering the duration of intent as a factor in culpability offers a way out.[64] In other words, they would allow time for deliberation to factor into a "how bad" inquiry that could be paired with the "how many" question. If it is possible to scale the severity of an offense to match culpability, effectively grafting a continuous variable onto the integer count, the number of instances matters less.

Yet sometimes everything *does* turn on the counting question, as the insurance litigation following 9/11 illustrated.[65] Were the terrorist attacks on the north and south towers of the World Trade Center—a coordinated

attack involving two commercial aircraft that were separately hijacked—
one occurrence for insurance purposes, or two? The answer would determine whether coverage would be capped at $3.5 billion or doubled to
reach $7 billion.[66] To complicate matters, the attacks occurred as the rel-
evant insurance contracts were being negotiated, and only one insurer had
issued a final policy. The US Court of Appeals for the Second Circuit af-
firmed federal district court rulings following a two-phase jury trial that
reached different answers for different insurers: the 9/11 attack on the towers constituted "one occurrence" for most of the insurers, but "two occurrences" for a few of them.[67]

At one level, questions like these are straightforward matters of statutory or contractual interpretation that can be resolved by clearer definitions. But they also illustrate the pervasive tendency to use discrete chunks
like "offenses" or "occurrences" to organize the world—a tendency that
raises questions about how to bound and isolate these phenomena. These
efforts at individuation must be informed by the goals that led to the use
of enumeration in the first place.[68] For example, one commentator has suggested that "per occurrence" limits in insurance contracts generally represent efforts to control exposure to an insured's highly correlated losses.[69]
If "occurrences" are meant to connote independent (uncorrelated) losses,
then the statistical relationship among losses could provide a way of deciding what should count as a single occurrence, at least in the absence of
evidence the parties intended otherwise.[70]

Defining Denominators

Similar individuation problems arise when legal consequences depend
on *how much of* something (such as a property interest or a legal entitlement) has been affected by another party's actions. A basic but surprisingly
difficult initial task involves defining the interest or entitlement at issue,
against which we can measure the complained-of impact. The most well-
known manifestation of this "denominator problem" (although, as we will
see, hardly the only one) appears in regulatory takings law.

Fractions in Takings Law

The Supreme Court's recent decision in *Murr v. Wisconsin* squarely confronted this individuation problem.[71] The four Murr siblings received two
adjacent parcels of land along the St. Croix River in Wisconsin: one from
their parents and one from their parents' plumbing business. One of these

parcels contained a cabin that the family had used recreationally for many years. The siblings wanted to improve and relocate the cabin, which had become prone to flooding. To finance this project, they sought to sell the other parcel as a building lot. There was only one problem: under a state law enacted many years earlier to protect the river area, each lot was too small to sell or develop separately. Undersized lots like the ones the Murrs acquired had been grandfathered in when the law was originally adopted, but with a proviso: if adjacent undersized lots came under common owner-ship, as happened when the Murr siblings received their two-part gift, then the lots would be merged into one and could no longer be sold or devel-oped separately.

The Murrs argued that this restriction amounted to a "taking" of their property under the US Constitution. The strength of their claim hinged on an odd question: should the Murr siblings' property be considered one parcel or two? The answer matters under the Supreme Court's rather quirky doctrines surrounding "regulatory" or "implicit" takings.[72] Unlike explicit exercises of eminent domain in which the government openly announces it is condemning property (as it did in *Kelo*), implicit takings occur when the government acts in a regulatory or other permissible capacity but so signifi-cantly affects property interests as to trigger the constitutional requirement that it compensate the owner. Most ordinary government actions that im-pact property values in some way do not require compensation. However, the Supreme Court has developed a set of tests for determining when the government has, in the words of Justice Holmes, gone "too far."[73]

In *Lucas v. South Carolina Coastal Council*, the Supreme Court held that restrictions that remove "all economically beneficial use" constitute per se takings that will always require just compensation, except where they merely reflect background limitations on title.[74] But if *not all* economically viable use is eliminated by the regulation, the more lenient multifactor test developed in *Penn Central Transportation Co. v. New York City* applies.[75] Together these two rules create a sharp cliff in governmental liability: full compensation is required when the last increment of value is drained away, but eliminating *nearly all* of the value might not be enough to trigger any compensation requirement at all.[76]

The liability cliff created by the *Lucas* rule interacts powerfully with the unit-of-analysis issue discussed earlier. It is impossible to say whether "all" value has been taken from someone's property without answering the question "all of what?" In takings parlance, this question has been dubbed "the denominator problem."[77] Although the *Lucas* test raises the denomi-nator problem with particular clarity, denominators matter even when government action is measured against the more amorphous *Penn Central* standard. The first *Penn Central* factor, "the economic impact of the regulation," requires some implicit base against which to judge the burden's magnitude, while the second factor, "the extent to which the regulation has interfered with distinct investment-backed expectations," depends on how those "distinct" interests are defined and bounded.[78]

When it comes to defining the denominator, two fairly clear principles bracket the spectrum of possibilities. First, it seems uncontroversial that the denominator cannot be reverse-engineered from the regulation itself to encompass only those rights that the regulation removed. For example, if a regulation prohibits landowners from keeping llamas on their property, an owner cannot claim that "all" of her "llama-keeping estate" has been destroyed. This would constitute "conceptual severance"—a term coined by Margaret Jane Radin to refer to an illegitimate form of disaggregation.[79] In *Tahoe-Sierra Preservation Council v. Tahoe Regional Planning Agency*, a case involving a moratorium on development, the Court similarly rejected landowners' efforts to subdivide their property interests into time slices defined by the moratorium itself in order to make out a *Lucas* taking.[80] Second, at the other extreme, the Court seems unwilling to countenance a denominator made up of all of a landowner's assets, no matter where they may be located.[81] The risk that the Court is concerned with here seems to map onto what Steven Eagle has called "conceptual agglomeration"—the opposite of "conceptual severance."[82]

In between these extremes, we run into situations like *Murr*. If an owner has two adjacent lots and all value is taken from (only) one of them, has the owner lost everything (triggering *Lucas*'s per se rule) or only half of everything (leaving the case to be resolved under *Penn Central's* multifactor test)? The Murr siblings argued that each parcel should be considered separately when conducting the takings analysis. Since they were not allowed to separately sell or develop the parcel that did not have the cabin on it, they argued that all value was taken from it.[83] Wisconsin argued that the two lots together, now a single merged lot under state law, should be the denominator. In a 5–3 decision in *Murr*, the Court eschewed any categorical approach to this question, choosing instead to apply a multifactor test to the denominator question itself. The factors to be considered include "the treatment of the land, in particular how it is bounded or divided, under state and local law"; "the physical characteristics of the landowner's property"; and "the value of the property under the challenged regulation, with special attention to the effect of burdened land on the value of other holdings."[84] This last factor seems to implicate the kinds of complementarities and indivisibilities that we have been considering throughout this book.

In addition to disputes about how to construct the *denominator*, the *Lucas* rule's sharp liability cliff generates disputes over what goes in the *numerator*. In *Lucas* itself, conservation legislation prohibited owners from building anything on their land, in an area where owners had previously been permitted to construct substantial and expensive dwellings. The state trial court found that all economically viable use had been destroyed, and the Supreme Court did not revisit this finding.[85] But as Justice Blackmun and Justice Stevens both noted in dissent, the land clearly was not "valueless": an unbuilt lot could have (for example) added yard space for a neighbor or served as a campsite.[86] The Court has since indicated that the government cannot dodge a compensation requirement by leaving a peppercorn or mere "token interest" behind.[87] But the line between what will count as constructively "all" and what falls short is unclear, and both parties will have an interest in adjusting the numerator to suit their arguments.

These difficulties might cause us to question the discontinuities baked into the underlying doctrine. Why should the law consider the loss of *all* of something (however defined) to be worse than an economically equivalent (or greater) loss that represents merely a portion of something? Perhaps, as Frank Michelman posited, there is something especially demoralizing about losing an *entire thing* due to government action.[88] If so, however, we need to have some sense of what essential cohesiveness gives a particular interest or set of interests its status as a distinct, discrete thing. Or perhaps, to pick up another thread emphasized by Michelman, it is easier to tell when *all* of something is gone and to settle up accounts based on it than it is to worry over partial losses—in part because total losses are simply rarer events.[89] Yet unless we know what counts as a thing in the first place, we cannot tell whether it is entirely gone.

Other Denominator Problems

The denominator problem of takings law renown is just one manifestation of a family of similar issues that crop up in a variety of areas of law. For example, many issues in election law, especially when it comes to drawing boundaries for voting districts, concern denominator specification. The voting rules that apply to annexation in the local government context similarly present problems of legitimate and illegitimate methods of arriving at the relevant denominator. In both cases, a lumpy on-off result is at stake—who will win the election or whether the annexation will occur. Whether one's favored result will be achieved depends not just on the absolute number of votes in favor, but also on how that number compares to the votes cast within the relevant unit.

Other constitutional issues involve how much the exercise of a particular constitutional right has been burdened, which again requires defining the relevant domain. How widely (in space, time, or subject matter) should we draw the frame around the relevant impacts to determine if the government has gone over the line?[90] For instance, it is impossible to tell whether free speech has been impermissibly infringed by limits on when and where it can be carried out without knowing both where a particular type of speech is forbidden *and* where it is permitted. And here, the unit of analysis can prove decisive. In *Schad v. Borough of Mt. Ephraim*, for example, the Supreme Court struck down an ordinance that totally excluded live entertainment (including nonobscene nude dancing) from a municipality. In so doing, it rejected the claim that ample live entertainment opportunities *outside* the municipality would save the ordinance's validity and distinguished an earlier case that merely dispersed adult uses *within* a jurisdiction.[91]

A New Jersey Supreme Court decision, *Borough of Sayreville v. 35 Club, L.L.C.*, took up a similar question.[92] The court had previously held that a state statute that regulated the placement of sexually oriented businesses was permissible under the US and New Jersey Constitutions only "if there are adequate alternative channels of the communication of this type of speech."[93] But must all these alternative channels be located within the state? Maybe not. In *Sayreville*, the court held that it was permissible to define the relevant market area to include some areas outside the state.[94] As Kenneth Stahl observes, this approach "makes one community's right to exclude adult uses contingent on other communities permitting them," which seems to set up a race to exclude uses first.[95]

In other instances, courts must consider how different restrictions stack together or offset each other. If a cumulative regulatory burden is impermissible, how should the various restrictions that contribute to it be evaluated, and in what order? Analogous aggregation and offsetting issues surface when law is applied to private conduct. If a private residential community bans sex offenders within its borders, should the prevalence of similar bans in the area cut against the validity of these restrictions?[96] Or consider disability rights laws that require employers to provide reasonable accommodations. If accommodating some number of disability-related requests can be managed without significantly impairing an employer's operations, but the cumulative effect of several such requests imposes an unreasonable burden, what is the legally required response to the sequence of requests?[97]

More broadly, antidiscrimination law prompts questions about whether impacts should be evaluated based on individual outcomes or net effects on a given group—which produces further questions about group definition and the scope of time and activities that should be considered together or broken apart. Indeed, one cannot even assess whether an area is segregated or integrated, economically or racially, without specifying whether one is examining the composition of an entire metropolitan area, a city, a neighborhood, a block, or an individual household.[98]

Other examples abound. Assessing a firm's market power for antitrust purposes customarily turns on how the relevant product market is defined—in other words, the denominator.[99] The outcome of a copyright infringement case may depend in part on how much of a particular work was taken, an inquiry that requires setting the denominator—a single episode of *Seinfeld*, for example, or the entire series?[100] In patent law, the calculation of damages under the Patent Act hinges on how the infringing "article of manufacture" is defined—a whole smartphone or just the infringing screen?[101] The evaluation of environmental impacts for regulatory purposes depends on whether effects are evaluated per smokestack, per plant, or based on a larger "bubble" of industrial activity.[102] A recent dispute over the Dakota Access Pipeline involved a similar issue: how the Army Corps of Engineers should delineate the "Area of Potential Effects" for purposes of evaluating impacts under the National Historic Preservation Act—the whole pipeline or each water crossing?[103]

Denominators matter in all of these cases because the fractions that they help define serve as inputs into legal thresholding. If every incremental input or effect had the same precisely scaled legal outcome no matter how it was grouped together with or split apart from other actions or impacts, these questions of aggregation would not play a role in legal analysis. But because the law embeds discontinuities, questions of lumping and slicing can be outcome determinative. The next chapter will consider how law's work of bundling and unbundling interacts with the economic principle that actions should be assessed based on their marginal impacts. These questions are relevant not only to litigated disputes but also to legislation and regulation.

TWELVE

Legal Bundles

A cricket ball sails out of an unfenced cricket field and brains a pedestrian, Paula.[1] At trial, forensic experts testify that the ball exited the field at an altitude of seven feet ten inches. It is undisputed that putting up an eight-foot fence—one high enough to have prevented this accident—would have cost the cricket club only $1,000 and would have saved an expected $1,200 in accident costs over the useful life of the fence. Invoking the "Hand formula," which assesses negligence by comparing the costs and benefits of a given precaution,[2] the lawyer for Paula's estate declares this "an open and shut case of negligence liability." But is it? And should it be?

These questions are surprisingly hard ones for reasons that relate to aggregation. Notice first that there is nothing inevitable about treating the full eight feet of fencing as an indivisible unit when assessing the cricket club's behavior. Once we disaggregate that single lumpy all-or-nothing choice into incremental choices about fence heights, the simple case starts to look less airtight. Suppose the cricket club proves that only the first six feet of fence height are actually worthwhile, delivering $1,100 in accident savings while costing only $800 in lumber and labor. The last two feet, by contrast, require an extra $200 in construction costs only to save a marginal $100 in accident costs. Thus, even though it was negligent for the cricket club not to build a six-foot fence, it would not have been negligent for it to stop at six feet—and a six-foot fence would not have stopped the fateful ball. Thus, the cricket club asserts, it would be clearly wrong to hold it liable for Paula's death, since its *negligence* did not cause the accident.

Which perspective will dominate—treating the unbuilt fence as a single unit or breaking it down into its component parts? This precaution-bundling problem has an important structural feature that connects it to the take-it-or-leave-it offers we saw earlier in the book: it involves the potential commingling of elements that add value (the first six feet) with those that subtract value (the last two feet). Should the plaintiff be allowed to graft the part of the fence that would have been worthwhile to build (the first six feet) to the unworthwhile increment that would have stopped the accident (the last two feet)? Or should the defendant be permitted to break these two components apart so it can benefit from an efficiency analysis that it chose to ignore when it built no fence at all? The answer ultimately depends on the specific architecture and purpose of negligence liability, but it cannot be derived without first recognizing the role of aggregation.

Strategic bundling and unbundling efforts are not unique to tort law; they can be found in many other legal contexts as well. This chapter will examine the structure of these problems and show how they crop up in other areas before circling back to the cricket field. Spoiler alert: the cricket club should lose this one!

Grading and Mixing

A brief detour into the history of grain markets in Chicago offers a useful metaphor for some of law's bundling dilemmas. As recounted by William Cronon in *Nature's Metropolis*, the Chicago Board of Trade began to address the problem of dirty, low-quality, and adulterated grain shipments in 1857 by establishing a formal grading system for wheat and other grains, which was then refined over the next few years.[3] Heterogeneity *within* grades, however, presented a problematic opportunity: the operator of a grain elevator could mix together grain from a higher grade with grain from a lower grade and sell the entire batch as higher grade.[4] The "extra" goodness of the better wheat within the higher grade—the amount by which it surpassed the minimum level required for its grade—could absorb some of the inadequacies of wheat brought in from a lower grade when the two were mixed, so that the mixture's average would remain above the bar for the higher category.

Aggregation made this strategy work; if each individual piece of grain could be graded separately, the problem could not occur. But because quantities of grain were graded collectively, only the average quality of the batch mattered. Lower-quality grains could effectively free ride on what might be viewed as a form of excess capacity in the quality dimension—the gaps between the grade minimum and the grain that exceeded that level. The practice was viewed with opprobrium, presumably because it allocated gains to players who gamed the system at the expense of other market participants. As Cronon explains:

What made [grade] mixing particularly objectionable was the uniquely powerful position of elevator operators, who could earn large sums of money by manipulating the physical partitions between grain bins so as to profit from the conceptual partitions between grain grades. By mixing grain to bring it as close as possible to the lower boundary of a grade, elevators could capture the hidden value of intragrade variation for themselves, an act that seemed both dishonest and unfair.[5]

But the basic move of mixing more and less favorable elements together is hardly unusual, and it can take more benign forms. Yoram Barzel noted a different problem with heterogeneity among identically priced goods: if the price of apples, for example, is set without regard to minor quality variations, people will pick over the supply to try to get the best deals.[6] A store might address the issue by bundling sets of apples at random and forcing customers to an all-or-nothing choice. The solution isn't perfect: the bundles may require people to buy a larger quantity of apples than they would prefer, and some customers will lose increments of surplus as a result. Yet bundling can add value for consumers as a whole if it keeps people from wasting a lot of time picking through apples in the supermarket.[7] It also delivers consistent value to all customers, whether or not they are lucky enough to arrive right after a new produce shipment. It may even prevent some sharp elbows at the produce bin.

Concerns about picking and choosing also supported the demarcation of land into rectangular parcels by government survey, an approach championed by Thomas Jefferson and carried out in much of the US.[8] As Gary Libecap and Dean Lueck explain, one advantage attributed to the rectangular system was that it "would prevent gaps and gores, making the buyer take the good land with the bad" rather than allowing owners to "gerrymander the claim" in ways that would leave behind unclaimed pieces of poor land, as occurred under the metes and bounds system.[9] Making the land lumpier made it more valuable for owners as a whole. The different normative reactions that such cases elicit compared with grain mixing suggests that good-with-bad bundling cannot be evaluated in the abstract, but requires considering the incentives that the bundling creates as well as its distributive effects. The same is true when we turn to contexts where law does the bundling itself or makes judgments about the bundles that private parties create.

As the examples above show, bundles are often constructed in response to thresholds or discontinuities—whether in the background rules of the game or in the reservation prices of consumers. In the grain context, the grades defined the operative thresholds, and elevator operators bundled in an effort to put as much grain as possible over a given grade line. In the supermarket, the threshold is a consumer's willingness to pay for apples, and bundles must be designed to make it over that line for enough customers. For land, the package as a whole must be attractive enough to attract landowners—and here, the reciprocal benefits of standardized parcels may help to boost the bottom line. In the cricket fence context, the threshold that motivates the bundling is a negligence standard that compares the costs and benefits of untaken precautions. In other contexts, the threshold might be set by a methodology like cost-benefit analysis, or by the willingness of a decision-making body to pass legislation or approve regulations.

Bundling matters in all of these cases precisely because it can produce different outcomes than applying a given threshold item by item or increment by increment. Yet increment-by-increment decision making—marginal analysis—is a foundational principle of economics, and one that might seem to cast doubt on legal bundling. The next section explains.

Bundling and Marginal Analysis

One of the most basic lessons of economics is that analysis must be conducted "at the margin."[10] Whether you are deciding how high to build a fence, how many widgets to make, or how many cookies to eat, a surefire way to get the wrong answer is to continue building, manufacturing, or eating until your *total* costs begin to outweigh your *total* benefits. That stopping point will be much too late in any situation where marginal costs are rising, marginal benefits are falling, or both. Under these conditions, which are highly typical, the first units in the sequence will have a much more favorable ratio of benefits to costs than the later units in the sequence. In making decisions about each subsequent unit, what matters is whether the benefits *of that unit* outweigh the costs *of that unit*. As soon as the answer stops being yes, it's time to immediately stop adding units.

Continuing beyond that point will mean adding units that are more costly than beneficial, even though it may take some time for the deficits that they introduce to eat away the surplus of benefits over costs associated with the earlier units and bring the total cost-benefit ratio into the red. Thus, if a cost-benefit analysis requires only that *total* benefits for a given regulation exceed *total* costs, this leaves lawmakers room to go beyond the optimal point and include elements that subtract value at the margin.

Bundling and Line Drawing

Suppose that the EPA is deciding which asbestos-containing products to ban and which ones to permit.[11] The products vary both in how hazardous they are and how useful they are, relative to other available alternatives. Suppose they can be listed on a schedule based on their overall cost-benefit ratio, taking into account the potential substitutes (and *their* dangers). At the top of the list is the product that is least useful relative to its dangers— perhaps something like asbestos-based artificial snow, which was at one time used for seasonal decorations and movie special effects but has been replaced by safer substitutes. As we move down the list, the products become more useful, less hazardous, or both—asbestos-flocked ceiling insulation; asbestos-based tiles; asbestos brake liners, pipes, roofing, and so on. At the bottom of the list are products so useful relative to the harms they cause that the costs of banning them would exceed the benefits.

Imagine an agency regulator has to draw a line somewhere in this list to indicate which products will be allowed and which will be banned. Marginal analysis suggests that she should draw the line underneath the last product of which it can be said that its hazards are excessive relative to its value (thus, the benefits of the ban outweigh its costs). But if she follows a rule of continuing down the list until the total costs of the asbestos regulation *as a whole* start to outweigh its benefits, she may keep on going well past this point. Here we return again to the question of the appropriate unit of analysis. If the ban *for each product* must be separately justified on a cost-benefit analysis, then we get the line in the right place, at least if we assume that the product level is the right unit of analysis. But is it? Perhaps there are subproducts that have slightly different characteristics and different cost-benefit ratios—should marginal analysis be applied to each of them as well?

In the background lurks another question: why assume that the binary ban/allow decision is the right one? If the ban is broken down into different degrees of restriction, each of which have to be justified for each subproduct based on marginal analysis, we will get yet different answers. Economies of scale or similar factors that make regulation easier to produce or enforce in particular chunks can inform the conceptually best way to frame the unit of analysis. Is a ban easier to administer than a restriction, for example? Is it more cost effective to restrict all varieties of one product line rather than draw fine distinctions among them? The malleability of such considerations leaves room for strategizing. As Jennifer Nou and Edward

Stiglitz observe, "a strategic agency could . . . bundle a rule with high benefits and low costs with other rules it wishes to pursue that, standing alone, would not meet a cost-benefit criterion."[12] Other pressures push agencies in the direction of "tactical splitting," as Nou and Stiglitz also detail.[13]

Administrative agencies do face some constraints on their ability to craft regulatory bundles. In *Corrosion Proof Fittings v. EPA*, the US Court of Appeals for the Fifth Circuit vacated the EPA's proposed asbestos regulation, in part for failing to consider alternatives that would be less burdensome than completely banning a wide array of asbestos-containing products.[14] Likewise, OSHA's revised Air Contaminants Standard, which set forth exposure limits for 428 substances, was vacated by an Eleventh Circuit decision, *AFL-CIO v. OSHA*, on the grounds that it "lumped together substances and affected industries and provided such inadequate explanation that it is virtually impossible for a reviewing court to determine if sufficient evidence supports the agency's conclusions."[15] For example, the court pointed out that the agency "did not cite any studies whatsoever for its aluminum welding fumes standard, or its vegetable oil mist standard."[16] Although the agency's lumping in *AFL-CIO* appears to have been motivated primarily by a desire to quickly update a large number of standards in a single rule-making procedure, the court was concerned that some of the standards could not have withstood scrutiny if considered alone.[17]

Nonetheless, lawmakers and regulators often have considerable discretion to lump and split.[18] Nou and Stiglitz's work probes how and why agencies bundle and unbundle regulations.[19] Legislation, too, can draw within its compass elements that might not hold up if considered in isolation. In upholding zoning classifications against a facial challenge in *Village of Euclid v. Ambler Realty*, for example, the Supreme Court explained that laws will not be invalidated simply because prohibitions "include individual cases that may turn out to be innocuous in themselves" given the need for "a reasonable margin to ensure effective enforcement" and the reality that "in some fields, the bad fades into the good by such insensible degrees that the two are not capable of being readily distinguished and separated in terms of legislation."[20]

Legislative strategies like logrolling also involve strategically packaging together favorable and unfavorable elements into a single up-down choice.[21] The potential to exploit this opportunity has led most states to enact single-subject restrictions—a move that predictably generates debate about the bounds of a "single subject."[22] Yet although restrictions on subject matter limit the domain of bundling, they do not really address the foundational issue: *any* package compiled for an up-down decision may contain negative-value components, whether on the same subject or a different one.

In any event, bundling may be necessary to get legislation through the political process. For example, Senator Robert La Follette and then-Representative Mike Monroney commented on the virtues of package assembly in the context of the Legislative Reorganization Act of 1946: Monroney suggested that passage was accomplished in part by pairing "ice cream" provisions, like increased pay, with "spinach" changes to committee organization.[23] Likewise, "grandfathering" provisions may be essential to gathering the political will to protect common-pool resources. This can make reform lumpier: it becomes possible only by including all the bundled components, including some that may be inefficient on their own.[24]

Reconsidering Production Functions

The stylized asbestos example above assumed diminishing marginal returns to increments of reform, with each product ban on the list appearing less worthwhile than the one before. The same was true of the cricket fence: the last two feet had a less favorable cost-benefit ratio than the first six. Diminishing returns like these present the classic scenario for applying marginal analysis. But as this book has emphasized throughout, sometimes marginal returns *don't* diminish but rather increase, perhaps in a dramatic all-at-once fashion, as more inputs are added. This lumpiness lurks behind some instances of judicial deference to legislative judgments.

In *Berman v. Parker*, for example, the Supreme Court rejected a landowner's challenge to an exercise of eminent domain aimed at redeveloping a "blighted" area. Even though the challenger's store was concededly not itself blighted, the Court upheld the legislative choice to redevelop the area as a whole rather than on a "piecemeal" or "structure-by-structure" basis.[25] The condemnation's scope was seemingly premised on the idea that redeveloping the entire area would bring lumpy or discontinuous gains—a premise that could justify including nonblighted properties that would not be good candidates for condemnation on their own.

Increasing returns to scale exist in many other contexts as well. If increasing funding to a low-performing school district does no good until a critical threshold is surpassed, but then brings substantial gains, evaluating the effects of just the first few funding increments would lead to the wrong conclusion. Conversely, *removing* an increment of funding may carry disproportionately large (or small) consequences, depending on the production function for translating inputs into regulatory outputs.[26] Thus, a too-narrow framing of the unit of analysis can miss cumulative effects, where additional doses of reform make the earlier doses more potent.

The shape of the production function may not always be evident at first. Consider the Moving to Opportunity studies mentioned in chapter 9, which tracked outcomes for families who received housing vouchers to move to lower-poverty neighborhoods.[27] The initial results were disappointing. Despite improvements in some areas, such as mental health, the hoped-for gains in earnings and employment did not materialize. Most observers were ready to conclude that changing the neighborhood environment was simply not a worthwhile policy intervention.[28] But as more time passed, researchers could examine the long-term outcomes of children who were younger at the time of the move, and who had therefore experienced longer periods of exposure to the lower-poverty neighborhood. This group, unlike the earlier cohort, showed significant gains, including increased earnings and higher college attendance rates.[29] Where a smaller temporal bundle failed, a larger temporal bundle succeeded—but it took many years to find that out.

Judicial deference to regulatory and legislative line drawing may reflect a sensitivity to indivisibilities or economies of scale that make it important to tackle some problems in a unified, blanket, or long-term way—judgments that are typically the domain of legislators or regulators. Yet by leaving line drawing up to the political branches, policy components that are inefficient or disadvantageous at the margin may be allowed to cannibalize some of the surplus from the components that are worthwhile. The larger the excess of benefits over costs for the worthwhile increments, the larger the flaws of the unworthwhile increments may be without sinking the overall package. Large and discrete unfavorable add-ons may become targets of challenge or of legislative amendment, but many value-draining measures may fly under the radar.

How much should we worry about these forms of bundling? In the legislative or administrative realm, errors may involve doing too much or doing too little about a given problem. If we think that inaction or insufficient action is systematically punished less severely than excessive action, that could provide a reason to accept bundling that embeds some inefficient increments.[30] The best defense against such a stratagem is to move the law as close as possible to the optimum point. That way, no surplus is left on the table in the form of untaken worthwhile reforms that would provide cover for bundled worthless elements. For the same reason, we might expect optimal laws to be more durable than enactments that overreach. If a law overreaches, an opponent could later show gains from eliminating its unworthwhile components—and could also bundle in the elimination of some of its worthwhile elements. If a law achieves optimality, however, there will be no room to gain from scaling it back.

Even so, the potential for strategic behavior remains. Moving the policy baseline forward through partial reforms may effectively constrain the size of the next available change that would satisfy a cost-benefit analysis—especially if the steps in which regulators must move are inherently chunky.[31] Thus, incremental moves might in some cases stymie rather than catalyze further moves.[32] Here, as elsewhere, manipulating the unit of analysis—unifying or subdividing moves—can expand or contract the opportunities for others to act.

Lumps of Precaution

Let us return now to the cricket field, where the principle of marginal analysis offers a starting point for assessing our fence issue. If negligence means failing to take increments of precaution that would have been worth their cost in reducing accidents, then determining liability might seem to boil down to the following two-step procedure: (1) identify the point beyond which adding fence height costs more in labor and lumber than it saves in accident costs—that is, the optimal fence height; and (2) see if the defendant's failure to build a fence of that height caused the accident. In our example, the optimal fence would have been just six feet tall. The cricket club built no fence at all, but the ball that hit Paula flew out of the field at a height of seven feet ten inches. So even if the cricket club had done exactly what it should have—build a six-foot fence—Paula's accident still would have happened. This analysis might seem to give a clear win to the cricket club if the jurisdiction applies a negligence rule. After all, the club's *negligence* did not cause the accident.[33]

The fact that an accident-stopping eight-foot fence would have produced total benefits greater than total costs seems like a red herring, since the last two feet would have reduced rather than added to the fence's net benefits. The neatly stacked fence heights with known costs and projectile-stopping properties enable us to partition the defendant's untaken precaution—the failure to build any fence at all—into two parts: a negligent omission (failing to construct the first six feet) and an efficient omission (failing to build beyond six feet). Because the forensic evidence can pinpoint the height of the exiting ball with certainty, we can immediately see that it was merely the cricket club's efficient omission, and not its negligent omission, that was responsible for the accident. The correct result would seem to be no liability.

But not so fast. The fact that six feet rather than eight feet is the correct stopping point for the cricket club's fence does not, on its own, tell us what the legal response should be to a cricket club that never started building a fence at all. Answering that question requires careful attention to the incentives we are trying to create. Put differently, it is not self-evident that the cricket club is entitled to partition its efficient omission from its negligent omission, when it did not undertake that segmenting work itself by actually building the optimal fence. The fact that the cricket club could not be held liable if its only omission were an efficient one (not building above six feet) does not necessarily mean it should be off the hook when it has commingled that efficient omission with a negligent one (by building no fence at all). The two omissions might instead be lumped together as a unified failing capable of producing liability, at least under some circumstances.

If that possibility sounds odd or unfair, consider some other legal contexts where we take exactly that unifying move for granted—drunk driving, for example. A single sip of beer may separate the driver who is just over the legal limit from the driver who is just below that line. But the over-the-limit driver cannot demand that her legal exposure be limited to the marginal effects attributable to that single sip. Had she actually stayed under the line, she would have been in the clear. But having crossed it, her intoxication is treated (without comment) as an indivisible unit, one that she is not entitled to partition into its "below the limit" and "above the limit" subparts. Indeed, when we think intuitively about what a drunk driver did wrong, we come up with an answer like "downing three drinks in rapid succession and then getting behind the wheel" not "taking one last tiny sip." Here, we might see the legal limit as marking out a safe harbor that a driver can only claim if she actually stays within it, rather than evidence of a societal judgment that people should never be held accountable for increments of harm caused by blood alcohol levels below that limit. Having crossed the line, the driver forfeits the protective benefits that her below-the-line conduct would otherwise have enjoyed.[34]

Regulatory takings law seems to operate similarly. The government can regulate in many ways that negatively impact the value of private property without having to pay compensation to the owner, but if it goes "too far" under the applicable doctrinal tests, it has committed a taking and must pay just compensation. As in the drunk driving context, we can imagine a line that the government might or might not cross. Until it crosses the line, no compensation is due. If it does cross the line, however, it must pay just compensation for all that it has taken, not just the too-far increment. Just as the drunk driver's intoxication is treated as an indivisible unit that she is not entitled to partition into above- and below-limit segments, the government's act of committing a regulatory taking may be regarded as a unitary event that the government cannot partition into its not-too-far and too-far components.

The results can be stark, especially when considered in light of the *Lucas* total taking rule discussed in the previous chapter. Justice Scalia, writing for the majority in *Lucas*, conceded that the doctrine could at times generate an "all-or-nothing" result in which "the landowner with 95% loss will get nothing, while the landowner with total loss will recover in full."[35] There is more than one way to break down that cliff. One approach, most prominently associated with the work of Richard Epstein, would be to "continuize" takings law so that all diminutions in value require appropriately scaled compensation.[36] Alternatively, some commentators have proposed takings valuation approaches that would effectively isolate just the "too far" portion for compensation.[37] The all-or-nothing effect is already softened in cases where preexisting or potential land use regulations (i.e., constraints that reduce value without requiring compensation) help define the baseline against which takings compensation will be assessed.[38]

We may tolerate or even embrace cliff effects in some areas of law. A key reason is to provide appropriate levels of deterrence. If a drinking driver knew that the consequences of going a little bit over the line would be limited to the incremental societal harm on the far side of the line, she might not try very hard to stay under the limit. A regulatory takings doctrine that requires compensation only for the over-the-line increment would be open to a similar criticism: If the government pays nothing until it goes too far, and then only pays for the too-far increment, it will err on the side of "too far" every time, since it internalizes no benefit from going less far (it pays zero, no matter how close to the too-far line it may be, as long as it does not go over).[39] The same might be said of potential injurers who are deciding which precautions to take. The incentive to take due care will be sharper if failing to do so means not only risking the harms that come from the negligent omission, but also giving up the law's protection against liability relating to efficient omissions.

There are, however, significant social costs to injurers overshooting as well as undershooting due care. It is socially costly for people to be careless, but it is also socially costly for people to be too careful.[40] This is why we do not have speed limits set at three miles per hour, require cars to be built like tanks, or mandate the wearing of body armor at all times.[41]

Thus, to use a dichotomy employed by Robert Cooter, the law may wish to charge accurate "prices" for negligent behavior rather than apply punitive "sanctions."[42] To hold an injurer like the cricket club liable for *everything* that happens when it has been negligent—not just the escaping ball that struck Paula, but also freak accidents involving balls that exit the field at a height no feasible fence could possibly stop—can visit extraordinarily harsh punishment on those who have fallen just a little bit short. Not only might this seem unfair, it could induce people to take excessive precautions if they are uncertain exactly where the line between negligent and non-negligent conduct falls, or if they fear errors by courts.

Yet even if the goal is to set prices for conduct that exactly match the social harm that the actor creates, these prices still must be set appropriately. As Mark Grady has carefully demonstrated and as I have elaborated in other work, both a system that holds negligent injurers liable for all the harm they cause (whether or not it is caused by the actor's negligence) *and* a system that limits liability to the marginal effects of the negligence will misprice conduct and distort incentives.[43] Grady's analysis makes the case for an intermediate approach that would impose liability on a negligent defendant only if the plaintiff can identify an untaken precaution that satisfies two criteria: (1) it would have prevented the accident; and (2) considered as a unit, the precaution's benefits in accident reduction exceed its costs. In short, the precaution as a whole must be both causally effective and cost effective. Under such a regime, liability would follow in the hypothetical that began this chapter, where the club constructed no fence at all, the ball sailed out at just under eight feet, and the eight foot fence, taken as a whole, would have been cost justified. But a pedestrian brained by a ball exiting the field at a height of thirty feet would have no claim, because a thirty-foot fence would not be worth its cost, even when compared with nothing at all.

Significantly, this "unified untaken precaution" (UUP) approach, as I term it, evaluates precautions in the lumps that the plaintiff presents them and does not allow a defendant to, say, disaggregate an unbuilt tall fence into shorter increments of fencing for segment-by-segment marginal evaluation. Although the fence example involves the unifying of physical segments for evaluation, the same point applies to other kinds of untaken half-measures that the defendant might argue would have been sufficient to meet its duty of due care. For example, if a particular gauge of safety netting would have been worth its cost in accident reductions, the defendant cannot counter with a claim that a less robust version of the netting would have met the due care standard and would have not stopped the accident—

unless, of course, the defendant had actually installed the less robust type of netting.

There are important incentive effects associated with this approach, which have been discussed in detail elsewhere.[44] The intuitive point is that defendants who are trying to decide whether to err on the side of taking too much care or too little care will be inclined to take too little care if they get a free pass for everything that due care would not have prevented. Conversely, defendants may be inclined to take too much care if they are on the hook for everything that happens as a result of their conduct even if no feasible amount of precaution could have prevented it. Grady's intermediate solution makes those two kinds of errors look equally costly to defendants, at least under certain assumptions, so that they do their best to dead-center their conduct on due care.

The better defendants do at that task, the lower their potential exposure will be under the UUP approach. This follows from the requirement that the plaintiff show that the benefits of the untaken precaution (considered as a unit) exceed its costs. That showing will only be possible if the defendant fell short of the optimal level of precaution. Suppose that the cricket club had constructed the optimal six-foot fence. In that case, there would have been no way that a plaintiff could identify an untaken precaution that would have been cost justified and also would have stopped the ball in question since it simply wasn't worth building above six feet. The no-fence club in our original example was vulnerable to the showing that Paula's estate made, because the excess of benefits over costs in the first six feet of (unbuilt) fencing effectively granted some additional "running room" to add unworthwhile elements before costs would begin to exceed benefits. By failing to construct any fence at all, the cricket club leaves itself open to the lumpy precaution that fits into the gap created by its own shortfall.

The smaller the shortfall, the smaller that gap will be, and the harder it will be for a plaintiff to identify an untaken precaution that meets the two requirements of causal effectiveness and cost effectiveness. Thus, a cricket club that constructed a five-foot fence might very well win against Paula's estate, because it would not be possible to show that adding three more feet of fencing would be cost justified, even when all three feet were treated as a unit. The opportunities open to a plaintiff under this approach are very much like the opportunities that a legislator or regulator has to bundle some very valuable reforms with some negative-value ones and sell the whole package as an improvement. In both cases, the fewer the increments of valuable work left undone, the fewer the opportunities one leaves open for a counterparty to smuggle in unworthwhile elements along with the worthwhile ones.

The UUP standard is also easy for courts to administer. There is no need to calculate the exact location of the due care line in the abstract—an enterprise that is generally impossible.[45] Instead, a court can simply look at whether an untaken precaution exists that would have stopped this accident and that is also cost effective on the whole.[46] Consistent with this point, we might understand due care as a step good that, like a bridge, generates certain societal benefits when (and only when) it is provided by defendants in full. These benefits, which include reduced information costs, entitle nonnegligent defendants to a safe harbor from liability for efficient accidents.[47] Because defendants who fall short need not be extended this same immunity, tort law is free to shape their liability in the ways that best achieve its objectives.

The UUP approach raises another question, however. What kinds of untaken precautionary steps can be unified together as a single "precaution" for purposes of making the necessary UUP showings?[48] As the fence example shows, the UUP binds together two untaken increments: a cost-justified increment that is not causally connected to the accident (first six feet) and a marginally unjustified increment that is causally connected to the accident (last two feet). Surely a plaintiff cannot meld a completely unrelated failing of the cricket club (like its failure to maintain the brakes on the club car) together with an inefficient precaution that would have stopped the plaintiff's accident (such as a much higher fence) to meet the twin criteria of causal effectiveness and cost effectiveness. But what is the limiting principle?

As a first cut, we might look for indicia of natural unity. The inability to articulate a cognizable single precaution that incorporates both components would rule out combinations like the bad brakes and the ultra-tall fence. But we have come too far in the book to suppose that a search for natural unity will always yield clear answers. Information costs suggest another way of gaining traction on the question. We might look for instances in which the untaken precautionary steps are so closely related that it would typically be difficult or costly to disentangle which subset was responsible for the accident. Treating these entwined untaken steps as a unified precaution economizes on information costs and underscores the information function that is performed when an actor takes due care. Once the efficient steps have actually been taken, it is no longer difficult to tell whether they were sufficient to prevent the accident.

Risky Bundles

The cricket fence example was atypical in that it permitted certainty about whether a given accident would have been prevented by a fence of a given height. In many scenarios, by contrast, we know only that a given accident would have been prevented with some probability if the actor were not negligent. To use one of Robert Cooter and Ariel Porat's examples, suppose that the negligent heating of a vat used to make hot chocolate can cause a valve to crack and cause harm.[49] But the valve would crack a certain amount of the time even when heated nonnegligently. Figuring out what to do about such cases involves another form of aggregation, one that asks what set of accidents—or potential accidents—should be held in mind when assessing liability.

Scenario Bundling

To start, it is important to see the implicit scenario bundling that underlies much of tort analysis. First, think of precautions that are durable, such as equipping a boat with a piece of safety equipment such as a life buoy.[50] These precautions are temporally lumpy (they last a relatively long time, at least compared to human actions that must be repeated again and again) and indivisible (they are entirely present or entirely absent and cannot be scaled up or down in response to external circumstances).[51] Because of these characteristics, the calculation that determines whether it would be negligent to omit a given piece of safety equipment is based on a bundle of all of the scenarios that will unfold while the precaution is in place. For example, the preventative measure of putting a life buoy on a boat before it goes out to sea cannot be altered during the boat's journey depending on conditions that later develop.[52] The buoy on board in calm, predator-free waters is bundled with the buoy on board in stormy, shark-infested waters.[53]

This bundling carries interesting implications. For one thing, it means that the buoy may be required by a Hand formula analysis based on the conditions in which it is very likely to help (calm, predator-free waters) even though there are other conditions in which it is unlikely to do any good (stormy, shark-filled waters). If it were feasible to conjure up the life buoy selectively, and prorate its cost accordingly, it might turn out to be cost justified only some of the time. On this account, the life buoy is a bit like an eight-foot cricket fence that *cannot* be constructed at any lower height.

The portions of the precautionary technology with a favorable cost-benefit profile (the first six feet of the cricket fence or the buoy on smooth shark-less waters) are bundled together with portions that would have an unfavorable cost-benefit profile if considered on their own (the last two feet of cricket fence or the buoy on board when swells are high and sharks circle).

Here we see how better technologies for customizing the availability of certain precautions might bring advantages, though not without removing some of the incidental benefits that accrue when durable precautions are more continually present. Imagine for a moment a fanciful "Uber for life buoys" that can deliver a life buoy (via hypersonic drone) exactly when it is likely to be most useful but reallocates it to other ships when the circumstances are such that it would not do any good. This would be an improvement in targeting the precaution to its most cost-effective uses, but could have unacceptable distributive or expressive implications (imagine the life buoy is whisked away just as the storm begins to threaten the lives of a crew of bad swimmers, based on the low probability that it would be capable of saving their lives). Put differently, there are facets of lumpiness here as in other contexts that we take for granted and benefit from, even if greater efficiency could be achieved from a more surgical slicing of precautions and states of the world.

This is not to suggest that scenario bundling always produces excessive levels of precaution. The flip side of the point above is that there may be precautions that would do a great deal of good in certain (relatively rare) states of the world, but they are not cost justified on a Hand formula analysis. This is because it is impossible to supply them *only* in the states of the world for which they are highly efficacious without also having them around in the many other states of the world in which they are not cost justified. Again, if it were possible to conjure up the precaution only in the useful states of the world, at a prorated price, this would clearly be required on a Hand formula analysis—but because it is not, the precaution can be omitted without negligence liability.

For instance, think of a self-driving car that is very reliable in avoiding errors (much better than a human driver) but on rare occasions makes mistakes that cause accidents. One way to keep these accidents from occurring would be to always have a licensed driver available to override the machine's reactions. Although it might be clear that the driver would be worthwhile if she could be present only at those critical points of failure, it might be much less clear whether her full-time presence is cost justified. And even if it is cost justified today, when large proportions of the adult population know how to drive, will it be cost justified in a few decades when (presumably) a far smaller proportion will possess that skill?

The lumpiness of precautions and the implicit bundling of scenarios also limits the ability of potential victims to strike deals that would personalize or tailor the precautionary efforts of the potential injurers with whom they interact. Suppose some passengers on a boat or airplane would like to forgo certain safety equipment in exchange for a lower ticket price. This is not possible if the boat or plane must be equipped or not equipped; it cannot be equipped for some and not for others. Jennifer Arlen makes this point in the context of medical malpractice. In theory, it might seem possible to allow individual patients to contract with health care providers over liability arrangements, so that they could execute a liability waiver in exchange for a lower-cost procedure.[54] But Arlen points out that inputs into medical care tend to be lumpy (investments in equipment, training, and so on), so that it is not possible for health care providers to selectively scale back their precaution levels in light of particular patients' waivers.[55] As a result, Arlen argues, precaution levels represent a kind of public good, with attendant concerns about free riding.[56]

Bundling Uncertainty

The lumpiness and implicit scenario bundling associated with durable precautions has another set of implications that relate to problems of uncertain causation. Consider again the case of the life buoy on board. Suppose that a case comes to trial in which the life buoy was absent, which was clearly negligent, but the accident scenario involved a weak swimmer who fell into stormy, shark-filled waters and sank instantly from view; all the evidence suggested that a life buoy would have done no good.[57] Should we be concerned about letting the defendant boat operator off the hook here? Perhaps not. As Grady points out, failing to supply the buoy still generates a real risk of liability since its absence under better conditions is very likely to make a difference. The inability of the defendant to choose precautions separately in the two states of the world helps to preserve appropriate incentives.[58] The boat owner might be let off the hook this time, but he cannot be persistently negligent without serious consequences.

But suppose we imagine a boat, *The Dangercraft*, that only plies stormy, sharky waters while perpetually carrying a crew of terrible swimmers.[59] It is possible that failing to provide a life buoy on such a boat is not actually Hand-formula negligent at all, since death is so likely for a person who falls overboard, regardless of flotation devices. Let us assume, however, that the buoy is so inexpensive and occasionally so effective that it is negligent not to include it. Yet in any given instance, it is overwhelmingly likely that a man overboard from *The Dangercraft* would have died anyway, whether the life buoy were present or absent. If tort law's usual more-likely-than-not standard ("preponderance of the evidence") is used to determine liability, the operator of *The Dangercraft* will never be called to account for its negligence in failing to provide a life buoy on board. This presents a problem that Saul Levmore has termed "recurring misses."[60] If the bundle of scenarios associated with an untaken precaution does not contain sufficient instances in which a defendant will be charged for her negligence, she will not be sufficiently deterred from being negligent.[61]

The Dangercraft may seem fanciful, but there are more realistic contexts in which recurring misses may be troublesome. Consider medical subfields in which patients face high background risks of dying even if their doctors do everything exactly right. A doctor who is negligent in this context will never be the more-likely-than-not cause of a patient's death, yet her negligence may indeed make the difference between life and death in, say, 10 percent of cases. Tort law has evolved some ways to address this well-recognized problem, such as allowing for recovery of "loss of a chance" or providing a probabilistic partial recovery.[62] But these approaches fit uneasily with a tort system that is premised on matching up wrongs and recoveries on a one-to-one basis.

An alternative would take us back to the analogy of thresholding in image manipulation that was introduced in the previous chapter—the process of translating a continuous variable (grayscale shading), pixel by pixel, into the binary of black and white.[63] A globally applied threshold will produce unacceptable results where, for example, light or shadow falls across a portion of the image, making all pixels in a given region darker or lighter than the threshold that works best elsewhere in the image.[64] The key to successfully picking out foreground from background is to see which pixels are *local* standouts—hence, thresholding methods examine pixel neighborhoods to determine the appropriate local threshold.[65] Translated into the tort realm, this would suggest lowering the liability threshold in contexts with high background risk to pick out those instances that were most likely to have been caused by the injurer's negligence.

Here, instead of tort law's more-likely-than-not inquiry, we might ask a slightly different question: Is the strength of the causal connection between the harm and the defendant in the case before the court stronger or weaker *than the average causal connection* between defendants engaged in this type of activity and harms of this type? To return to *The Dangercraft*, we would ask not whether it is more likely than not that the missing buoy caused an overboard sailor's death, but rather whether *this* overboard sailor's death was more likely to have been caused by the missing life buoy than the *typical* overboard sailor's death occurring under the dangerous conditions in which the boat regularly operates. If we are trying to match up defendants who cause harm with the harm that they cause, it is the *relative* strength of the causal connection, and not its absolute strength, that should matter.

Likewise, in the medical malpractice context we would want to identify the harms that were the most likely ones, among those occurring in a particular specialized high-risk setting, to have been caused by a doctor's error. That might be done by lowering the liability threshold to something close to the *average* causal connection between a doctor's negligence and negative medical outcomes in that subfield. If a doctor's negligence would, if repeated, cause death in twenty cases out of one hundred, a court might ask whether in the case before it the causal connection between negligence and harm exceeds the baseline causal connection of 20 percent (or, perhaps, exceeds that baseline by some particular margin). This corresponds to the intuitive inquiry of whether there will be better opportunities than this one to hold the defendant to account for her risk-generating behavior.[66] Just as the thresholds for converting grayscale pixels to black and white need to be adjusted within portions of an image to compensate for the effects of light and shadow, the relevant thresholds for assigning liability may require adjustment under certain background risk conditions.

This chapter has illustrated how legal thresholding is sensitive to choices about bundling and packaging—whether of laws, regulations, precautions, or risk. This sensitivity can prompt a great deal of strategic bundling and unbundling. While these efforts often look like illegitimate efforts to game the system, some carry hidden benefits. The possibility that other actors will exploit bundling opportunities can usefully induce parties to act in socially valuable ways—to do their best to select optimal precautions, for example—in order to close those windows of strategic opportunity.

Conclusion

This book has shown that a large set of real-world situations can be better understood if recast in terms of aggregation and division, complementarities and indivisibilities. But we need not accept lumps and slices as we find them. There is room to innovate, invent, recut, and reconfigure—to do our own lumping and slicing. Even where indivisibilities are products of natural phenomena or are constructed by others, we can find ways to respond more intelligently to them. In the spirit of fostering configuration entrepreneurship, this last chapter distills ten broad lessons for policy makers, academics, and individuals. Although these points are stated simply, they are meant to spur serious thought about configuration problems and to encourage habits of mind that can creatively confront the challenges that lumps and slices present.

1. Mind the Lump. The most basic lesson of this book is that many goods and bads do not come about in smoothly increasing increments, but rather in large chunks or steps. Because a linear relationship between inputs and outcomes is often simply assumed without comment in economic analysis, developing a mental habit of asking "what if the effects are nonlinear?" can often transform the conversation. This is true whether the topic is an entrepreneurial effort, a conservation initiative, a charity drive, an educational program, or the allocation of welfare funding.

Sometimes the lumpiness of a given goal is evident to all, but people fail to appreciate how the shape of the production function changes the prospects for cooperation. For example, the Prisoners' Dilemma may be erroneously invoked where lumpy goods are involved, even though its logic does not apply in that context. In other cases, the lumpiness of a given good means that contributions stop making things better (or that negative impacts stop making things worse) beyond a certain point. It is important to have a complete bridge, but it is just as important to know when to stop building. Recognizing both threshold and plateau effects can change how problems are perceived.

Closely related to lumpiness is the idea that improvements may require large leaps rather than steady climbs. Often, it is not possible to get to a better result incrementally, but only through an all-or-nothing shift. Recall the vineyards that can only be successfully changed to residential housing if the shift is total, or the person who is struggling to adopt a new pattern of behavior.[1] Small changes might mean descending the local "hill" of optimality and making things worse rather than better. But if a large leap to a higher peak across the valley can be made all at once, matters might be made much better. Minding the lump can mean making the leap.

2. Survey the Structure. Whether a problem involves dividing a resource into pieces or assembling a fragmented resource, what really must be assembled is cooperation from those who have control over the resource. The same is true when collective goals are at issue. How easy or hard it will be to assemble the necessary cooperation depends on production functions, participation requirements, and payoff structures. Identifying how these components operate in a given context, be it land assembly or radio spectrum, will determine the difficulty of achieving a cooperative solution through private, noncoercive means. In the land assembly context, for example, much turns on the required degree of contiguity among parcels, the specified shape of the overall aggregation, and the degree to which the assembly is tethered to a particular geospatial location—all of which determine the specificity of the participation requirements.

The use of coercion radically changes the structure of assembly and division problems by overriding the lack of consent of some or all parties to the reconfiguration. It also ushers in information problems about whether reconfiguration actually adds value, all things considered. Thus, it is important to separate situations in which private solutions are likely to be possible from those in which the use of coercion is truly essential. Finding ways to expand the first category of cases through innovations in property law that make property holdings more contingent represents an important avenue for research and policy development.

3. Question the Unit. Another key lesson that emerges from this book's analysis is that the units in which goods, services, and conditions arrive are rarely inevitable. Often they are artifacts of past economic pressures or assumptions that have become less compelling as technological conditions have changed. This points to a strategy that many in the slicing economy have already begun to exploit: ask whether there is another way to divide or configure the good or service. Sometimes this means redefining the real object of interest. Cars look lumpy, but transportation is sliceable.

In other cases, units are constructed to serve some doctrinal or political purpose. For example, assessing what counts as "the denominator" for regulatory takings analysis or evaluating untaken precautions in tort law requires making background choices about what belongs together as a unit. Here, questioning the unit of analysis can be an important litigation strategy. Likewise, legislative or regulatory bundles can be engineered in ways that encompass unworthwhile as well as worthwhile elements. Breaking down the bundle can generate different outcomes.

4. Manage the Menu. A recurring theme of the book is the power of menus, which construct the choice sets to which people respond. Although earlier work has identified a variety of psychological effects that menus can produce, my focus here has been on the chunkiness of the choice intervals themselves. The number and placement of these intervals can have powerful effects on behavior, whether we are talking about production levels for a widget factory, housing options, or soft drink sizes at the local convenience store. Recognizing how the granularity of choice interacts with externalities and internalities offers new ways to gain traction on social and intrapersonal problems. In some instances, a chunky choice can push an actor whose behavior has spillovers on others (or on other selves) closer to the social optimum. In other cases, the opposite effect results. Investigating which effect dominates in particular settings and examining how small changes in incentive structures might tip the balance in the other direction represent important and understudied domains for policy research.

Gaps that appear in menus as a result of legal restrictions also deserve special attention. We should ask whether they correspond to meaningful discontinuities in the world or whether they represent missing alternatives that people would otherwise prefer. Sometimes the point of a gap is to creature pressure toward existing nodes by effectively embedding a take-it-or-leave-it (TIOLI) offer—or, more precisely, a lump-it-or-leave-it (LIOLI) offer. Both designers and users of menus should attend to these pressures. People often respond to an overly chunky menu by adjusting other dimensions. Square footage minimums for housing units can trigger adjustments in household size. Step-like price jumps demanded by vending machine technology may be smoothed by changes in the size of candy bars, a continuous variable. And in the criminal law context, the counting problem introduced by a volley of shots in a warehouse can be eased by introducing culpability considerations that make the number of offenses less decisive.[2]

5. Build Better Bundles. The flip side of questioning the units or the menus that others have devised is to build (or seek out) better bundles to achieve one's purposes. Bundling can serve strategic purposes where it effectively operates as a TIOLI (or LIOLI) offer to another party. It can also raise the stakes associated with particular acts, as we saw where rules effectively bundle together different instances of a given behavior. Alternatively, bundles can lower the stakes (and reduce regret or sunk-cost behaviors) by enabling people to derive at least some benefit from the bundled thing. Recognizing how bundles operate as lumpy offers can make policies and negotiations (including intrapersonal ones) more effective.

6. Segment Strategically. Like building better bundles, segmentation is a strategy that can be employed to alter the menus that other people (or other selves) confront. The ability to partition food, money, or other resources can alter the way that choice menus are perceived and help to buttress social norms facilitating informal solutions to commons problems. It is easier to divide a pie that has already been sliced. Segmentation can also help to fortify self-control, both by marking out a (permeable) barrier that requires a conscious act to break through, and by keeping small slips from becoming larger ones. A focus on segmentation can also suggest new alternatives for accessing goods and services, where one's own demand is not sufficient to justify outright ownership.

7. Cut Yourself Some Slack. Much of the analysis in this book has discussed ways to make better use of the excess capacity lurking in lumpy goods. Slicing up things differently can add value, whether we are talking about physical resources or time commitments. Yet as the technology for repurposing slivers of capacity improves, the heretofore hidden virtues of maintaining some slack capacity must also be taken into account. Having some unused capacity serves to create option value as well as reserves for meeting unexpected surges and stresses in many contexts, from work arrangements to industrial capacity to personal scheduling to decisions about how to configure the home.[3] These benefits, which ease the stresses of everyday life and help people absorb various shocks, are largely unrecognized and fortuitous by-products of existing *imprecisions* in resource slicing.

As slicing technologies improve, it becomes increasingly possible to get rid of slack—but this does not mean it is always advisable. Seeing where and how slack creates value can help firms and families avoid the pitfalls of putting every stray resource sliver to work.

8. Start Seeing Standardization. Lumpiness sometimes manifests itself in standardization that limits variety, whether of product sizes, colors of Model Ts, or land tenure forms. Although there may often be good reasons to limit customization, doing so also imposes costs. Law, policy, and markets often create binaries or limited slates of alternatives. As elsewhere, those menu design choices should be open to question—something that only becomes possible once we recognize them *as* choices.

Debates about the *numerus clausus* principle in property law pick up this theme, but questions of standardization range much more broadly. For example, Sonia Katyal has recently explored this topic in the context of sex and gender, where binaries have long prevailed.[4] In a recent novel by Ian McEwan, *Nutshell*, the protagonist (a fetus) draws a connection between Henry Ford's famous anti-customization statement and the sex binary: "Pink or blue—a minimal improvement on Henry Ford's offer of cars of any colour as long as they were black. Only two sexes. I was disappointed."[5] To see standardization, then, is to recognize the possibility of more alternatives. Indeed, McEwan's narrator goes on to note that a "social media site famously proposes seventy-one gender options—neutrois, two spirit, bigender . . . any colour you like, Mr. Ford."[6]

9. Compare Competing Complementarities. Lumpiness often involves complementarities, like those between right and left shoes or among segments of a bridge. Many social dilemmas pit competing complementarities (or alleged complementarities) against each other. Recasting disagreements in these terms can transform debate and keep people from simply talking past each other. For example, there are complementarities associated with residing in the same place over time. But there are also spatial complementarities associated with large-scale development, which can require disrupting the temporal complementarities. Understanding that there are complementarities on both sides of the debate can help to pin down what is really at issue.

To take another example, consider the question of whether property is usefully conceived as a "bundle of sticks" or, equivalently, a "bundle of rights." This conceptualization, associated with the work of the legal realists, and, more recently, the law and economics movement, has come under sustained attack.[7] The reason: calling property a "bundle" implies that there is no irreducible core to property, that it instead consists of nothing more than a loosely assembled and endlessly disaggregable pile of use rights.[8] In other words, the bundle of sticks metaphor seems to neglect complementarities among property rights; it fails to treat the full suite of rights as a coherent, indivisible whole.

But defenders of the bundle approach understand complementarities—they simply disagree about which ones are most important. In a complex society, there are not just complementarities *within* property holdings but also *among* property holdings. In order for certain societal projects and goals to be achieved on a broad scale, individual owners must cede some measure of control—that is, give up some sticks. What property theory needs most, and what a focus on lumpiness can provide, is a way to weigh these two sets of conflicting complementarities against each other. The approaches presented in this book, which include attention to production functions, show how such comparisons might proceed.

10. Identify Interactions. As this book has emphasized, aggregation and division problems exist in virtually every area of law and every domain of life. This makes it important to trace how lumpiness and divisibility in different arenas can impact configuration issues in other arenas or create spillovers for seemingly unrelated decisions. For example, new ways of slicing up jobs or homes may also slice away legal protections or cut apart social arrangements that were built on traditional models. Recognizing interactions helps to identify places where innovative rebundling may be required.

Even the purchase of an ordinary lumpy good can have surprising implications for an individual's consumption of other, more granular goods. Rod Garratt gives the example of a beer drinker who buys *less* beer when the price of beer drops, because doing so enables him to afford a car—a lumpy expenditure—without giving up beer altogether.[9] As lumps break down (it is possible to buy private automobile transportation in thin slices, for instance), consumer activity in seemingly unrelated domains may change in unexpected ways. Preferences for monetary lumps may change too, if money no longer needs to be spent in unified chunks. By the same token, stickiness in one arena may block configuration entrepreneurship in other domains. If apartments or condos adopt a blanket rule against pets, for instance, or require residents to choose between having a parking space all the time or none of the time, innovations like pet sharing and car sharing may be slower to take hold.[10]

Some of the most profound interactions among different forms of aggregation and division can be observed in the city. The city's density (its aggregation of people) creates markets thick enough to support new ways of slicing up resources like transportation and housing. In addition, existing lumps of development in a city influence where other potential assemblies of land uses (and land users) will end up. The same interaction can be seen between development and the fragmentation or aggregation of open space,[11] and of habitats.[12] In all of these interlocking domains, we are concerned not just with how much we have in total, but also how it is configured.

This book's tour of slices and lumps has been far from comprehensive, and the points emphasized in this conclusion illustrate rather than exhaust the lessons one might take away from the study of aggregation and division. The concepts and strategies developed here are general ones, but I hope readers will find ways to refine and adapt them for particular contexts. Lumpiness, as we have seen, operates variously as an impediment and as a lever. Indivisibilities—and prospects of overcoming them or strategically employing them—are everywhere. What this book has aimed to do is make these ubiquitous features of everyday life visible, so that they can be surmounted, countered, harnessed, transformed, or simply better understood.

ACKNOWLEDGMENTS

This book brings together, refines, and extends ideas that I have been working on for many years. I first formulated the book's organizing theme of division and aggregation—slices and lumps—when I was invited by my colleague (then Dean) Saul Levmore to present the 2008 Coase Lecture at the University of Chicago Law School. As I struggled to come up with a topic worthy of the event, I stumbled upon a framing that captivated me. I found that it not only connected up much of my prior thinking but also opened up new questions and avenues for research. The idea for this book has been percolating in the background ever since.

Although my ideas have continued to evolve during this book's long gestation and I have reworked material extensively throughout, pieces of the analysis have made prior appearances in print. Traces of my 2008 Coase Lecture, "Slices and Lumps," can be found throughout the book. Chapters 1 and 11 incorporate portions of "Lumpy Property," *University of Pennsylvania Law Review* 160 (2012): 1955–93. Chapter 2 builds on multiple prior works, including "Common Interest Tragedies," *Northwestern University Law Review* 98 (2004): 907–90, and "Revealing Options," *Harvard Law Review* 118 (2005): 1399–488. Chapters 3 and 4 include material adapted from "Slicing Spontaneity," *Iowa Law Review* 100 (2015): 2365–88. Chapters 5 and 6 build on my prior work on willpower and time preferences and incorporate some material appearing in "Personalizing Precommitment," *University of Chicago Law Review* 86 (2019): 433–57. Chapter 7 includes bits and pieces from "Unbundling Risk," *Duke Law Journal* 60 (2011): 1285–365. Portions of chapter 9 draw on "Property in Housing," *Academia Sinica Law Journal* 12 (2013): 31–78. Chapter 10 incorporates portions of "Agglomerama," *B.Y.U. Law Review* 2014 (2015): 1373–414.

Chapters 11 and 12 incorporate and adapt material from "Accidents and Aggregates," *William & Mary Law Review* 59 (2018): 2371–445.

This book has benefited enormously from the thoughtful input of many people, including my wonderful colleagues at the institutions where I have taught (University of Chicago Law School, University of Illinois College of Law, and University of Texas School of Law) and visited (University of Virginia School of Law, New York University School of Law, and Yale Law School) and at the many other schools where I have been privileged to present my work and discuss my ideas with students and faculty. Although I could never assemble a list long enough to thank everyone I should, I owe special thanks for helpful comments and conversations to Matthew Adler, Ellen Aprill, Douglas Baird, Omri Ben-Shahar, Lynn Blais, Richard Brooks, Yun-chien Chang, James Hines, William Hubbard, Heather Hughes, Tim Iglesias, Leo Katz, Adam Kolber, Saul Levmore, Daniel Markovits, Jonathan Masur, Richard McAdams, Edward McCaffery, Manisha Padi, Ariel Porat, Eric Rasmusen, Daria Roithmayr, Carol Rose, Richard Schragger, Lior Strahilevitz, Thomas Ulen, and David Weisbach. I am also grateful for feedback I received on draft chapters of this book in workshops at American University Washington College of Law, Arizona College of Law, Loyola Law School Los Angeles, Yale Law School, the University of Chicago Law School, and the University of Michigan Law School.

My research at the University of Chicago Law School has been supported by the Harold J. Green Faculty Fund and the SNR Denton Fund and has been greatly advanced by first-rate research assistants. Especially important to the early stages of this work were Catherine Kiwala and Eric Singer (both of the JD class of 2010), Prisca Kim (JD, 2011), and Aaron Benson (JD, 2012). More recently, the manuscript has benefited from the excellent work of Nicole LaBell (JD, 2020), Beth Macnab (JD, 2020), and Victoria Wang (MA Social Science, 2018). I am also grateful for the encouragement of the late Christopher Rhodes of the University of Chicago Press who convinced me to submit a book proposal, as well as for the guidance of my editor, Chuck Myers. My greatest thanks, as always, goes to Christopher Fennell, who has contributed untold slices of time and patience to helping me with this lumpy work.

NOTES

INTRODUCTION

1. This question has received some academic attention. See Das-Friebel et al., "Hypothetical Use of Superpowers"; Tyler Cowen, "The Macroeconomics of Superman," *Marginal Revolution* (blog) June 7, 2006, http://marginalrevolution.com/marginal revolution/2006/06/the_macroeconom.html.
2. In a world without transaction costs, these feats (and others) could be accomplished effortlessly, sans capes. See Coase, "Problem of Social Cost."
3. Taylor and Ward, "Chickens, Whales, and Lumpy Goods," 353.
4. See Gene Sloan, "Silversea Ship Silver Spirit Cut in Half to Make Room for New Midsection," *USA Today*, March 20, 2018.
5. See Sloan.
6. See Frank, *Production Theory*, 117. This is not to suggest that economists have wholly ignored indivisibilities. They haven't: sophisticated treatments of the topic exist. But the economic analysis that features in most legal scholarship generally assumes linear relationships. There are exceptions, of course, some of which will be discussed in this book, but lumpiness remains underappreciated.
7. See, e.g., Frank, 117 (observing that "the tools of algebra and mathematical analysis usually fail to be of much use in analyzing the effects of indivisible commodities"); Bobzin, *Indivisibilities*, 1 ("Even advanced works on microeconomic theory . . . refrain from the consideration of indivisible goods and factors to provide a structure for the analysis where relatively simple mathematical methods can be applied.").
8. See, e.g., Arrow and Hahn, *General Competitive Analysis*, 62.
9. Mas-Colell, "Non-Convexity," 655. The horse and oat example is from Walras, *Elements of Pure Economics*, 95, quoted in Mas-Colell, 655. See also Frank, *Production Theory*, 117.
10. Bobzin, *Indivisibilities*, 2 (footnote omitted).
11. Hannibal, *Spine of the Continent*, xiii.

CHAPTER ONE

1. See Waldfogel, *Tyranny of the Market* (examining how fixed costs limit product availability); Mas-Colell, "Non-Convexity," 656 (describing labor specialization as a response to indivisibilities in learning skills). Indeed, were it not for scale economies,

each of us could "assemble in our own backyards all of the manufactured goods whose services we would like to consume." Scarf, "Allocation of Resources," 114–15.

2. See Coase, "Problem of Social Cost," 15.

3. Wicksteed, *Common Sense*, 97–98.

4. For work analyzing Solomon's decision, see, e.g., Brams and Taylor, *Fair Division*, 6–7 and n2; R. Brooks, "Relative Burden," 282 and nn62–64.

5. See, e.g., Young, *Equity*, 13–14.

6. See, e.g., Benkler, "Sharing Nicely."

7. Recharge, https://recharge.co/; see Michael Liedtke, "App to Book Hotel Rooms by the Minute May Expand to Chicago," *Chicago Sun-Times*, May 9, 2018.

8. See, e.g., Jennifer Jolly, "Online Matchmaking, but with Dogs as Dates," *Well* (blog), *New York Times*, November 12, 2015, https://well.blogs.nytimes.com/2015/11/12/online-matchmaking-but-with-dogs-as-dates/.

9. BorrowMyDoggy.com, https://www.borrowmydoggy.com.

10. See Prabhat, "'Borrow My Doggy.com.'"

11. See Young, "Dividing the Indivisible," 904, 906; see also Frank, *Production Theory*, 32 (giving the example of "an industrial heat exchanger with a two-million-ton capacity," which if split, would comprise "two piles of steel scrap and other debris," not "two heat exchangers with a capacity of a million tons apiece").

12. See Frank, *Production Theory*, 32 (listing four different senses in which a commodity might be considered "indivisible" including "where a given amount of a commodity cannot be physically divided into fractional parts in any meaningful sense").

13. For a helpful discussion of production functions, see Oliver, Marwell, and Teixeira, "Theory of the Critical Mass."

14. See Oliver, Marwell, and Teixeira, 525–28 and fig. 1 (depicting and describing a variety of production functions).

15. See, e.g., Taylor and Ward, "Chickens, Whales, and Lumpy Goods"; R. Hardin, "Group Provision of Step Goods"; Hampton, "Free-Rider Problems."

16. R. Hardin, *Collective Action*, 59.

17. See Hardin, 59–60.

18. Wicksteed, *Common Sense*, 82–83.

19. See, e.g., Hampton, "Free-Rider Problems, 249–50 (discussing "steppy" collective goods, for which contributions in particular increments will add value, and "mixed structure" collective goods, which may require an initially large production step but could then be improved in smaller increments).

20. See Oliver, Marwell, and Teixeira, "Theory of the Critical Mass," 527–28 and fig. 1(a).

21. For graphical representations and analyses of possible land assembly scenarios, see, e.g., McDonald, "What Is Public Use?," 15–19; Fennell, "Taking Eminent Domain Apart," 972–75.

22. Definitions of lumpiness vary in breadth. Compare Hampton, "Free-Rider Problems," 248–50 (equating "lumpy goods" with "pure step goods" and distinguishing both from hybrid forms like multistep and mixed goods) with Levi, *Of Rule and Revenue*, 57–58 (recognizing the possibility of "lumpy goods with sloping risers" that exhibit linearity "after the initial production threshold is crossed").

23. See Oliver, Marwell, and Teixeira, "Theory of the Critical Mass," 525–28; Fennell, "Common Interest Tragedies," 971–78.

24. See Faden, *Economics of Space and Time*, 208, 213.

25. R. Hardin, *Collective Action*, 65–66.

26. See Taylor and Ward, "Chickens, Whales, and Lumpy Goods," 353.
27. Bostedt, "Threatened Species." For discussion and additional examples, see Buchholz, Cornes, and Rübbelke, "Public Goods and Public Bads."
28. Bostedt's analysis is not framed in this way, but it does imply at least one form of lumpiness. Bostedt, "Threatened Species," 61 (citing surveys indicating a widespread preference for the existence of the wolf regardless of its numbers, which would be consistent with a sharp step at the level of species sustainability).
29. Smith, "Law of Things," 1693; see also Fennell, "Lumpy Property."
30. See, e.g., Smith, "Property and Property Rules," 1728, 1754–55 (discussing property as delegation); Smith, "Law of Things," 1711–12 (noting property's "persistence").
31. Such changes may reshape property expectations. See Nash and Stern, "Property Frames," 484.
32. See G. Alexander, "Objects of Art" (using examples from the work of artist Félix González-Torres that evolve with audience participation).
33. Van Inwagen, *Material Beings*, 104.
34. See Van Inwagen, 33–37.
35. Rogers and McAvoy, "Mule Deer Impede Pando's Recovery."
36. Coase, "Nature of the Firm."
37. See Delia Falconer, "The Radical Plan to Split Sydney into Three," *Guardian*, April 10, 2018.
38. See, e.g., Moore, *Act and Crime*, 366, 388; M. Kelman, "Interpretative Construction," 600–20.
39. See chapter 11.
40. See, e.g., Adler, *Well-Being and Fair Distribution*, 405–75; Fennell and Stark, "Taxation over Time." Related philosophical questions surround the durability and cohesiveness of personal identity. See Parfit, *Reasons and Persons*.
41. This feature of nonrival goods enables increasing returns to scale that can fuel exponential economic growth, as more people make use of the good as an input to production. See Romer, "Endogenous Technological Change."
42. Some nonrival goods, like cleaning up a neighborhood or tidying a shared apartment, do not have this lumpy quality, assuming that greater and lesser degrees of cleanliness can be meaningfully enjoyed. See Frohlich and Oppenheimer, "With a Little Help," 109; Lunney, "Discrete Public Goods," 6–16.
43. Thompson, "Lumpy Goods and Cheap Riders," 434.
44. See Conley and Yoo, "Nonrivalry and Price Discrimination," 1804, 1808–9 (observing that all consumers of indivisible creative products consume the same output— the full unit) (citing Samuelson, "Aspects of Public Expenditure Theories," 336).
45. See, e.g., Lunney, "Discrete Public Goods," 5–6; Thompson, "Lumpy Goods and Cheap Riders," 433–34.
46. See Lunney, "Discrete Public Goods," 10–18; Thompson, "Lumpy Goods and Cheap Riders," 434. For a less optimistic account, see R. Hardin, "Group Provision of Step Goods."
47. See, e.g., Baumol and Sidak, "The Pig in the Python," 385; Spulber and Yoo, "Access to Networks," 913.
48. Waldfogel, *Tyranny of the Market*, 21–28, 100–107; see also Faden, *Economics of Space and Time*, 213.
49. See Anderson, *Long Tail*.
50. See Waldfogel, *Tyranny of the Market*, 134–38.
51. A caveat to this point will be discussed in chapter 7, where the nature of the work

is *itself* inherently lumpy. See Van Echtelt, Glebbeek, and Lindenberg, "New Lumpiness of Work."

52. See, e.g., Landers, Rebitzer, and Taylor, "Rat Race Redux."

53. This is one of several examples discussed in Shavell, "Contractual Holdup and Legal Intervention," 327–28. Gandolfini's per episode pay was reportedly increased from an initial contractual level of $400,000 to over $800,000. See Reuters, "*Sopranos* Kingpin Set for Raise," March 18, 2003, http://www.cnn.com/2003/SHOWBIZ/TV/03/18/television.sopranos.reut/.

54. See Singer, "Competitive Public Contracts" (proposing "competitive dual sourcing" for public contracts).

55. Calabresi, *Costs of Accidents*, 136–38.

56. See Weisbach, "Disability Law," 98.

57. See Ginsburg, Masur, and McAdams, "Temporary Law," 316.

58. See, e.g., Leo Katz, *Why the Law Is So Perverse*, 139–55.

59. See Nou and Stiglitz, "Regulatory Bundling," 1202–03 (discussing "rule-production costs").

60. Merrill and Smith, "Optimal Standardization," 26.

61. See generally Merrill and Smith. This account has not gone unquestioned. See, e.g., Robinson, "Personal Property Servitudes," 1484–88.

62. See Davidson, "Standardization and Pluralism," 1601–3, 1644–50 (discussing limited property forms as "regulatory platforms").

CHAPTER TWO

1. Kelo v. City of New London, 545 U.S. 469 (2005).

2. For a detailed analysis of the *Kelo* decision and its aftermath, see Somin, *Grasping Hand*.

3. See Smith, "Property and Property Rules," 1729.

4. See Merrill, "Economics of Public Use," 72–93; Bell and Parchomovsky, "Reconfiguring Property," 1049–51.

5. This trade-off between investment efficiency (getting people to optimally develop and maintain their property) and allocative efficiency (getting property into the hands of those who value it most highly) is well framed in Posner and Weyl, "Another Name for Monopoly."

6. See, e.g., Heller, "Tragedy of the Anticommons" (examining the effects of multiple necessary permits to open new storefront businesses in post-Soviet Russia); Chang and Fennell, "Partition and Revelation" (considering problems in the partition of land among co-owners).

7. See Kominers and Weyl, "Assembly of Complements"; see also Winn and McCarter, "Who's Holding Out?," 184–85 (finding in an experimental study that even weak competition, in the form of an imperfect substitute, was effective against seller holdout problems).

8. See Kominers and Weyl, "Assembly of Complements," 362.

9. See Kominers and Weyl, 362.

10. On the difficulties presented by changes over time in the efficient scale of use, see, e.g., Bell and Parchomovsky, "Reconfiguring Property," 1024; Fennell, "Commons, Anticommons, Semicommons," 48.

11. Shmanske and Packey, "Lumpy Demand," 72.

12. Shmanske and Packey, 72.

13. See, e.g., Nash, "Trading Species," 20–25; Tewksbury et al., "Corridors Affect Plants, Animals"; Gilbert-Norton et al., "Corridor Effectiveness."

14. On the effects of past ownership on the options open to current owners, see Larissa Katz, "Exclusion and Exclusivity," 307–8.

15. See R. Epstein, "Justified Monopolies," 108–9.

16. See Merrill, "Economics of Public Use," 75.

17. See Kominers and Weyl, "Assembly of Complements," 361.

18. Not all uses of eminent domain involve reconfiguration of property. For example, the government might condemn a single parcel of land that it plans to use as a site for a post office.

19. For the potential relevance of secrecy in land assembly, see Kelly, "'Public Use' Requirement."

20. See Merrill, "Economics of Public Use," 75.

21. See Calabresi and Melamed, "Property Rules, Liability Rules," 1092, 1106, 1116.

22. Both theoretical and empirical scholarship support this intuitive proposition. See, e.g., Kominers and Weyl, "Assembly of Complements"; Miceli and Sirmans, "Holdout Problem"; Collins and Isaac, "Holdout," 800–801. Some recent empirical work finds support for land assembly frictions in the premiums paid for parcels that were destined for assembly. See Brooks and Lutz, "Today's City," 71–72 (finding, based on a dataset of 2.3 million parcels in Los Angeles County over the period 1999–2011, premiums of 15 to 40 percent for parcels that subsequently became part of a land assembly compared with land that was not subsequently assembled); Cunningham, "Estimating the Holdout Problem" (finding, using data from Seattle, that subsequently assembled land sold for a premium of 18 percent). For experimental work suggesting that strategic behavior by buyers (low offers) is responsible for much of the inefficiency surrounding assembly efforts, see Winn and McCarter, "Who's Holding Out?"

23. See Calabresi and Melamed, "Property Rules, Liability Rules," 1092, 1108–9.

24. The basic constitutional standard is fair market value, which is what a willing buyer would pay a willing seller. See, e.g., United States v. 564.54 Acres of Land, 441 U.S. 506, 511 (1979). However, many owners receive more than the constitutional minimum due to statutory protections or negotiated agreements. See Garnett, "Neglected Political Economy," 121–36.

25. Fair market value tends to undercompensate owners for a number of reasons. See, e.g., Fennell, "Taking Eminent Domain Apart." For a challenge to the extent of undercompensation as well as its normative significance, see B. Lee, "Just Undercompensation." For a response, see Fennell, "Just Enough."

26. On whether and how the government attends to payments it makes for condemnations, see Levine-Schnur and Parchomovsky, "Is the Government Fiscally Blind?"; Levinson, "Making Government Pay."

27. On the inverse risks of property rules and liability rules, see R. Epstein, "A Clear View."

28. Kominers and Weyl, "Assembly of Complements," 361.

29. Webb, *Railroad Construction*, 3.

30. Webb, 557–65.

31. See Kominers and Weyl, "Assembly of Complements," 362 n10.

32. Shapiro, "Navigating the Patent Thicket," 120.

33. See Lichtman, "Patent Holdouts," 2; see also Merges, *Justifying Intellectual Property*, 162–76 (using the metaphor of a bridge to make this point).

34. The term "patent troll" has been attributed to Peter Detkin, who coined it in 2001 when he was a lawyer at Intel. Heller, *Gridlock Economy*, 218 n34.

35. See Lemley and Shapiro, "Patent Holdup," 2008–10; Lichtman, "Patent Hold-outs," 4.

36. See, e.g., Lemley and Shapiro, "Patent Holdup," 2008–10.

37. See Lemley and Shapiro, 2008–9; Ian Austen, "BlackBerry Service to Continue," *New York Times*, March 4, 2006.

38. eBay v. MercExchange, L.L.C., 547 U.S. 388 (2006).

39. *eBay*, 547 U.S. at 396–97 (Kennedy, J., concurring).

40. See, e.g., Dukeminier et. al., *Property*, 169; Golden Press v. Rylands, 235 P.2d 592, 595 (Colo. 1951).

41. Mannillo v. Gorski, 255 A.2d 258, 264 (N.J. 1969).

42. *Mannillo*, 255 A.2d at 264.

43. Parchomovsky and Siegelman, "Selling Mayberry."

44. See Parchomovsky and Siegelman, 119–24.

45. See Parchomovsky and Siegelman, 119–24.

46. Kuo and Means, "Collective Coercion," 1615–20.

47. Kuo and Means, 1618.

48. For a broad examination of divide and conquer strategies (and some mechanisms for resisting them), see Posner, Spier, and Vermeule, "Divide and Conquer."

49. Cf. Schelling, "Models of Segregation" (describing unraveling dynamics in which moves trigger further moves).

50. Parchomovsky and Siegelman, "Selling Mayberry," 128–29.

51. For a recent overview and extreme proposal along these lines, see Posner and Weyl, *Radical Markets*, 30–79. Some of the many earlier scholarly treatments include, e.g., Holland and Vaughn, "Evaluation of Self-Assessment"; Tideman, "Improving Urban Land Use," 52–69; Levmore, "Self-Assessed Valuation"; Bell and Parchomovsky, "Takings Reassessed," 300–306; Fennell, "Revealing Options"; Chang, "Self-Assessment of Takings Compensation."

52. This application has been a primary focus of the literature on self-assessed valuation. See, e.g., the sources cited in note 51 above.

53. See, e.g., Plassmann and Tideman, "Marginal Cost Pricing." For example, if the property tax rate is higher than the perceived chance of having one's property condemned, there is an incentive to undervalue the property. See Chang, "Self-Assessment of Takings Compensation" (positing this as the primary cause for undervaluation in Taiwan's self-assessment system, which was in force from 1954 to 1977).

54. See, e.g., Chang and Fennell, "Partition and Revelation."

55. For a survey of judicial partition rules in different countries, see Chang and Fennell, app. A, http://lawreview.uchicago.edu/sites/lawreview.uchicago.edu/files/02_Chang-Fennell_SYMP_APPX.pdf, archived at https://perma.cc/P752-7CVL.

56. See, e.g., Miceli and Sirmans, "Partition of Real Estate," 789.

57. See, e.g., Johnson v. Hendrickson, 24 N.W.2d 914, 916 (S.D. 1946).

58. See, e.g., Ark Land Co. v. Harper, 599 S.E.2d 754, 761 (W. Va. 2004).

59. See Bell and Parchomovsky, "Theory of Property," 601.

60. Cake-cutting games have been explored extensively in the literature. See, e.g., Brams and Taylor, *Fair Division*, 8–29; Baumol, *Superfairness*, 15–16, 66.

61. See, e.g., Young, "Dividing the Indivisible," 911–12.

62. See, e.g., Landeo and Spier, "Shotguns and Deadlocks."

63. See Landeo and Spier, 146–47.
64. Chang and Fennell, "Partition and Revelation."
65. See Chang and Fennell.
66. See, e.g., Blume and Rubinfeld, "Compensation for Takings," 618–20.
67. See Heller and Hills, "Land Assembly Districts."
68. See Harris, "Owning and Dissolving Strata Property."
69. Michelman, "Ethics, Economics and the Law of Property," 6, 9; Michelman, "Is the Tragedy of the Common Inevitable?"
70. See, e.g., Heller, *Gridlock Economy*; Heller, "Tragedy of the Anticommons"; Heller and Eisenberg, "Can Patents Deter Innovation?"
71. See, e.g., Heller, "Tragedy of the Anticommons"; Heller, "Boundaries of Private Property," 1165–69.
72. See, e.g., Heller, "Boundaries of Private Property," 1170–74; Parisi, "Entropy in Property," 603–13; Smith, "Language of Property," 1143 and n137.
73. Michelman, "Is the Tragedy of the Common Inevitable?"
74. 467 U.S. 229 (1984). In *Midkiff*, the difficulty in gaining the cooperation of the landowners was apparently primarily due to federal tax liability that would have been triggered by a voluntary sale. See 467 U.S. at 233.
75. See Honoré, *Making Law Bind*, 187–88.
76. See Bell and Parchomovsky, "Of Property and Antiproperty."
77. See Fennell, "Commons, Anticommons, Semicommons."
78. See, e.g., Schulz and Lueck, "Contracting for Control" (discussing contractual alternatives for managing large-scale resources such as habitats and firescapes).
79. See Libecap, "Contracting for Property Rights," 156–65.
80. See Libecap, 162–63; see also Libecap and Smith, "Petroleum Property Rights."
81. See, e.g., Heller, "Boundaries of Private Property," 1173–82.
82. Heller, 1165–66, 1169; see also Parisi, "Entropy in Property," 595–96, 627.
83. See Larissa Katz, "Red Tape and Gridlock," 120–21.
84. See Kominers and Weyl, "Assembly of Complements."
85. See generally Fennell, "Fee Simple Obsolete."

CHAPTER THREE

1. See Judy Kuhlman, "Children Reach in Pockets for Oklahoma City Zoo Judy the Elephant Popular Campaign," *NewsOK*, April 24, 1994; "Elephant, OC Zoo Attraction for 50 Years, Dies," *Tulsa World*, October 9, 1997.
2. To be precise, she was a *local* public good since her benefits were localized to a relatively small area. See Cornes and Sandler, *Theory of Externalities*, 24.
3. For discussion of these attributes, see, e.g., Cornes and Sandler, 6–7; E. Ostrom, *Understanding Institutional Diversity*, 23–24 and fig. 1.3.
4. For the idea that goods can be valued in part for their "option value," see Weisbrod, "Collective-Consumption Services," 472–73.
5. G. Hardin, "Tragedy of the Commons."
6. See, e.g., Coase, "Lighthouse in Economics."
7. See E. Ostrom, *Governing the Commons*.
8. On the use of focal points to solve coordination problems, see McAdams, *Expressive Powers of Law*, 22–56; Schelling, *Strategy of Conflict*, 53–80, 89–118.
9. See Taylor and Ward, "Chickens, Whales, and Lumpy Goods," 353; R. Hardin, "Group Provision of Step Goods"; Hampton, "Free-Rider Problems."
10. See Taylor and Ward, "Chickens, Whales, and Lumpy Goods," 353.

11. See, e.g., Demsetz, "Toward a Theory," 354–55; Ostrom and Ostrom, "Theory for Institutional Analysis," 159.
12. Chong, *Collective Action*, 15–20.
13. See, e.g., Baird, Gertner, and Picker, *Game Theory and the Law*; Skyrms, *The Stag Hunt*; McAdams, *Expressive Powers of Law*, 29–42.
14. See, e.g., McAdams, *Expressive Powers of Law*, 42–44.
15. See McAdams, "Beyond the Prisoners' Dilemma," 210–11.
16. See, e.g., Tewksbury et al., "Corridors Affect Plants, Animals"; Gilbert-Norton et al., "Corridor Effectiveness."
17. The shape as well as the size of habitat patches determines their value to species. See, e.g., Nash, "Trading Species," 20–25; Olson, Murphy, and Thornton, "Habitat Transaction Method," 28–30.
18. See, e.g., L. Cohen, "Holdouts and Free Riders."
19. See Frohlich and Oppenheimer, "With a Little Help," 117–18.
20. Popkin, "Political Entrepreneurs," 21; see also Chong, *Collective Action*, 14–15.
21. See, e.g., Elster, *Cement of Society*, 27–28 and fig. 1.3; Baird, Gertner, and Picker, *Game Theory and the Law*, 19–22, 33–34.
22. See generally E. Ostrom, *Governing the Commons*.
23. See Dawes and Thaler, "Anomalies: Cooperation," 188 (describing this type of public goods game).
24. See Elster, *Cement of Society*, 27–28 and fig 1.3.
25. See Oliver, Marwell, and Teixeira, "Theory of the Critical Mass," 533–34 (explaining that when contributions follow a linear production function, "everyone will contribute either everything possible or nothing," depending on the slope of the line).
26. Kickstarter, "What Are the Basics?," https://help.kickstarter.com/hc/en-us/articles/115005028514-What-are-the-basics- ("No one will be charged for a pledge towards a project unless it reaches its funding goal.").
27. See, e.g., Elster, *Cement of Society*, 42; Palfrey and Rosenthal, "Discrete Public Goods," 173, 191.
28. See Dawes et al., "Organizing Groups for Collective Action," 1174.
29. See Larissa Katz, "Governing through Owners."
30. See, e.g., Thompson, "Lumpy Goods and Cheap Riders."
31. See, e.g., Cornes and Sandler, *Theory of Externalities*; E. Ostrom, *Understanding Institutional Diversity*.
32. See Ciriacy-Wantrup and Bishop, "'Common Property' as a Concept" (emphasizing the significance of limited access to common property).
33. See, e.g., Eggertsson, "Open Access versus Common Property."
34. Benkler, "Sharing Nicely," 336; Benkler, *Wealth of Networks*, 100–101.
35. See, e.g., Linda Babcock et al., "Biased Judgments."
36. On the significance of monitoring, see E. Ostrom, *Governing the Commons*, 45, 94–100.
37. Ayres, Raseman, and Shih, "Peer Comparison Feedback."
38. Ellickson, *Order without Law*, 55–56.
39. Lewis, *Convention*, 96.
40. Popkin, "Political Entrepreneurs," 18.
41. On focal points, see McAdams, *Expressive Powers of Law*, 22–56; Schelling, *Strategy of Conflict*, 53–80, 89–118.
42. Government agencies charge grazing fees keyed to the "animal unit month"—the amount that a cow and her calf (or one horse, or five sheep or goats) consume in

one month. See US Department of the Interior, Bureau of Land Management, "BLM and Forest Service Announce 2018 Grazing Fees," January 30, 2018.

43. E. Ostrom, *Governing the Commons*, 174.

44. See, e.g., E. Ostrom, *Understanding Institutional Diversity*, 228–33 and table 8.2 (providing a catalog of "choice rules" for allocating common-pool resources, including allocations based on location, time slot, quantity, and resource attributes).

45. On the effects of technological change on the prospects for property rights, see Anderson and Hill, *Not So Wild, Wild West*, 27.

46. For a discussion and critique of such purpose-based distinctions, see Harris and Millerd, "Food Fish."

47. Felicity Barringer, "Bottling Plan Pushes Groundwater to Center Stage in Vermont," *New York Times*, August 21, 2008, A14.

48. See Fennell, "Adjusting Alienability," 1427–33.

49. See Main and Hannah, *Site Furnishings*, 98.

50. See Main and Hannah, 98; Samantha Melamed, "Is LOVE Park Inclusive—or Hostile? How the 'War on Sitting' Is Changing Public Spaces," *Philadelphia Inquirer*, May 31, 2018.

51. Soarigami, https://www.soarigami.com/.

52. Natalie Paris, "Plane Diverted after Row over Reclining Seat Device," *The Telegraph*, August 26, 2014.

53. "Pricing," Divvy Bikes, https://www.divvybikes.com/pricing.

54. "How It Works," Divvy Bikes, https://www.divvybikes.com/how-it-works.

55. See Benkler, "Sharing Nicely," 336.

56. "Volunteering with One Brick Is as Easy as 1, 2, 3," One Brick: Chicago, http://chicago.onebrick.org.

57. See, e.g., "Unwrapped," Oxfam America, https://www.oxfamgifts.com/gift-category/all-gifts/.

58. Hale, "Nonrenewable Resources," 381.

59. "Eddie Cantor and the Origin of the March of Dimes," March of Dimes, http://www.marchofdimes.org/mission/eddie-cantor-and-the-origin-of-the-march-of-dimes.aspx.

60. "Eddie Cantor and the Origin of the March of Dimes."

61. Cialdini and Schroeder, "Legitimizing Paltry Contributions"; see Andrews et al., "Legitimization of Paltry Favors" (conducting a meta-analysis of nineteen studies and finding consistent positive effects in face-to-face treatments that involved immediate monetary contributions).

62. See Andrews et al., "Legitimization of Paltry Favors," 66.

63. Goswami and Urminsky, "When Should the Ask Be a Nudge?"

64. Goswami and Urminsky, 842.

65. Goswami and Urminsky, 842 (citing Andreoni, "Impure Altruism").

66. See Andrews et al., "Legitimization of Paltry Favors," 66.

67. Goswami and Urminsky, "When Should the Ask Be a Nudge?," 842.

68. Goswami and Urminsky, 842.

69. See Goswami and Urminsky, 842.

70. Andreoni and Petrie, "Public Goods Experiments," 1606, 1618–20, and fig. 3.

71. See, e.g., Fiala and Noussair, "Charitable Giving" (reviewing literature and presenting findings showing that defaults had no effect).

72. See Goswami and Urminsky, "When Should the Ask Be a Nudge?," 838–39 (describing a field experiment in which default amounts were customized based on each donor's past contributions).

73. Benkler, *Wealth of Networks*, 101.
74. See Benkler, 102.
75. See E. Ostrom, *Governing the Commons*, 203–5 (noting the relevance to monitoring of "physical attributes of the resource itself" and the visibility of appropriation actions); Cass and Edney, "Commons Dilemma" (finding in an experimental simulation involving a self-replenishing resource that making resource units visible moved harvesting strategies closer to the optimum).
76. See Libecap and Lueck, "Land Demarcation Systems."
77. See Anderson and Hill, *Not So Wild, Wild West*, 116–17 (citing Libecap, "Economic Variables," 345–46).
78. G. Epstein et al., "Governing the Invisible Commons," 347.
79. E. Ostrom, "General Framework," 421 (citing Schlager, Blomquist, and Tang, "Mobile Flows").
80. For a detailed account, see Greenberg, *Feathered River across the Sky*.
81. Stoke et al., *Student Reactions to Study Facilities*, 15; see also Sommer, *Personal Space*, 77–78.
82. Anderson and Hill, *Not So Wild, Wild West*, 170.
83. Anderson and Hill, 231 n33.
84. See, e.g., Andreoni and Petrie, "Public Goods Experiments," 1619 (observing that "poorly chosen categories may reduce contributions or may have no effect on shifting contributions at all").
85. Benkler, *Wealth of Networks*, 102.
86. McAdams, *Expressive Powers of Law*, 22–56.
87. LaManna and Eason, "Effects of Landmarks."
88. LaManna and Eason, 473.
89. See McAdams, *Expressive Powers of Law*, 88–90 (discussing LaManna and Eason, "Effects of Landmarks," as well as human landmarking and boundary construction).
90. On difficulties with lumpiness in norms, see Vermeule, "The Invisible Hand," 1431–38.
91. There may be exceptions. See, e.g., Landes and Posner, "Indefinitely Renewable Copyright," 485–86 (observing that overuse of an image could cause "confusion, the tarnishing of the image, or sheer boredom on the part of the consuming public").
92. See, e.g., Lunney, "Discrete Public Goods."
93. See Lunney, 23 and n31.
94. See Lunney, 23–24.
95. See Lunney, 25–26 (arguing that "King should have stated his own reservation price").
96. Frohlich and Oppenheimer, "With a Little Help," 118.
97. Lunney, "Discrete Public Goods," 26 n37.
98. See Coase, "Lighthouse in Economics."
99. For ideas along these lines see, e.g., Netanel, "Noncommercial Use Levy," 43–44; Litman, "Sharing and Stealing," 30–35. For further analysis, see, e.g., Liu, "Copyright Complements"; W. Fisher, *Promises to Keep*, 199–258.
100. Private subscription services like Netflix and music licensing services like ASCAP operate on a similarly bundled basis and require a similar all-or-nothing decision about payment and access.
101. For different take on this question, see Liu, "Copyright Complements," 1038–39. The answer turns on how elastic the demand is for the complementary good in

question—with implications for both efficiency and equity. See W. Fisher, *Promises to Keep*, 217–23.

CHAPTER FOUR

1. C. Rose, "Comedy of the Commons," 769.
2. See Buchanan and Stubblebine, "Externality," 374–77.
3. This core point was made in a different context in Gergen, "Open Terms," 1013–19.
4. See, e.g., Greg Ip, "Stock Prices Switch to Decimals from Fractions, Raising Concerns," *Wall Street Journal*, August 28, 2000. I thank Daria Roithmayr for bringing this example to my attention.
5. See Arthur Levitt, US Securities and Exchange Commission Chairman, Testimony Concerning Decimal Pricing in the Securities and Options Market, Hearings before the Subcommittee on Finance and Hazardous Materials, Committee on Commerce, US House of Representatives, June 13, 2000.
6. See, e.g., Paul Kedrosky, "Fractions, Decimals, and the Math of Markets," *The Street*, May 16, 2003; Ip, "Stock Prices Switch."
7. See Andrew Ackerman, "SEC Finalizes 'Tick Size' Pilot for Smaller-Company Stock," *Wall Street Journal*, May 6, 2015; Griffith and Roseman, "Making Cents of Tick Sizes"; see also Plott et al., "Tick Size."
8. See, e.g., DellaVigna, "Psychology and Economics," 353–56 (discussing a variety of "menu effects," including a tendency to excessively diversify across choices or avoid choice altogether when the menu contains many options); Sydnor, "(Over)Insuring Modest Risks," 194–95 (discussing possible "menu effects" for insurance deductibles, such as inferring appropriateness from available choices or avoiding the highest and lowest options).
9. See Buchanan and Stubblebine, "Externality"; Haddock, "Irrelevant Externality Angst"; Frischmann and Lemley, "Spillovers."
10. See Haddock, "Irrelevant Externality Angst," 10–11 (providing a similar example involving a forest).
11. See Haddock, 10–11.
12. See Buchanan and Stubblebine, "Externality," 374; Haddock, "Irrelevant Externality Angst," 10–11.
13. More specifically, an externality like Gina's does not qualify as a "Pareto-relevant externality," which Buchanan and Stubblebine define as one that exhibits the potential for "gains from trade." Buchanan and Stubblebine, "Externality," 374–77. Such potential gains exist only where the party affected by the externality would be willing to pay the actor producing it enough to alter her behavior. See Buchanan and Stubblebine, 380–81.
14. See Dukeminier et al., *Property*, 49 (observing that if an actor does not change her behavior after taking an external effect into account, the effect is no longer an "externality" but may still be distributively unfair).
15. See Haddock, "Irrelevant Externality Angst," 9–10 (noting the public good characteristics of a forest that is viewable by those passing by).
16. Frischmann and Lemley, "Spillovers," 269.
17. Frischmann and Lemley, 269–70.
18. See Coase, "Problem of Social Cost," 15–16.
19. There are some exceptions. See, e.g., Gergen, "Open Terms," 1013–19; Lunney, "Discrete Public Goods."

20. This follows the general tendency in economics to ignore indivisibilities in modeling in order to simplify the mathematics. See, e.g., Bobzin, *Indivisibilities*, 1.
21. For similar graphs, see, e.g., Mankiw, *Principles of Economics*, 198, fig. 2; Cowen and Tabarrok, *Modern Principles: Microeconomics*, 172, fig. 9.2, panel B.
22. This graph assumes there are no positive externalities produced by the draws, so the marginal private benefit line is also the marginal social benefit line.
23. Such a graph would show a marginal social benefit line lying above the marginal private benefit line. See, e.g., Mankiw, *Principles of Economics*, 199, fig. 3.
24. Mankiw, 201 (emphasis removed); see also Cowen and Tabarrok, *Modern Principles: Microeconomics*, 170–74.
25. For a different way of illustrating the effects of lumpiness on choices that involve externalities, see Gergen, "Open Terms," 1014, diagram 1.
26. If transaction costs were zero, then chunkiness would not provide the indicated advantage because the parties would bargain to the socially preferred position on their own. Coase, "Problem of Social Cost," 8.
27. See Gergen, "Open Terms," 1013–15 and n55.
28. See Gergen, 1013–19.
29. See Gergen, 1010–11, 1015 (explaining how oil and gas leases are structured to induce lessees to begin lumpy investments).
30. This fence-building example was inspired by (but diverges from) one in Buchanan and Stubblebine, "Externality."
31. For related observations, see Tisdell, *Environmental Economics*, 31. A Pareto improvement is a change that makes at least one person better off while making no one worse off.
32. See Taylor and Ward, "Chickens, Whales, and Lumpy Goods," 353.
33. Chapter 5 will examine this point in the context of intrapersonal dilemmas.
34. Pigouvian taxes attempt to align private and social payoffs by charging the actor with the difference; subsidies can similarly be used to encourage acts with positive spillovers. See Pigou, *Economics of Welfare*, 192–96.
35. C. Rose, "Comedy of the Commons," 769–70.
36. This advantage is dampened when the offering party is uncertain about her counterparty's valuation. For discussion of TIOLI bargaining dynamics, see, e.g., Ayres and Talley, "Solomonic Bargaining," 1049–50.
37. See Jolls, Sunstein, and Thaler, "Behavioral Approach," 21–23. For variation in rejection rates among different societies, see Joseph Henrich et al., "In Search of *Homo Economicus*," 75.
38. See Walras, *Elements of Pure Economics*, 95.
39. On the strategic advantages for workers of outlawing certain bargains, see, e.g., R. Hardin, "Utilitarian Logic of Liberalism," 58–62.
40. See Banerjee and Duflo, *Poor Economics*, 9–16.
41. A high-profile example was Mayor Bloomberg's effort to limit soda sizes in New York City—an initiative that was struck down as being beyond the authority of the city's Board of Health. Michael Grynbaum, "New York's Ban on Big Sodas Is Rejected by Final Court," *New York Times*, June 26, 2014.
42. See, e.g., Geier, Rozin, and Doros, "Unit Bias."
43. The academic literature on this topic is voluminous. See, e.g., R. Epstein, *Bargaining with the State*; K. Sullivan, "Unconstitutional Conditions"; Schauer, "Too Hard"; Cass R. Sunstein, "Why the Unconstitutional Conditions Doctrine Is an Anachro-

nism"; Hamburger, "Unconstitutional Conditions"; Berman, "Coercion without Baselines."

44. See R. Epstein, *Bargaining with the State*, 183 (referencing this sort of "empirical guess" in the land use exactions context).

45. See Koontz v. St. Johns River Water Management District, 570 U.S. 595, 633–34 (2013) (Kagan, J., dissenting) (observing that a local governmental body will be motivated to simply deny land use permits if discussions about potential conditions on development will generate costly litigation).

CHAPTER FIVE

1. Prelec, "Values and Principles," 134–35.

2. See Ainslie, *Picoeconomics*, 160–64.

3. Ainslie, 161–62.

4. For an intrapersonal saga involving selves identified with each calendar month, see Tim Urban, "Doing a TED Talk: The Full Story," *Wait but Why* (blog), March 2, 2016, https://waitbutwhy.com/2016/03/doing-a-ted-talk-the-full-story.html.

5. Thaler and Shefrin, "Economic Theory of Self-Control."

6. See Parchomovsky and Siegelman, "Selling Mayberry," 128–29.

7. See DellaVigna and Malmendier, "Paying Not to Go to the Gym."

8. Köszegi and Rabin, "Revealed Mistakes and Revealed Preferences," 206–7.

9. See, e.g., Rasmusen, "Internalities and Paternalism."

10. On the continuity of personal identity over time and the connections between successive versions of oneself, see Parfit, *Reasons and Persons*, 314–15.

11. See Herrnstein and Prelec, "Melioration," 251.

12. Milkman, Minson, and Volpp, "Hunger Games."

13. S. King, "Quitter's Inc."

14. StickK, http://www.stickk.com.

15. "FAQ, Commitment Contracts, Stakes," StickK, https://www.stickk.com/faq/stakes/ Commitment+Contracts. See Rachlin, "Self-Control" (1974), 100 (proposing a similar technique where a lapser's money would go to a disliked political party).

16. Studies consistently show a "portion size effect," although the mechanisms that produce it are unclear. See English, Lasschuijt, and Keller, "Mechanisms of the Portion Size Effect."

17. See Wertenbroch, "Consumption Self-Control."

18. See, e.g., Geier, Rozin, and Doros, "Unit Bias," 521.

19. Cheema and Soman, "Effect of Partitions."

20. Cheema and Soman.

21. Kennedy-Hagan et al., "Pistachio Shells as a Visual Cue."

22. See Roose, Van Kerckhove, and Huyghe, "Honey They Shrank the Food!" (presenting a meta-analysis of past work on food granularity and the results of a new study involving adult participants); Marchiori, Waroquier, and Klein, "Split Them!" (finding that splitting cookies reduced consumption among first and fifth graders).

23. Marchiori, Waroquier, and Klein, "Split Them!," 254. Another possible mechanism relates to the smaller bite sizes that people may take when eating smaller items. See Weijzen et al., "Sensory Specific Satiety."

24. See, e.g., E. Robinson et al., "Smaller Plates."

25. Libotte, Siegrist, and Bucher, "Influence of Plate Size," 94–96.

26. See Libotte, Siegrist, and Bucher, 94–96 (suggesting that people are likely to self-

ration starchy foods, and thus more likely to use the extra space for vegetables, at least if they are undistracted).

27. "Choose My Plate," US Department of Agriculture, https://www.choosemyplate
.gov/; see Sunstein, "Empirically Informed Regulation," 1378–79.

28. Cass and Edney, "The Commons Dilemma," 374.

29. Cass and Edney, 378, 383. The opposite effect, overharvesting, was observed when resource units were invisible in common-pool conditions. Cass and Edney, 378.

30. See Roose, Van Kerckhove, and Huyghe, "Honey They Shrank the Food!"

31. Roose, Van Kerckhove, and Huyghe, 215–17; see also Bui, Tangari, and Haws, "Health 'Halos'" (finding that undivided packages containing sixteen discrete pieces led to more consumption than when subdivided into packets of four items for items perceived as healthy [granola bites] but not for items perceived as unhealthy [cookies]).

32. The researchers had a different interpretation. Roose, Van Kerckhove, and Huyghe, "Honey They Shrank the Food!," 212, 217–18 (arguing that the physical partitioning of food leads to a self-control conflict around eating, producing restraint among certain eaters, whereas the bundling of food into small packages does not trigger such a conflict). See also Bui, Tangari, and Haws, "Health 'Halos'" (suggesting that people may rely on internal self-control for unhealthy foods but eat apparently healthy foods without restraint).

33. See Herrnstein et al., "Utility Maximization and Melioration," 150 (defining an "internality" as a "within-person externality").

34. See Gul and Pesendorfer, "Temptation and Self Control."

35. See, e.g., O'Donoghue and Rabin, "Studying Optimal Paternalism," 189–90 (presenting an example in which both naive and sophisticated actors behave the same way—but for different reasons).

36. O'Donoghue and Rabin, 189–90.

37. Chen and Schwartz, "Intertemporal Choice," 5–6.

38. O'Donoghue and Rabin, "Studying Optimal Paternalism," 190.

39. See O'Donoghue and Rabin, 190. On the rationality of addiction, see Becker and Murphy, "Theory of Rational Addiction"; Gruber and Köszegi, "Is Addiction 'Rational'?"

40. See, e.g., John, Donnelly, and Roberto, "Sugary-Drink Portion Limits"; Dobson, Chakraborty, and Seaton, "Containing Big Soda."

41. Benkler, "Sharing Nicely," 336.

42. Mullainathan and Shafir, Scarcity, 84–85.

43. Mullainathan and Shafir, 84–85.

44. Mullainathan and Shafir, 84–85.

45. Mullainathan and Shafir, 85.

46. See Mullainathan and Shafir, 69–86 (describing scarcity as a lack of slack).

47. See Schelling, Choice and Consequence, 79.

48. Cirillo, The Pomodoro Technique.

49. Cirillo, 30–39.

50. See Gergen, "Open Terms," 1015–16.

51. Bolker, Writing Your Dissertation; see also Jensen, Write No Matter What, 17–21 (advising spending at least fifteen minutes per day on a writing project).

52. See, e.g., Ainslie, Picoeconomics, 142–73; Bénabou and Tirole, "Willpower and Personal Rules."

53. See Ainslie, Breakdown of Will, 112–13.

54. Mullainathan and Shafir, *Scarcity*, 212.
55. On the bundling and stake-raising character of rules, see, e.g., Bénabou and Tirole, "Willpower and Personal Rules," 851–52; Ainslie, *Picoeconomics*, 192–93. On the distinction between acts and patterns, see Rachlin, "Self-Control: Beyond Commitment," 115–17; see also Rachlin, *Science of Self-Control*, 60–65; Herrnstein and Prelec, "Melioration," 236–37.
56. See Rachlin, *Science of Self-Control*, 72–74 and fig. 3.5 (2000) (discussing and illustrating "the primrose path from sobriety to alcoholism") (citing Herrnstein and Prelec, "Theory of Addiction").
57. Rachlin, *Science of Self-Control*, 63–64.
58. Rachlin, 60–62.
59. See, e.g., Bénabou and Tirole, "Willpower and Personal Rules"; Schelling, *Choice and Consequence*, 76.
60. See, e.g., Ainslie, *Breakdown of Will*, 113–16, 148–49.
61. Cochran and Tesser, "'What the Hell' Effect"; see Herman and Polivy, "Dieting as an Exercise," 466–71.
62. Herman and Polivy, "Dieting as an Exercise," 469.
63. See Cochran and Tesser "'What the Hell' Effect," 109 (suggesting focusing on a longer time period); Herman and Polivy, "Dieting as an Exercise," 468–69 (noting drawbacks of a longer focal period).
64. See Herman and Polivy, "Dieting as an Exercise," 470–71.
65. Ainslie, "Beyond Microeconomics," 148–49.
66. See Ainslie, 148–49.
67. See Ainslie, 148–49 (quoting James, *Principles of Psychology*, 565, on a similar expansion of excuses to drink).
68. See, e.g., Ainslie, *Breakdown of Will*, 143–60; Cowen, "Self-Constraint versus Self-Liberation."
69. For some ideas along these lines, see Herman and Polivy, "Dieting as an Exercise," 469–70 (dietary plans that build in some amount of cheating); Kivetz and Simonson, "Self-Control for the Righteous" (precommitments to future indulgent expenditures).
70. Rachlin, *Science of Self-Control*, 65–69.
71. Ian Ayres, "Vegetarianism as a Sometimes Thing," *Freakonomics* (blog), June 19, 2009, http://freakonomics.com/2009/06/19/vegetarianism-as-a-sometimes-thing/.
72. Merrill and Smith, "Optimal Standardization," 27.

CHAPTER SIX
1. Warren and Tyagi, *Two-Income Trap*, 164–66.
2. See Prelec and Loewenstein, "The Red and the Black."
3. Kahneman and Varey, "Psychology of Utility," 147.
4. See, e.g., Friedman, *Theory of the Consumption Function*, 26–31, 220–21; Modigliani and Brumberg, "Utility Analysis"; Ando and Modigliani, "'Life Cycle' Hypothesis."
5. See, e.g., Thaler and Loewenstein, "Intertemporal Choice," 98–99.
6. See Fetherstonhaugh and Ross, "Framing Effects," 195.
7. See, e.g., Laibson, "Hyperbolic Discount Functions," 27; Chen and Schwartz, "Intertemporal Choice," 35.
8. Banerjee and Duflo, *Poor Economics*, 183–84. This example is discussed further in chapter 9.
9. Banerjee and Duflo, 193–94.

10. Banerjee and Duflo, 193–94. See also Duflo, Kremer, and Robinson, "Nudging Farmers to Use Fertilizer."

11. Mullainathan and Shafir, *Scarcity*, 208 (finding, in a small pilot program run with IFMR Trust, "a surprising number of people eager to save in this way").

12. Besley and Levenson, "Informal Finance," 50.

13. There are a variety of ways to determine the order in which group members get access to the funds, including randomization and bidding. See Besley and Levenson, 50.

14. See Palmer, *Smart Money*, 209–10.

15. Besley and Levenson, "Informal Finance," 50.

16. 26 U.S.C. § 25B; see "Retirement Savings Contributions Credit (Saver's Credit)," Internal Revenue Service, August 6, 2018, https://www.irs.gov/retirement-plans/plan -participant-employee/retirement-savings-contributions-savers-credit.

17. "Individual Development Accounts," Office of the Comptroller of the Currency, Community Developments Fact Sheet (January 2018), https://www.occ.gov/topics/ community-affairs/publications/fact-sheets/fact-sheet-individual-development -accounts.pdf.

18. Libson, "Retirement Savings Problem," 233.

19. Libson, 233.

20. Libson, 238–39.

21. Laibson, "Golden Eggs and Hyperbolic Discounting."

22. Another delumping alternative is the reverse mortgage, which enables an older homeowner who has built up home equity to receive payments that draw down that equity. At the end of the homeowner's life, or when the house is sold, proceeds from the home's sale repay the mortgage. This model can transform an overly lumpy piece of real estate into a useful stream of income, but it has not been very popular—perhaps because it would dispossess remaining family members who expected to hold onto the family home. See Palmer, *Smart Money*, 140–42.

23. See Mian and Sufi, "Household Debt and Defaults," 257 ("Existing homeowners borrowed aggressively against the rise in home equity values through cash-out refinancing and home equity loans, and this behavior explains the substantial rise in the household debt to GDP ratio from 2000 to 2007.").

24. Soman and Cheema, "Earmarking and Partitioning."

25. Soman and Cheema, S16.

26. Soman and Cheema, S16–S17.

27. Soman and Cheema, S16–S17.

28. Soman and Cheema, S19. The children's pictures also helped participants with the lower savings target avoid opening an envelope at all (something that was much easier to accomplish when the amount being saved was low than when it was high).

29. Soman and Cheema, S19.

30. Soman and Cheema, S19.

31. See Shefrin and Thaler, "Behavioral Life-Cycle Hypothesis," 613–20.

32. Soman and Cheema, "Earmarking and Partitioning," S20–S21 (quoting blogger Chris Peterson, who expressed a desire for banking software that could segment a single bank account).

33. Dave Ramsey, "How the Debt Snowball Method Works," Dave Ramsey (blog) https://www.daveramsey.com/blog/how-the-debt-snowball-method-works.

34. The IRS cumulative 2017 filing season report for the week ending December 29, 2017, showed 151,916,000 returns processed, with 111,873,000 receiving refunds—

about 73.6 percent. "Filing Season Statistics for Week Ending December 29, 2017," 2017 Filing Season Statistics, Internal Revenue Service. See also Jones, "Inertia and Overwithholding."

35. See e.g., Jones, "Inertia and Overwithholding"; Fennell, "Hyperopia in Public Finance"; Ayers, Kachelmeier, and Robinson, "Interest-Free Loans."

36. See Souleles, "Response of Household Consumption" (examining the marginal propensity to consume tax refunds).

37. See, e.g., Jones, "Inertia and Overwithholding"; Thaler and Benartzi, "Save More Tomorrow," S185.

38. Internal Revenue Service, "Publication 505 (2018) Tax Withholding and Estimated Tax" ("The deadline for putting [a new W-4] into effect is the start of the first payroll period ending 30 or more days after you turn it in.").

39. See Government Accountability Office, Report to the Joint Committee on Taxation, "Advance Earned Income Tax Credit: Low Use and Small Dollars Paid Impede IRS's Efforts to Reduce High Noncompliance," 3 (August, 2007).

40. Government Accountability Office, 3. The GAO report also referenced an IRS-funded study identifying another concern: that recipients might mistakenly receive too much in advance and have to pay it back at filing time.

41. The Advance EITC was repealed by the Education Jobs and Medicaid Assistance Act of 2010, Public Law No. 111-226, 124 Stat. 2389.

42. See Romich and Weisner, "How Families View and Use the EITC," 1248.

43. The average refund for the 2017 filing season, as of December 29, 2017, was $2,895. "Filing Season Statistics for Week Ending December 29, 2017," 2017 Filing Season Statistics, Internal Revenue Service.

44. See, e.g., Halpern-Meekin et al., *It's Not Like I'm Poor*, 45; Karelis, *Persistence of Poverty*, 71.

45. See Halpern-Meekin et al., *It's Not Like I'm Poor*, 43–48; Romich and Weisner, "How Families View and Use the EITC," 1259–60; Smeeding, Phillips, and O'Connor, "EITC," 1198; Goodman-Bacon and McGranahan, "EITC Recipients," 29; Souleles, "Response of Household Consumption," 952–53.

46. See, e.g., Romich and Weisner, "How Families View and Use the EITC," 1257.

47. See, e.g., Smeeding, Phillips, and O'Connor, "EITC," 1198; Matthew Frankel, "The Average American's 2017 Tax Refund—and How They'll Spend It," *USA Today*, May 2, 2017.

48. Hayashi, "Refund Anticipation Loans," 7 (reporting that in 2008 "44% of EITC recipients obtained a [refund anticipation loan] or [refund anticipation check], as compared with only 7% of non-EITC recipients").

49. See Hayashi, 7; Theodos et al., "Who Needs Credit."

50. For discussion of hyperopic behavior, see Fennell, "Hyperopia in Public Finance"; Kivetz and Simonson, "Self-Control for the Righteous," 201, 214.

51. See Hayashi, "Refund Anticipation Loans," 8; Theodos et al., "Who Needs Credit," 33.

52. See Theodos et al., "Who Needs Credit," 40.

53. See Theodos et al., 40.

54. See Hayashi, "Refund Anticipation Loans," 10.

55. See "Frequently Asked Questions about Splitting Federal Income Tax Refunds," Internal Revenue Service, https://www.irs.gov/refunds/frequently-asked-questions -about-splitting-federal-income-tax-refunds.

56. A more raid-proof form of partitioning might involve channeling some of the

refund money into an individual development account from which withdrawals would be more difficult. Theodos et al., "Who Needs Credit," 40–41.

57. Theodos et al., 40.

58. See, e.g., Holt, "Periodic Payment"; Halpern-Meekin et al., *It's Not Like I'm Poor*, 112–13.

59. See Kearney et al., "Making Savers Winners," 3 ("In the year 2008, 42 states and the District of Columbia offered state lotteries, bringing in roughly $60 billion in sales, or more than $540 per household nationwide."); Clotfelter and Cook, *Selling Hope*, 215–19 (discussing lotteries as a revenue source).

60. Lottery tickets are almost always bad bets, although in rare instances a lottery pot grows large enough to give the ticket a positive expected value—until taxes are taken into account. See Lawsky, "On the Edge," 930 n106.

61. Kearney et al., "Making Savers Winners," 3.

62. See, e.g., McCaffery, "Why People Play Lotteries."

63. See McCaffery; Cohen, "Lure of the Lottery."

64. Kwang, "Why Do People Buy Lottery Tickets?"; see McCaffery, "Why People Play Lotteries," 99–105.

65. See McCaffery, "Why People Play Lotteries," 102–5; Friedman and Savage, "Choices Involving Risk," 299; see also Clotfelter and Cook, *Selling Hope*, 75–77 (citing and discussing Friedman and Savage).

66. See, e.g., Kearney et al., "Making Savers Winners," 4–5; Garratt, "Lotteries and the Law of Demand," 166.

67. See Friedman and Savage, "Choices Involving Risk," 294–97 and figs. 2 and 3 (discussing and illustrating kinked utility curves that could reconcile lottery play and insurance); see also Lawsky, "On the Edge," 933, fig. 4 and 935, fig. 5.

68. Fels, "Insurance and Gambling Motives," 3.

69. Fels, 2 (citing Kwang, "Why Do People Buy Lottery Tickets?").

70. See Fels, 2.

71. See Fels, 3 (citing Nyman, "Value of Health Insurance").

72. Although these accounts have a centuries-long history and are common in a number of other countries, they have only recently begun to receive significant attention in the US. See, e.g., Kearney et al., "Making Savers Winners" (surveying current and historical examples). A nonprofit called the Doorways to Dreams Fund has worked to introduce prize-linked savings in the US. See Kearney et al., 14–18; Palmer, *Smart Money*, 212–14.

73. See Cole, Iverson, and Tufano, "Can Gambling Increase Savings?" (finding evidence suggesting prize-linked savings accounts offered by a bank in South Africa "increase[d] net savings" and substituted for National Lottery play); Atalay et al., "Prize-Linked Savings," 87 (finding in an online experiment that introducing a prize-linked savings [PLS] account "increases total savings quite dramatically (on average by 12% points), and that the demand for the PLS account comes from reductions in lottery expenditures and current consumption"); Filiz-Ozbay et al., "Do Lottery Payments Induce Savings Behavior" (finding in a lab experiment that a lottery payout option led to greater rates of payment deferral, which the researchers used to proxy for savings behavior).

74. American Savings Promotion Act, Public Law No. 113-251, enacted December 18, 2014, 128 Stat. 2888. For discussion of state laws relating to prize-linked savings accounts and potential legislative directions for the future, see Watford, "Save Now, Win Later."

75. Qualifying savings can take the form of "a savings account, certificate of deposit, IRA, prepaid card, savings bond, or Treasury Direct account." Save Your Refund, https://saveyourrefund.com/home/.

76. Fetherstonhaugh and Ross, "Framing Effects," 203.

77. Alm, Jackson, and McKee, "Deterrence and Beyond," 319, 323–24.

78. Fabbri, Barbieri, and Bigoni, "Ride Your Luck!"

79. See Koen Smets, "There Is More to Behavioral Economics Than Biases and Fallacies," *Behavioral Scientist*, July 24, 2018 (describing mixed results in lottery studies, including ones involving health and work incentives).

80. Vashistha, Cutrell, and Thies, "Snowball Sampling."

81. Cristina Caron, "United Airlines Pauses Lottery for Bonuses after Employees Rebel Online," *New York Times*, March 5, 2018.

82. See Mollner and Weyl, "Lottery Equilibrium" (modeling the choice that people might make between a divisible good such as corn and an indivisible one like a house).

83. See Mollner and Weyl, 14–15.

84. Thirty-two states had formal diversion programs as of 2015. Elissa Cohen et al., *Welfare Rules Databook: State TANF Policies as of July 2015*, US Department of Health and Human Services, Administration for Children and Families, Office of Planning, Research, and Evaluation, OPRE Report 2016-67, September 2016, 11–12.

85. See Cohen et al., 32–38, table I.A.1 (detailing state diversion programs, including "period of TANF ineligibility after receiving diversion payment").

86. See Hamrick and Andrews, "SNAP Participants' Eating Patterns," 2.

87. See Hamrick and Andrews, 2; Goldin, Homonoff, and Meckel, "Is There an Nth of the Month Effect?"

88. See Hamrick and Andrews, "SNAP Participants' Eating Patterns," 15.

89. See Banerjee and Duflo, *Poor Economics*, 9–13 (discussing and diagramming poverty traps, and noting the potential for disagreement about whether one exists in a given context).

90. Banerjee and Duflo, 9–13.

91. Banerjee and Duflo, 221–23 (discussing and illustrating situations in which surmounting a particular "hump" of funding enables a business to become profitable).

92. See generally Karelis, *Persistence of Poverty*.

93. See Karelis, 77–78. Karelis argues that his analysis does not implicate lumpy goods, since the first increments are not completely valueless on their own. Karelis, 119–22. But this only means that the good's production function is not a single step; the upsurge in value when the final increment is added is consistent with the idea of lumpiness as used here.

94. Super, "Political Economy of Entitlement," 655–58.

95. For related analysis, see Ball, *Critical Mass*, 317–19 and fig. 13.5 (citing Campbell and Ormerod, "Dynamics of Crime") (discussing and depicting how changes in social deprivation can produce large or small differences in crime levels, depending on starting positions).

96. They also connect to much-studied philosophical questions about whether and how to aggregate benefits and harms across people. For the role of lumpiness in making these judgments, see Brennan, "Moral Lumps."

97. See, e.g., S. Kelman, "In-Kind Transfers," 57.

CHAPTER SEVEN

1. Bureau of Labor Statistics, "Economic News Release: Contingent and Alternative Employment Arrangements—May 2017," June 7, 2018.

2. Board of Governors of the Federal Reserve System, *Report on the Economic Well-Being of U.S. Households in 2017* (May 2018).

3. See Chen et al., "Value of Flexible Work."

4. See C. Alexander, "Legal Avoidance."

5. Mullainathan and Shafir, *Scarcity*, 84–85.

6. See Mas-Colell, "Non-Convexity," 656.

7. Landers, Rebitzer, and Taylor, "Rat Race Redux."

8. Van Echtelt, Glebbeek, and Lindenberg, "New Lumpiness of Work."

9. Van Echtelt, Glebbeek, and Lindenberg, 507.

10. Van Echtelt, Glebbeek, and Lindenberg, 498.

11. Williams, Platt, and Lee, "Disruptive Innovation," 13.

12. Van Echtelt, Glebbeek, and Lindenberg, "New Lumpiness of Work," 508.

13. Van Echtelt, Glebbeek, and Lindenberg, 497.

14. See Gergen, "Open Terms," 1015–16.

15. It is possible that new business models, such as relay drivers who take over from each other at designated points, could break down such chunks—if autonomous vehicles do not make human drivers obsolete first.

16. See Iliev and Welch, "Model of Operational Slack," 4.

17. See Iliev and Welch, 4, 14.

18. Frank, *Production Theory*, 33.

19. Sandra G. Boodman, "Is Your Surgeon Double-Booked?," *Washington Post*, July 10, 2017.

20. See, e.g., Rifkin, *Age of Access*, 32; Gibson and Lizeieri, "Friction and Inertia."

21. See, e.g., Sue Shellenberger, "Don't Get Too Used to Your Own Desk," *Wall Street Journal*, May 15, 2018; Lawrence Biemiller, "Does the Faculty Office Have a Future?," *Chronicle of Higher Education*, May 6, 2018.

22. See Shellenberger, "Your Own Desk."

23. See Brown, "Claiming a Corner at Work"; Morrison and Macky, "Shared Office Spaces," 105.

24. Hirst, "Settlers, Vagrants and Mutual Indifference."

25. See Shellenberger, "Don't Get Too Used to Your Own Desk."

26. Ripstein, "Beyond the Harm Principle," 218.

27. Ripstein, 218; see also Larissa Katz, "Exclusion and Exclusivity," 303 (discussing Ripstein's example).

28. Shoup, *High Cost of Free Parking*, 434–53.

29. See Powanga and Powanga, "Timeshare Ownership," 69–74.

30. See Robert Reich, "The Sharing Economy Will Be Our Undoing," *Salon*, August 25, 2015.

31. Aguiar, et al., "Leisure Luxuries."

32. See J. Rose, *Free Time*, 93–111.

33. Zerubavel, *Seven Day Circle*, 35–43.

34. Mas and Pallais, "Valuing Alternative Work Arrangements," 3726, 3745 (finding "a strong aversion to jobs that permit employer discretion in scheduling," which the authors found "is due to aversion to working nonstandard hours, rather than unpredictability in scheduling").

35. See Hamermesh and Stancanelli, "Long Workweeks and Strange Hours," 1016 (find-

ing, based on time diary data, that "more than 1 in every 3 workers perform some weekend work in the United States compared to 1 in 5 in France, Germany, and the Netherlands; and more than 1 in 4 workers work at night (between 10 p.m. and 6 a.m.) in the United States compared to 1 in 14 in France, 1 in 7 in Germany, and 1 in 10 in the Netherlands").

36. Prescott, "Improving Access to Justice."
37. See Warren and Tyagi, *Two-Income Trap*, 59–62.
38. By analogy, many elderly people prefer independent living over sharing a home with their adult children. See, e.g., Costa, *Evolution of Retirement*, 106–32; Ellickson, *Household*, 82.
39. The Jumpstart Our Business Startups (JOBS) Act was signed into law on April 5, 2012. Title III of the Act addresses crowdfunding.
40. Banerjee and Duflo, *Poor Economics*, 221.
41. "When a Novelist Holds an IPO," *Freakonomics* (blog), August 1, 2008, http://freakonomics.com/2008/08/01/when-a-novelist-holds-an-ipo/.
42. Milton Friedman discussed the idea in his 1962 book, *Capitalism and Freedom*, 102–4. For a dystopian fictional take, see Kollin and Kollin, *Unincorporated Man*.
43. See Alonso and Watt, "Efficient Distribution of Copyright Income," 81, 89.
44. Some efforts along these lines have been attempted in the music industry, although they appear to have encountered difficulty remaining sustainable. See Ian Youngs, "Music Fans Buy a Slice of Stars," *BBC News*, September 14, 2010.
45. Shiller, *New Financial Order*, 107–13; see Purdy, "Freedom-Promoting Approach to Property," 1272–78 (discussing Shiller's ideas);
46. Steven D. Levitt, "Let's Just Get Rid of Tenure (Including Mine)," *Freakonomics* (blog), March 3, 2007, http://freakonomics.com/2007/03/03/lets-just-get-rid-of-tenure/.
47. Cooter and Porat, "Anti-Insurance," 218–21.
48. Cf. Cooter and Porat, 218–21.
49. See, e.g., Hemel, "Pooling and Unpooling."
50. See, e.g., Estlund, "What Should We Do after Work?"; Chase, *Peers Inc.*, 60.
51. Banerjee and Duflo, *Poor Economics*, 223–26.
52. Banerjee and Duflo, 230.
53. Banerjee and Duflo, 230.
54. See Ellenberg, *How Not to Be Wrong*, 233–37 (recounting and discussing this quote).
55. Put differently, money may generate more utility in the state of the world in which one's team has won. See Cook and Graham, "Demand for Insurance and Protection," 143, 149 n14.
56. See, e.g., Loewenstein and Prelec, "Preferences for Sequences"; Loewenstein and Sicherman, "Do Workers Prefer Increasing Wage Profiles?" For a concise overview, see Frederick, Loewenstein, and O'Donoghue, "Time Discounting and Time Preference," 28–29.
57. See Loewenstein and Prelec, "Preferences for Sequences," 91.
58. On adaptation, see Kahneman and Varey, "Psychology of Utility." On the greater pain associated with changes coded as losses rather than those coded as failures to achieve gains, see, e.g., Shafir and Tversky, "Decision Making." For the application of this idea to the preferences for improving sequences, see Loewenstein and Prelec, "Preferences for Sequences," 92.
59. Loewenstein and Prelec, "Preferences for Sequences," 92–93. Saving the best episodes for later also allows people to derive value from anticipation. See Loewenstein, "Anticipation."

60. Loewenstein and Sicherman, "Do Workers Prefer Increasing Wage Profiles?"; Neumark, "Rising Earnings Profiles"; see Frederick, Loewenstein, and O'Donoghue, "Time Discounting and Time Preference," 31.
61. Loewenstein and Sicherman, "Do Workers Prefer Increasing Wage Profiles?" 69–70.
62. Loewenstein and Sicherman, 75.
63. Similarly, lump sums may be difficult to self-assemble. See chapter 6.
64. The life-cycle hypothesis (the idea that people can easily spread their lifetime earnings across the life cycle, regardless of when the money is earned) has been rebutted by behavioral findings. See Shefrin and Thaler, "Behavioral Life-Cycle Hypothesis"; see also Fennell and Stark, "Taxation over Time," 6–21.
65. See, e.g., Rachlin, *Science of Self-Control*, 60–62.
66. See Heyman, *Addiction*, 116–24 (discussing a hypothetical presented by Richard Herrnstein).
67. Heyman, 156–57.
68. Machina, "Dynamic Consistency," 1645, 1659. See Machina generally for an exploration of the degree to which preferences are contingent on whether other preferences have been satisfied—that is, are "nonseparable."

CHAPTER EIGHT

1. For one provider's guide to large-scale meat purchases, including images showing the refrigerator space required, see "Buying Half a Cow. How Much Beef Is It?," Clover Meadows Beef, http://www.clovermeadowsbeef.com/buying-half-a-cow/.
2. Crowd Cow, https://www.crowdcow.com/; see also "Frequently Asked Questions," Crowd Cow, https://www.crowdcow.com/faq.
3. For examples of both kinds of aggregation, see J. Lee, "Gaining Assurances."
4. Wicksteed, *Common Sense*, 99–100, 108–9.
5. Wicksteed, 109.
6. The term "sharing economy" is often criticized, although many writers continue to use it because it has gained such currency. See, e.g., Davidson and Infranca, "Urban Phenomenon," 216 n1. Alternatives abound. For example, Umair Haque uses the apt term "microchunking" to capture new approaches to unbundling goods and services. Haque, *New Capitalist Manifesto*, 128–31, 137.
7. See, e.g., Rifkin, *Zero Marginal Cost Society*, 234–40; Lobel, "Law of the Platform," 95; Kreiczer-Levy, "Share, Own, Access," 174–77.
8. See, e.g., Baumeister and Wangenheim, "Access versus Ownership."
9. Baumeister and Wangenheim, 7–8.
10. See Wicksteed, *Common Sense*, 120–21.
11. Chase, *Peers Inc.*, 44 (explaining how by "slicing" and "aggregating," platforms "create a right-sized asset and give access to it"); see Roth, *Who Gets What*, 101–6 (examining how speed thickens matching markets).
12. Hayek, "Use of Knowledge," 526–28.
13. The gains from specialization can themselves be attributed to indivisibilities, whether in production processes or in skills. Scarf, "Allocation of Resources," 115; Mas-Colell, "Non-Convexity," 656.
14. The amount of time a car sits idle is often cited as evidence of inefficiency. See, e.g., Rifkin, *Zero Marginal Cost Society*, 228 ("The average vehicle in the United States is idle 92 percent of the time, making it an extremely inefficient fixed asset.") (endnote omitted). But a car's idleness is only inefficient if there is some better way to make use of the car or its components, or of the space that it takes up.

15. For a fictional account of the (real) challenges of New York City's street parking system, see Quindlen, *Alternate Side*, 33–35.
16. Strahilevitz, "Right to Abandon," 387.
17. See Brian Solomon, "FlightCar to Shut Down, Sell Technology to Mercedes-Benz," *Forbes*, July 14, 2016.
18. Omni, https://www.beomni.com/; see Josh Constine, "Omni Storage Now Earns You Money by Renting Out Your Stuff," *TechCrunch*, October 24, 2017.
19. See, e.g., Lobel, "Law of the Platform," 108; Chase, *Peers Inc.*, 73–78.
20. See Benkler, *Wealth of Networks*, 81–82.
21. Strahilevitz, "Wealth without Markets," 1498.
22. Strahilevitz, 1499.
23. Strahilevitz, 1499.
24. "Frequently Asked Questions," Clean the World, https://cleantheworld.org/faq/.
25. See Lobel, "Law of the Platform," 109 ("In many ways, the platform [as a mode of access] tilts the balance away from altruistic/communal interactions to marketable/commodified exchanges.").
26. See Horton and Zeckhauser, "Owning, Using and Renting," 3 (explaining that "for owners, the possibility of rental creates a new opportunity cost for their own usage").
27. See Strahilevitz, "Wealth without Markets," 1498.
28. Lobel, "Law of the Platform" 108–9.
29. See Horton and Zeckhauser, "Owning, Using and Renting" (discussing and modeling long-run changes in ownership decisions under various assumptions).
30. See Benkler, "Sharing Nicely," 276–77, 297.
31. Johnson, "Economics and Sociality," 1952.
32. Johnson, 1952.
33. See Benkler, "Sharing Nicely," 297 (defining "fine-grained" and "large-grained" lumpy goods).
34. See Horton and Zeckhauser, "Owning, Using and Renting," 19–21 (discussing the implications of economies of scale for ownership patterns).
35. Dillon, De Weerdt, and O'Donoghue, "Paying More for Less" (finding evidence consistent with this explanation, as well as with several others, including self-rationing, inattention, and intra-household coordination issues).
36. See Dillon, De Weerdt, and O'Donoghue, 47–51.
37. "FAQs," GivnGo, https://www.givngo.com/faq/.
38. Kreiczer-Levy, "Consumption Property," 83 (quoting an explanatory video from NeighborGoods that rhetorically asks "does everyone on your block need to own a lawnmower?"); Kreiczer-Levy, "Share, Own, Access," 198.
39. See Iliev and Welch, "Model of Operational Slack."
40. See, e.g., Horton and Zeckhauser, "Owning, Using and Renting," 32.
41. Perlacia, Duml, and Saebi, "Collaborative Consumption," 6.
42. See Clewlow and Mishra, "Disruptive Transportation," 1 ("Parking represents the top reason that urban ride-hailing users substitute a ride-hailing service in place of driving themselves (37%).").
43. See, e.g., Clewlow and Mishra, 26; Gehrke, Felix, and Reardon, "Fare Choices," 13.
44. See Schaller, "Empty Seats, Full Streets," 12.
45. Horton and Zeckhauser, "Owning, Using and Renting," 2–3.
46. See Horton and Zeckhauser, 22.
47. Horton and Zeckhauser, 22, 27.

48. Waldfogel, *Tyranny of the Market*; The Rolling Stones, "You Can't Always Get What You Want," on *Let It Bleed* (London Records, 1969).
49. Waldfogel, *Tyranny of the Market*, 14–20.
50. Ford, *My Life and Work*, 72; see also Waldfogel, *Tyranny of the Market*, 119–20.
51. See Hall, *Cities in Civilization*, 409–10 (quoting Ford, *My Life and Work*, 72).
52. Seabright, *Company of Strangers*, 159.
53. Anderson, *Long Tail*.
54. See Anderson.
55. Waldfogel, *Tyranny of the Market*, 21–28, 100–107.
56. See Waldfogel, 134–38.
57. See Waldfogel, 131–46.
58. Waldfogel, 23–26.
59. Waldfogel, 164.
60. Agence France-Presse, "Japanese Noodle Company Invents Noise Cancelling Fork to Mask Offensive Slurping," *South China Morning Post*, October 25, 2017.
61. Ayres, "Voluntary Taxation and Beyond," 3–4.
62. The spatial modeling of product differentiation—the idea that products can be arrayed in virtual space based on their characteristics—was introduced in Hotelling, "Stability in Competition." See also, e.g., Waldfogel, *Tyranny of the Market*, 13–20; Yoo, "Economics of Product Differentiation."
63. Bar-Gill, "Bundling and Consumer Misperception."
64. Varian, "Pricing Information Goods," 23. Product "tying"—requiring consumers to use proprietary ink cartridges for a laser printer, for example—could facilitate price discrimination in another way, by allowing the manufacturer to identify heavier users of the product. See Bowman, "Tying Arrangements," 23–24 (explaining how a tied product could operate as a "counting device" for price discrimination purposes).
65. Varian, "Pricing Information Goods," 23.
66. Chris Dixon, "How Bundling Benefits Sellers and Buyers," *cdixon* (blog), July 8, 2012, http://cdixon.org/2012/07/08/how-bundling-benefits-sellers-and-buyers/.
67. Dixon.
68. See Dixon (noting qualifications).
69. See Waldfogel, "Golden Age," 210–11 (discussing advantages of bundling when digital products can be delivered to more consumers at zero marginal cost and "consumers' valuations of products are not (perfectly) positively correlated").
70. Frank, *Production Theory*, 33; see also Frank, "Assortment Problem."
71. Orzach and Stano, "Supersizing."
72. Orzach and Stano, 7–9 (providing a similar numerical example).
73. Orzach and Stano, 8–9.
74. Orzach and Stano, 11–12.
75. Orzach and Stano, 11–12.
76. The nonrefundable event ticket, coupled with a desire not to attend the event, is a standard example in the sunk-cost literature. See, e.g., Nozick, *Nature of Rationality*, 21–24.
77. Nozick, 21–24; see also Rachlin, *Science of Self-Control*, 141–42.
78. Soman and Gourville, "Transaction Decoupling."
79. The question of whether people feel the loss of an entire discrete "thing" more acutely than an economically equivalent drop in overall value recurs in the regulatory takings context. See chapter 11.
80. Levy and Young, "The Real Thing."

81. On the "single coin" constraint, see Levy and Young. On the limits of vending machines, see Allen, *Secret Formula*, 301.
82. See Levy and Young, "The Real Thing," 785–86.
83. See Levy and Young, 786; Allen, *Secret Formula*, 301.
84. Allen , *Secret Formula*, 301–3
85. Allen, 301.
86. See Levy and Young, "The Real Thing," 786.
87. Levy and Young, 786 n35.
88. Levy and Young, 787–89. Coke machines were ultimately redesigned to take multiple coins—a move that built in flexibility going forward by enabling future price changes "at zero marginal cost." Levy and Young.
89. Allen, *Secret Formula*, 301.
90. See Gould, "Phyletic Size Decrease in Hershey Bars."
91. See Levy and Young, "The Real Thing," 795–96.

CHAPTER NINE
1. Oliver Wainwright, "Chilean Architect Alejandro Aravena Wins 2016 Pritzker Prize," *Guardian*, January 13, 2016.
2. Wainwright.
3. Wainwright. See Sennett, *Building and Dwelling* 228–30 (discussing Aravena's work and the potential of "shell" structures more generally).
4. Wainwright, "Chilean Architect Alejandro Aravena."
5. Vargas, "Incremental User Built Housing."
6. R. Hardin, *Collective Action*, 59.
7. See, e.g., "Tiny Homes," *Curbed*, http://www.curbed.com/tiny-homes.
8. Fennell, *Unbounded Home*.
9. See Coase, "Nature of the Firm." For analyses applying Coase's theory of efficient firm boundaries to real property contexts, see Ellickson, "Property in Land," 1332–34; Demsetz, "Toward a Theory," 358.
10. See Fenster, "Community by Covenant," 11–12.
11. Cf. Groth, *Living Downtown*, 126–27 (explaining that for rooming houses, "the surrounding sidewalks and stores functioned as parts of each resident's home"); Infranca, "Spaces for Sharing," 7–13.
12. Infranca, "Spaces for Sharing," 7–13.
13. See Liu Chang, "Bathrooms for Hutong Dwellers Planned," *China Daily*, August 5, 2004, http://www.chinadaily.com.cn/english/doc/2004–08/05/content_359010.htm; "Living on the Lawn FAQs," Office of the Dean of Students, University of Virginia, https://odos.virginia.edu/living-lawn-faqs.
14. See, e.g., "Laneway Housing Approved by Vancouver Council," *CBC News*, July 29, 2009 (quoting Vancouver councillor Raymond Louie's observation that permitting laneway garages to be converted to dwelling units "will allow people to age in place"); "Accessory Dwelling Units Text Amendment," Community Planning and Economic Development, Minneapolismn.gov (providing information on Minneapolis's 2014 zoning amendment permitting accessory dwelling units).
15. Nesterly, https://www.nesterly.io/; see Katharine Schwab, "The Airbnb for Affordable Housing Is Here," *Fast Company*, November 21, 2017, https://www.fastcompany.com/90151804/the-airbnb-for-affordable-housing-is-here.
16. Such efforts may not turn out to be as effective as envisioned. See DellaVigna and Malmendier, "Paying Not to Go to the Gym."

17. See, e.g., Field, "Investment in Urban Slums," 280; Besley, "Property Rights and Investment Incentives," 906–7; Besley and Ghatak, "Property Rights and Economic Development."
18. Galiani and Schargrodsky, "Property Rights for the Poor," 706. Titling was also associated with reductions in household size and increased education of children. Galiani and Schargrodsky, 708–10.
19. Erica Field, "Community Public Goods," 842–46.
20. Field, 858–59.
21. See, e.g., Infranca, "Housing Changing Households"; Gabbe, "Lens of Size"; Stern and Yager, "21st Century SROs"; Been, Gross, and Infranca, "Responding to Changing Households."
22. See Stern and Yager, "21st Century SROs"; Been, Gross, and Infranca, "Responding to Changing Households."
23. See, e.g., Been, Gross, and Infranca, "Responding to Changing Households."
24. See, e.g., Infranca, "Housing Changing Households."
25. Lee Romney, "San Francisco Approves 220-Square-Foot Apartments," Los Angeles Times, November 21, 2012; see also Gabbe, "Lens of Size."
26. See Stern and Yager, "21st Century SROs," 28; see also Been, Gross, and Infranca, "Responding to Changing Households," 40–41 (reporting in 2014 that Washington DC, Denver, and Austin all followed the International Building Code's minimum dwelling size of 220 square feet, with Seattle also using that minimum as a default, while at that time New York City remained "an outlier").
27. International Code Council, R304.1, Minimum Habitable Room Area (2015).
28. International Code Council, R304.1.
29. Caplin et al., Housing Partnerships, 6.
30. See Rose-Ackerman, "Inalienability," 959 n79; R. Hardin, "Utilitarian Logic of Liberalism," 58–62.
31. See Karelis, Persistence of Poverty, and the related discussion in chapter 6.
32. See Banerjee and Duflo, Poor Economics, 9–16. I thank Kay Dannenmaier for flagging this parallel.
33. See Caplin et al., Housing Partnerships.
34. See Fennell, "Homeownership 2.0," for an overview of existing and proposed approaches.
35. In most US cities, explicit size minima are less likely to act as binding constraints on small units than other regulatory restrictions that make building small units infeasible. See Been, Gross, and Infranca, "Responding to Changing Households," 61.
36. Ellickson, Household, 76–84; Ellickson, "Unpacking the Household," 287–92.
37. See, e.g., Ellickson, "Unpacking the Household," 260, 287–92; O'Flaherty, City Economics, 348–49.
38. See Stern and Yager, "21st Century SROs," 4 (observing that single adults may live with roommates not out of choice but out of necessity).
39. This is not a fundamentally new phenomenon—the practice of taking in boarders for extra cash has a long history. See Groth, Living Downtown, 121.
40. See Fennell, "Owners and Outlaws," 248–50.
41. Desmond, Evicted.
42. See Mariana Ionova, "The $80-a-Week, 60-Square-Foot Housing Solution That's Also Totally Illegal," Next City, June 3, 2013.
43. Chhaya Community Development Corporation, "Illegal Dwelling Units," 1, 3.
44. See Chhaya Community Development Corporation, 4, 9.

45. For accounts of the fire, see, e.g., Benjamin Wallace-Wells, "What Happened, Exactly, in Oakland's Ghost Ship Fire?," *New Yorker*, December, 13, 2016; J. Weston Phippen, "What Caused the Deadly Oakland Warehouse Fire?," *Atlantic*, December 5, 2016.
46. See, e.g., Glaeser and Gyourko, "Economic Implications of Housing Supply," 5–8 (discussing geographical and regulatory constraints on housing production).
47. Glaeser and Gyourko, 5–8; Glaeser, Gyourko, and Saks, "Why Is Manhattan So Expensive?"
48. See, e.g., Paul Krugman, "Wrong Way Nation," editorial, *New York Times*, August 24, 2014; Schleicher, "Stuck!"
49. See, e.g., Glaeser and Gyourko, "Economic Implications of Housing Supply."
50. The fraction has recently been falling and is closer to one in five as of this writing. See Kingsley, "Trends in Housing Problems," 2–3 ("Among low-income renters with housing needs, the share receiving assistance dropped from 24 percent in 2005 to 21 percent in 2015.").
51. The 2017 average HUD monthly expenditure for the Housing Choice Voucher Program was $753 ($9,036 annually); the average for all HUD housing programs was $693 ($8,316 annually). US Department of Housing and Urban Development, Office of Policy Development and Research, Assisted Housing: National and Local, https://www.huduser.gov/portal/datasets/assthsg.html.
52. Ellen, "Housing Low-Income Households," 784.
53. Super, "Political Economy of Entitlement," 655–58.
54. Ellen, "Housing Low-Income Households," 783. The Nesterly platform may represent a step in this direction. See note 15 above and accompanying text.
55. See Vargas, "Incremental User Built Housing," 4 (discussing the 2007 Elemental Renca project: "Each house was designed to grow incrementally inside within a structural shell. In reality, the organized community managed to find additional subsidy from private funding to build the complete house from the beginning.").
56. Banerjee and Duflo, *Poor Economics*, 183–84.
57. This relates to the long-running debate over whether "people-based" or "place-based" strategies are superior. See, e.g., Crane and Manville, "People or Place?," 2.
58. See, e.g., Seicshnaydre, "Missed Opportunity," 176.
59. See Ellen and Yager, "Federal Rental Housing Policy," 104 (noting the "tension . . . between serving as many households as possible and supporting housing in high-opportunity neighborhoods").
60. Chetty, Hendren, and Katz, "Exposure to Better Neighborhoods." The effects on those who moved as adolescents were slightly negative. Chetty, Hendren, and Katz, 858.
61. In 2017, the average time nationwide on the waiting list for a Housing Choice Voucher was thirty-two months. The average wait times are longer in some areas: seventy-five months in San Francisco and sixty-eight months in New York City. US Department of Housing and Urban Development, Office of Policy Development and Research, Assisted Housing: National and Local, https://www.huduser.gov/portal/datasets/assthsg.html.
62. See Department of Housing and Urban Development, "Final Rule on Small Area Fair Market Rents," *Federal Register* 81 (November 16, 2016): 80567–87. There are other barriers to voucher use in high-opportunity areas, including landlords who refuse to accept vouchers and time limits for using vouchers.

63. Collinson and Ganong, "Changes in Housing Voucher Design," 66.
64. See S. Kelman, "In-Kind Transfers," 57.
65. See Daniel Hamermesh, "How Far Should Your Sympathies Go?," *Freakonomics* (blog), February 6, 2009, http://freakonomics.com/2009/02/06/how-far-should -your-sympathies-go/?c_page=2 (suggesting that society may manifest a "second-hand endowment effect" in which more resources will be spent to keep people from losing things than to generate gains for them).

CHAPTER TEN

1. See Glaeser, *Cities, Agglomeration, and Spatial Equilibrium*, 1.
2. Glaeser, 1 ("The foremost question of urban economics is why cities exist.").
3. As of the 2010 census, 80.7 percent of the US population lived in urban areas. US Census Bureau, "Growth in Urban Population Outpaces Rest of Nation, Census Bureau Reports," News Release, March 12, 2012. For global urbanization statistics and projections, see "World Urbanization Prospects 2018," United Nations Department of Economics and Social Affairs, Population Division, https://esa.un.org/unpd/ wup/.
4. Davidson and Infranca, "Urban Phenomenon."
5. See, e.g., Schleicher, "City as a Law and Economic Subject," 1528–29.
6. See, e.g., Bettencourt, "Origins of Scaling in Cities," 1438; Brinkman, "Structure of Cities."
7. See West, *Scale*, 319–21 (emphasizing the physical nature of cities and their inhabitants).
8. See, e.g., Karlsson, "Clusters."
9. West, *Scale*, 321.
10. See Artle, "Space Economy," 167–69 (noting that the commonly used linear approach "is not capable of dealing with indivisibilities, and, hence, with increasing and decreasing returns to scale, or with external economies and diseconomies—the very phenomena which location theorists consider basic in any attempt to explain why urban areas exist and continue to grow"); West, *Scale*, 355 (decrying the assumption that "any urban characteristic . . . scales *linearly* with population size" given the city's "most essential feature and the very point of its existence, namely, that it is a collective emergent agglomeration resulting from *nonlinear* social and organizational interactions").
11. Hopkins, *Urban Development*, 28 (emphasis omitted).
12. See, e.g., Benkler, "Commons and Growth."
13. For recent legal scholarship on this topic, see, e.g., Schleicher, "City as a Law and Economic Subject"; Parchomovsky and Siegelman, "Cities, Property, and Positive Externalities," 251–52; Rodriguez and Schleicher, "Location Market"; see also C. Rose, "Comedy of the Commons," 766–71.
14. Marshall, *Principles of Economics*, Book IV, ch. X, § 3 (8th ed. 1920).
15. See Duranton and Puga, "Micro-Foundations," 2066; see also Henderson, "Urban Scale Economies," 243–48.
16. Glaeser, *Cities, Agglomeration, and Spatial Equilibrium*, 6–8, 117.
17. See Glaeser, Kolko and Saiz, "Consumers and Cities," 135–36.
18. Duranton and Puga, "Micro-Foundations," 2066 (emphasis omitted).
19. Duranton and Puga, 2067–86.
20. See, e.g., Waldfogel, *Tyranny of the Market*, 165; Parchomovksy and Siegelman, "Cities, Property, and Positive Externalities," 237–40.

21. See Duranton and Puga, "Micro-Foundations," 2086–98; Schleicher, "City as a Law and Economic Subject," 1521–23; Rauch and Schleicher, "Like Uber," 939–40.
22. These innovations both depend on density and promise to alleviate some of its negative effects. See Davidson and Infranca, "Urban Phenomenon," 227–32; Rauch and Schleicher, "Like Uber," 940–41.
23. See Duranton and Puga, "Micro-Foundations," 2098–109.
24. Marshall, *Principles of Economics*, Book IV, ch. X, § 3.
25. Hsieh and Moretti, "Housing Constraints and Spatial Misallocation."
26. Albouy et al., "Optimal Distribution," 2 ("Our simulations suggest that large American cities may be undersized by about a third, causing about twice too many sites to be developed and more than half of the U.S. urban population to be misallocated.").
27. Albouy et al., 2.
28. Albouy et al., 2; see also Schleicher, "Stuck!"
29. Glaeser and Gyourko, "Economic Implications of Housing Supply," 23.
30. See Emily Badger, "Why Don't People Who Can't Afford Housing Just Move Where It's Cheaper?," The Upshot, *New York Times*, May 15, 2018.
31. See, e.g., Albouy et al., "Optimal Distribution."
32. Garratt, "Tale of Two Cities."
33. Garratt uses the Canadian examples of Toronto and Eden Mills to illustrate the more preferred and less preferred city, respectively.
34. Garratt.
35. See Nick deWilde, "A Startup Jobseeker's Guide for Moving to San Francisco," *Tradecraft*, June 28, 2018 (emphasizing the importance of building a "runway" of time to find a job in the Bay Area).
36. Garratt, "A Tale of Two Cities."
37. Seabright, *Company of Strangers*, 112.
38. See Jacobs, *Death and Life*, 152–77.
39. For discussion and analysis of this literature, see Garnett, *Ordering the City*, 49–76.
40. Buchanan and Stubblebine, "Externality," 371.
41. See Fennell, "Slicing Spontaneity," 2378–82; Gergen, "Open Terms," 1013–19.
42. To be sure, these actions could be done to different degrees, such as creating a more or less elaborate rose garden. But the choice may be binary in practice if the minimum level necessary to satisfy the actor's own preferences exceeds the level that anyone else would be willing to pay to enjoy. See Haddock, "Irrelevant Externality Angst," 10–11; Buchanan and Stubblebine, "Externality," 374.
43. Frischmann and Lemley, "Spillovers," 269.
44. See Fennell, "Agglomerama."
45. See Fennell, "Fee Simple Obsolete"; Posner and Weyl, "Another Name for Monopoly."
46. See Artle, "Space Economy," 168 (explaining potential distortions in location choices and how "indivisibilities, as it were, upset the price mechanism as an efficient allocator").
47. On the characteristics of public goods, see, e.g., Cornes and Sandler, *Theory of Externalities*, 6–7.
48. See Tideman, "Integrating Land-Value Taxation."
49. See, e.g., Rothschild and White, "Analytics of the Pricing."
50. See, e.g., Been, "'Exit' as a Constraint," 478–83.
51. See, e.g., Fennell and Peñalver, "Exactions Creep."

52. Euclidian zoning is named for Euclid, Ohio, the municipality involved in the land-mark Supreme Court case upholding zoning, Village of Euclid v. Ambler Realty Co., 272 U.S. 365 (1926).

53. See, e.g., Jacobs, *Dark Age Ahead*, 153–57; Porter, Phillips, and Lassar, *Flexible Zoning*, 11; Acker, "Performance Zoning."

54. See Wendy Lee and Roland Li, "Mountain View's Unusual Rule for Facebook: No Free Food," SFChronicle.com, July 23, 2018. See also Nellie Bowles, "San Francisco Officials to Tech Workers: Buy Your Lunch," *New York Times*, July 31, 2018 (reporting on a recently proposed San Francisco ordinance that would ban company cafeterias in newly constructed corporate offices).

55. For an extended discussion of the ideas in this section, see Fennell, "Fee Simple Obsolete."

56. See, e.g., United States v. Westinghouse Elec. & Mfg. Co., 339 U.S. 261, 272 (1950) (Jackson, J., dissenting) (observing that the government's "inherent condemnation power, by its very nature, is a perpetual option to take, at any time, any property it needs").

57. See, e.g., Hong, "Assembling Land," 3.

58. Kerr and Kominers, "Agglomerative Forces and Cluster Shapes."

59. Kerr and Kominers, 877–78.

60. Kerr and Kominers, 877–79, 898.

61. Duranton and Kerr, "Logic of Agglomeration," 359.

62. Duranton and Kerr, 359–60.

63. See Rodriguez and Schleicher, "Location Market," 647 (distinguishing agglomeration effects that operate at the regional level from "microagglomerations" at the scale of groups of stores or residents).

64. See, e.g., Fischel, "Zoning, Nonconvexities"; Cooter, "Decentralized Law," 1687.

65. For the mountain range metaphor for nonconvexities, see, e.g., Fischel, "Zoning, Nonconvexities," 176–77; Cooter, "Decentralized Law," 1687. Cf. Margolis, *Patterns, Thinking and Cognition*, 32–36 (discussing "hill-jumping" in evolutionary theory).

66. Ellickson and Been, *Land Use Controls*, 40.

67. Ellickson and Been, 40. Another possibility is that a developer succeeds in incrementally introducing a use that advances her own interests but devalues the area. See Fischel, "Zoning, Nonconvexities," 176–77.

68. Ellickson and Been, *Land Use Controls*, 40.

69. See, e.g., Schelling, *Micromotives and Macrobehavior*, 147–66.

70. See, e.g., Garnett, "Neglected Political Economy," 119–20 (describing losses to communities caused by expressways cutting through parish boundaries).

71. See Grisolía, López, and Ortúzar, "Burying the Highway." The term "community severance" refers not only to the severing of residential communities, but also the severing of communities from nearby services and amenities, such as shopping areas.

72. See Bell and Parchomovsky, "Reconfiguring Property," 1064–65.

73. See Parchomovsky and Siegelman, "Selling Mayberry."

74. See Fennell, "Forcings," 1356; cf. Bell and Parchomovsky, "Partial Takings," 2067–78 (proposing that an individual owner harmed by a partial taking be able to force the government to take—and compensate for—the balance of her property as well).

75. See, e.g., Banner, *Who Owns the Sky?*, 296.

76. See Banner, 296.

77. For example, the federal Fair Housing Act prohibits both public and private actors from discriminating along protected dimensions in providing access to housing. 42 U.S.C. § 3601 et seq.
78. See Zhang, "Cultural Paradigms," 355–60.

CHAPTER ELEVEN

1. Popov v. Hayashi, 2002 WL 31833731 (Cal Super. Ct. Dec. 18, 2002).
2. *Popov*, 2002 WL 31833731 at *8.
3. See Parchomovsky, Siegelman, and Thel, "Equal Wrongs," 740 ("Split-the-difference remedies are exceedingly unusual."); Helmholz, "Equitable Division," 322–27 (noting limited examples of equitable division in cases involving joint finders).
4. See, e.g., Leo Katz, *Why the Law Is So Perverse*, 139–55.
5. See Katz, 145–51; Kolber, "Smoothing Vague Laws." For an exploration of apportionment between litigants as contrasted with "winner-take-all" resolutions, see Coons, "Compromise as Precise Justice."
6. See, e.g., Parchomovsky, Siegelman, and Thel, "Equal Wrongs"; Chang, "214 Jurisdictions."
7. See, e.g., Johnson v. Hendrickson, 24 N.W.2d 914, 916 (S.D. 1946).
8. See, e.g., Kolber, "Smooth and Bumpy Laws"; Slemrod, "Buenas Notches."
9. For an overview of image thresholding, see Bovik, *Image and Video Processing*, 39–43. On legal thresholding, which renders continuous variables into binaries, see, e.g., Porat and Posner, "Aggregation and Law," 8; Leo Katz, *Why the Law Is So Perverse*, 157–81; Kolber, "Smoothing Vague Laws," 281.
10. How frequently this scenario will occur depends on how values, such as levels of shading, are distributed. See Bovik, *Image and Video Processing*, 41, fig. 4 (using image histograms to illustrate "well-separated modes" versus "poorly separated or indistinct modes"). In law, the cases that make it to trial may tend to cluster around breakpoints. See Priest and Klein, "Selection of Disputes for Litigation," 13–17.
11. See, e.g., Leo Katz, *Why the Law Is So Perverse*, 139–56; Kolber, "Smooth and Bumpy Laws"; see also Cooter, "Prices and Sanctions" (examining how sanctions introduce discontinuities).
12. See, e.g., R. Fisher et al., "Adaptive Thresholding"; Bovik, *Image and Video Processing*, 43–55.
13. See, e.g., Honoré, "Responsibility and Luck," 549–50; Grady, "Res Ipsa Loquitur," 899–90.
14. Juries may, however, "forgive" certain lapses. Grady, "American Negligence Rule."
15. Rex v. Smith, 11 Cr. App. R. 229, 84 L.J.K.B. 2153 (1915). For a detailed analysis, see S. Sullivan, "Probative Inference."
16. See S. Sullivan, "Probative Inference," 29–30.
17. See Sullivan, 31–32 (noting that the jury deliberated only eighteen minutes before finding Smith guilty).
18. See Sullivan, 30.
19. Sullivan, 35–37 (analyzing *Rex v. Smith* using the analogy of marbles drawn from urns).
20. Grady, "Efficient Negligence," 402.
21. See Schauer and Zeckhauser, "Degree of Confidence," 28 (contrasting criminal law's focus on the "discrete event" with employment contexts in which patterns of conduct are often deemed relevant).

22. Schauer and Zeckhauser, 48–52.
23. Schauer and Zeckhauser, 48–52.
24. Ayres and Unkovic, "Information Escrows."
25. Project Callisto, https://www.projectcallisto.org/; see Ian Ayres, "Meet Callisto, the Tinder-Like Platform That Aims to Fight Sexual Assault," *Washington Post*, October 9, 2015.
26. See, e.g., Ayres, "Meet Callisto."
27. Ayres, "Voluntary Taxation and Beyond," 38–43.
28. Ayres, 38–39.
29. S. Sullivan, "Probative Inference," 38–43.
30. Sullivan, 41–42.
31. On the question of whether it is possible to draw stochastic connections between events like the tub drownings without relying on propensity interferences, compare Sullivan, 42–43, with Rothstein, "Doctrine of Chances."
32. Harel and Porat, "Aggregating Probabilities across Cases."
33. Harel and Porat, 266–71. See also Schauer, "Sanctions for Acts."
34. See, e.g., Honoré, "Responsibility and Luck," 549–50.
35. See, e.g., Waldron, "Moments of Carelessness."
36. Grady alludes to this problem he observes that "many slips are like so many peas in a pod; the efficient ones look the same as the uneconomic ones." Grady, "Res Ipsa Loquitur," 905–6.
37. See Shavell, *Economic Analysis of Accident Law*, 21–26.
38. See, e.g., Grady, "Why Are People Negligent?," 309.
39. See Grady, 309.
40. See Grady, 309. Grady describes tort law as placing a "stochastic tax" on negligent activity, given the wide range of possible outcomes—from jury forgiveness to high damage awards. Grady, "American Negligence Rule," 48–49.
41. Cooter and Porat, "Lapses of Attention," 350–55.
42. Farnsworth and Grady, *Torts*, 158.
43. See Farnsworth and Grady, 158 (posing but not answering this question).
44. Cooter and Porat, "Lapses of Attention," 352–53.
45. Cooter and Porat, 352–53.
46. Cooter and Porat, *Getting Incentives Right*, 61–62, 68.
47. See, e.g., Nadler, "Blaming as a Social Process," 15–31.
48. Cooter and Porat, *Getting Incentives Right*, 61–62.
49. Cooter and Porat, 60–73.
50. Cooter and Porat, "Lapses of Attention," 339–48.
51. Grady, "American Negligence Rule," 36–37.
52. See "Drivewise from Allstate," Allstate, https://www.allstate.com/drive-wise.aspx; "Drive Safe and Save," State Farm, https://www.statefarm.com/insurance/auto/discounts/drive-safe-save/mobile-app.
53. Strahilevitz, "How's My Driving?"
54. On the analogy between manufacturing defects and human lapses, see Goldberg and Zipursky, "Strict Liability in Fault," 773–74; Cooter and Porat, *Getting Incentives Right*, 65.
55. See, e.g., Abbott, "The Reasonable Computer," 4.
56. Cooter and Porat are, in effect, urging an orchards to orchards comparison—one that would either aggregate behavior into larger patterns or look at the use of durable "second-order" precautions designed to produce particular patterns over time.

Cooter and Porat, *Getting Incentives Right*, 70–72; Cooter and Porat, "Lapses of Attention," 339–48.

57. See Waldron, "Moments of Carelessness," 387–89.

58. See, e.g., Keating, "Products Liability as Enterprise Liability," 74. For historical background and a critique of enterprise liability, see Priest, "Invention of Enterprise Liability."

59. Brown v. Ohio, 432 U.S. 161 (1977). For discussion of the "number of offenses" question raised by the case, see Moore, *Act and Crime*, 366, 386–88.

60. *Brown*, 432 U.S. at 169–70.

61. *Brown*, 432 U.S. at 169–70.

62. For discussion of this scenario, see Moore, *Act and Crime*, 365, 380, 389–90; see also Alexander and Ferzan, "Culpable Acts," 399 (discussing an example involving six shots aimed at an individual).

63. For discussion and criticism of the "volume discount," see Moore, *Act and Crime*, 390 n51; Alexander and Ferzan, "Culpable Acts," 399–400.

64. Alexander and Ferzan, "Culpable Acts," 400–401.

65. See Murray, "Law of Describing Accidents."

66. See SR International Business Insurance Co. v. World Trade Center Properties, LLC, 467 F.3d 107 (2d Cir. 2006).

67. See *SR International*, 467 F.3d 107.

68. On philosophical approaches to individuation, see, e.g., Moore, *Act and Crime*, 356–90.

69. Murray, "Law of Describing Accidents."

70. Murray.

71. Murr v. Wisconsin, 137 S. Ct. 1933 (2017).

72. On terminology for this category of takings, see Krier and Sterk, "Implicit Takings," 40–41.

73. Pennsylvania Coal v. Mahon, 260 U.S. 393, 415 (1922).

74. Lucas v. South Carolina Coastal Council, 505 U.S. 1003, 1027 (1992).

75. Penn Central Transportation Co. v. New York City, 438 U.S. 104 (1978). A separate per se test applies to permanent physical occupations and physical appropriations of property. See Loretto v. Teleprompter Manhattan CATV Corp., 458 U.S. 419 (1982); Horne v. Dept. of Agriculture, 135 S. Ct. 2419 (2015).

76. See *Lucas*, 505 U.S. at 1019–20 n8.

77. Michelman, "Property, Utility, and Fairness," 1192–93 (identifying the issue of denominator definition).

78. See *Penn Central*, 438 U.S. at 124. The third Penn Central factor is "the character of the governmental action," 438 U.S. at 124, which may also depend on choosing an implicit frame of reference.

79. Radin, "Liberal Conception of Property," 1674–78.

80. Tahoe-Sierra Pres. Council v. Tahoe Regional Planning Agency, 535 U.S. 302, 331 (2002).

81. See *Lucas*, 505 U.S. at 1016–17 n7 (describing as "insupportable," a denominator that included all of the landowner's "other holdings in the vicinity"). For a contrary view, see Dagan, "Takings and Distributive Justice," 782–84.

82. Eagle, *Regulatory Takings*, ch. 7, § 7-7(b)(2).

83. This characterization is questionable. In fact, they could have built a house on the currently empty lot, or a house that straddled the two lots, if they destroyed the existing cabin. See *Murr*, 137 S. Ct. at 1941.

84. *Murr*, 137 S. Ct. at 1945–46.
85. *Lucas*, 505 U.S. at 1020 and n9.
86. *Lucas*, 505 U.S. at 1043–44 (Blackmun, J., dissenting); 505 U.S. at 1065 n3 (Stevens, J., dissenting); see also 505 U.S. at 1076 (Statement of Souter, J.) (stating that the writ of certiorari should have been dismissed as improvidently granted, "because the questionable conclusion of total deprivation cannot be reviewed").
87. Palazzolo v. Rhode Island, 533 U.S. 606, 631 (2001).
88. Michelman, "Property, Utility, and Fairness," 1232–34 (discussing this rationale, while recognizing that the assumptions underlying it "are surely debatable").
89. See Michelman, 1234; see also Michelman, 1214 (discussing "settlement costs").
90. See Levinson, "Framing Transactions in Constitutional Law."
91. Schad v. Borough of Mt. Ephraim, 452 U.S. 61, 71–77 (1981) (distinguishing Young v. American Mini Theaters, 427 U.S. 50 (1976)).
92. Borough of Sayreville v. 35 Club, L.L.C., 33 A.3d 1200 (2012).
93. *Sayreville*, 33 A.3d at 1202 (citing Twp. of Saddle Brook v. A.B. Family Ctr., Inc., 722 A.2d 530, 596–97 (1999)).
94. *Sayreville*, 33 A.3d at 1203.
95. Stahl, "Challenge of Inclusion," 511.
96. See Mulligan v. Panther Valley Property Owners Assn., 766 A.2d 1186, 1192–93 (N.J. App. 2001).
97. For an examination of this question, see Porter, "Cumulative Hardship."
98. See, e.g., Ellickson, "Optimal Social Composition," 204–6.
99. See, e.g., Pitofsky, "New Definitions of Relevant Market." For criticism of the market definition approach, see, e.g., Kaplow, "Why (Ever) Define Markets?"
100. Castle Rock Entertainment v. Carol Pub. Group, 150 F.3d 132, 138 (2d Cir. 1998) ("For the purposes of the quantitative copying analysis we shall treat *Seinfeld*—a discrete, continuous television series—as a single work"); see also Civility Experts Worldwide v. Molly Manners, LLC, 167 F. Supp.3d 1179, 1193 (D. Colo. 2016) (expressing concern about the unit-of-analysis reasoning in *Castle Rock*). For an examination of the denominator problem as it arises throughout copyright law, see Kaminski and Rub, "Copyright's Framing Problem."
101. See Samsung Electronics Co. v. Apple Inc. 137 S. Ct. 429 (2016).
102. See Chevron U.S.A., Inc. v. Nat. Res. Def. Council, Inc., 467 U.S. 837 (1984).
103. Standing Rock Sioux Tribe v. U.S. Army Corps of Engineers, 205 F. Supp.3d 4, 30–32 (D.D.C. 2016).

CHAPTER TWELVE
1. This is a standard example, prompted by the facts of Bolton v. Stone, [1951] A.C. 850, 1 All. E.R. 1078 (H.L.) rev'g [1950] 1 K.B. 201. See, e.g., Farnsworth and Grady, *Torts*, 147–48; Kahan, "Causation and Incentives," 428–29.
2. The Hand formula was famously articulated by Judge Learned Hand in United States v. Carroll Towing, 159 F.2d 169 (2d Cir. 1947). The formula calls for comparing the burden (B) of an untaken precaution (such as the unbuilt fence) against the probability of injury (P) multiplied by the expected magnitude of loss (L). If B is less than $P \times L$, it is negligent not to take the precaution. 159 F.2d at 173.
3. Cronon, *Nature's Metropolis*, 116–19.
4. Cronon, 134–35.
5. Cronon, 135 (footnote omitted).
6. Barzel, *Economic Analysis of Property Rights*, 103.

7. See Barzel, 103 (noting the gains that would be possible under competitive conditions "were all buyers to choose randomly from the available selection").
8. See Dukeminier et al., *Property*, 706–8.
9. Libecap and Lueck, "Land Demarcation Systems," 286–87.
10. See, e.g., Hovenkamp, "Marginalist Revolution," 306–14.
11. See Masur and Posner, "Cost-Benefit Analysis," 953–61 (discussing Corrosion Proof Fittings v. EPA, 947 F.2d 1201 (5th Cir. 1991)).
12. Nou and Stiglitz, "Regulatory Bundling," 1207.
13. Nou and Stiglitz, 1208.
14. *Corrosion Proof Fittings*, 947 F.2d at 1215–17.
15. AFL-CIO v. OSHA, 965 F.2d 962, 986 (11th Cir. 1992).
16. *AFL-CIO*, 965 F.2d at 976 (citations omitted).
17. See *AFL-CIO*, 965 F.2d at 971–72.
18. For example, *Corrosion Proof Fittings* is generally regarded as an outlier. See Masur and Posner, "Cost-Benefit Analysis," 953–55 (describing but disagreeing with the scholarly response).
19. Nou and Stiglitz, "Regulatory Bundling."
20. Village of Euclid v. Ambler Realty, 272 U.S. 365, 388–89 (1926).
21. See Gilbert, "Single Subject Rules" (discussing logrolling, which involves vote trading, as well as riders that are tacked onto otherwise popular measures).
22. See Gilbert.
23. See Quirk and Binder, *Legislative Branch*, 48–51 (citing *Congressional Record*, July 25, 1946, 10048).
24. See C. Rose, "Evolution of Property Rights," 97 (citing the claims of existing stakeholders and "grandfathering" considerations as among the reasons why "changes in environmental regulation often have a distinctly lumpy character").
25. Berman v. Parker, 348 U.S. 26, 34–35 (1954).
26. See, e.g., Nash, Ruhl, and Salzman, "Production Function of the Regulatory State" (developing the idea of a "regulatory production function" to examine the effects of incremental funding changes).
27. For a succinct overview of the Moving to Opportunity research, see Jonathan Rothwell, "Sociology's Revenge: Moving to Opportunity (MTO) Revisited," Brookings, Social Mobility Memos (May 6, 2015).
28. See Rothwell.
29. See Chetty, Hendren, and Katz, "Exposure to Better Neighborhoods."
30. "Action" need not imply more regulation; actions can move in a deregulatory direction as well. Masur and Posner, "Cost-Benefit Analysis," 946–47.
31. The chunkiness of available moves depends in part on the relationship between the fixed and variable costs of making a change. See Gilbert, "Optimal Entrenchment of Legal Rules."
32. Incremental changes also alter political coalitions in ways that can increase the likelihood of future changes. See Levmore, "Problem with Incrementalism." Slicing early reforms in ways that alter the cost-benefit balance of future changes offers a counterweight to these effects.
33. See, e.g., Kahan, "Causation and Incentives," 428–29; Cooter and Porat, *Getting Incentives Right*, 23.
34. This result is not inevitable. The law could be made more continuous in its effects by punishing people only for the marginal impacts of their over-the-limit conduct. Kolber, "Smoothing Vague Laws," 293.

35. *Lucas*, 505 U.S. at 1019–20 n8. As Justice Scalia emphasizes, however, an owner whose property has lost most (but not all) of its value might qualify for compensation under the *Penn Central* test.
36. See, e.g., R. Epstein, *Takings*.
37. See Kmiec, "Regulatory Takings," 75; see also Costonis, "Accommodation Power."
38. See Serkin, "Meaning of Value," 692–94.
39. It is not clear, however, that governments actually pay attention to discontinuous payment obligations. For an empirical study that raises doubts about the significance of a liability cliff in the eminent domain context, see Levine-Schnur and Parchomovsky, "Is the Government Fiscally Blind?"
40. This point was emphasized by Guido Calabresi, whose approach to accidents calls for minimizing the sum of accident costs, prevention costs, and administrative costs. Calabresi, *Costs of Accidents*, 26–31.
41. See Calabresi, *Ideals, Beliefs, Attitudes*, 9.
42. Cooter, "Prices and Sanctions."
43. Grady, "New Positive Economic Theory"; Fennell, "Accidents and Aggregates."
44. Grady, "New Positive Economic Theory"; Fennell, "Accidents and Aggregates."
45. See Grady, "Discontinuities and Information Burdens," 660.
46. Grady, 661.
47. On safe harbors in law, see Morse, "Safe Harbors, Sure Shipwrecks."
48. I thank Michael Livermore and Mildred Robinson for pressing me on this point.
49. Cooter and Porat, *Getting Incentives Right*, 20.
50. See Grady, "Marginal Causation and Injurer Shirking," 16–20, 26 (discussing the significance of durability and divisibility in precautions).
51. See Grady, 26.
52. Grady, 16–17 (using an example involving a life buoy and heterogeneity in swimming ability).
53. Grady terms this a "victim-aggregating effect." Grady, 26.
54. See Thaler and Sunstein, *Nudge*, 207–9.
55. Arlen, "Contracting over Liability," 992–93 and n97.
56. Arlen, 989–1000.
57. The facts here are an embellished version of those in New York Central R.R. v. Grimstad, 264 F. 334 (2d Cir. 1920), another tort law staple.
58. See Grady, "Marginal Causation and Injurer Shirking," 16–20.
59. Cf. Grady, 19 (presenting a hypothetical in which a boat owner can strategically tailor the provision of a life preserver to the swimming abilities of the boat's crew).
60. Levmore, "Probabilistic Recoveries."
61. Levmore, 706.
62. See, e.g., Herskovits v. Group Health Cooperative of Puget Sound, 664 P.2d 474, 486–87 (Wash. 1983) (Pearson, J., concurring) (drawing on analysis in J. King, "Causation, Valuation, and Chance"); Matsuyama v. Birnbaum, 890 N.E.2d 819, 832–33 (Mass. 2008).
63. See, e.g., Bovik, *Image and Video Processing*, 39–43.
64. See R. Fisher et al., "Adaptive Thresholding" (describing and depicting thresholding techniques capable of addressing an image with "a strong illumination gradient").
65. See R. Fisher et al.; Bovik, *Image and Video Processing*, 42–55 (discussing use of "region correction algorithms").
66. The question of whether there is a better scenario or better plaintiff is a common one in tort (and other) law and can explain a variety of doctrines. See, e.g., Levmore,

"Probabilistic Recoveries" (discussing the problem of "recurring misses," which assumes a dearth of opportunities to hold the defendant to account).

CONCLUSION

1. See Ellickson and Been, *Land Use Controls*, 40 (vineyard example); Heyman, *Addiction*, 156–58 (contrasting local and global optima).
2. See Alexander and Ferzan, "Culpable Acts," 400–401.
3. See, e.g., Spulber and Yoo, "Access to Networks," 913; Iliev and Welch, "Model of Operational Slack."
4. Katyal, "*Numerus Clausus* of Sex." For discussion of *numerus clausus* as it applies to identity more generally, see Clarke, "Identity and Form," 768–69.
5. McEwan, *Nutshell*, 143.
6. McEwan, 144.
7. For some background on the debate, see Klein and Robinson, "Property: A Bundle of Rights?"; Merrill and Smith, "What Happened," 365–66.
8. See, e.g., Smith, "Law of Things," 1697–700.
9. Garratt, "Indivisibility," 249.
10. I thank Lior Strahilevitz for this example.
11. Tankel, "Importance of Open Space," 69.
12. See, e.g., Nash, "Trading Species" (examining implications of habitat configuration).

BIBLIOGRAPHY

Abbott, Ryan. "The Reasonable Computer: Disrupting the Paradigm of Tort Liability." *George Washington Law Review* 86 (2018): 1–45.

Abramowicz, Michael. "The Law-and-Markets Movement." *American University Law Review* 49 (1999): 327–431.

Acker, Frederick. "Performance Zoning." *Notre Dame Law Review* 67 (1991): 363–401.

Adler, Matthew D. *Well-Being and Fair Distribution: Beyond Cost-Benefit Analysis.* New York: Oxford University Press, 2012.

Aguiar, Mark, Mark Bils, Kerwin Kofi Charles, and Erik Hurst. "Leisure Luxuries and the Labor Supply of Young Men." National Bureau of Economic Research Working Paper No. 23552, June 2017. http://www.nber.org/papers/w23552.

Ainslie, George. "Beyond Microeconomics: Conflict among Interests in a Multiple Self as a Determinant of Value." In *The Multiple Self,* edited by Jon Elster, 133–75. Cambridge: Cambridge University Press, 1986.

———. *Breakdown of Will.* Cambridge: Cambridge University Press, 2001.

———. *Picoeconomics: The Strategic Interaction of Successive Motivational States within the Person.* Cambridge: Cambridge University Press, 1992.

Albouy, David, Kristian Behrens, Frédéric Robert-Nicoud, and Nathan Seegert. "The Optimal Distribution of Population across Cities." National Bureau of Economic Research Working Paper No. 22823, November 2016. http://www.nber.org/papers/w22823.

Alexander, Charlotte S. "Legal Avoidance and the Restructuring of Work." *Research in the Sociology of Organizations* 47 (2016): 311–32.

Alexander, Gregory S. "Objects of Art; Objects of Property." *Cornell Journal of Law and Public Policy* 26 (2017): 461–68.

Alexander, Larry, and Kimberly Kessler Ferzan. "Culpable Acts of Risk Creation." *Ohio State Journal of Criminal Law* 5 (2008): 375–405.

Allen, Frederick. *Secret Formula: How Brilliant Marketing and Relentless Salesmanship Made Coca-Cola the Best-Known Product in the World.* Paperback ed. New York: Harper-Business, 1995.

Alm, James, Betty Jackson, and Michael McKee. "Deterrence and Beyond: Toward a Kinder, Gentler IRS." In *Why People Pay Taxes: Tax Compliance and Enforcement,* edited by Joel Slemrod, 311–29. Ann Arbor: University of Michigan Press, 1992.

Alonso, Jorge, and Richard Watt. "Efficient Distribution of Copyright Income." In *The*

Economics of Copyright: Developments in Research and Analysis, edited by Wendy J. Gordon and Richard Watt, 81–103. Cheltenham, UK: Edward Elgar, 2003.

Anderson, Chris. *The Long Tail: Why the Future of Business Is Selling Less of More.* New York: Hyperion, 2006.

Anderson, Terry L., and Peter J. Hill. *The Not So Wild, Wild West: Property Rights on the Frontier.* Stanford, CA: Stanford Economics and Finance, 2004.

Ando, Albert, and Franco Modigliani. "The 'Life Cycle' Hypothesis of Saving: Aggregate Implications and Tests." *American Economic Review* 53 (1963): 55–84.

Andreoni, James. "Impure Altruism and Donations to Public Goods: A Theory of Warm-Glow Giving." *Economic Journal* 100 (1990): 464–77.

Andreoni, James, and Ragan Petrie. "Public Goods Experiments without Confidentiality: A Glimpse into Fund-Raising." *Journal of Public Economics* 88 (2004): 1605–23.

Andrews, Kyle R., Christopher J. Carpenter, Allison S. Shaw, and Franklin J. Boster. "The Legitimization of Paltry Favors Effect: A Review and Meta-Analysis." *Communication Reports* 21 (2008): 59–69.

Arlen, Jennifer. "Contracting over Liability: Medical Malpractice and the Cost of Choice." *University of Pennsylvania Law Review* 158 (2010): 957–1023.

Arrow, Kenneth J., and F. H. Hahn. *General Competitive Analysis.* San Francisco: Holden-Day, 1971.

Artle, Roland. "Public Policy and the Space Economy of the City." In *Cities and Space: The Future Use of Urban Land,* edited by Lowdon Wingo Jr. Baltimore: Johns Hopkins Press, 1963.

Atalay, Kadir, Fayzan Bakhtiar, Stephen L. Cheung, and Robert Slonim. "Savings and Prize-Linked Savings Accounts." *Journal of Economic Behavior and Organization* 107 (2014): 86–106.

Ayers, Benjamin C., Steven J. Kachelmeier, and John R. Robinson. "Why Do People Give Interest-Free Loans to the Government? An Experimental Study of Interim Tax Payments." *Journal of the American Taxation Association* 21, no. 2 (1999): 55–74.

Ayres, Ian. "Voluntary Taxation and Beyond: The Promise of Social-Contracting Voting Mechanisms." *American Law and Economics Review* 19 (2017): 1–48.

Ayres, Ian, Sophie Raseman, and Alice Shih. "Evidence from Two Large Field Experiments That Peer Comparison Feedback Can Reduce Residential Energy Usage." *Journal of Law, Economics, and Organization* 29 (2013): 992–1022.

Ayres, Ian, and Eric Talley. "Solomonic Bargaining: Dividing a Legal Entitlement to Facilitate Coasean Trade." *Yale Law Journal* 104 (1995): 1027–117.

Ayres, Ian, and Cait Unkovic. "Information Escrows." *Michigan Law Review* 111 (2012): 145–96.

Babcock, Linda, George Loewenstein, Samuel Issacharoff, and Colin Camerer. "Biased Judgments of Fairness in Bargaining." *American Economic Review* 85 (1995): 1337–43.

Baird, Douglas G., Robert H. Gertner, and Randal C. Picker. *Game Theory and the Law.* Cambridge, MA: Harvard University Press, 1994.

Ball, Philip. *Critical Mass: How One Thing Leads to Another.* 1st American ed. New York: Farrar, Straus and Giroux, 2004.

Banerjee, Abhijit V., and Esther Duflo. *Poor Economics: A Radical Rethinking of the Way to Fight Global Poverty.* Paperback ed. New York: PublicAffairs, 2012.

Banner, Stuart. *Who Owns the Sky? The Struggle to Control Airspace from the Wright Brothers On.* Cambridge, MA: Harvard University Press, 2008.

Bar-Gill, Oren. "Bundling and Consumer Misperception." *University of Chicago Law Review* 73 (2006): 33–61.

Barzel, Yoram. *Economic Analysis of Property Rights*. 2nd ed. Cambridge: Cambridge University Press, 1997.

Baumeister, Christoph, and Florian v. Wangenheim. "Access versus Ownership: Understanding Consumers' Consumption Mode Preference." Working Paper, July 7, 2014. https://papers.ssrn.com/abstract=2463076.

Baumol, William J. *Superfairness: Applications and Theory*. Cambridge, MA: MIT Press, 1986.

Baumol, William J., and J. Gregory Sidak. "The Pig in the Python: Is Lumpy Capacity Investment Used and Useful?" *Energy Law Journal* 23 (2002): 383–99.

Becker, Gary S., and Kevin M. Murphy. "A Theory of Rational Addiction." *Journal of Political Economy* 96 (1988): 675–700.

Been, Vicki. "'Exit' as a Constraint on Land Use Exactions: Rethinking the Unconstitutional Conditions Doctrine." *Columbia Law Review* 91 (1991): 473–545.

Been, Vicki, Benjamin Gross, and John Infranca. "Responding to Changing Households: Regulatory Challenges for Micro-Units and Accessory Dwelling Units." NYU Furman Center Working Paper, January 2014. http://furmancenter.org/research/publication/responding-to-changing-households-regulatory-challenges-for-micro-units-and.

Bell, Abraham, and Gideon Parchomovsky. "Of Property and Antiproperty." *Michigan Law Review* 102 (2003): 1–70.

———. "Partial Takings." *Columbia Law Review* 117 (2017): 2043–94.

———. "Reconfiguring Property in Three Dimensions." *University of Chicago Law Review* 75 (2008): 1015–70.

———. "Takings Reassessed." *Virginia Law Review* 87 (2001): 277–318.

———. "A Theory of Property." *Cornell Law Review* 90 (2005): 531–616.

Bénabou, Roland, and Jean Tirole. "Willpower and Personal Rules." *Journal of Political Economy* 112 (2004): 848–86.

Benkler, Yochai. "Commons and Growth: The Essential Role of Open Commons in Market Economies" (Reviewing *Infrastructure: The Social Value of Shared Resources* by Brett M. Frischmann). *University of Chicago Law Review* 80 (2013): 1499–555.

———. "Sharing Nicely: On Shareable Goods and the Emergence of Sharing as a Modality of Economic Production." *Yale Law Journal* 114 (2004): 273–358.

———. *The Wealth of Networks: How Social Production Transforms Markets and Freedom*. New Haven, CT: Yale University Press, 2006.

Berman, Mitchell N. "Coercion without Baselines: Unconstitutional Conditions in Three Dimensions." *Georgetown Law Journal* 90 (2001): 1–112.

Besley, Timothy. "Property Rights and Investment Incentives: Theory and Evidence from Ghana." *Journal of Political Economy* 103 (1995): 903–37.

Besley, Timothy, and Maitreesh Ghatak. "Property Rights and Economic Development." In Vol. 5, *Handbook of Development Economics*, edited by Dani Rodrik and Mark Rosenzweig, 4525–95. The Netherlands: North-Holland, 2010.

Besley, Timothy, and Alec R. Levenson. "The Role of Informal Finance in Household Capital Accumulation: Evidence from Taiwan." *Economic Journal* 106 (1996): 39–59.

Bettencourt, Luís M. A. "The Origins of Scaling in Cities." *Science* 340, no. 6139 (June 21, 2013): 1438–41.

Blume, Lawrence, and Daniel Rubinfeld. "Compensation for Takings: An Economic Analysis." *California Law Review* 72 (1984): 569–628.

Bobzin, Hagen. *Indivisibilities: Microeconomic Theory with Respect to Indivisible Goods and Factors*. Heidelberg: Physica-Verlag, 1998.

Bolker, Joan. *Writing Your Dissertation in Fifteen Minutes a Day: A Guide to Starting, Revising, and Finishing Your Doctoral Thesis*. New York: Henry Holt, 1998.

Bollen, Nicolas P. B., and Jeffrey A. Busse. "Tick Size and Institutional Trading Costs: Evidence from Mutual Funds." *Journal of Financial and Quantitative Analysis* 41 (2006): 915–37.

Bostedt, Göran. "Threatened Species as Public Goods and Public Bads." *Environmental and Resource Economics* 13 (1999): 59–73.

Bovik, Alan C. *Handbook of Image and Video Processing.* 2nd ed. Boston: Elsevier Academic Press, 2005.

Bowman, Ward S., Jr. "Tying Arrangements and the Leverage Problem." *Yale Law Journal* 67 (1957): 19–36.

Brams, Steven J., and Alan D. Taylor. *Fair Division: From Cake-Cutting to Dispute Resolution.* Cambridge: Cambridge University Press, 1996.

Brennan, Samantha. "Moral Lumps." *Ethical Theory and Moral Practice* 9 (2006): 249–63.

Brinkman, Jeffrey C. "Congestion, Agglomeration, and the Structure of Cities." *Journal of Urban Economics* 94 (2016): 13–31.

Brooks, Leah, and Byron Lutz. "From Today's City to Tomorrow's City: An Empirical Investigation of Urban Land Assembly." *American Economic Journal: Economic Policy* 8 (2016): 69–105.

Brooks, Richard R. W. "The Relative Burden of Determining Property Rules and Liability Rules: Broken Elevators in the Cathedral." *Northwestern University Law Review* 97 (2002): 267–317.

Brown, Graham. "Claiming a Corner at Work: Measuring Employee Territoriality in Their Workspaces." *Journal of Environmental Psychology* 29 (2009): 44–52.

Buchanan, James M., and Wm. Craig Stubblebine. "Externality." *Economica* 29 (1962): 371–84.

Buchholz, Wolfgang, Richard Cornes, and Dirk Rübbelke. "Public Goods and Public Bads." *Journal of Public Economic Theory* 20 (2018): 525–40.

Bui, My (Myla), Andrea Heintz Tangari, and Kelly L. Haws. "Can Health 'Halos' Extend to Food Packaging? An Investigation into Food Healthfulness Perceptions and Serving Sizes on Consumption Decisions." *Journal of Business Research* 75 (2017): 221–28.

Calabresi, Guido. *The Costs of Accidents: A Legal and Economic Analysis.* New Haven, CT: Yale University Press, 1970.

———. *Ideals, Beliefs, Attitudes, and the Law: Private Law Perspectives on a Public Law Problem.* Syracuse, NY: Syracuse University Press, 1985.

Calabresi, Guido, and A. Douglas Melamed. "Property Rules, Liability Rules, and Inalienability: One View of the Cathedral." *Harvard Law Review* 85 (1972): 1089–128.

Campbell, Michael, and Paul Ormerod. "Social Interaction and the Dynamics of Crime." Working Paper, 1997.

Caplin, Andrew, Sewin Chan, Charles Freeman, and Joseph Tracy. *Housing Partnerships: A New Approach to a Market at a Crossroads.* Cambridge, MA: MIT Press, 1997.

Cass, Robert C., and Julian J. Edney. "The Commons Dilemma: A Simulation Testing the Effects of Resource Visibility and Territorial Division." *Human Ecology* 6 (1978): 371–86.

Chang, Yun-chien. "Self-Assessment of Takings Compensation: An Empirical Study." *Journal of Law, Economics, and Organization* 28 (2012): 265–85.

———. "214 Jurisdictions in the World Get It Wrong: Fractional Ownership and Internal Auction in the Good-Faith Purchase Problem." Working Paper, August 8, 2018. https://ssrn.com/abstract=3208458.

Chang, Yun-chien, and Lee Anne Fennell. "Partition and Revelation." *University of Chicago Law Review* 81 (2014): 27–51.

Chase, Robin. *Peers Inc.: How People and Platforms Are Inventing the Collaborative Economy and Reinventing Capitalism.* New York: PublicAffairs, 2015.

Cheema, Amar, and Dilip Soman. "The Effect of Partitions on Controlling Consumption." *Journal of Marketing Research* 45 (2008): 665–75.

Chen, M. Keith, Judith A. Chevalier, Peter E. Rossi, and Emily Oehlsen. "The Value of Flexible Work: Evidence from Uber Drivers." *Journal of Political Economy* (forthcoming). https://doi.org/10.1086/702171.

Chen, M. Keith, and Alan Schwartz. "Intertemporal Choice and Legal Constraints." *American Law and Economics Review* 14 (2012): 1–43.

Chetty, Raj, Nathaniel Hendren, and Lawrence F. Katz. "The Effects of Exposure to Better Neighborhoods on Children: New Evidence from the Moving to Opportunity Experiment." *American Economic Review* 106 (2016): 855–902.

Chhaya Community Development Corporation. "Illegal Dwelling Units: A Potential Source of Affordable Housing in New York City." August 14, 2008. http://chhayacdc.org/wp-content/uploads/2008/10/Illegal-Dwelling-Units-A-Potential-Source-of-Affordable-Housing-in-New-York-City.pdf.

Chong, Dennis. *Collective Action and the Civil Rights Movement.* Chicago: University of Chicago Press, 1991.

Cialdini, Robert B., and David A. Schroeder. "Increasing Compliance by Legitimizing Paltry Contributions: When Even a Penny Helps." *Journal of Personality and Social Psychology* 34 (1976): 599–604.

Ciriacy-Wantrup, S. V., and Richard C. Bishop. "'Common Property' as a Concept in Natural Resources Policy." *Natural Resources Journal* 15 (1975): 713–27.

Cirillo, Francesco. *The Pomodoro Technique: The Acclaimed Time-Management System That Has Transformed How We Work.* New York: Currency, 2018.

Clarke, Jessica A. "Identity and Form." *California Law Review* 103 (2015): 747–839.

Clewlow, Regina R., and Gouri Shankar Mishra. "Disruptive Transportation: The Adoption, Utilization, and Impacts of Ride-Hailing in the United States." UC Davis Institute of Transportation Studies, Research Report UCD-ITS-RR-17-07, October 2017. https://itspubs.ucdavis.edu/wp-content/themes/ucdavis/pubs/download_pdf.php?id=2752.

Clotfelter, Charles, and Philip J. Cook. *Selling Hope: State Lotteries in America.* Cambridge, MA: Harvard University Press, 1989.

Coase, R. H. "The Lighthouse in Economics." *Journal of Law and Economics* 17 (1974): 357–76.

———. "The Nature of the Firm." *Economica*, n.s., 4 (1937): 386–405.

———. "The Problem of Social Cost." *Journal of Law and Economics* 3 (1960): 1–44.

Cochran, Winona, and Abraham Tesser. "The 'What the Hell' Effect: Some Effects of Goal Proximity and Goal Framing on Performance." In *Striving and Feeling: Interactions among Goals, Affect, and Self-Regulation*, edited by Leonard L. Martin and Abraham Tesser, 99–120. Mahwah, NJ: Lawrence Erlbaum Associates, 1996.

Cohen, Lloyd. "Holdouts and Free Riders." *Journal of Legal Studies* 20 (1991): 351–62.

———. "The Lure of the Lottery." *Wake Forest Law Review* 36 (2001): 705–45.

Cole, Shawn Allen, Benjamin Charles Iverson, and Peter Tufano. "Can Gambling Increase Savings? Empirical Evidence on Prize-Linked Savings Accounts." Saïd Business School Working Paper 2014-10, August 8, 2017. https://papers.ssrn.com/abstract=2441286.

Collins, Sean M., and R. Mark Isaac. "Holdout: Existence, Information, and Contingent Contracting." *Journal of Law and Economics* 55 (2012): 793–814.

Collinson, Robert, and Peter Ganong. "How Do Changes in Housing Voucher Design

Affect Rent and Neighborhood Quality?" *American Economic Journal: Economic Policy* 10, no. 2 (2018): 62–89.

Conley, John, and Christopher Yoo. "Nonrivalry and Price Discrimination in Copyright Economics." *University of Pennsylvania Law Review* 157 (2009): 1801–30.

Cook, Philip J., and Daniel A. Graham. "The Demand for Insurance and Protection: The Case of Irreplaceable Commodities." *Quarterly Journal of Economics* 91 (1977): 143–56.

Coons, John E. "Compromise as Precise Justice." *California Law Review* 68 (1980): 250–62.

Cooter, Robert D. "Decentralized Law for a Complex Economy: The Structural Approach to Adjudicating the New Law Merchant." *University of Pennsylvania Law Review* 144 (1996): 1643–96.

———. "Prices and Sanctions." *Columbia Law Review* 84 (1984): 1523–60.

Cooter, Robert D., and Ariel Porat. "Anti-Insurance." *Journal of Legal Studies* 31 (2002): 203–32.

———. *Getting Incentives Right: Improving Torts, Contracts, and Restitution.* Princeton, NJ: Princeton University Press, 2014.

———. "Lapses of Attention in Medical Malpractice and Road Accidents." *Theoretical Inquiries in Law* 15 (2014): 329–58.

Cornes, Richard, and Todd Sandler. *The Theory of Externalities, Public Goods, and Club Goods.* Cambridge: Cambridge University Press, 1986.

Costa, Dora L. *The Evolution of Retirement: An American Economic History, 1880–1990.* Chicago: University of Chicago Press, 1998.

Costonis, John J. "'Fair' Compensation and the Accommodation Power: Antidotes for the Taking Impasse in Land Use Controversies." *Columbia Law Review* 75 (1975): 1021–82.

Cowen, Tyler. "Self-Constraint versus Self-Liberation." *Ethics* 101 (1991): 360–73.

Cowen, Tyler, and Alex Tabarrok, *Modern Principles: Microeconomics.* New York: Worth Publishers, 2010.

Crane, Randall, and Michael Manville. "People or Place? Revisiting the Who versus the Where of Urban Development." *Land Lines*, July 2008.

Cronon, William. *Nature's Metropolis: Chicago and the Great West.* New York: W. W. Norton, 1991.

Cunningham, Chris. "Estimating the Holdout Problem in Land Assembly." Federal Reserve Bank of Atlanta Working Paper No. 2013-19, December 2013. https://www.frbatlanta.org/research/publications/wp/2013/19.

Dagan, Hanoch. "Takings and Distributive Justice." *Virginia Law Review* 85 (1999): 741–804.

Das-Friebel, Ahuti, Nikita Wadhwa, Merin Sanil, Hansika Kapoor, and Sharanya V. "Investigating Altruism and Selfishness through the Hypothetical Use of Superpowers." *Journal of Humanistic Psychology*, April 13, 2017. https://doi.org/10.1177/0022167817699049.

Davidson, Nestor M. "Standardization and Pluralism in Property Law." *Vanderbilt Law Review* 61 (2008): 1597–663.

Davidson, Nestor M., and John J. Infranca. "The Sharing Economy as an Urban Phenomenon." *Yale Law and Policy Review* 34 (2016): 215–79.

Dawes, Robyn M., John M. Orbell, Randy T. Simmons, and Alphons J. C. Van de Kragt. "Organizing Groups for Collective Action." *American Political Science Review* 80 (1986): 1171–85.

Dawes, Robyn M., and Richard H. Thaler. "Anomalies: Cooperation." *Journal of Economic Perspectives* 2, no. 3 (Summer 1988): 187–97.

DellaVigna, Stefano. "Psychology and Economics: Evidence from the Field." *Journal of Economic Literature* 47 (2009): 315–72.

DellaVigna, Stefano, and Ulrike Malmendier. "Paying Not to Go to the Gym." *American Economic Review* 96 (2006): 694–719.

Demsetz, Harold. "Toward a Theory of Property Rights." AEA Papers and Proceedings, *American Economic Review* 57 (1967): 347–59.

Desmond, Matthew. *Evicted: Poverty and Profit in the American City*. New York: Crown Publishers, 2016.

Dillon, Brian, Joachim De Weerdt, and Ted O'Donoghue. "Paying More for Less: Why Don't Households in Tanzania Take Advantage of Bulk Discounts?" LICOS Discussion Paper No. 396/2017, May 10, 2017. https://ssrn.com/abstract=2989027.

Dobson, Paul W., Ratula Chakraborty, and Jonathan S. Seaton. "Containing Big Soda: Countering Inducements to Buy Large-Size Sugary Drinks." *Journal of Business Research* 75 (2017): 185–91.

Duflo, Esther, Michael Kremer, and Jonathan Robinson. "Nudging Farmers to Use Fertilizer: Theory and Experimental Evidence from Kenya." *American Economic Review* 101 (2011): 2350–90.

Dukeminier, Jesse, James E. Krier, Gregory S. Alexander, Michael H. Schill, and Lior Jacob Strahilevitz. *Property*. 8th ed. New York: Wolters Kluwer Law and Business, 2014.

Duranton, Gilles, and William R. Kerr. "The Logic of Agglomeration." In *The New Oxford Handbook of Economic Geography*, edited by Gordon L. Clark, Maryann P. Feldman, Meric S. Gertler, and Dariusz Wójcik, 347–65. Oxford: Oxford University Press, 2018.

Duranton, Gilles, and Diego Puga. "Micro-Foundations of Urban Agglomeration Economies." In Vol. 4, *Handbook of Regional and Urban Economics*, edited by J. V. Henderson and J. E. Thisse, 2063–117. N.p.: Elsevier, 2004.

Eagle, Steven J. *Regulatory Takings*. 5th ed. New Providence, NJ: LexisNexis Matthew Bender, 2012.

Eggertsson, Thráinn. "Open Access versus Common Property." In *Property Rights: Cooperation, Conflict, and Law*, edited by Terry L. Anderson and Fred S. McChesney, 73–89. Princeton, NJ: Princeton University Press, 2003.

Ellen, Ingrid Gould. "Housing Low-Income Households: Lessons from the Sharing Economy?" *Housing Policy Debate* 25 (2015): 783–84.

Ellen, Ingrid Gould, and Jessica Yager. "Race, Poverty, and Federal Rental Housing Policy." In *HUD at 50: Creating Pathways to Opportunity*, 103–31. Washington, DC: US Department of Housing and Urban Development, Office of Policy Development and Research, 2015. https://www.huduser.gov/hud50th/HUDat50Book.pdf.

Ellenberg, Jordan. *How Not to Be Wrong: The Power of Mathematical Thinking*. New York: Penguin, 2014.

Ellickson, Robert C. *The Household: Informal Order around the Hearth*. Princeton, NJ: Princeton University Press, 2008.

———. *Order without Law: How Neighbors Settle Disputes*. Cambridge, MA: Harvard University Press, 1991.

———. "Property in Land." *Yale Law Journal* 102 (1993): 1315–400.

———. "The Puzzle of the Optimal Social Composition of Neighborhoods." In *The Tiebout Model at Fifty: Essays in Public Economics in Honor of Wallace Oates*, edited by William A. Fischel, 199–209. Cambridge, MA: Lincoln Institute of Land Policy, 2006.

———. "Unpacking the Household: Informal Property Rights around the Hearth." *Yale Law Journal* 116 (2006): 226–329.

Ellickson, Robert C., and Vicki L. Been. *Land Use Controls: Cases and Materials.* 3rd ed. New York: Aspen Publishers, 2005.

Elster, Jon. *The Cement of Society: A Study of Social Order.* Cambridge: Cambridge University Press, 1989.

English, Laural, Marlou Lasschuijt, and Kathleen L. Keller. "Mechanisms of the Portion Size Effect: What Is Known and Where Do We Go from Here?" *Appetite* 88 (2015): 39–49.

Epstein, Graham, Irene Pérez, Michael Schoon, and Chanda Meek. "Governing the Invisible Commons: Ozone Regulation and the Montreal Protocol." *International Journal of the Commons* 8 (2014): 337–60.

Epstein, Richard A. *Bargaining with the State.* Princeton, NJ: Princeton University Press, 1993.

———. "A Clear View of *The Cathedral*: The Dominance of Property Rules." *Yale Law Journal* 106 (1997): 2091–120.

———. "Justified Monopolies: Regulating Pharmaceuticals and Telecommunications." *Case Western Reserve Law Review* 56 (2005): 103–34.

———. *Takings: Private Property and the Power of Eminent Domain.* Cambridge, MA: Harvard University Press, 1985.

Estlund, Cynthia. "What Should We Do after Work? Automation and Employment Law." *Yale Law Journal* 128 (2018): 254–326.

Fabbri, Marco, Paolo Nicola Barbieri, and Maria Bigoni. "Ride Your Luck! A Field Experiment on Lottery-Based Incentives for Compliance." Quaderni—Working Paper DSE No. 1089, November 20, 2016. https://papers.ssrn.com/abstract=2881465.

Faden, Arnold M. *Economics of Space and Time: The Measure-Theoretic Foundations of Social Science.* Ames: Iowa State University Press, 1977.

Farnsworth, Ward, and Mark F. Grady. *Torts: Cases and Questions.* 2nd ed. Austin, TX: Wolters Kluwer Law and Business, 2009.

Fels, Markus. "A Note on the Equality of Insurance and Gambling Motives." Working Paper, March 30, 2017. https://papers.ssrn.com/abstract=2943324.

Fennell, Lee Anne. "Accidents and Aggregates." *William & Mary Law Review* 59 (2018): 2371–444.

———. "Adjusting Alienability." *Harvard Law Review* 122 (2009): 1403–65.

———. "Agglomerama." *Brigham Young University Law Review* 2014 (2015): 1373–414.

———. "Common Interest Tragedies." *Northwestern University Law Review* 98 (2003): 907–90.

———. "Commons, Anticommons, Semicommons." In *Research Handbook on the Economics of Property Law,* edited by Kenneth Ayotte and Henry E. Smith, 35–56. Cheltenham, UK: Edward Elgar, 2011.

———. "Fee Simple Obsolete." *New York University Law Review* 91 (2016): 1457–516.

———. "Forcings." *Columbia Law Review* 114 (2014): 1297–372.

———. "Homeownership 2.0." *Northwestern University Law Review* 102 (2008): 1047–118.

———. "Hyperopia in Public Finance." In *Behavioral Public Finance,* edited by Edward J. McCaffery and Joel Slemrod, 141–71. New York: Russell Sage Foundation, 2006.

———. "Just Enough." *Columbia Law Review Sidebar* 113 (2013) 109–22. https://columbialawreview.org/wp-content/uploads/2016/05/Fennell-113-Colum.-L.-Rev-109.pdf.

Bibliography / 283

———. "Lumpy Property." *University of Pennsylvania Law Review* 160 (2012): 1955–93.

———. "Options for Owners and Outlaws." *Brigham-Kanner Property Rights Conference Journal* 1 (2012): 239–62.

———. "Revealing Options." *Harvard Law Review* 118 (2005): 1399–488.

———. "Slicing Spontaneity." *Iowa Law Review* 100 (2015): 2365–88.

———. "Taking Eminent Domain Apart." *Michigan State Law Review* (2004): 957–1004.

———. *The Unbounded Home: Property Values beyond Property Lines.* New Haven, CT: Yale University Press, 2009.

Fennell, Lee Anne, and Eduardo M. Peñalver. "Exactions Creep." *Supreme Court Review* 2013 (2014): 287–358.

Fennell, Lee Anne, and Kirk J. Stark. "Taxation over Time." *Tax Law Review* 59 (2005): 1–64.

Fenster, Mark. "Community by Covenant, Process, and Design: Cohousing and the Contemporary Common Interest Community." *Journal of Land Use & Environmental Law* 15 (1999): 3–54.

Fetherstonhaugh, David, and Lee Ross. "Framing Effects and Income Flow Preferences in Decisions about Social Security." In *Behavioral Dimensions of Retirement Economics,* edited by Henry J. Aaron, 187–209. Washington, DC: Brookings Institution Press, 1999.

Fiala, Lenka, and Charles N. Noussair. "Charitable Giving, Emotions, and the Default Effect." *Economic Inquiry* 55 (2017): 1792–812.

Field, Erica. "Property Rights and Investment in Urban Slums." *Journal of the European Economic Association* 3 (2005): 279–90.

———. "Property Rights, Community Public Goods, and Household Time Allocation in Urban Squatter Communities: Evidence from Peru." *William & Mary Law Review* 45 (2004): 837–87.

Filiz-Ozbay, Emel, Jonathan Guryan, Kyle Hyndman, Melissa Schettini Kearney, and Erkut Y. Ozbay. "Do Lottery Payments Induce Savings Behavior: Evidence from the Lab." National Bureau of Economic Research Working Paper No. 19130, June 2013. http://www.nber.org/papers/w19130.

Fischel, William A. "Zoning, Nonconvexities, and T. Jack Foster's City." *Journal of Urban Economics* 35 (1994): 175–81.

Fisher, Robert, Simon Perkins, Ashley Walker, and Erik Wolfart. "Adaptive Thresholding." In *Hypermedia Image Processing Reference.* Online ed. 2004. http://homepages.inf.ed.ac.uk/rbf/HIPR2/adpthrsh.htm.

Fisher, William W., III. *Promises to Keep: Technology, Law, and the Future of Entertainment.* Stanford, CA: Stanford University Press, 2004.

Ford, Henry. *My Life and Work.* With Samuel Crowther. Garden City, NY: Doubleday, Page and Co., 1922.

Frank, Charles R., Jr. "A Note on the Assortment Problem." *Management Science* 11 (1965): 724–26.

———. *Production Theory and Indivisible Commodities.* Princeton, NJ: Princeton University Press, 1969.

Frederick, Shane, George Loewenstein, and Ted O'Donoghue. "Time Discounting and Time Preference: A Critical Review." In *Time and Decision: Economic and Psychological Perspectives on Intertemporal Choice,* edited by George Loewenstein, Daniel Read, and Roy F. Baumeister, 13–86. New York: Russell Sage Foundation, 2003.

Friedman, Milton. *Capitalism and Freedom.* Chicago: University of Chicago Press, 1962.

———. *A Theory of the Consumption Function.* Princeton, NJ: Princeton University Press, 1957.

Friedman, Milton, and L. J. Savage. "The Utility Analysis of Choices Involving Risk." *Journal of Political Economy* 56 (1948): 279–304.

Frischmann, Brett M., and Mark A. Lemley. "Spillovers." *Columbia Law Review* 107 (2007): 257–301.

Frohlich, Norman, and Joe A. Oppenheimer. "I Get by with a Little Help from My Friends." *World Politics* 23 (1970): 104–20.

Gabbe, C. J. "Looking through the Lens of Size: Land Use Regulations and Micro-Apartments in San Francisco." *Cityscape* 17 (2015): 223–37.

Galiani, Sebastian, and Ernesto Schargrodsky. "Property Rights for the Poor: Effects of Land Titling." *Journal of Public Economics* 94 (2010): 700–729.

Garnett, Nicole Stelle. "The Neglected Political Economy of Eminent Domain." *Michigan Law Review* 105 (2006): 101–50.

———. *Ordering the City: Land Use, Policing, and the Restoration of Urban America.* New Haven, CT: Yale University Press, 2010.

Garratt, Rodney J. "Indivisibilities, Inferior Goods, and Giffen Goods." *Canadian Journal of Economics* 30 (1997): 246–51.

———. "Lotteries and the Law of Demand." In *New Insights into the Theory of Giffen Goods,* edited by W. J. M. Heijman and Pierre von Mouche, 161–71. Berlin: Springer, 2012.

———. "A Tale of Two Cities and a Giffen Good." *Canadian Journal of Economics* 38 (2005): 49–56.

Gehrke, Stephen R., Alison Felix, and Timothy Reardon. "Fare Choices: A Survey of Ride-Hailing Passengers in Metro Boston; Report No. 1." Metropolitan Area Planning Council Research Brief, February 2018.

Geier, Andrew B., Paul Rozin, and Gheorghe Doros. "Unit Bias: a New Heuristic That Helps Explain the Effect of Portion Size on Food Intake." *Psychological Science* 17 (2006): 521–25.

Gergen, Mark P. "The Use of Open Terms in Contract." *Columbia Law Review* 92 (1992): 997–1081.

Gibson, Virginia A., and Colin M. Lizieri. "Friction and Inertia: Business Change, Corporate Real Estate Portfolios and the U.K. Office Market." *Journal of Real Estate Research* 22 (2001): 59–79.

Gilbert, Michael D. "Optimal Entrenchment of Legal Rules." Virginia Law and Economics Research Paper No. 2017-10, May 17, 2017. https://ssrn.com/abstract=2970164.

———. "Single Subject Rules and the Legislative Process." *University of Pittsburgh Law Review* 67 (2006): 803–70.

Gilbert-Norton, Lynne, Ryan Wilson, John R. Stevens, and Karen H. Beard. "A Meta-Analytic Review of Corridor Effectiveness." *Conservation Biology* 24 (2010): 660–68.

Ginsburg, Tom, Jonathan S. Masur, and Richard H. McAdams. "Libertarian Paternalism, Path Dependence, and Temporary Law." *University of Chicago Law Review* 81 (2014): 291–359.

Glaeser, Edward L. *Cities, Agglomeration, and Spatial Equilibrium.* Oxford: Oxford University Press, 2008.

Glaeser, Edward L., and Joseph Gyourko. "The Economic Implications of Housing Supply." *Journal of Economic Perspectives* 32, no. 1 (Winter 2018): 3–30.

Glaeser, Edward L., Joseph Gyourko, and Raven Saks. "Why Is Manhattan So Expensive? Regulation and the Rise in Housing Prices." *Journal of Law and Economics* 48 (2005): 331–69.

Glaeser, Edward L., Jed Kolko, and Albert Saiz. "Consumers and Cities." In *The City as an Entertainment Machine*, edited by Terry N. Clark. Lanham, Md.: Lexington Books, 2011.

Goldberg, John C. P., and Benjamin C. Zipursky. "The Strict Liability in Fault and the Fault in Strict Liability." *Fordham Law Review* 85 (2016): 743–88.

Goldin, Jacob, Tatiana Homonoff, and Katherine Meckel. "Is There an Nth of the Month Effect? The Timing of SNAP Issuance, Food Expenditures, and Grocery Prices." Working Paper, February 25, 2016. Archived at https://perma.cc/WAA8-JAMQ.

Goodman-Bacon, Andrew, and Leslie McGranahan. "How Do EITC Recipients Spend Their Refunds?" *Economic Perspectives* 32, no. 2 (2008): 17–32.

Goswami, Indranil, and Oleg Urminsky. "When Should the Ask Be a Nudge? The Effect of Default Amounts on Charitable Donations." *Journal of Marketing Research* 53 (2016): 829–46.

Gould, Stephen Jay. "Phyletic Size Decrease in Hershey Bars." In *Hen's Teeth and Horse's Toes*, 313–19. New York: W. W. Norton, 1983.

Grady, Mark F. "The American Negligence Rule." *Valparaiso Law Review* (forthcoming).

———. "Discontinuities and Information Burdens" (Reviewing *The Economic Structure of Tort Law* by William M. Landes and Richard A. Posner). *George Washington Law Review* 56 (1988): 658–78.

———. "Efficient Negligence." *Georgetown Law Journal* 87 (1998): 397–419.

———. "Marginal Causation and Injurer Shirking." *Journal of Tort Law* 7 (2014): 1–33.

———. "A New Positive Economic Theory of Negligence." *Yale Law Journal* 92 (1983): 799–829.

———. "Res Ipsa Loquitur and Compliance Error." *University of Pennsylvania Law Review* 142 (1994): 887–947.

———. "Why Are People Negligent? Technology, Nondurable Precautions, and the Medical Malpractice Explosion." *Northwestern University Law Review* 82 (1988): 293–334.

Greenberg, Joel. *A Feathered River across the Sky: The Passenger Pigeon's Flight to Extinction.* New York: Bloomsbury, 2014.

Griffith, Todd G., and Brian S. Roseman. "Making Cents of Tick Sizes: An Investigation of the 2016 U.S. SEC Tick Size Pilot on Limit Order Book Liquidity." Working Paper, July 2018. https://papers.ssrn.com/abstract=2888657.

Grisolía, José M., Francisco López, and Juan de Dios Ortúzar. "Burying the Highway: The Social Valuation of Community Severance and Amenity." *International Journal of Sustainable Transportation* 9 (2015): 298–309.

Groth, Paul. *Living Downtown: The History of Residential Hotels in the United States.* Berkeley: University of California Press, 1994.

Gruber, Jonathan, and Botond Köszegi. "Is Addiction 'Rational'? Theory and Evidence." *Quarterly Journal of Economics* 116 (2001): 1261–303.

Gul, Faruk, and Wolfgang Pesendorfer. "Temptation and Self Control." *Econometrica* 69 (2001): 1403–35.

Haddock, David D. "Irrelevant Externality Angst." *Journal of Interdisciplinary Economics* 19 (2007): 3–18.

Hale, Benjamin. "Nonrenewable Resources and the Inevitability of Outcomes." *The Monist* 94 (2011): 369–90.

Hall, Peter. *Cities in Civilization.* 1st American ed. New York: Pantheon Books, 1998.

Halpern-Meekin, Sarah, Jennifer Sykes, Laura Tach, and Kathryn Edin. *It's Not Like I'm Poor: How Working Families Make Ends Meet in a Post-Welfare World.* Oakland: University of California Press, 2015.

Hamburger, Philip. "Unconstitutional Conditions: The Irrelevance Of Consent." *Virginia Law Review* 98 (2012): 479–577.

Hamermesh, Daniel S., and Elena Stancanelli. "Long Workweeks and Strange Hours." *ILR Review* 68 (2015): 1007–18,

Hampton, Jean. "Free-Rider Problems in the Production of Collective Goods." *Economics & Philosophy* 3 (1987): 245–73.

Hamrick, Karen S., and Margaret Andrews. "SNAP Participants' Eating Patterns over the Benefit Month: A Time Use Perspective." *PLOS One* 11, no. 7 (July 13, 2016): 1–18.

Hannibal, Mary Ellen. *The Spine of the Continent: The Race to Save America's Last, Best Wilderness.* Paperback ed. Guilford, CT: Lyons Press, 2013.

Haque, Umair. *The New Capitalist Manifesto: Building a Disruptively Better Business.* Boston: Harvard Business Review Press, 2011.

Hardin, Garrett. "The Tragedy of the Commons." *Science* 162, no. 3859 (Dec. 13, 1968): 1243–48.

Hardin, Russell. *Collective Action.* Baltimore: Johns Hopkins University Press, 1982.

———. "Group Provision of Step Goods." *Behavioral Science* 21 (1976): 101–6.

———. "The Utilitarian Logic of Liberalism." *Ethics* 97 (1986): 47–74.

Harel, Alon, and Ariel Porat. "Aggregating Probabilities across Cases: Criminal Responsibility for Unspecified Offenses." *Minnesota Law Review* 94 (2009): 261–310.

Harris, Douglas C. "Owning and Dissolving Strata Property." *University of British Columbia Law Review* 50 (2017): 935–69.

Harris, Douglas C., and Peter Millerd. "Food Fish, Commercial Fish, and Fish to Support a Moderate Livelihood: Characterizing Aboriginal and Treaty Rights to Canadian Fisheries." *Arctic Review on Law and Politics* 2 (2010): 82–107.

Hayashi, Andrew T. "The Effects of Refund Anticipation Loans on Tax Filing and EITC Takeup." Virginia Law and Economics Research Paper 2016-9, October 27, 2016. https://ssrn.com/abstract=2801591.

Hayek, F. A. "The Use of Knowledge in Society." *American Economic Review* 35 (1945): 519–30.

Heller, Michael A. "The Boundaries of Private Property." *Yale Law Journal* 108 (1999): 1163–223.

———. *The Gridlock Economy: How Too Much Ownership Wrecks Markets, Stops Innovation, and Costs Lives.* New York: Basic Books, 2008.

———. "The Tragedy of the Anticommons: Property in the Transition from Marx to Markets." *Harvard Law Review* 111 (1998): 621–88.

Heller, Michael A., and Rebecca S. Eisenberg. "Can Patents Deter Innovation? The Anticommons in Biomedical Research." *Science* 280, no. 5364 (May 1, 1998): 698–701.

Heller, Michael, and Rick Hills. "Land Assembly Districts." *Harvard Law Review* 121 (2008): 1465–527.

Helmholz, R. H. "Equitable Division and the Law of Finders." *Fordham Law Review* 52 (1983): 313–28.

Hemel, Daniel J. "Pooling and Unpooling in the Uber Economy." *University of Chicago Legal Forum* 2017 (2017): 265–86.

Henderson, J. Vernon. "Urban Scale Economies." In *Handbook of Urban Studies,* edited by Ronan Paddison. London: SAGE, 2001.

Henrich, Joseph, Robert Boyd, Samuel Bowles, Colin Camerer, Ernst Fehr, Herbert Gintis, and Richard McElreath. "In Search of *Homo Economicus*: Behavioral Experiments in 15 Small-Scale Societies." AEA Papers and Proceedings, *American Economic Review* 91 (2001): 73–78.

Herman, C. Peter, and Janet Polivy. "Dieting as an Exercise in Behavioral Economics." In *Time and Decision: Economic and Psychological Perspectives on Intertemporal Choice*, edited by George Loewenstein, Daniel Read, and Roy Baumeister, 459–89. New York: Russell Sage Foundation, 2003.

Herrnstein, Richard J., George F. Loewenstein, Drazen Prelec, and William Vaughan. "Utility Maximization and Melioration: Internalities in Individual Choice." *Journal of Behavioral Decision Making* 6 (1993): 149–85.

Herrnstein, Richard J., and Drazen Prelec. "Melioration." In *Choice over Time*, edited by George Loewenstein and Jon Elster, 235–63. New York: Russell Sage Foundation, 1992.

———. "A Theory of Addiction." In *Choice over Time*, edited by George Loewenstein and Jon Elster, 331–60. New York: Russell Sage Foundation, 1992.

Heyman, Gene M. *Addiction: A Disorder of Choice*. Cambridge, MA: Harvard University Press, 2009.

Hirst, Alison. "Settlers, Vagrants and Mutual Indifference: Unintended Consequences of Hot-Desking." *Journal of Organizational Change Management* 24 (2011): 767–88.

Holland, Daniel M., and William M. Vaughn. "An Evaluation of Self-Assessment under a Property Tax." In *The Property Tax and Its Administration*, edited by Arthur D. Lynn. Madison: University of Wisconsin Press, 1969.

Hong, Yu-hung. "Assembling Land for Urban Development: Issues and Opportunities." In *Analyzing Land Readjustment: Economics, Law, and Collective Action*, edited by Yu-hung Hong and Barrie Needham. Cambridge, MA: Lincoln Institute of Land Policy, 2007.

Honoré, Tony. *Making Law Bind: Essays Legal and Philosophical*. Oxford: Clarendon Press, 1987.

———. "Responsibility and Luck." *Law Quarterly Review* 104 (1988): 530–53.

Hopkins, Lewis D. *Urban Development: The Logic of Making Plans*. Washington, DC: Island Press, 2001.

Holt, Steve. "Periodic Payment of the Earned Income Tax Credit Revisited." *Brookings Metropolitan Policy Program*, December 2015.

Horton, John J., and Richard J. Zeckhauser. "Owning, Using and Renting: Some Simple Economics of the 'Sharing Economy.'" National Bureau of Economic Research Working Paper No. 22029, February 2016. http://www.nber.org/papers/w22029.

Hotelling, Harold. "Stability in Competition." *Economic Journal* 39 (1929): 11–57.

Hovenkamp, Herbert. "The Marginalist Revolution in Legal Thought." *Vanderbilt Law Review* 46 (1993): 305–59.

Hsieh, Chang-Tai, and Enrico Moretti. "Housing Constraints and Spatial Misallocation." National Bureau of Economic Research Working No. 21154, Revised May 2017. http://www.nber.org/papers/w21154.

Iliev, Peter, and Ivo Welch. "A Model of Operational Slack: The Short-Run, Medium-Run, and Long-Run Consequences of Limited Attention Capacity." *Journal of Law, Economics, and Organization* 29 (2013): 2–34.

Infranca, John. "Housing Changing Households: Regulatory Challenges for Micro-Units and Accessory Dwelling Units." *Stanford Law and Policy Review* 25 (2014): 53–90.

———. "Spaces for Sharing: Microunits amid the Shift from Ownership to Access." *Fordham Urban Law Journal* 43 (2016): 1–30.

Jacobs, Jane. *Dark Age Ahead*. New York: Random House, 2004.

———. *The Death and Life of Great American Cities*. New York: Random House, 1961.

James, William. *The Principles of Psychology*. New York: Henry Holt, 1890.

Jensen, Joli. *Write No Matter What: Advice for Academics*. Chicago: University of Chicago Press, 2017.

John, Leslie K., Grant E. Donnelly, and Christina A. Roberto. "Psychologically Informed Implementations of Sugary-Drink Portion Limits." *Psychological Science* 28 (2017): 620–29.

Johnson, Eric E. "The Economics and Sociality of Sharing Intellectual Property Rights." *Boston University Law Review* 94 (2014): 1935–95.

Jolls, Christine, Cass R. Sunstein, and Richard H. Thaler. "A Behavioral Approach to Law and Economics." In *Behavioral Law and Economics*, edited by Cass R. Sunstein, 13–58. Cambridge: Cambridge University Press, 2000.

Jones, Damon. "Inertia and Overwithholding: Explaining the Prevalence of Income Tax Refunds." *American Economic Journal: Economic Policy* 4, no. 1 (2012): 158–85.

Kahan, Marcel. "Causation and Incentives to Take Care under the Negligence Rule." *Journal of Legal Studies* 18 (1989): 427–47.

Kahneman, Daniel, and Carol Varey. "Notes on the Psychology of Utility." In *Interpersonal Comparisons of Well-Being*, edited by Jon Elster and John E. Roemer, 127–63. Cambridge: Cambridge University Press, 1991.

Kaminski, Margot E., and Guy A. Rub. "Copyright's Framing Problem." *UCLA Law Review* 64 (2017): 1102–81.

Kaplow, Louis. "Why (Ever) Define Markets?" *Harvard Law Review* 124 (2010): 437–517.

Karelis, Charles. *The Persistence of Poverty: Why the Economics of the Well-Off Can't Help the Poor*. New Haven, CT: Yale University Press, 2007.

Karlsson, Charlie. "Clusters." In *The New Palgrave Dictionary of Economics*, edited by Palgrave Macmillan. Online ed. London: Palgrave Macmillan, 2016.

Katyal, Sonya. "The *Numerus Clausus* of Sex." *University of Chicago Law Review* 84 (2017): 389–494.

Katz, Larissa. "Exclusion and Exclusivity in Property Law." *University of Toronto Law Journal* 58 (2008): 275–315.

———. "Governing through Owners: How and Why Formal Private Property Rights Enhance State Power." *University of Pennsylvania Law Review* 160 (2012): 2029–59.

———. "Red Tape and Gridlock." *Canadian Journal of Law and Jurisprudence* 23 (2010): 99–123.

Katz, Leo. *Why the Law Is So Perverse*. Chicago: University of Chicago Press, 2011.

Kearney, Melissa Schettini, Peter Tufano, Jonathan Guryan, and Erik Hurst. "Making Savers Winners: An Overview of Prize-Linked Savings Products." National Bureau of Economic Research Working Paper No. 16433, October 2010. http://www.nber.org/papers/w16433.

Keating, Gregory C. "Products Liability as Enterprise Liability." *Journal of Tort Law* 10 (2017): 41–97.

Kelly, Daniel B. "The 'Public Use' Requirement in Eminent Domain Law: A Rationale Based on Secret Purchases and Private Influence." *Cornell Law Review* 92 (2006): 1–65.

Kelman, Mark. "Interpretative Construction in the Substantive Criminal Law." *Stanford Law Review* 33 (1981): 591–673.

Kelman, Steven. "A Case for In-Kind Transfers." *Economics & Philosophy* 2, no. 1 (April 1986): 55–73.

Kennedy-Hagan, K., J. E. Painter, C. Honselman, A. Halvorson, K. Rhodes, and K. Skwir. "The Effect of Pistachio Shells as a Visual Cue in Reducing Caloric Consumption." *Appetite* 57 (2011): 418–20.

Kerr, William R., and Scott Duke Kominers. "Agglomerative Forces and Cluster Shapes." *Review of Economics and Statistics* 97 (2015): 877–99.

King, Joseph H., Jr. "Causation, Valuation, and Chance in Personal Injury Torts Involving Preexisting Conditions and Future Consequences." *Yale Law Journal* 90 (1981): 1353–97.

King, Stephen. "Quitters Inc." In *Night Shift*, 220–40. New York: Doubleday and Company, 1978.

Kingsley, G. Thomas. "Trends in Housing Problems and Federal Housing Assistance." Urban Institute, October 2017. https://www.urban.org/sites/default/files/publication/94146/trends-in-housing-problems-and-federal-housing-assistance.pdf.

Kivetz, Ran, and Itamar Simonson. "Self-Control for the Righteous: Toward a Theory of Precommitment to Indulgence." *Journal of Consumer Research* 29 (2002): 199–217.

Klein, Daniel B., and John Robinson. "Property: A Bundle of Rights? Prologue to the Property Symposium." *Econ Journal Watch* 8 (2011): 193–204.

Kmiec, Douglas W. "Regulatory Takings: The Supreme Court Runs out of Gas in *San Diego*." *Indiana Law Journal* 57 (1982): 45–81.

Kolber, Adam J. "Smooth and Bumpy Laws." *California Law Review* 102 (2014): 655–90.

———. "Smoothing Vague Laws." In *Vagueness and Law: Philosophical and Legal Perspectives*, edited by Geert Keil and Ralf Poscher, 275–95. Oxford: Oxford University Press, 2016.

Kollin, Dani, and Eytan Kollin. *The Unincorporated Man*. New York: Tor, 2009.

Kominers, Scott Duke, and E. Glen Weyl. "Holdout in the Assembly of Complements: A Problem for Market Design." *American Economic Review* 102 (2012): 360–65.

Köszegi, Botond, and Matthew Rabin. "Revealed Mistakes and Revealed Preferences." In *The Foundations of Positive and Normative Economics: A Handbook*, edited by Andrew Caplin and Andrew Schotter, 193–209. Oxford: Oxford University Press, 2008.

Kreiczer-Levy, Shelly. "Consumption Property in the Sharing Economy." *Pepperdine Law Review* 43 (2015): 61–123.

———. "Share, Own, Access." *Yale Law and Policy Review* 36 (2017): 155–218.

Krier, James E., and Stewart E. Sterk. "An Empirical Study of Implicit Takings." *William & Mary Law Review* 58 (2016): 35–95.

Kuo, Susan S., and Benjamin Means. "Collective Coercion." *Boston College Law Review* 57 (2016): 1599–637.

Kwang, Ng Yew. "Why Do People Buy Lottery Tickets? Choices Involving Risk and the Indivisibility of Expenditure." *Journal of Political Economy* 73 (1965): 530–35.

Laibson, David. "Golden Eggs and Hyperbolic Discounting." *Quarterly Journal of Economics* 112 (1997): 443–78.

———. "Hyperbolic Discount Functions, Undersaving, and Savings Policy." National Bureau of Economic Research Working Paper No. 5635, June 1996. http://www.nber.org/papers/w5635.

LaManna, Justin, and Perri K. Eason. "Effects of Landmarks on Territorial Establishment." *Animal Behavior* 65 (2003): 471–78.

Landeo, Claudia, and Kathryn Spier. "Shotguns and Deadlocks." *Yale Journal on Regulation* 31 (2014): 143–87.

Landers, Renée M., James B. Rebitzer, and Lowell J. Taylor. "Rat Race Redux: Adverse Selection in the Determination of Work Hours in Law Firms." *American Economic Review* 86 (1996): 329–48.

Landes, William M., and Richard A. Posner. "Indefinitely Renewable Copyright." *University of Chicago Law Review* 70 (2003): 471–518.

Lawsky, Sarah B. "On the Edge: Declining Marginal Utility and Tax Policy." *Minnesota Law Review* 95 (2011): 904–52.

Lee, Brian Angelo. "Just Undercompensation: The Idiosyncratic Premium in Eminent Domain." *Columbia Law Review* 113 (2013): 593–655.

Lee, Julia Y. "Gaining Assurances." *Wisconsin Law Review* 2012 (2012): 1137–75.

Lemley, Mark A, and Carl Shapiro. "Patent Holdup and Royalty Stacking." *Texas Law Review* 85 (2007): 1991–2049.

Levi, Margaret. *Of Rule and Revenue*. Berkeley: University of California Press, 1988.

Levine-Schnur, Ronit, and Gideon Parchomovsky. "Is the Government Fiscally Blind? An Empirical Examination of the Effect of the Compensation Requirement on Eminent-Domain Exercises." *Journal of Legal Studies* 45 (2016): 437–69.

Levinson, Daryl J. "Framing Transactions in Constitutional Law." *Yale Law Journal* 111 (2002): 1311–90.

———. "Making Government Pay: Markets, Politics, and the Allocation of Constitutional Costs." *University of Chicago Law Review* 67 (2000): 345–420.

Levmore, Saul. "Interest Groups and the Problem with Incrementalism." *University of Pennsylvania Law Review* 158 (2010): 815–58.

———. "Probabilistic Recoveries, Restitution, and Recurring Wrongs." *Journal of Legal Studies* 19 (1990): 691–726.

———. "Self-Assessed Valuation Systems for Tort and Other Law." *Virginia Law Review* 68 (1982): 771–861.

Levy, Daniel, and Andrew T. Young. "'The Real Thing': Nominal Price Rigidity of the Nickel Coke, 1886–1959." *Journal of Money, Credit, and Banking* 36 (2004): 765–99.

Lewis, David K. *Convention: A Philosophical Study*. Cambridge, MA: Harvard University Press, 1969.

Libecap, Gary D. "Contracting for Property Rights." In *Property Rights: Cooperation, Conflict, and Law*, edited by Terry L. Anderson and Fred S. McChesney, 142–67. Princeton, NJ: Princeton University Press, 2003.

———. "Economic Variables and the Development of the Law: The Case of Western Mineral Rights." *Journal of Economic History* 38 (1978): 338–62.

Libecap, Gary D., and Dean Lueck. "Land Demarcation Systems." In *Research Handbook on the Economics of Property Law*, edited by Kenneth Ayotte and Henry E. Smith, 257–95. Cheltenham, UK: Edward Elgar, 2011.

Libecap, Gary D., and James L. Smith. "The Economic Evolution of Petroleum Property Rights in the United States." *Journal of Legal Studies* 31 (2002): S589–S608.

Libotte, E., M. Siegrist, and T. Bucher. "The Influence of Plate Size on Meal Composition: Literature Review and Experiment." *Appetite* 82 (2014): 91–96.

Libson, Adi. "Confronting the Retirement Savings Problem: Redesigning the Saver's Credit." *Harvard Journal on Legislation* 54 (2017): 207–58.

Lichtman, Doug. "Patent Holdouts in the Standard-Setting Process." Academic Advisory Council Bulletin. Washington, DC: Progress and Freedom Foundation, May 2006. http://www.pff.org/issues-pubs/ip/bulletins/bulletin1.3patent.pdf.

Litman, Jessica. "Sharing and Stealing." *Hastings Communications and Entertainment Law Journal* 27 (2004): 1–50.

Liu, Jiarui. "Copyright Complements and Piracy-Induced Deadweight Loss." *Indiana Law Journal* 90 (2015): 1011–45.

Lobel, Orly. "The Law of the Platform." *Minnesota Law Review* 101 (2016): 87–166.

Loewenstein, George. "Anticipation and the Valuation of Delayed Consumption." *Economic Journal* 97 (1987): 666–84.

Loewenstein, George F., and Drazen Prelec. "Preferences for Sequences of Outcomes." *Psychological Review* 100 (1993): 91–108.

Loewenstein, George, and Nachum Sicherman. "Do Workers Prefer Increasing Wage Profiles?" *Journal of Labor Economics* 9 (1991): 67–84.

Lunney, Glynn, Jr. "Copyright, Private Copying, and Discrete Public Goods." *Tulane Journal of Technology and Intellectual Property* (2009): 1–30.

Machina, Mark J. "Dynamic Consistency and Non-Expected Utility Models of Choice under Uncertainty." *Journal of Economic Literature* 27 (1989): 1622–68.

Main, Bill, and Gail Greet Hannah. *Site Furnishings: A Complete Guide to the Planning, Selection and Use of Landscape Furniture and Amenities.* Hoboken, NJ: John Wiley and Sons, 2009.

Mankiw, N. Gregory. *Principles of Economics.* 7th ed. Stamford, CT: Cenage Learning, 2015.

Marchiori, David, Laurent Waroquier, and Olivier Klein. "'Split Them!' Smaller Item Sizes of Cookies Lead to a Decrease in Energy Intake in Children." *Journal of Nutrition Education and Behavior* 44 (2012): 251–55.

Margolis, Howard. *Patterns, Thinking, and Cognition: A Theory of Judgment.* Chicago: University of Chicago Press, 1987.

Marshall, Alfred. *Principles of Economics.* 8th ed. London: Macmillan and Co., 1920. http://www.econlib.org/library/Marshall/marP.html.

Mas, Alexandre, and Amanda Pallais. "Valuing Alternative Work Arrangements." *American Economic Review* 107 (2017): 3722–59.

Mas-Colell, A. "Non-Convexity." In Vol. 3, *The New Palgrave: A Dictionary of Economics,* edited by John Eatwell, Murray Milgate, and Peter Newman, 653–61. London: Macmillan, 1987.

Masur, Jonathan S., and Eric A. Posner. "Cost-Benefit Analysis and the Judicial Role." *University of Chicago Law Review* 85 (2018): 935–86.

McAdams, Richard H. "Beyond the Prisoners' Dilemma: Coordination, Game Theory, and Law." *Southern California Law Review* 82 (2009): 209–58.

———. *The Expressive Powers of Law: Theories and Limits.* Cambridge, MA: Harvard University Press, 2015.

McCaffery, Edward J. "Why People Play Lotteries and Why It Matters." *Wisconsin Law Review* 1994 (1994): 71–122.

McDonald, John F. "What Is Public Use? Eminent Domain and the Kelo Decision." *Cornell Real Estate Review* 5 (2007): 10–25.

McEwan, Ian. *Nutshell.* New York: Doubleday, 2016.

Merges, Robert P. *Justifying Intellectual Property.* Cambridge, MA: Harvard University Press, 2011.

Merrill, Thomas W. "The Economics of Public Use." *Cornell Law Review* 72 (1986): 61–116.

Merrill, Thomas W., and Henry E. Smith. "Optimal Standardization in the Law of Property: The *Numerus Clausus* Principle." *Yale Law Journal* 110 (2000): 1–70.

———. "What Happened to Property in Law and Economics?" *Yale Law Journal* 111 (2001): 357–98.

Mian, Atif, and Amir Sufi. "Household Debt and Defaults from 2000–2010: The Credit Supply View." In *Evidence and Innovation in Housing Law and Policy,* edited by Lee Anne Fennell and Benjamin J. Keys, 257–88. Cambridge: Cambridge University Press, 2017.

Miceli, Thomas J., and C. F. Sirmans. "The Holdout Problem, Urban Sprawl, and Eminent Domain." *Journal of Housing Economics* 16 (2007): 309–19.

———. "Partition of Real Estate; or, Breaking Up Is (Not) Hard to Do." *Journal of Legal Studies* 29 (2000): 783–96.

Michelman, Frank I. "Ethics, Economics and the Law of Property." In *Ethics, Economics, and the Law*, edited by J. Roland Pennock and John W Chapman. NOMOS XXIV. New York: New York University Press, 1982.

———. "Is the Tragedy of the Common Inevitable?" Remarks Presented at the Association of American Law Schools Annual Meeting, Property Panel, January 1985.

———. "Property, Utility, and Fairness: Comments on the Ethical Foundations of 'Just Compensation' Law." *Harvard Law Review* 80 (1967): 1165–258.

Milkman, Katherine L., Julia A. Minson, and Kevin G. M. Volpp. "Holding the Hunger Games Hostage at the Gym: An Evaluation of Temptation Bundling." *Management Science* 60 (2014): 283–99.

Modigliani, Franco, and Richard Brumberg. "Utility Analysis and the Consumption Function: An Interpretation of Cross-Section Data." In *Post-Keynesian Economics*, edited by Kenneth K. Kurihara, 388–436. New Brunswick, NJ: Rutgers University Press, 1954.

Mollner, Joshua, and E. Glen Weyl. "Lottery Equilibrium." Working paper, April 6. 2018. https://ssrn.com/abstract=3157918.

Moore, Michael S. *Act and Crime*. Oxford: Oxford University Press, 1993.

Morrison, Rachel L., and Keith A. Macky. "The Demands and Resources Arising from Shared Office Spaces." *Applied Ergonomics* 60 (2017): 103–15.

Morse, Susan C. "Safe Harbors, Sure Shipwrecks." *U.C. Davis Law Review* 49 (2016): 1385–430

Mullainathan, Sendhil, and Eldar Shafir. *Scarcity: The New Science of Having Less and How It Defines Our Lives*. Reprint, New York: Picador, 2014.

Murray, Michael. "The Law of Describing Accidents: A New Proposal for Determining the Number of Occurrences in Insurance." *Yale Law Journal* 118 (2009): 1484–544.

Nadler, Janice. "Blaming as a Social Process: The Influence of Character and Moral Emotion on Blame." *Law and Contemporary Problems* 75, no. 2 (2012): 1–31.

Nash, Jonathan Remy. "Trading Species: A New Direction for Habitat Trading Programs." *Columbia Journal of Environmental Law* 32 (2007): 1–40.

Nash, Jonathan Remy, J. B. Ruhl, and James Salzman. "The Production Function of the Regulatory State: How Much Do Agency Budgets Matter?" *Minnesota Law Review* 102 (2017): 695–759.

Nash, Jonathan Remy, and Stephanie M. Stern. "Property Frames." *Washington University Law Review* 87 (2010): 449–504.

Netanel, Neil Weinstock. "Impose a Noncommercial Use Levy to Allow Free Peer-to-Peer File Sharing." *Harvard Journal of Law & Technology* 17 (2003): 1–84.

Neumark, David. "Are Rising Earnings Profiles a Forced-Saving Mechanism?" *Economic Journal* 105 (1995): 95–106.

Nou, Jennifer, and Edward H. Stiglitz. "Regulatory Bundling." *Yale Law Journal* 128 (2019): 1174–1245.

Nozick, Robert. *The Nature of Rationality*. Princeton, NJ: Princeton University Press, 1993.

Nyman, John A. "The Value of Health Insurance: The Access Motive." *Journal of Health Economics* 18 (1999): 141–52.

O'Donoghue, Ted, and Matthew Rabin. "Studying Optimal Paternalism, Illustrated by a Model of Sin Taxes." AEA Papers and Proceedings, *American Economic Review* 93 (2003): 186–91.

O'Flaherty, Brendan. *City Economics*. Cambridge, MA: Harvard University Press, 2005.

Oliver, Pamela, Gerald Marwell, and Ruy Teixeira. "A Theory of the Critical Mass. I. Interdependence, Group Heterogeneity, and the Production of Collective Action." *American Journal of Sociology* 91 (1985): 522–56.

Olson, Todd G., Dennis D. Murphy, and Robert D. Thornton. "The Habitat Transaction Method: A Proposal for Creating Tradable Credits in Endangered Species Habitat." In *Building Economic Incentives into the Endangered Species Act*, edited by Hank Fischer and Wendy E. Hudson, 3rd ed. Washington, DC: Defenders of Wildlife, 1994.

Orzach, Ram, and Miron Stano. "Supersizing: The Illusion of a Bargain and the Right-to-Split." Working Paper, May 2018. https://ssrn.com/abstract=3189901.

Ostrom, Elinor. "A General Framework for Analyzing Sustainability of Social-Ecological Systems." *Science* 325, no. 5939 (July 24, 2009): 419–22.

———. *Governing the Commons: The Evolution of Institutions for Collective Action.* Cambridge: Cambridge University Press, 1990.

———. *Understanding Institutional Diversity.* Princeton, NJ: Princeton University Press, 2005.

Ostrom, Vincent, and Elinor Ostrom. "A Theory for Institutional Analysis of Common Pool Problems." In *Managing the Commons*, edited by Garrett Hardin and John Baden. San Francisco: W. H. Freeman, 1971.

Palfrey, Thomas R., and Howard Rosenthal. "Participation and the Provision of Discrete Public Goods: A Strategic Analysis." *Journal of Public Economics* 24 (1984): 171–93.

Palmer, Andrew. *Smart Money: How High-Stakes Financial Innovation Is Reshaping Our World—for the Better.* New York: Basic Books, 2015.

Parchomovsky, Gideon, and Peter Siegelman. "Cities, Property, and Positive Externalities." *William & Mary Law Review* 54 (2012): 211–61.

———. "Selling Mayberry: Communities and Individuals in Law and Economics." *California Law Review* 92 (2004): 75–146.

Parchomovsky, Gideon, Peter Siegelman, and Steve Thel. "Of Equal Wrongs and Half Rights." *New York University Law Review* 82 (2007): 738–89.

Parfit, Derek. *Reasons and Persons.* Oxford: Oxford University Press, 1984.

Parisi, Francesco. "Entropy in Property." *American Journal of Comparative Law* 50 (2002): 595–632.

Perlacia, Anna Soler, Valeria Duml, and Tina Saebi. "Collaborative Consumption: Live Fashion, Don't Own It; Developing New Business Models for the Fashion Industry." Working Paper, October 27, 2016. https://papers.ssrn.com/abstract=2860021.

Pigou, A. C. *The Economics of Welfare.* 4th ed. London: Macmillan, 1932.

Pitofsky, Robert. "New Definitions of Relevant Market and the Assault on Antitrust." *Columbia Law Review* 90 (1990): 1805–64.

Plassmann, Florenz, and T. Nicolaus Tideman. "Marginal Cost Pricing and Eminent Domain." *Foundations and Trends in Microeconomics* 7 (2011): 1–110.

Plott, Charles, Richard Roll, Han Seo, and Hao Zhao. "Tick Size, Price Grids, and Market Performance: Stable Matches as a Model of Market Dynamics and Equilibrium." California Institute of Technology Social Science Working Paper No. 1435, February 9, 2018. https://ssrn.com/abstract=3122558.

Popkin, Samuel L. "Political Entreprenuers and Peasant Movements in Vietnam." In *Rationality and Revolution*, edited by Michael Taylor, 9–61. Cambridge: Cambridge University Press, 1988.

Porat, Ariel, and Eric A. Posner. "Aggregation and Law." *Yale Law Journal* 122 (2012): 2–69.

Porter, Douglas R., Patrick L. Phillips, and Terry J. Lassar. *Flexible Zoning: How It Works.* Washington, DC: Urban Land Institute, 1988.

Porter, Nicole Buonocore. "Cumulative Hardship." *George Mason Law Review* (forthcoming).

Posner, Eric A., Kathryn E. Spier, and Adrian Vermeule. "Divide and Conquer." *Journal of Legal Analysis* 2 (2010): 417–71.

Posner, Eric A., and E. Glen Weyl. "Property Is Only Another Name for Monopoly." *Journal of Legal Analysis* 9 (2017): 51–123.

———. *Radical Markets: Uprooting Capitalism and Democracy for a Just Society.* Princeton, NJ: Princeton University Press, 2018.

Posner, Richard A., and William M. Landes. "Indefinitely Renewable Copyright." *University of Chicago Law Review* 70 (2003): 471–518.

Powanga, Atupele, and Luka Powanga. "An Economic Analysis of a Timeshare Ownership." *Journal of Retail and Leisure Property* 7 (2008): 69–83.

Prabhat, Devyani. "'BorrowMyDoggy.Com': Rethinking Peer-to-Peer Exchange for Genuine Sharing." *Journal of Law and Society* 45 (2018): 84–98.

Prelec, Drazen. "Values and Principles: Some Limitations on Traditional Economic Analysis." In *Socio-Economics: Toward a New Synthesis,* edited by Amitai Etzioni and Paul R. Lawrence, 131–45. Armonk, NY: M. E. Sharpe, 1991.

Prelec, Drazen, and George Loewenstein. "The Red and the Black: Mental Accounting of Savings and Debt." *Marketing Science* 17 (1998): 4–28.

Prescott, J. J. "Improving Access to Justice in State Courts with Platform Technology." *Vanderbilt Law Review* 70 (2017): 1993–2050.

Priest, George L. "The Invention of Enterprise Liability: A Critical History of the Intellectual Foundations of Modern Tort Law." *Journal of Legal Studies* 14 (1985): 461–527.

Priest, George L., and Benjamin Klein. "The Selection of Disputes for Litigation." *Journal of Legal Studies* 13 (1984): 1–55.

Purdy, Jedediah. "A Freedom-Promoting Approach to Property: A Renewed Tradition for New Debates." *University of Chicago Law Review* 72 (2005): 1237–98.

Quindlen, Anna. *Alternate Side.* New York: Random House, 2018.

Quirk, Paul J., and Sarah A. Binder. *The Legislative Branch.* New York: Oxford University Press, 2005.

Rachlin, Howard. *The Science of Self-Control.* Cambridge, MA: Harvard University Press, 2000.

———. "Self-Control." *Behaviorism* 2 (1974): 94–107.

———. "Self-Control: Beyond Commitment." *Behavioral and Brain Sciences* 18 (1995): 109–21.

Radin, Margaret Jane. "The Liberal Conception of Property: Cross Currents in the Jurisprudence of Takings." *Columbia Law Review* 88 (1988): 1667–96.

Rasmusen, Eric. "Internalities and Paternalism: Applying the Compensation Criterion to Multiple Selves across Time." *Social Choice and Welfare* 38 (2012): 601–15.

Rauch, Daniel E., and David Schleicher. "Like Uber, but for Local Governmental Law: The Future of Local Regulation of the Sharing Economy." *Ohio State Law Journal* 76 (2015): 901–63.

Rifkin, Jeremy. *The Age of Access: The New Culture of Hypercapitalism, Where All of Life Is a Paid-For Experience.* New York: Jeremy P. Tarcher/Putnam, 2000.

———. *The Zero Marginal Cost Society: The Internet of Things, the Collaborative Commons, and the Eclipse of Capitalism.* New York: Palgrave Macmillan, 2014.

Ripstein, Arthur. "Beyond the Harm Principle." *Philosophy & Public Affairs* 34 (2006): 215–45.

Robinson, E., S. Nolan, C. Tudur-Smith, E. J. Boyland, J. A. Harrold, C. A. Hardman, and J. C. G. Halford. "Will Smaller Plates Lead to Smaller Waists? A Systematic Review and Meta-Analysis of the Effect that Experimental Manipulation of Dishware Size Has on Energy Consumption." *Obesity Reviews* 15 (2014): 812–21.

Robinson, Glen O. "Personal Property Servitudes." *University of Chicago Law Review* 71 (2003): 1449–523.

Rodriguez, Daniel B., and David Schleicher. "The Location Market." *George Mason Law Review* 19 (2012): 637–64.

Rogers, Paul C., and Darren J. McAvoy, "Mule Deer Impede Pando's Recovery: Implications for Aspen Resilience from a Single-Genotype Forest." *PLOS One*, October 17, 2018. https://doi.org/10.1371/journal.pone.0203619.

Romer, Paul M. "Endogenous Technological Change." *Journal of Political Economy* 98 (1990): S71–S102.

Romich, Jennifer L., and Thomas Weisner. "How Families View and Use the EITC: Advance Payment versus Lump Sum Delivery." *National Tax Journal* 53 (2000): 1245–65.

Roose, Gudrun, Anneleen Van Kerckhove, and Elke Huyghe. "Honey They Shrank the Food! An Integrative Study of the Impact of Food Granularity and Its Operationalization Mode on Consumption." *Journal of Business Research* 75 (2017): 210–20.

Rose, Carol M. "The Comedy of the Commons: Custom, Commerce, and Inherently Public Property." *University of Chicago Law Review* 53 (1986): 711–81.

———. "Evolution of Property Rights." In Vol. 2, *The New Palgrave Dictionary of Economics and the Law*, edited by Peter Newman, 93–98. London: Macmillan Reference, 1998.

Rose, Julie L. *Free Time*. Princeton, NJ: Princeton University Press, 2016.

Rose-Ackerman, Susan. "Inalienability and the Theory of Property Rights." *Columbia Law Review* 85 (1985): 931–69.

Roth, Alvin E. *Who Gets What—and Why*. Boston: Houghton Mifflin Harcourt, 2015.

Rothschild, Michael, and Lawrence J. White. "The Analytics of the Pricing of Higher Education and Other Services in Which the Customers Are Inputs." *Journal of Political Economy* 103 (1995): 573–86.

Rothstein, Paul F. "Comment: The Doctrine of Chances, Brides of the Bath and a Reply to Sean Sullivan." *Law Probability & Risk* 14 (2015): 51–66.

Samuelson, Paul A. "Aspects of Public Expenditure Theories." *Review of Economics and Statistics* 40 (1958): 332–38.

Scarf, Herbert E. "The Allocation of Resources in the Presence of Indivisibilities." *Journal of Economic Perspectives* 8, no. 4 (1994): 111–28.

Schaller, Bruce. "Empty Seats, Full Streets: Fixing Manhattan's Traffic Problem." Schaller Consulting, December 21, 2017. http://schallerconsult.com/rideservices/emptyseats.htm.

Schauer, Frederick. "Sanctions for Acts or Sanctions for Actors?" University of Virginia School of Law Public Law and Legal Theory Research Paper 2018-41, July 2018. http://www.ssrn.com/abstract=3212111.

———. "Too Hard: Unconstitutional Conditions and the Chimera of Constitutional Consistency." *Denver University Law Review* 72 (1995): 989–1005.

Schauer, Frederick, and Richard Zeckhauser. "On the Degree of Confidence for Adverse Decisions." *Journal of Legal Studies* 25 (1996): 27–52.

Schelling, Thomas C. *Choice and Consequence*. Cambridge, MA: Harvard University Press, 1984.

———. *Micromotives and Macrobehavior.* New York: W. W. Norton, 1978.

———. "Models of Segregation." AEA Papers and Proceedings, *American Economic Review* 59 (1969): 488–93.

———. *The Strategy of Conflict.* New York: Oxford University Press, 1969.

Schlager, Edella, William Blomquist, and Shui Yan Tang. "Mobile Flows, Storage, and Self-Organized Institutions for Governing Common-Pool Resources." *Land Economics* 70 (1994): 294–317.

Schleicher, David. "The City as a Law and Economic Subject." *University of Illinois Law Review* 2010 (2010): 1509–63.

———. "Stuck! The Law and Economics of Residential Stagnation." *Yale Law Journal* 127 (2017): 78–154.

Schulz, Karen Bradshaw, and Dean Lueck. "Contracting for Control of Landscape-Level Resources." *Iowa Law Review* 100 (2015): 2507–49.

Seabright, Paul. *The Company of Strangers: A Natural History of Economic Life.* Princeton, NJ: Princeton University Press, 2004.

Seicshnaydre, Stacy. "Missed Opportunity: Furthering Fair Housing in the Housing Choice Voucher Program." *Law and Contemporary Problems* 79 (2016): 173–97.

Sennett, Richard. *Building and Dwelling: Ethics for the City.* New York: Farrar, Straus and Giroux, 2018.

Serkin, Christopher. "The Meaning of Value: Assessing Just Compensation for Regulatory Takings." *Northwestern University Law Review* 99 (2005): 677–742.

Shafir, Eldar, and Amos Tversky. "Decision Making." In Vol. 3, *An Invitation to Cognitive Science: Thinking,* edited by Edward E. Smith and Daniel N. Osherson. 2nd ed. Cambridge, MA: MIT Press, 1995.

Shapiro, Carl. "Navigating the Patent Thicket: Cross Licenses, Patent Pools, and Standard Setting." In Vol. 1, *NBER Innovation Policy and the Economy,* edited by Adam B. Jaffe, Josh Lerner, and Scott Stern, 119–50. Cambridge, MA: MIT Press, 2001.

Shavell, Steven. "Contractual Holdup and Legal Intervention." *Journal of Legal Studies* 36 (2007): 325–54.

———. *Economic Analysis of Accident Law.* Cambridge, MA: Harvard University Press, 1987.

Shefrin, Hersh M., and Richard H. Thaler. "The Behavioral Life-Cycle Hypothesis." *Economic Inquiry* 26 (1988): 609–43.

Shiller, Robert J. *The New Financial Order: Risk in the 21st Century.* Princeton, NJ: Princeton University Press, 2003.

Shmanske, Stephen, and Daniel Packey. "Lumpy Demand and the Diagrammatics of Aggregation." *Journal of Economic Education* 30 (1999): 64–74.

Shoup, Donald C. *The High Cost of Free Parking.* Chicago: Planners Press, 2005.

Skyrms, Brian. *The Stag Hunt and the Evolution of Social Structure.* Cambridge: Cambridge University Press, 2004.

Singer, Eric M. "Competitive Public Contracts." *Virginia Law Review* 102 (2016): 1297–354.

Slemrod, Joel. "Buenas Notches: Lines and Notches in Tax System Design." *eJournal of Tax Research* 11 (2013): 259–83.

Smeeding, Timothy M., Katherin Ross Phillips, and Michael O'Connor. "The EITC: Expectation, Knowledge, Use, and Economic and Social Mobility." *National Tax Journal* 53 (2000): 1187–210.

Smith, Henry E. "The Language of Property: Form, Context, and Audience." *Stanford Law Review* 55 (2003): 1105–91.

———. "Property and Property Rules." *New York University Law Review* 79 (2004): 1719–98.

———. "Property as the Law of Things." *Harvard Law Review* 125 (2012): 1691–726.

Soman, Dilip, and Amar Cheema. "Earmarking and Partitioning: Increasing Saving by Low-Income Households." *Journal of Marketing Research* 48 (2011): S14–S22.

Soman, Dilip, and John T. Gourville. "Transaction Decoupling: How Price Bundling Affects the Decision to Consume." *Journal of Marketing Research* 38 (2001): 30–44.

Somin, Ilya. *The Grasping Hand: Kelo v. City of New London and the Limits of Eminent Domain.* Chicago: University of Chicago Press, 2015.

Sommer, Robert. *Personal Space: The Behavioral Basis of Design.* Revised ed. Bristol, England: Bosko Books, 2007.

Souleles, Nicholas S. "The Response of Household Consumption to Income Tax Refunds." *American Economic Review* 89 (1999): 947–58.

Spulber, Daniel F., and Christopher S. Yoo. "Access to Networks: Economic and Constitutional Connections." *Cornell Law Review* 88 (2003): 885–1024.

Stahl, Kenneth A. "The Challenge of Inclusion." *Temple Law Review* 89 (2017): 487–534.

Stern, Eric, and Jessica Yager. "21st Century SROs: Can Small Housing Units Help Meet the Need for Affordable Housing in New York City?" NYU Furman Center Working Paper, January 31, 2018. http://furmancenter.org/research/publication/21st-century -sros-can-small-housing-units-help-meet-the-need-for-affordable.

Stoke, Stuart M., Robert F. Grose, David W. Lewit, Michael Olmstead, and Bulkeley Smith Jr. *Student Reactions to Study Facilities: With Implications for Architects and College Administrators.* A Report to the Presidents of Amherst College, Mount Holyoke College, Smith College, and the University of Massachusetts, 1960.

Strahilevitz, Lior Jacob. "'How's My Driving' for Everyone (and Everything?)." *New York University Law Review* 81 (2006): 1699–765.

———. "The Right to Abandon." *University of Pennsylvania Law Review* 158 (2010): 355–420.

———. "Wealth without Markets?" (Reviewing *The Wealth of Networks* by Yochai Benkler). *Yale Law Journal* 116 (2007): 1472–516.

Sullivan, Kathleen M. "Unconstitutional Conditions." *Harvard Law Review* 102 (1989): 1413–506.

Sullivan, Sean P. "Probative Inference from Phenomenal Coincidence: Demystifying the Doctrine of Chances." *Law, Probability and Risk* 14 (2015): 27–50.

Sunstein, Cass R. "Empirically Informed Regulation." *University of Chicago Law Review* 78 (2011): 1349–430.

———. "Why the Unconstitutional Conditions Doctrine Is an Anachronism (with Particular Reference to Religion, Speech, and Abortion)." *Boston University Law Review* 70 (1990): 593–621.

Super, David. "The Political Economy of Entitlement." *Columbia Law Review* 104 (2004): 633–729.

Sydnor, Justin. "(Over)Insuring Modest Risks." *American Economic Journal: Applied Economics* 2 (2010): 177–99.

Tankel, Stanley B. "The Importance of Open Space in the Urban Pattern." In *Cities and Space: The Future Use of Urban Land,* edited by Lowdon Wingo Jr., 57–71. Baltimore: Johns Hopkins Press, 1963.

Taylor, Michael, and Hugh Ward. "Chickens, Whales, and Lumpy Goods: Alternative Models of Public-Goods Provision." *Political Studies* 30 (1982): 350–70.

Tewksbury, Joshua J., Douglas J. Levey, Nick M. Haddad, Sarah Sargent, John L. Orrock, Aimee Weldon, Brent J. Danielson, Jory Brinkerhoff, Ellen I. Damschen, and Patricia Townsend. "Corridors Affect Plants, Animals, and Their Interactions in Fragmented Landscapes." *Proceedings of the National Academy of Sciences of the United States of America* 99 (2002): 12923–26.

Thaler, Richard H., and Shlomo Benartzi. "Save More Tomorrow: Using Behavioral Economics to Increase Employee Saving." *Journal of Political Economy* 112 (2004): S164–S187.

Thaler, Richard H., and George Loewenstein. "Intertemporal Choice." In *The Winner's Curse: Paradoxes and Anomalies of Economic Life*, edited by Richard H. Thaler, 50–62. New York: Free Press, 1992.

Thaler, Richard H., and Hersh M. Shefrin. "An Economic Theory of Self-Control." *Journal of Political Economy* 89 (1981): 392–406.

Thaler, Richard H., and Cass R. Sunstein. *Nudge: Improving Decisions about Health, Wealth, and Happiness.* New Haven, CT: Yale University Press, 2008.

Theodos, Brett, Rachel Brash, Jessica F. Compton, Nancy M. Pindus, and C. Eugene Steuerle. "Who Needs Credit at Tax Time and Why: A Look at Refund Anticipation Loans and Refund Anticipation Checks." Urban Institute, October 2010. https://www .urban.org/research/publication/who-needs-credit-tax-time-and-why-look-refund -anticipation-loans-and-refund-anticipation-checks.

Thompson, Fred. "Lumpy Goods and Cheap Riders: An Application of the Theory of Public Goods to International Alliances." *Journal of Public Policy* 7 (1987): 431–49.

Tideman, T. Nicolaus. "Integrating Land-Value Taxation with the Internalization of Spatial Externalities." *Land Economics* 66 (1990): 341–55.

———. "Three Approaches to Improving Urban Land Use." PhD dissertation, University of Chicago, 1969.

Tisdell, Clem. *Environmental Economics: Policies for Environmental Management and Sustainable Development.* Aldershot, England: Edward Elgar, 1993.

Van Echtelt, Patricia E., Arie C. Glebbeek, and Siegwart M. Lindenberg. "The New Lumpiness of Work: Explaining the Mismatch between Actual and Preferred Working Hours." *Work, Employment and Society* 20 (2006): 493–512.

Van Inwagen, Peter. *Material Beings.* Ithaca, NY: Cornell University Press, 1990.

Vargas, Arq. Ana Christina. "Incremental User Built Housing; Elemental Projects and Similar Housing in Santiago, Chile." SIGUS Lab MIT, December 2014. http://web.mit .edu/incrementalhousing/articlesPhotographs/pdfs/Vargas_Report-R.pdf.

Varian, Hal R. "Economics of Networked Information: Pricing Information Goods." In *Scholarship in the New Information Environment*, edited by Carol Hughes, 19–24. Mountain View, CA: Research Libraries Group, 1996.

Vashistha, Aditya, Edward Cutrell, and William Thies. "Increasing the Reach of Snowball Sampling: The Impact of Fixed versus Lottery Incentives." Working Paper, March 2015, https://www.microsoft.com/en-us/research/wp-content/uploads/2016/02/Vashistha -CSCW2015-snowball.pdf.

Vermeule, Adrian. "The Invisible Hand in Legal and Political Theory." *Virginia Law Review* 96 (2010): 1417–52.

Waldfogel, Joel. "How Digitization Has Created a Golden Age of Music, Movies, Books, and Television." *Journal of Economic Perspectives* 31, no. 3 (Summer 2017): 195–214.

———. *The Tyranny of the Market: Why You Can't Always Get What You Want.* Cambridge, MA: Harvard University Press, 2007.

Waldron, Jeremy. "Moments of Carelessness and Massive Loss." In *Philosophical Foundations of Tort Law*, edited by David G. Owen, 387–408. Oxford: Oxford University Press, 1995.

Walras, Léon. *Elements of Pure Economics*. Translated by William Jaffé. London: George Allen and Unwin, 1954.

Warren, Elizabeth, and Amelia Warren Tyagi. *The Two-Income Trap: Why Middle-Class Mothers and Fathers Are Going Broke*. New York: Basic Books, 2003.

Watford, Ann E. "Save Now, Win Later: Removing Statutory Barriers to Prize-Linked Savings Initiatives." *Vanderbilt Law Review* 67 (2014): 907–56.

Webb, Walter Loring. *Railroad Construction: Theory and Practice; A Text-Book for the Use of Students in Colleges and Technical Schools, and a Hand-Book for the Use of Engineers in Field and Office*. 7th ed. London: Chapman and Hall, 1922.

Weijzen, P. L. G., D. G. Liem, E. H. Zandstra, and C. de Graaf. "Sensory Specific Satiety and Intake: The Difference between Nibble- and Bar-Size Snacks." *Appetite* 50 (2008): 435–42.

Weisbach, David A. "Toward a New Approach to Disability Law." *University of Chicago Legal Forum* 47 (2009): 47–102.

Weisbrod, Burton A. "Collective-Consumption Services of Individual-Consumption Goods." *Quarterly Journal of Economics* 78 (1964): 471–77.

Wertenbroch, Klaus. "Consumption Self-Control by Rationing Purchase Quantities of Virtue and Vice." *Marketing Science* 17 (1998): 317–37.

West, Geoffrey. *Scale: The Universal Laws of Growth, Innovation, Sustainability, and the Pace of Life in Organisms, Cities, Economies, and Companies*. New York: Penguin, 2017.

Wicksteed, Philip H. *The Common Sense of Political Economy*. London: Macmillan, 1910.

Williams, Joan C., Aaron Platt, and Jessica Lee. "Disruptive Innovation: New Models of Legal Practice." *Hastings Law Journal* 67 (2015): 1–84.

Winn, Abel M., and Matthew W. McCarter. "Who's Holding Out? An Experimental Study of the Benefits and Burdens of Eminent Domain." *Journal of Urban Economics* 105 (2018): 176–85.

Yoo, Christopher S. "Intellectual Property and the Economics of Product Differentiation." In *Research Handbook on the Economics of Intellectual Property Law*, edited by Ben Depoorter and Peter Menell. Cheltenham, UK: Edward Elgar, forthcoming.

Young, H. Peyton. "Dividing the Indivisible." *American Behavioral Scientist* 38 (1995): 904–20.

———. *Equity: In Theory and Practice*. Princeton, NJ: Princeton University Press, 1994.

Zerubavel, Eviatar. *The Seven Day Circle: The History and Meaning of the Week*. New York: Free Press, 1985.

Zhang, Taisu. "Cultural Paradigms in Property Institutions." *Yale Journal of International Law* 41 (2016): 347–413.

INDEX

Page numbers in italics indicate figures.

indivisibilities (*continued*)
63; and slicing, 227; and social policy,
4; strategic, 233; in supply and demand,
21, 22–23; and technology, 3; temporal,
120, 122; types of, 5; and urban economics, 172–74, 183, 188, 264n10; use
of term, 9, 11–12; in workplace, 120,
121–24, 127, 135, 237n1, 258n13. *See
also* complementarities; divisibilities;
step goods
Infranca, John J., 172
innovation: and cities, 173, 180; and
divisibilities, 7; and housing, 108, 155;
lumpiness, 7; and policies, 232–33; and
public finance, 114; support of, 132. *See
also* entrepreneurship
inputs/outputs, 12–15
insurance and risk-bearing, 113–14, 131,
164–65, 198, 200–202. *See also* health
insurance
intellectual property, 22, 33–35, 70. *See also*
copyright; patents
interactions, identifying, 232
intrapersonal dilemmas, 6, 83, 84–101;
aggregation and division, impact on, 6;
lumpiness in, 84; lumping and slicing
solutions, 91–101; and lumpy goals,
84–85, 87, 101; and mixed patterns,
101; participation requirements, 86–89;
payoffs, 90–91, 95, 98; and production
functions, 85–86; and risky behavior,
4, 197–98; rules, exceptions, acts,
patterns, 98–101; and segmenting, 84,
91–93, 95–98; and self-control, 6, 85,
91, 94, 97–98, 250n32; strategic menu
construction, 93–95
investment efficiency, 240n5
investments, lumpy, 248n29

Jacobs, Jane, 177–78
Jefferson, Thomas, 210
jobs. *See* work and workplace
JOBS Act. *See* Jumpstart Our Business Start-
ups (JOBS) Act
Johnson, Eric E., 142
judicial decisions. *See* law
judicial partition. *See* partition, judicial
Jumpstart Our Business Startups (JOBS)
Act, 130, 257n39

Karelis, Charles, 117, 255n93
Karlan, Dean, 90
Katyal, Sonia, 231
Kearney, Melissa Schettini, 112
Kelo v. City of New London, 27, 32, 203
Kerr, William R., 185–86
Kindle, 150
King, Stephen, 62, 90, 91
Knee Defender, 56
Kominers, Scott Duke, 33, 185
Köszegi, Botond, 89
Kreiczer-Levy, Shelly, 143
Kuo, Susan S., 36
Kwang, Ng Yew, 113

Laibson, David, 106
land assembly: and agglomeration, 7; and
aggregation/division, 28, 42; blocked,
167; and cooperation, 228; and eminent domain, 5; graphical representations of, 238n21; and holdin, 88; and
holdouts, 33, 241n22; and lumpiness,
15–16, 22, 26, 188; options, 42–44;
participation/participants, 48, 181, 228;
problems, 29–44, *43*; and reconfiguration, 28, 42–44; scenarios, 238n21;
secrecy in, 241n19; and valuations, 15,
32, 38. *See also* cities; eminent domain
land use: and co-location, 187; controls,
182; permits, 31–32, 83, 249n45; pricing, 183; within and among cities, 172,
177–78, 182, 187–88, 233
lapses: in attention, 195–200; in self-
control, 99–100
law, 190–207, 208–26; binary outcomes,
191; cliffs, 7, 189, 190–207; continu-
ized, 191; counting problems, 200–202;
and discontinuities, 210–11; double
jeopardy clause, 201; economic analysis
of, 3; grandfathering, 214; individuation
problems, 202; indivisible entitlements, 191; judicial decisions, 7, 27, 34;
lumpiness in/of, 24–26, 189, 195–200;
and order, 25; safe harbors, 217, 221,
272n47; and unbundling, 7, 207
Legislative Reorganization Act, 214
Lemley, Mark A., 180
Levenson, Alec R., 105
Levitt, Steven D., 131